THE EPIDEMIC STREETS

The Epidemic Streets

INFECTIOUS DISEASE AND THE RISE OF PREVENTIVE MEDICINE, 1856–1900

ANNE HARDY

CLARENDON PRESS · OXFORD

Oxford University Press, Walton Street, Oxford OX2 6DP
Oxford New York
Athens Auckland Bangkok Bombay
Calcutta Cape Town Dar es Salaam Delhi
Florence Hong Kong Istanbul Karachi
Kuala Lumpur Madras Madrid Melbourne
Mexico City Nairobi Paris Singapore
Taipei Tokyo Toronto
and associated companies in
Berlin Ibadan

Oxford is a trade mark of Oxford University Press

Published in the United States by
Oxford University Press Inc., New York

First published 1993

British Library Cataloguing in Publication Data
Data available

Library of Congress Cataloging in Publication Data
Hardy, Anne, Dr.
The epidemic streets: infectious disease and the rise of preventive medicine, 1856-1900 / Anne Hardy.
p. cm.
Includes bibliographical references.
1. Communicable diseases—England—London—History—19th century.
2. Medicine, Preventive—England—London—History—19th century.
3. Epidemiology—England—London. I. Title.
[DNLM: 1. Communicable Disease—history—London. 2. Preventive Medicine—history—London. WC 11 FE5 H2e 1993]
RA643.7.G7H37 1993 614.4'4212'09034—dc20 93-28155
ISBN 0-19-820377-2

3 5 7 9 10 8 6 4

Printed in Great Britain
on acid-free paper by
Ipswich Book Co. Ltd.,
Ipswich, Suffolk

For my parents

Acknowledgements

This book has its origins in my doctoral thesis for Oxford University, and it was the support and encouragement of my supervisors, Max Hartwell and Peter Mathias, that set me on the path to the book. I am much indebted to Michael Brock, former Warden of Nuffield College, Oxford, and its Fellows, and to the Wellcome Trust, for the fellowships which allowed me to undertake the further research which the development of the thesis made necessary. I am grateful to W. F. Bynum and David Reeder for their advice and support at a crucial moment in the book's history, and to Simon Szreter, without whose unstinting generosity of time, advice, and encouragement the final manuscript would not have reached the publisher. I owe extensive debts to the staff of several libraries: the former staff of the Southwark Collection, then in Newington Public Library, who gave me access to their basement archive when I was writing the thesis; the staff of the former Greater London Council Members' Library, who supplied endless runs of medical-officer-of-health reports with patience and good humour; the staff of the Radcliffe Science Library, especially those in the Lancaster Room, who have trudged many miles for me, and have always met my requests and queries with courtesy and efficiency. Edith Gilchrist of the Royal Free Hospital kindly gave me access to the London Fever Hospital records; and the resources of the Wellcome Institute Library were invaluable.

I would like to thank the editors of *Medical History* for allowing me to use material first published in my article, 'Urban famine or urban crisis? Typhus in the Victorian city', *Medical History*, 32 (1988) and the editors of *Social History of Medicine* similarly, for allowing the use of material first published in my article 'Rickets and the rest: child-care, diet and the infectious children's diseases, 1850–1914', *Social History of Medicine*, 5 (1992).

I am fortunate to have had the support of my family throughout my research and the writing of this book. My parents provided moral support and practical assistance in ways too numerous to detail. My husband, Henry Hardy, sorted out word-processor problems and listened to professional anxieties with exemplary patience. Ellen and Michael, who have not known life without a working mother, have learnt to manage her with tact and humour. The writing of this book saved my sanity during their babyhood: their company makes me profoundly grateful that deadly epidemics of childhood infections are at this moment essentially a terror of the past.

Anne Hardy

February 1993

Contents

List of Figures

List of Tables

List of Abbreviations

CSFH	Commission on Smallpox and Fever Hospitals
ICPD	Interdisciplinary Committee on Physical Deterioration
LCC	London County Council
LGB	Local Government Board
LFH	London Fever Hospital
LFHAR	London Fever Hospital Annual Report
MAB	Metropolitan Asylums Board
MABAR	Metropolitan Asylums Board Annual Report (Statistical Committee)
MABMP	Metropolitan Asylums Board Minutes of Proceedings
MOH	Medical Officer of Health
MOAR	Medical Officer (of Health)'s Annual Report
MOQR	Medical Officer's Quarterly Report
MRC	Medical Research Committee
NAPT	National Association for the Prevention of Tuberculosis
PC	Privy Council
PLCAR	Poor Law Commission Annual Report
PP	Parliamentary Papers
RCHWC	Royal Commission on the Housing of the Working Classes
RCMWS	Royal Commission on the Metropolitan Water Supply
RCV	Royal Commission on Vaccination
RGAR	Registrar-General's Annual Report
RGDS	Registrar-General's Decennial Supplement
SCALDI	Select Committee on Artisans' and Labourers' Dwellings
VAR	Vestry Annual Report
VM	Vestry Minutes

Introduction

> Anything may be proved by statistics and . . . anything may be seen by the aid of a microscope . . . Upon this subject of epidemics, we want facts and faithful records.
>
> (Quaesitor, *Lancet*, 1855)

The epidemic streets haunted nineteenth-century Britain. From them, the Victorians feared, epidemic diseases would escape to ravage the rest of society. The idea originated with the fever nest, the house or group of houses so devastatingly described by Charles Dickens in *Bleak House* from which the inhabitants were for month after month carried out by dozens, dead and dying. Such houses were at the heart of the terrible slum Tom-All-Alone's, every drop of whose 'corrupted blood' spread infection and contagion somewhere, through every order of society, 'up to the proudest of the proud, and to the highest of the high'.[1] First with fever in the 1830s, then with cholera after 1832, disease outbreaks began to be associated with particular streets, sometimes even with particular houses. By the 1890s specific place-associations were thought to have been established for several diseases: tuberculosis, typhus, typhoid, and diphtheria. It was on the basis of such observations that public-health reform and the science of epidemiology had developed in the intervening period. Both these movements emerged during the 1830s and 1840s, and provided the effective background for the development of a national public-health administration designed to reduce the incidence and mortality of infectious diseases in the years after 1850.

For many years the decline in the death-rates from the common infectious diseases which began in the 1870s was attributed to the new science and technology of public health. In 1976, however, Thomas McKeown published *The Modern Rise of Population*, in which he argued that population growth in Western Europe since 1700 was the result of a decline in deaths from the infectious diseases.[2] In his view, this decline was primarily due to improved nutrition; and a central plank of this argument rested on his interpretation of the English registration data from the period 1837–1914. McKeown's work has been widely influential, stimulating historians of many different backgrounds to inquire into the mechanisms of the demographic transition, and into the effects of nutrition on human health.[3] McKeown's basic thesis has, however, recently been challenged by Simon Szreter, in a reappraisal of the very diverse

* Place of publication is London throughout, unless otherwise shown.

[1] Charles Dickens, *Bleak House* (Harmondsworth, 1971), 364, 683.

[2] Thomas McKeown, *The Modern Rise of Population* (1976).

[3] See R. I. Rotberg and T. K. Rabb (eds.), *Hunger and History: The Impact of Changing Food Production and Consumption on Society* (Cambridge, 1985).

literature which now exists on the history of health and public health in the Victorian period. In Szreter's view, social intervention, not improved nutrition, was the critical determinant of the nineteenth-century decline in mortality.[4] Szreter's polemic has provoked fresh discussion of McKeown's thesis, and provides the context of historical debate for this book, which sets out to examine the behaviour of the infectious diseases in the later nineteenth-century, and the part which preventive medicine played in reducing the toll of deaths they exacted.[5]

Despite McKeown's thesis, the investigation of the local and particular circumstances of death and disease in the cities, towns, and countryside of Victorian England has been largely neglected.[6] The history of health can be approached in various ways, since it variously casts light on the evolution of a country's government and institutions, on its population history, on its intellectual development, and on its social attitudes and popular beliefs. It is only relatively recently that the history of mortality has become an issue for historians, and the focus of speculation and research; within the subject as a whole there is a sharp division in interest between the early modern period on the one hand, and the nineteenth century and after on the other. This division has no doubt been brought about partly by the intrinsic tendency of historians to specialize in time, but also by the very different natures of the sources available for the two periods, and by the different questions they raise. The result has been, however, the evolution of two contrasting historical styles. Inspired by the late Andrew Appleby's fascination with the interrelationship between famine, disease, and mortality, students of the early modern period have concentrated on painstaking local and particular studies, through which a deep and satisfactory, if at times contradictory and confusing, picture of mortality and morbidity and their social context in the past is being steadily built up.[7] By contrast, historians of the more recent period have been more individualistic, developing no consistent approach or focus of interest; our knowledge of the workings of disease and death since 1850 is more random and, because of the existence of national statistical series and immense literary sources, more general than for the years between 1560 and 1830.

Most existing accounts of nineteenth-century society's response to the problem of epidemic disease focus on sanitary reform, on the struggles to achieve

[4] Simon Szreter, 'The importance of social intervention in Britain's mortality decline *c.*1850–1914: a reinterpretation of the role of public health', *Social History of Medicine*, 1 (1988), 1–37.

[5] Further discussion of the historical arguments on the 19th cent. mortality decline has been reserved for the concluding chapter.

[6] Pioneering essays are to be found in R. E. Woods and J. Woodward (eds.), *Urban Disease and Mortality* (1983).

[7] This is evident in the important collection of essays recently issued in tribute to Andrew Appleby: John Walter and Roger Schofield (eds.), *Famine, Disease and the Social Order in Early Modern Society* (Cambridge, 1989).

clean water and air, effective sewage disposal, and decent housing.[8] By contrast, the contributions of epidemiology, and of the public-health administration, have received little direct attention, while the diseases themselves, which constituted the core of the public-health problem, have for the most part been ignored.[9] The aim of this book is to redress the balance; to describe the historical behaviour of the most important nineteenth-century infectious diseases, to assess the relative contribution of different factors to their prevalence and fatality, and to lay a foundation-stone for more detailed investigations of local patterns of disease-incidence and behaviour in the years between 1850 and 1914. In this story sanitary reform has a role, but the characteristics of the different diseases and the administrative measures which were taken against them play the greater part.

McKeown identified eight major infections as contributing to the nineteenth-century mortality decline. These eight constituted the major part of the group of diseases recognized by nineteenth-century observers as being 'preventable', whether because they were accepted as directly contagious or because they were thought to be associated with insanitary conditions. With the exception of respiratory tuberculosis, they were designated as 'miasmatic' diseases in the registrar-general's classification. Officially, therefore, they were considered to be associated with remediable environmental conditions. These are the diseases discussed in the chapters that follow. All were endemic, and periodically epidemic, and all were major contributors to the high death-rates experienced by Victorian cities in particular. Whooping cough, measles, scarlet fever, and diphtheria were all serious and life-threatening diseases for young children; smallpox was a classic killer among all age-groups. Typhoid and typhus, although very different in their etiology, were the 'filth diseases' which made the century notorious; and tuberculosis was an insidious, chronic infection which left almost no one untouched. In the 1860s, just when the late-Victorian sanitary administration was beginning its work, these diseases as a group contributed nearly 30 per cent of the total annual deaths in England and Wales. By 1900 nearly all were declining as causes of death, and their share of annual mortality had dropped to under 20 per cent.[10] Once the epidemiological profiles of these diseases are set in historical context, a broad range of factors can be seen to have contributed to the reduction of their fatality.

Two other diseases which concerned the Victorian authorities are not considered here. Infant diarrhoea has a hugely complex history, and merits more detailed attention than can be given here; only towards the very end of the period did the preventive authorities begin to regard it as a less than hopeless

[8] A. S. Wohl, *Endangered Lives: Public Health in Victorian Britain* (1983); W. Luckin, *Pollution and Control: A Social History of the Thames* (Bristol, 1987).

[9] Exceptions to this generalization are studies by Gillian Cronje and F. B. Smith on tuberculosis, and by Bill Luckin on the diarrhoeal diseases (in *Pollution and Control*) and on typhus: see Bibliography.

[10] McKeown, *Modern Rise*, 50–76.

proposition. Cholera, which in popular memory has marked the nineteenth century for its own, has been omitted with some regret.[11] Like plague before it, it was an occasional invader, and its irruptions on to the English scene were transitory. Furthermore, its principal incursions took place before the preventive administration existed. The epidemic of 1866 was largely confined to London, and thereafter the disease failed to make any serious breach in Britain's sanitary defences: in demographic terms, cholera was only of minor significance as a cause of death in the later nineteenth century.

The campaign against endemic infectious disease which began in England in the 1850s was fought essentially at local-government level. Infectious disease was viewed as a local problem, to be dealt with by local authorities. The establishment of local sanitary departments, spearheaded by medical officers of health (MOHs), marks the beginning of serious preventive medicine in England. Medical officers of health had been appointed by various local authorities, notably Liverpool and the City of London, since 1847, but it was not until 1856 that they existed in sufficient numbers to form a regular sanitary organization. Under the Metropolis Local Management Act 1855, London's new civil vestries were each required to appoint a medical officer. In 1856 forty-eight officers took up appointments in the city, forming a unique specialist body with responsibility for, and interest in, infectious disease. Sixteen years later, under the Public Health Act 1872, medical officerships were instituted in all urban and rural sanitary districts, creating over a thousand new posts and extending preventive authority throughout the country.[12]

The working brief which the medical officers of health established for themselves was taken in part from the example of John Simon's programme as MOH for the City of London, and in part from the instruction contained in the Metropolis Local Management Act. The latter required them to ascertain the existence of diseases, especially epidemic diseases, and to determine the local causes and the most effective means of checking or preventing their spread.[13] From the mid-1850s, therefore, infectious disease was the recognized focus of a preventive programme. The medical officers were assisted in their labours by sanitary (or nuisance) inspectors, who carried out routine investigations and inspections. Initially most sanitary departments were small. In the early decades many medical officers had only one inspector, but by the 1890s many urban MOHs were directing a staff of a dozen or more. While the

[11] A chapter devoted to cholera in an earlier draft of this book was sacrificed for reasons of space. A revised version is published separately as 'Cholera, quarantine and the English preventive system, 1850–1895', *Medical History*, 37 (July 1993).

[12] Sidney Chave, *Recalling the Medical Officer of Health* (1987); Anne Hardy, 'Public health and the expert: the London Medical Officers of Health, 1856–1900', in R. M. Mcleod (ed.), *Government and Expertise: Specialists, Administrators, and Professionals, 1860–1919* (Cambridge, 1988), 128–42; Dorothy Watkins, 'The English revolution in social medicine, 1889–1911', unpublished Ph.D thesis, University of London (1984).

[13] R. S. Lambert, *Sir John Simon, 1816–1904, and English Social Administration* (Bristol, 1965); *Metropolis Local Management Act* 1855; 18 & 19 Vict., c. 120, s. cxxxii.

medical officers occasionally encountered obstruction from the local authorities who employed them, and were not immune to professional ambition and discontent, it is clear none the less that they were highly effective in implementing sanitary reform and in developing policies for the control of infectious disease.[14]

The basic preventive unit of the medical officer and his sanitary department was supplemented at both national and local level. Two national bodies were associated with the business of prevention. The General Register Office collected and made available the demographic data from which the medical officers assessed the health of their districts;[15] the Medical Department of the Privy Council (the Local Government Board after 1871) kept an eye on local and national health developments, and investigated specific health problems. Although the central medical department had little direct influence on local sanitary affairs, it provided a national perspective on preventive problems, and its reports provide important insights into preventive concerns and the development of preventive strategies.

At the local level a range of philanthropic and official initiatives supported or complemented the work of the preventive authorities. Clergymen, nursing sisters, pharmacists, dispensary doctors, general practitioners, Poor Law officials, and voluntary workers provided medical officers with information about disease outbreaks and insanitary conditions. Fever and smallpox hospitals had been established in the eighteenth century, and provided valuable isolation facilities for poor patients in many cities. Such provision was greatly extended in London after 1867, following the establishment of the Metropolitan Asylums Board, whose ambitious hospital-building programme enabled the isolation of infectious cases to become an integral part of metropolitan preventive policy. In London, and to a lesser extent in the provinces, where such institutions were less common, the isolation hospitals provided an opportunity for the removal of foci of infection from the community as well as feedback to the local authorities on epidemic outbreaks.[16] Schools too, while they played a part in maintaining and promoting infectious disease, acted as information sources for the preventive authorities and served, in a limited way, as channels of health education.

The existence of these formal and informal networks of information, co-operation, and support were essential to the effective functioning of the local

[14] David Owen, *The Government of Victorian London 1855–1889: The Metropolitan Board of Works, the Vestries and the City Corporation*, ed. R. M. Macleod, (1982); Wohl, *Endangered Lives*, chap. 7; Hardy, 'Public health and the expert'; Dorothy Porter, 'Stratification and its discontents': professionalisation and conflict in the British public health service, 1848–1914', in E. Fee and R. M. Acheson (eds.), *A History of Education in Public Health* (Oxford, 1991).

[15] Simon Szreter, 'The GRO and the public health movement in Britain, 1837–1914', *Social History of Medicine*, Special Issue (Dec. 1991), 435–63.

[16] M. C. Buer, *Health, Wealth and Population in the Early Days of the Industrial Revolution* (1926), chaps. 14, 15; G. M. Ayers, *England's First State Hospitals* (1969); J. V. Pickstone, *Medicine and Industrial Society* (Manchester, 1985).

preventive authorities. Without these networks the task of interfering with the course of infectious disease would have been virtually impossible. The tradition of the Englishman's liberty and privacy, of his home as his castle, was one that the legislature was reluctant to breach, especially in respect of the well-to-do. For much of the period, therefore, and certainly until the notification of infectious-disease cases began to be introduced in the 1880s, the preventive authorities were handicapped by partial information, as well as by legislative provisions aimed more specifically at sanitary reform than at disease control. The Sanitary Act 1866 marked a turning point in one respect, for it gave the sanitary authorities valuable powers to order the cleaning and disinfection of premises if this would tend to prevent or check infectious disease.[17] The application of such measures still depended, however, on relevant information about disease incidence being available: notification of infectious-disease cases was not made compulsory nationally until 1899. The formal legislative structure within which preventive policy was developed remained in many respects unsatisfactory throughout the period.

Despite such handicaps, preventive policies became increasingly oriented towards disease. Three phases of development can be distinguished. Until 1865 environmental concerns were paramount. Between 1865 and the mid-1890s, however, the conceptual framework of disease theory on which preventive policies were based was significantly modified and consolidated. From the mid-1890s the fruits of the new orthodoxy, bacteriology, began to be incorporated into preventive work at local level. In this process of evolution, paradoxically, the great advances in the knowledge of disease causation and in theories of disease communication which took place in Europe after 1870 played little direct part. In England, disease theory was less important in determining preventive practice than practical observation tempered by political pragmatism. For example, although observation suggested that fever was associated with filth, perhaps with putrefaction or miasma, it had long been recognized that smallpox and measles were directly transmissible, and few insisted that they were associated with insanitary conditions; hence, although medical men generally inclined towards an environmentalist or 'miasmatic' explanation for most diseases, the possibility of diverse causation, including some form of contagionism, was tacitly admitted for others. As recent historians of the heroic period of public-health reform have shown, the English approach to preventable disease was based on theoretical compromise.[18]

The critical moment for English preventive policy occurred in 1865–6, when imported cattle plague (rinderpest) devastated cattle herds throughout the country. The belated adoption of a 'stamping-out' policy to eliminate cattle plague led, by almost purely practical analogy, to the development of a stamp-

[17] Sanitary Act 1866, 29 & 30 Vict., c. 99, ss. 22, 23.

[18] J. M. Eyler, *Victorian Social Medicine: The Ideas and Methods of William Farr* (1979), 103; Margaret Pelling, *Cholera, Fever and English Medicine 1825–1865* (Oxford, 1978), chap. 8.

ing-out formula for smallpox which was quickly applied thereafter to the other infectious diseases.[19] The measures by which stamping out was to be achieved in human, as distinct from animal, populations (notification, isolation, and disinfection) could not be exhaustively implemented, certainly not before 1900, but the concept of stamping out played a crucial part in shaping English preventive policy in the years after 1870. The phrase itself occurs repeatedly in the preventive literature of the period, and was widely applied to diseases other than smallpox. This new perspective, combined with the powers conferred under the 1866 Act, brought something of a revolution to the methods of sanitary departments, consolidating their activities and directing them more precisely towards the effective prevention of infectious disease.

The impact of preventive policy on the behaviour of the different infectious diseases, its effectiveness or ineffectiveness, forms an important theme of the succeeding chapters. The history of the infectious diseases in the Victorian period is inevitably, and inextricably, bound up with the evolution of English preventive medicine, and with the growing expertise of the medical officers of health. The sources available to the historian for the study of infectious diseases in Victorian society, for example, derive overwhelmingly from the public-health administration, and from medical men with an interest in preventive medicine. Thus the local nature of the preventive campaign, and contemporary concern with the local causes of disease, have in part determined this book's emphasis on the behaviour of the various diseases at grass-roots level.

London provided the bulk of the primary sources consulted, since it was here that a corpus of medical officers was first appointed, while the records of the infectious-disease hospitals were also valuable. Many of the specific statistical examples and local illustrations are drawn from London. The size and diversity of the city further justify its choice as the basic unit of study: not only did it offer a wide variety of disease habitats, but by virtue of its size and economic and medical importance, London exerted a significant demographic effect on national statistical series.[20] London's medical officers were the first professional group to meet the challenge of providing facts and faithful records about infectious disease, and their activities had national implications, both demographically and in establishing a model for the development of preventive techniques. Their observations form a unique source for the study of local disease experience, and for exploring the evolution of nineteenth-century preventive medicine. The appointment of the London medical officers in 1856 marks the beginning of preventive medicine in England, and sets the starting date for this study. The terminal date of 1900 was determined partly by the London

[19] Anne Hardy, 'Smallpox in London: factors in the decline of the disease in the nineteenth century', *Medical History*, 27 (1983), 122–3.

[20] R. I. Woods, P. A. Watterson, and J. H. Woodward, 'The causes of rapid infant mortality decline in England and Wales, 1861–1921, Part 1', *Population Studies*, 42 (1988), 357–8.

local-government reforms of that year, which altered the administrative districts, but also by the changing concerns of preventive medicine in the 1890s which legitimate 1900 as, in many senses, the end of an era. By 1900 the old concerns of disease control and sanitary reform were well on the way to being replaced by new scientific and domestic preoccupations, by bacteriological monitoring and maternal and child welfare.

The local perspective extends our understanding of the way disease affected the lives of ordinary people, and complements and modifies the understanding of historical disease processes presented by existing studies based on national data.[21] The infectious diseases are by no means a homogenous group, but differ in their means of transmission, infectivity, and behaviour. As Cyril Dixon noted in his magisterial study of smallpox, their control depends on the recognition of possible and probable sources of infection, on the routes by which they spread, and on the factors affecting the susceptibility of individuals exposed to them.[22] It was the local observation of disease behaviour which provided the epidemiological insights that made preventive medicine possible. The multiplicity of factors involved in the disease ecology of any community meant that progress towards a coherent, uniform preventive policy was relatively slow, and the success of that policy variable. None the less, in the years after 1860 these factors began to be uncovered, painfully, by England's medical officers of health, who had a professional interest in understanding what governed the behaviour of the infectious diseases.

[21] McKeown, *Modern Rise*; A. Mercer, *Disease, Mortality and Population in Transition* (Leicester, 1990).

[22] Cyril Dixon, *Smallpox* (1965), 298.

1

Whooping Cough

Much that is mysterious still clings to the origin of hooping cough.

(Edward Smith, 1854)

There is scarcely a nursery in which, to everyone's great discomfort, it is not known as a familiar and most unwelcome visitant.

(Charles West, 1885)

Whooping cough is an unpromising subject with which to open the argument of this book, for it was the only one of the major infectious diseases which failed to arouse any substantial preventive attention in the years up to 1900. It was, however, one of the great killers of nineteenth-century England, and was an almost universal childhood experience for all social classes.[1] It was a scourge that fell predominantly upon infants: two-thirds of its victims were under the age of 2 years. Of the ninety-nine diseases listed by the registrar-general in the decade 1844–53, it ranked as the seventh most fatal; of diseases considered to be related, only phthisis, pneumonia, and bronchitis (chest afflictions), typhus and scarlet fever (zymotic diseases), and convulsions (diseases of the nervous system) were more dangerous.[2] Its prominence was to become even more noticeable with the decline in scarlet-fever mortality after 1870.[3] Nevertheless, whooping cough death-rates fell slightly during the later nineteenth century: national death-rates peaked at around 1,500 per million under-15s in about 1870, and thereafter declined almost continuously, to *c.*1,000 in 1900.[4]

Whooping cough has long been recognized as an acute infectious disease, but much of its epidemiology was, and remains, obscure.[5] It is, nevertheless, one of the most interesting of the infectious childhood diseases in its historical behaviour and the course of its mortality decline. It is an endemic disease, with its own cycle, generally of biennial or triennial epidemics. Although this

[1] William Squire, 'Whooping cough', in Richard Quain (ed.), *A Dictionary of Medicine* (1882), 1,772.

[2] Edward Smith, 'English statistics of hooping-cough', *Medico-Chirurgical Transactions*, ns 37 (1854), 229.

[3] Charles Creighton, *A History of Epidemics in Britain*, 2 vols. (Cambridge, 1894), ii. 673.

[4] Thomas McKeown, *The Modern Rise of Population*, (1976), 96, table 5.3.

[5] Smith, 'English statistics', 227; W. W. C. Topley and G. S. Wilson (eds.), *Principles of Bacteriology, Virology and Immunity*, seventh edn. (1984), iii. 229. Modern epidemiological studies relate to populations in which the natural behaviour of the disease has been modified by vaccination programmes, and assessments of the behaviour of 'natural' whooping cough are based on studies made before 1940. See Mark G. Thomas, 'Epidemiology of pertussis', *Reviews of Infectious Diseases*, 11 (1989), 255–62.

TABLE 1.1: *Whooping-cough death-rates per 1,000 living under 5*

	1851-60	*1861-70*	*1871-80*	*1881-90*	*1891-1900*
England and Wales	3.62	3.77	3.65	3.37	3.09
London	7.15	6.53	6.02	5.34	4.21

Source: Registrar-general's decennial reports.

pattern generally appears on the national curve, the national trend was not always repeated at local level in the nineteenth century. There was, for example, no general coincidence of urban epidemics in time. Evidence from Scotland shows that only where towns were close together, like Edinburgh and Leith (so close as to be one), or Dundee and Perth, could a similar epidemic time-scale be observed. In Paisley and Greenock, only a few miles apart, the epidemic years were quite different.[6] In the south, too, this urban epidemic disparity was repeated: the major national epidemic of 1866, for example, did not affect London. The epidemic cycle varied between and within conurbations, and in individual cities there were series of years when no significant epidemic pattern was discernible. Thus the periodicity of epidemics in Aberdeen was 'somewhat ill-defined' before 1890, but clearly substantially biennial thereafter. In Edinburgh and Perth epidemics occurred generally every three years; in Glasgow every three to four; in Dundee every four.[7]

In London there was some variation in periodicity, with the pattern becoming more unstable as mortality began to fall in the early 1880s (Fig. 1.1). Within London, however, the different districts did not have a uniform experience of epidemic years: in the East End, for example, St George-in-the-East displayed a rather different pattern of epidemic years from Whitechapel and Bethnal Green (Fig. 1.2), although none of the three had consistently coincident epidemic patterns. Given the size of London, with each of these districts containing a population equivalent to a sizeable provincial town, this independence may not be surprising. With a disease like whooping cough, which is largely transmitted within the home, the rhythm of epidemics was probably to some extent governed by local community habits and patterns of domestic sociability.

While there were great annual variations in local mortality,[8] nineteenth-century whooping cough was most fatal in large urban areas and in mining communities.[9] In London mortality was nearly twice the national average in the 1850s, and remained significantly above it for the rest of the century. Yet

[6] James S. Laing, 'Whooping cough: its prevalence and mortality in Aberdeen', *Public Health*, 13 (1901–2), 586–7.

[7] Ibid. 596.

[8] F. B. Smith, *The People's Health* (1987), 233.

[9] *RGAR*, PP (1893–4), xxi, p. 14.

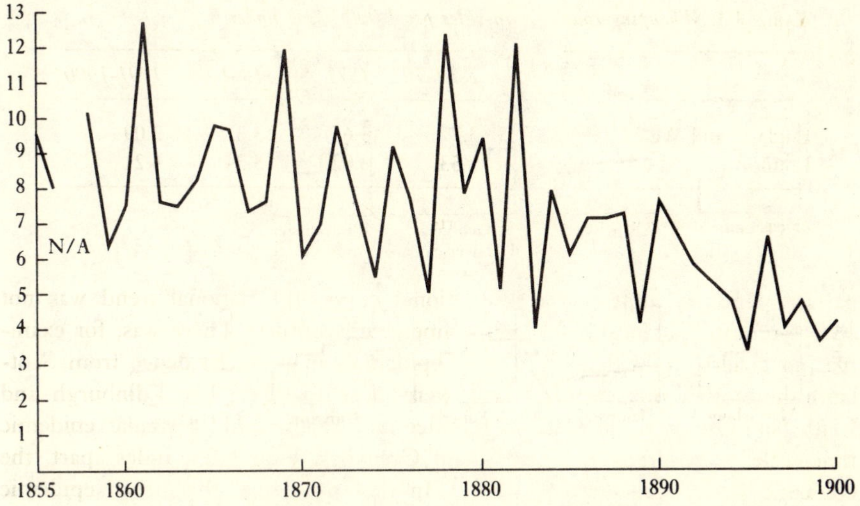

FIG. 1.1. *Whooping-cough deaths in London, 1855–1900, per 10,000 population.*

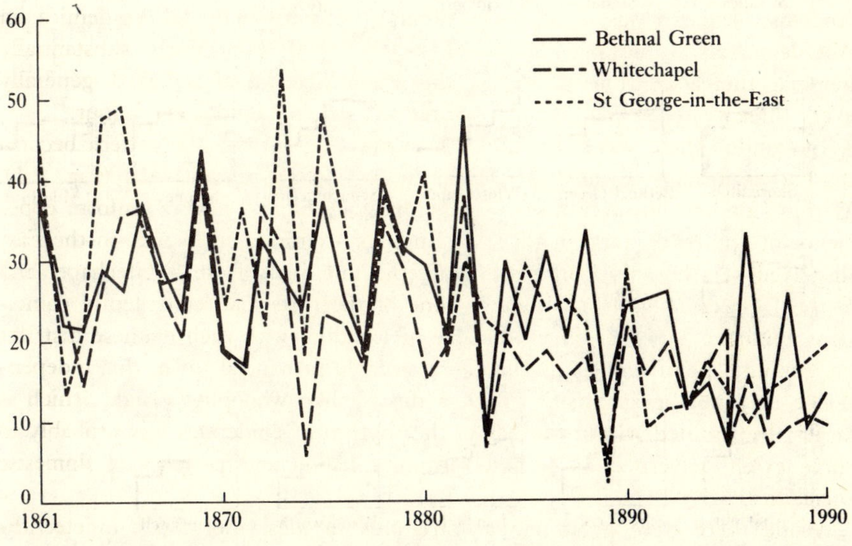

FIG. 1.2. *Whooping-cough deaths in three London districts, per 10,000 under 15.*

in London death-rates from whooping cough declined relatively much faster than in the country as a whole, and the decline was sharpest in those metropolitan districts which had suffered most severely in the 1850s (Fig. 1.3). In Scotland, similarly, the towns with the highest death-rates at mid-century were generally those where whooping-cough death-rates had fallen most by the

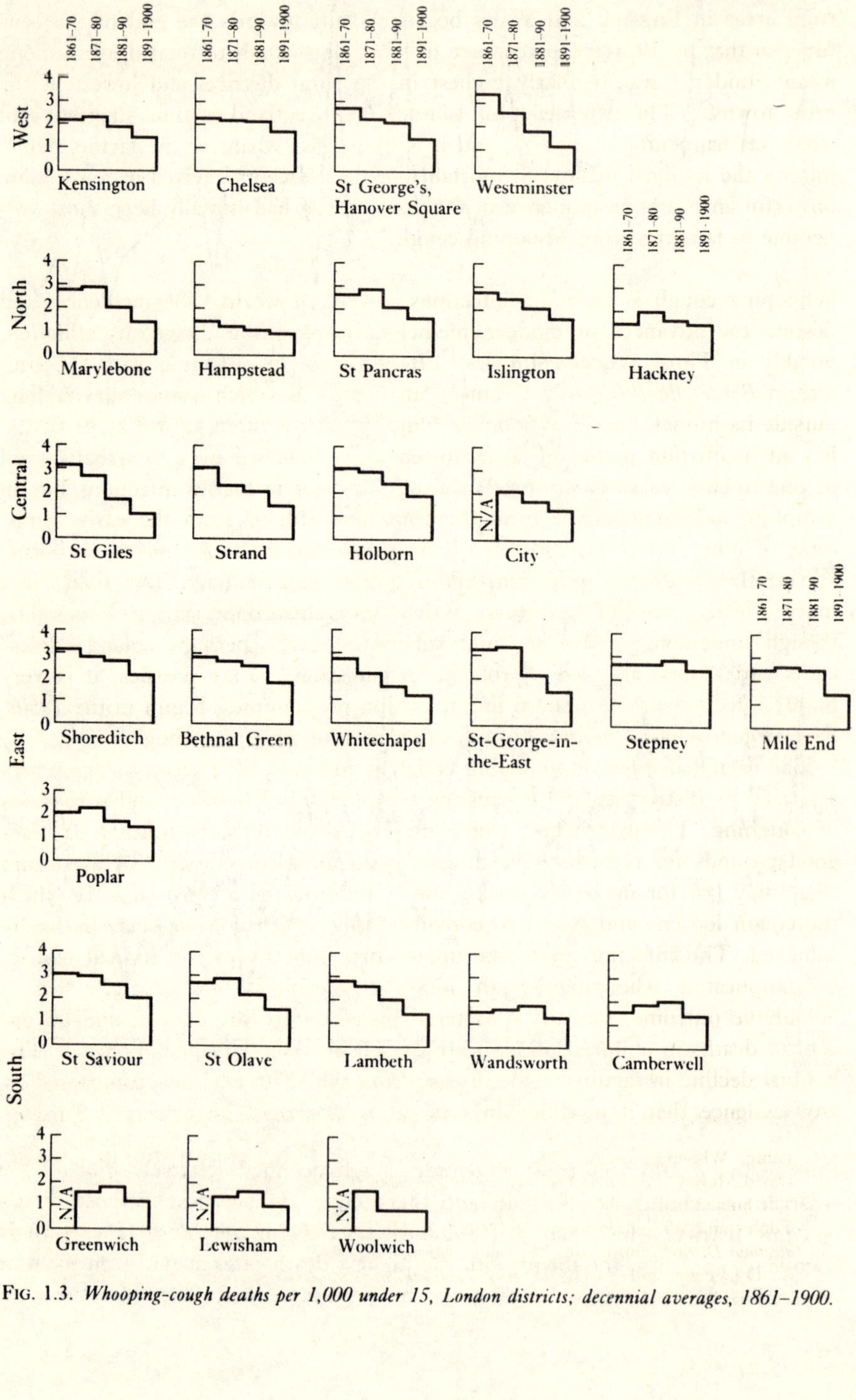

FIG. 1.3. *Whooping-cough deaths per 1,000 under 15, London districts; decennial averages, 1861–1900.*

century's end.[10] At the same time, the balance of fatality between urban and rural areas in England and Wales began to shift towards the end of the century, so that by 1921 the percentage of whooping-cough to total deaths among infants under 1 was regularly highest in the rural districts and lowest in the great towns.[11] The experience of London and Scotland is thus suggestive of what was happening elsewhere, and it is likely that whatever the factors determining the national decline in mortality, some elements exerted a much more powerful ameliorative influence in the areas which had initially been most vulnerable to fatalities from whooping cough.

Whooping cough is an acute infectious disease of world-wide incidence, and despite the advances of modern medicine it remains a dangerous affliction, notably in Third World countries.[12] It is caused by infection with the bacterium *Bordetella pertussis*, a Gram-negative bacillus which cannot survive long outside its human host.[13] Whooping cough (which is often known as pertussis) has an incubation period of seven-to-ten days, followed by a catarrhal period of one-to-two weeks (first stage), during which it is highly infectious but in symptom indistinguishable from the common cold, or from the early symptoms of other infectious diseases. Transmission seems to be mainly airborne, apparently by droplet infection, and requires close contact. The home is a more effective area of transmission than the schoolroom; and it is possible, though undemonstrated, that mild subclinical cases, perhaps among adolescents and adults, also play a role in transmission.[14] Like measles, it is very highly infectious; only modern immunization programmes, begun in the 1950s, have largely relieved children of the experience of whooping cough.

The catarrhal stage of whooping cough is followed by a second stage, characterized by distressing and exhausting symptoms, by vomiting, and paroxysms of coughing. These episodes, which may occur up to forty times a day, are good grounds for regarding the disease as an unwelcome visitor. This second stage may last for up to six weeks, and is followed by a third stage in which the cough loosens and ceases to convulse, after which convalescence is finally achieved. The infection may take up to three months to run its full course. Uncomplicated whooping cough may be alarming, but generally has a favourable outcome; secondary bacterial invasions are the danger, and 90 per cent of deaths in children under 3 are caused by secondary pneumonias.[15] The gradual decline in fatality of the disease from the 1870s was unaccompanied by any evidence that it modified in type. It was, and is, an extremely variable

[10] Laing, 'Whooping cough', 596.

[11] *RGDS* (1921), part III, p. xxxviii.

[12] David Morley, *Paediatric Priorities in the Developing World*, (1973), chap. 13.

[13] The human body is the sole known reservoir of *bordetella pertussis*.

[14] Topley and Wilson, *Principles*, iii. 464–8; F. H. Top and P. H. Wehrle (eds.), *Communicable and Infectious Diseases*, ninth edn., (St Louis, Miss., 1981), 468.

[15] R. D. Feigin and J. D. Cherry, *Textbook of Pediatric Infectious Diseases*, second edn. (Philadelphia, Pa., 1987), 1,230.

disease, at times so mild as to be almost indistinguishable from common cold, at others rapidly fatal. This variability of type is intrinsic to the disease, but a variety of other factors influence the outcome of infection, and an examination of these may contribute to our understanding of the historical pattern of the disease.

In the nineteenth century the epidemiology of whooping cough was even less clear than today. It was widely acknowledged to be an infectious disease,[16] but the origins and source of infection were unknown. While miasmatic concepts lingered into the closing years of the century, medical opinion was broadly expressed by William Squire, writing in Quain's *Dictionary of Medicine* (1882). To Squire, whooping cough was an infectious disease, readily propagated by '*fomites*', and frequently carried from house to house in the clothes of visitors. Those slightly affected or in the early stages of the disease were infectious; victims remained so throughout its course.[17] Naturally there was some disagreement on these points, notably on the length of the infectious period,[18] while research continued into the epidemiology of the disease. The search for the causative organism of whooping cough began in the 1860s,[19] but it was not until 1900 that it was first isolated by Bordet and Gengou; it was not grown *in vitro* until 1906, when its morphology and characteristics were finally established.[20] Meanwhile new theories of causation were floated from time to time; in the mid-1880s, for example, a Manchester surgeon, William Barlow,[21] came to favour the idea of a parasitic origin for the disease, and argued that the popular practice of taking children to inhale the vapours from the purifying tanks of gasworks, or of coal-tar, pointed in the same direction.[22]

The universal incidence of whooping cough in the nineteenth century was not matched by an equal catholicity of mortality. Contemporary observers were unanimous in their belief that fatalities occurred principally among the poorer classes; and this encouraged the view that sanitary circumstances were an important element in mortality, if not incidence.[23] August Hirsh recorded that it appeared impartially in all social circles, but was apparently more destructive among the poor than among the comparatively well-to-do.[24] During the major London epidemic of 1876, the registrar-general noted that, of 130 deaths registered in the week ending 19 February, only six could be ascribed to the affluent classes—'virtually all' the remaining deaths fell among the working classes.[25] Again, in 1878 the *Lancet* remarked that nearly all fatal cases were

[16] Charles West, *Lectures on the Diseases of Infancy and Childhood*, seventh edn. (1884), 500–1; Squire 'Whooping cough' 1,771.

[17] Squire, 'Whooping cough', 1,771.

[18] See below, n. 90.

[19] A. Hirsh, *Handbook of Geographical and Historical Pathology*, (1886), iii. 43.

[20] J. Bordet and O. Gengou, in *Annales de l'Institut Pasteur*, 20 (1906), 731 and 21 (1907), 720.

[21] Consultant Surgeon to the Pendleburn and Manchester Dispensary, General Hospital, and Dispensary for Sick Children.

[22] *Lancet* (1886), i. 966. For this practice see Smith, *People's Health*, 110.

[23] *Lancet* (1878), i. 945.

[24] Hirsch, *Handbook*, 39.

[25] *Lancet* (1876), i. 324.

among the working class.[26] These observations can be confirmed to some extent by the comparative death-rates of the various London districts in the 1850s and 1860s. To take the extreme example, the whooping-cough death-rate for St Giles was 97.8 per 10,000 living under 15 years old in 1851–60, but was a mere 33.5 in Hampstead (Fig. 1.3). None the less, mortality was not rigorously limited to the poorest: in 1868 whooping cough was markedly more fatal in the better-off Bloomsbury quarter of St Giles than it was in the slum districts in the south of the district.[27] In general, however, it is against a background of class-differential mortality that the factors affecting the historical pattern of whooping cough must be examined.

Among the factors determining a happy outcome to infection with pertussis, age is of primary importance. The younger the infant, the more serious whooping cough is likely to be. Babies are born without any natural immunity to the disease, and are therefore immediately vulnerable. In the 1850s it was estimated that 40 per cent of whooping-cough deaths occurred among infants under 1 year; 67 per cent among those under 2; and 95 per cent among the under-fives.[28] The figure of 68 per cent mortality under 2 was still being cited in the 1880s. In the later 1890s, over 97 per cent mortality occurred among the under-fives.[29] According to Charles West, young infants were less likely to contract whooping cough in the first three or four months of life; this he ascribed to their being kept more at home than other children.[30] Among the factors contributing to the class-differential mortality of this disease, the ability of better-class families to shield their younger members from family infection may have played a significant part.[31] Whooping-cough patients are probably most infectious during the first week of illness,[32] and domestic circumstances may thus play a significant part in the course which the disease runs through the family. It may also be that the intensity of individual cases is determined by the size of the infectious dose of the bacillus: the higher the dose, the more severe the disease.[33] Among the poorest classes in overcrowded housing, younger children were only too vulnerable to infection brought home by elder siblings or visitors. Such factors may explain the disproportionate class-differential in whooping-

[26] *Lancet* (1878), i. 945.

[27] *MOAR* St Giles (1868), 7.

[28] Smith, 'English statistics', 236.

[29] *RGAR*, PP 1900 xv, p. 26; PP 1901 xv, p. 24.

[30] Charles West, *The Mother's Manual of Children's Diseases* (1885), 141.

[31] Nevertheless, many middle-class families organized matters so that all children acquired an infectious disease at more or less the same time, so as to minimize domestic inconvenience: F. J. Waldo and D. Walsh, 'Murder by Measles', *Nineteenth Century*, 39 (1896), 957. This practice may help to account for Percy Stocks' finding, in the 1920s, that children in the middle-class districts of London contracted whooping cough at younger ages than those in poorer districts, and consequently a higher proportion of under-fives in well-to-do areas had had whooping cough than in poorer areas: P. Stocks, 'Some epidemiological features of whooping cough: a statistical investigation. Part Two.', *Lancet* (1933), i. 265–9.

[32] Thomas, 'Epidemiology of pertussis', 225–6.

[33] David Morley and Margaret Woodland, *See How They Grow: Monitoring Child Growth for Appropriate Health Care in Developing Countries* (1986), 94–5.

cough mortality, as well as the apparent influence of overcrowded housing conditions (see below). The greater winter whooping-cough mortality observed by Edward Smith may also have been in part a function of the greater likelihood of infection of very young infants, higher infective doses, and probably reduced nursing care, when siblings were cooped up at home by inclement weather and dark evenings: there was no correlation between mortality and the severity of winter conditions.[34]

The significance of good nursing care is considerable for whooping cough; in America today, indeed, infants under 1 year with whooping cough are hospitalized, so that they may be cared for by experienced staff, with proper nursing observation and attention to ventilation, nutritional intake, and the correct handling of paroxysms.[35] Nineteenth-century observers were equally aware of the need for special care in nursing whooping-cough cases; over-exertion or exposure to cold and damp, it was thought, could at any time alter the prospects even of favourable cases for the worse. 'Rest and warmth, with much individual care, and the utmost attention to a sufficiency of pure air, are requisite from the first', wrote William Squire;[36] thirty years later E. W. Goodall recommended a warm and well-ventilated room with a nourishing and easily digested diet.[37] All authorities admitted that no effective drugs were available to ease the paroxysms, and were unanimous in advising avoidance of cold and draughts.[38]

Observers with an epidemiological interest in the disease stressed the contribution of exposure to mortality among the poorer classes. Hirsh, for example, noted that the children of the comparatively well-to-do had better tending, 'and, in particular, are more protected from the harmful effects of the weather'.[39] The respiratory complications of whooping cough were recognized as generally more fatal than the disease itself.[40] Thus, of the thirty-five fatalities which Charles West recorded in his own practice, seventeen died of bronchitis or pneumonia, and eighteen from 'congestion of the brain, convulsions coming on in a fit of coughing, or from tubercular meningitis'.[41] Medical officers of health agreed that respiratory complications brought on by untimely exposure and insufficient nursing were a principal cause of high whooping-cough mortality.[42] Complaints were frequently heard of the way in which children were taken to dispensaries and out-patients' departments by train or omnibus, and could be heard whooping in railway stations and on

[34] Smith, 'English statistics', 241, 245–6.
[35] Top and Wehrle, *Communicable Diseases*, 468.
[36] Squire, 'Whooping cough', 1,774.
[37] E. W. Goodall and J. W. Washbourn, *A Manual of Infectious Diseases* (1908), 231–2.
[38] Squire, 'Whooping cough', 1,775, West, *Lectures*, 504–5; Goodall and Washbourn, *Manual*, 232.
[39] Hirsch, *Handbook*, iii. 39.
[40] *Lancet* (1878), i. 945.
[41] West, *Lectures*, 486.
[42] *MOAR* Camberwell (1857–8), 29; *MOQR* St George's, Southwark (1, 1858), 8; *MOQR* Whitechapel (1, 1880), 6; *MOAR* Clapham (1891), 112; *MOAR* Bow (1895), 185.

public conveyances.[43] Popular beliefs also contributed to such careless behaviour: many working-class people believed that medical remedies for whooping cough were of little avail, because the disease would run its course until May arrived; this belief, noted Samuel Lovett, was 'one of those nursery sayings which it seems impossible to get rid of'.[44] Recognized complications of whooping cough, such as pneumonia, bronchiectasis, secondary bacterial pneumonias, and mechanical damage to the lungs were certainly encouraged by such exposure. Indeed, authorities such as William Squire and Charles West expressly disapproved of the popular practice of taking whooping children to breathe in emissions from gasworks, on the grounds that the exposure involved was dangerous.[45]

If exposure was one important element in disproportionate working-class whooping-cough mortality, domestic living conditions were almost certainly another. In the 1890s James Laing discovered a direct correlation between size of house and whooping-cough mortality. In the one-roomed houses of Aberdeen, case mortality averaged 7.8 per cent, a figure greatly in excess of the average for all sizes of house, which stood at 4.7 per cent, and the disease was three-and-a-half times more fatal to children living in one-roomed houses than to children living in houses of five or more rooms.[46] As the *Lancet* had earlier observed, fatalities were largely confined to the classes whose living accommodation made the isolation and treatment of the patient 'simply impossible'.[47] William Rendle's belief that 'with fair management' whooping cough was 'by no means a destroying complaint',[48] is supported by the comparatively lower fatality among the better classes of the period, and by Charles West's injunction to avoid medication of all but the most serious cases.[49] Laing's results confirm the impossibility of nursing care of sufficiently high and sustained quality to save lives in the overcrowded living conditions of the Victorian poor.

Overcrowded living accommodation not only impaired the quality of nursing care, but may also have contributed to increased mortality through more severe infection. Contemporary observers were not unaware of this. Thus Robert Lee, formerly of the Great Ormond Street Hospital, drew attention in 1898 to the 'singular fact' that the more whooping-cough patients there were in one apartment, the more violent were their symptoms and the more difficult their relief. In the crowded courts of west-central London, he had often seen 'three or four children suffer in one room from the malady and it was usual in my experience for one or more to die'.[50]

[43] *Lancet* (1893), ii. 409; *MOQR* Whitechapel (1, 1880), 6; *MOAR* Clapham (1891), 112.
[44] *MOAR* St Giles (1875), 43.
[45] *Lancet* (1876), i. 324.
[46] Laing, 'Whooping cough', 595.
[47] *Lancet* (1876), i. 324.
[48] *MOQR* St George's, Southwark (1, 1858), 8.
[49] West, *Lectures*, 504, 510–11.
[50] *Lancet* (1898), i. 183.

William Squire, similarly, noted the 'aggravation of all symptoms' following the confinement of one or more sufferers in a single room.[51] Parents in such a situation also caught the disease, Lee claimed, even though they had had it in childhood. In fact this was not improbable, since childhood whooping cough does not, in fact, confer lifelong immunity, and adolescents and adults with declining immunity may develop the typical disease, or a brief atypical illness, when re-exposed to infection.[52] Lee, interestingly, inferred that the concentration of cases concentrated also the 'poison' of the disease.[53] Unfortunately the LCC medical officer, Shirley Murphy, who drew graphs of the relationship between overcrowding and mortality from a number of diseases in 1898, did not include whooping cough as a separate item.[54] No modern study has yet investigated the relationship between infective dose and severity of disease in whooping cough, but fatality rates for measles are significantly higher where several children have the disease simultaneously, and the risks of infection and heightened virulence of scarlet fever are also linked to the greater dose infection associated with overcrowded conditions.[55]

Lee was writing to oppose the creation of a special whooping-cough ward at the Great Ormond Street Hospital: he was afraid that it might create a 'powerful focus of infection' and do more harm than good.[56] Lee's language and views indicate how easily the epidemiological ideas of the 1860s and 1870s survived into the age of bacteriology where no bacteriological advances had been made. The idea of a dangerous concentration of whooping-cough 'poison', clearly still in Lee's mind in 1898, had its origins in the concept of whooping cough as a 'zymotic' or filth disease, even though it had only ever fitted doubtfully into this category. In the mid-1860s, for example, George Buchanan had observed of measles, scarlet fever, and whooping cough that only time would reveal accurately the effect of sewerage works and improved water-supply on these diseases, since their epidemics 'may revolve in long periods'. With respect to whooping cough, he noted, cautiously, 'some approach to regularity' in the way it declined as housing conditions (through sanitary works) improved.[57] Observation as well as theory governed the pronouncements of the best sanitarians.

While some allowance should be made for the influence of mid-nineteenth-century disease theory, Buchanan's statement is not without interest. It is

[51] Squire, 'Whooping cough', 1,774. Isabella Beeton's belief in whooping cough as 'a purely spasmodic disease' is also revealing in this context. In her view, it was 'only infectious through the faculty of imitation, a habit that all children are remarkably apt to fall into', and one which afflicted adults as well: *The Management of Children in Sickness and in Health* (1873), 33.

[52] Thomas, 'Epidemiology of pertussis', 257. [53] *Lancet* (1898), i. 183.

[54] *MOAR* LCC (1898), diagram 20.

[55] Peter Aaby *et al.*, 'Overcrowding and intensive exposure as determinants of measles mortality', *American Journal of Epidemiology*, 120 (1984), 49–63; B. B. Breese and C. Breese Hall, *Beta Haemolytic Streptococcal Diseases*, (Boston, 1978), 41.

[56] *Lancet* (1898), i. 183.

[57] George Buchanan, 'Results hitherto obtained in various parts of England by works and regulations designed to promote public health', *MOAR* PC, PP 1867 xxxvii. App. 2, p. 43.

noticeable, for example, that in London whooping-cough mortality was highest in the crowded and insanitary central and eastern districts, where slum clearances and in some cases the later influx of Jewish refugees substantially altered either the nature of local housing or the character and hygienic practices of the population. Other observers besides Buchanan noted a correlation between sanitary conditions and whooping-cough mortality. William Squire, whose practice at the North London Hospital for Diseases of the Chest and at St George's Dispensary, Hanover Square, made him familiar with the circumstances of respiratory illness and its seasonal patterns among the poor, defined spring as the major season for whooping-cough mortality. 'Cold', he noted, 'adds indirectly to the intensity of this disease . . . it is increased by overcrowding, bad ventilation, and the confinement of the sick in close apartments. All the hygienic defects which lead to rickets in that way add greatly to the bad effects of whooping cough.'[58] In the association between rickets and whooping cough may lie a further clue to the distribution of mortality from the latter, and to its association with insanitary conditions.

Rickets is widely accepted as being the result of dietary deficiency of vitamin D, resulting in defective growth of bone,[59] although it is primarily caused by insufficiency of sunlight, which permits the synthesis of calciferol, the calcifying hormone released into the bloodstream by the skin.[60] It is this that has led to rickets being nominated as the 'first air-pollution disease'.[61] Children deprived of sunlight need vitamin D in their diet (from animal or fish fats, or dairy products), and rickets affects those lacking a sufficiency from either source.[62] The nineteenth-century evidence linking rickets with deprivation of sunlight is certainly conclusive.[63] An investigation sponsored by the British Medical Association in 1889 showed the geographical distribution of the disease to be closely associated with large towns, and with industrial and mining areas. Thus not only London and its suburbs, but also the mining areas of Kent, Cornwall, Somerset, and north Essex showed a high incidence of rickets, as well as the industrial areas of Scotland and the North.[64] In London itself, only the wealthy residential districts of Belgravia and Mayfair were free of the disease, together with places in some of the 'high-lying outskirts':

[58] Squire, 'Whooping cough', 1,771.

[59] For rickets as a vitamin deficiency disease, see J. O. Forfar and G. C. Arneil (eds.), *A Textbook of Paediatric Medicine*, 3rd edn. (Edinburgh 1984), 1,299.

[60] Dame Harriette Chick, 'The discovery of vitamins', *Progress in Food and Nutrition Science*, 1 (1975), 10–13; Robert L. Summitt, *Comprehensive Pediatrics* (St Louis, Miss., 1990), 160. Other authorities accept the disease as being due to either dietary deficiency, or inadequate ultraviolet light, or to a combination of these factors: see e.g. Peter Wingate, *The Penguin Medical Encyclopaedia* (Harmondsworth, 1972), 363; H. Jolly and M. Levene, *Diseases of Children* (1985), 505–7.

[61] W. F. Loomis, 'Rickets', *Scientific American*, 6 (1970), 77–91.

[62] Wingate, *Encyclopaedia*, 363.

[63] *Pace* A. S. Wohl, *Endangered Lives: Public Health in Victorian Britain* (1984), 57.

[64] *British Medical Journal*, (1889), i. 114. I confess I am not able to explain the report's allusion to mining in East Anglia.

Brondesbury, Hampstead, Highbury, Stroud Green, Peckham, and Forest Hill, and the 'riparian and middle-class' Putney and Wandsworth. In the suburbs the concentration of rickets became less the further away from the centre; but everywhere else in the capital endured a more or less dense incidence of rickets.[65]

The social mix of most of the London districts obscures the exact class-incidence of rickets in the BMA survey, but there is evidence that the disease was not only present among the urban working classes. On coming to a London practice in the 1850s, for example, John Snow was struck by the number of cases of rickets he observed, not only among the poor, but extensively among the middle classes. In children in their second and third year, the characteristic outward curvature of the tibia and fibula 'seemed almost the rule'.[66] Although, according to Arthur Newsholme, the incidence of rickets was declining after 1870,[67] it remained one of the commonest disorders of childhood in English cities up to the 1920s. In 1909 the Great Ormond Street paediatrician Graham Still noted that 44.6 per cent of the children under 3 brought to his hospital practice presented with rickets, and cited figures of 30.3 per cent and over 50 per cent for Manchester and Edinburgh respectively.[68] While the high levels of pollution present in the air of Victorian London were no doubt a major contributor to this miserable picture, dietary inadequacies and social factors were also implicated. Margaret Ferguson, for example, found that the mothers of rachitic children studied in Glasgow nearly all admitted that they were unable to take their children out: either they had to go out to work themselves, or they had lodgers who demanded a great deal of attention, or, 'in not a few instances they had two or more young children and had no facilities for taking them out, being neither able to take both of them out nor to leave one of them at home'.[69] Other factors singled out by Ferguson are equally significant of the problems posed by young children, relative poverty, and restricted urban living: the housing of rachitic families was generally not only overcrowded, but had no easy access to the outer world, while the mother 'as a result of her unfavourable surroundings . . . has lost the vitality to contend against them';[70] a factor which probably further reduced her offsprings' chances of obtaining fresh air and all-important sunlight.

The significance of social factors is further suggested by some of the observed features of rickets at this period. Although it was often seen among children up to the age of 10, it was essentially a disease of infancy and childhood: clinically, it was most frequently observed between nine and eighteen

[65] *British Medical Journal*, (1889), i. 114.

[66] *Lancet* (1857), ii. 4.

[67] *MOAR* LGB, PP. 1914–15 xxv, p. 19. See also Arthur Newsholme, *Fifty Years in Public Health* (1935), 365.

[68] G. F. Still, *Common Disorders and Diseases of Childhood*, (1909), 82.

[69] M. Ferguson, 'A study of the social and economic factors in the causation of rickets', *MRC Special Report Series*, 20 (1917), 71.

[70] Ibid. 99.

months.[71] It was also apparently a seasonal disease. Ferguson's colleague, Leonard Findlay, noted evidence from independent observers and the out-patient departments of childrens' hospitals alike that cases became especially numerous in spring, and tailed off towards autumn.[72] The German specialist Von Hansemann found that almost all children born during the autumn and dying the following spring showed evidence of rickets, whereas those born in spring and dying in the autumn were free of the disease. In his experience the most severe examples of rickets were met with in children born in spring, who died at the age of 1 year.[73]

The age and seasonal incidence of rickets in young children, as reported by Leonard Findlay, is thus of particular interest with respect to the observed relationship between that disease and whooping cough, whose greatest mortality occurred in spring, and among children under 2. William Squire noted particularly that young children 'under defective hygienic conditions, or the subjects of rickets, are least likely to make the favourable recovery generally expected in uncomplicated whooping cough'. While the risk of unfavourable results from whooping cough diminished with each year of childhood, 'the impaired resistance of the chest walls in rickets may place a child of seven much in the state of another at two or three years old'.[74]

In more severe cases of whooping cough, the stamina of the child is evidently one of the critical factors in survival, and where rickets was present in any degree the child's stamina would be critically impaired. Thus the sanitary defects which, together with air pollution, had the effect of raising the incidence of rickets—dark housing and narrow streets, overcrowding, and indoor life—also contributed to raising the mortality from whooping cough.

Nutritional factors cannot, therefore, be ignored in considering whooping cough. Although the disease does not seem to be more severe in malnourished children, such children will not withstand a severe attack of it so well.[75] Where poorly nourished children suffer an attack of measles, which further reduces nutritional status, followed within a few months by one of whooping cough, their chances of succumbing to the latter are greatly increased.[76] In the nineteenth century it was observed that outbreaks of whooping cough frequently followed upon epidemics of measles, and vice versa.[77] The successive effects of these two infectious diseases on poorly nourished small children must often have resulted in a fatal outcome where the child had survived the first attack, for whooping cough also diminishes nutritional status, especially in infants. William Squire, for example, noted that the youngest children might escape with good sanitary surroundings and individual care, unless they were debilitated 'by previous illness such as measles, or a defective state of nutrition

[71] Ibid. (Introduction by Leonard Findlay), 17, 18. [72] Ibid. 20. [73] Ibid.
[74] Squire, 'Whooping cough', 1,774. [75] Morley, *Paediatric Priorities*, 238.
[76] See example in Morley and Woodland, *See How They Grow*, 93.
[77] *Lancet* (1886), i. 870; Creighton, *Epidemics*, ii. 674; Smith, *People's Health*, 107.

at the time of the attack'.[78] Where children experience whooping cough under the age of six months, they are unlikely to gain much weight in the following six months,[79] and even in older children recovery may take time. As Squire explained, the disease often lasts two months, 'and is followed by a tedious convalescence. The pulmonary deposits may originate tuberculosis, the disturbances of nutrition and innervation are long in being restored; some of the accidents of rickets never.'[80] The mortality of whooping cough was plainly increased through its interactions with other infectious childhood diseases, and with the nutritional status of its victims. The increasing concentration of whooping-cough fatalities among the under-fives during the later years of the century, at a time when overall mortality from the disease was falling slightly, may indicate small but significant improvements in general levels of nutrition among the working classes.

Declining death-rates from whooping cough were certainly not the result of any direct intervention by the medical profession or preventive authorities, for the disease aroused little interest among nineteenth-century practitioners and epidemiologists. Attention was primarily directed at treatment of the disease, and most of the literature reflects this.[81] During the 1860s there were calls for improved treatments, in view of its increasing ravages,[82] but it was not until the mid-1870s that 'practical epidemiology' in respect of it began to be considered.[83] Both the Registrar-General's Office and the Medical Department of the Local Government Board had only a cursory interest in whooping cough. Apart from Edward Smith's statistical essay of 1854, there are no epidemiological studies of the disease before 1901, when *Public Health* published James Laing's pioneering doctoral dissertation.[84] The general English medical apathy towards the disease was shared by the medical officers of health, who usually disclaimed all responsibility for both whooping cough and measles,[85] no doubt because both were known to be infectious before the nature of the disease was evident, and because care (or lack of it) within the home was felt to be an important factor in mortality.

Ignorance of the causal organism of whooping cough was not the reason for the apathy of the preventive authorities towards it. By the mid-1870s it was widely accepted that the disease was most infectious before its nature had become apparent.[86] As with measles, this made preventive action as regards the spread of the disease rather difficult. There was some argument in favour

[78] Squire, 'Whooping cough', 1,774.

[79] Morley and Woodland, *See How They Grow*, 96.

[80] Squire, 'Whooping cough', 1,773.

[81] See G. Hewitt, *The Pathology of Hooping Cough* (1855); (article by Edward Smith on 'Hooping Cough') Sir J. R. Reynolds (ed.), *A System of Medicine*, 2nd edn. (1870); Charles West, *Lectures*; William H. Barlow, 'The nature of whooping cough', *Lancet* (1886), i. 870, 915, 966. For a range of treatments current at the time, see Smith, *People's Health*, 108–9.

[82] *Lancet* (1860), i. 484, 530; (1861), i. 501.

[83] *Lancet* (1876), i. 181.

[84] Laing, 'Whooping cough', 585–99. See n. 7 above.

[85] *Lancet* (1882), i. 657.

[86] *Lancet* (1876), i. 181.

of taking victims into hospital, in the belief that hospital admission would decrease mortality, as the *Lancet* considered that it would undoubtedly do;[87] however, the fact that most of the worst cases were infants who could not be separated from their mothers acted as a deterrent to this course of action.[88] Medical officers of health occasionally suggested the desirability of isolating whooping-cough cases, but generally retracted before the problems posed by their lack of knowledge of the disease, especially of the length of the infectious period. In 1894 Weil stated his opinion that the disease was only contagious during the premonitary catarrhal stage, and later confirmed his hypothesis by experiment.[89] The problem of when the disease ceased to be infectious remained; and suggestions that whooping cough should be made a notifiable disease foundered on this obstacle.[90] Whooping-cough cases were accepted into neither the London Fever Hospital nor the Metropolitan Asylums Board hospitals in this period. Even when individual towns took advantage of the permissive clauses of the Infectious Diseases Notification Act 1889, and introduced the measure, the benefits were doubtful. In Aberdeen the result was apparently not a decrease but an increase in incidence, despite known cases being forbidden to move outside their homes during the infectious period.[91]

The traditional preventive measures of improved sanitation, isolation, disinfection, and hospital treatment were thus not only powerless against whooping cough, but were seen to be so by contemporaries. No concerted preventive effort was made to check the disease, yet it did begin to decline. With no observable alteration in the type of the disease or reduction in incidence, the national death-rate began its decline in about 1870. By the end of the century Laing was recording diminished case-fatality rates in Aberdeen. From an average of 10.5 per cent in the years 1882–9, Aberdeen's case-fatality rates fell to 5.3 per cent in 1890–1900. In 1897–1900 they were stable at 3.6 per cent, but during the major epidemic of 1901–2 mortality averaged only 2.8 per cent:[92] a favourable rate indeed when compared to the average 4.4 per cent fatality experienced in the 1920s before the introduction of sulphonamides.[93] Laing noted the reduction in case-mortality as 'the one gratifying feature' of the notification experiment.[94]

Laing was tempted to attribute the fall in case-mortality to the work of Aberdeen's sanitary department. Since the introduction of notification, they

[87] Ibid. 324. [88] Ibid.; *MOQR* Whitechapel (1, 1880), 6.

[89] *Public Health*, 9 (1896–7), 310.

[90] Ibid. 157. In fact, the duration of the infectious period in whooping cough varies. In an untreated patient the likelihood of a positive culture decreases from 95% in the first week to 50% or less in the fourth week, and positive cultures are unusual after the fifth week of the disease: Topley and Wilson, *Principles*, iii. 465.

[91] Laing, 'Whooping cough', 599. [92] Ibid. 592.

[93] G. F. Brooks and T. M. Buchanan, 'Pertussis in the United States', *Journal of Infectious Diseases*, 122 (1970), 123–5.

[94] Laing, 'Whooping cough', 599.

had supervised reported cases, issuing instructions on the hygienic treatment of patients, and warning against the dangers of exposure to cold.[95] In searching for reasons for the national decline in whooping-cough death-rates, it is equally tempting, if rash, to ascribe the decline in part at least to rising nursing standards. The fall in whooping-cough mortality was small before 1900, and it may possibly be that it reflects some such improvement with a disease in which, unlike its companions among the infectious diseases of childhood, the quality of nursing care is recognized as being of paramount importance. The experience of Aberdeen, with raised incidence and reduced case-fatality as a result of notification, certainly suggests this as a possibility; while the raised incidence no doubt reflected the concentration of infection in the home, any ill effects as regards individual cases seems to have been offset by improved nursing supervision.

For it seems likely that some improvement in the nursing care and even in the treatment of sick children occurred after 1850. This was probably largely confined to the better-off classes, rather than the poor, but it may have reached, unevenly, quite far down the social scale. The rise of the lower middle class at this period had an unknown effect on health and domestic practices; while the district nursing movement, the mothers' meetings, ladies' sanitary associations, and other middle-class efforts at improving the quality of domestic life for the poor cannot have been without effect in raising standards of some fraction of the uneducated working class.[96] Indeed, the awareness of the problems of children's diseases and of their nursing are likely to have been rising among middle-class women also at this period. The emerging medical speciality of paediatrics was partly responsible for this.[97] Thus Catharine Gladstone, later the author of an International Health Exhibition pamphlet on healthy nurseries and bedrooms, was as a young wife in the 1840s presented with 'Combe on Infancy' by Sir Charles Locock, and told to read and learn it by heart.[98]

The work of Charles West, the moving spirit behind the foundation of the Hospital for Sick Children in Great Ormond Street, was probably of central importance in these developments. West was acknowledged as the pioneer of a new approach to the care and treatment of children. In 1847 he was the first to deliver a systematic lecture course on the diseases of children at the Middlesex Hospital, with the aim of teaching the student to recognize them, and

95 Laing, 'Whooping cough', 599.

96 The work of Frank Prochaska has been enlightening in this regard, see F. K. Prochaska, 'Body and Soul: Bible nurses and the poor in Victorian London', *Historical Research* 60 (Oct. 1987), 336–48; also W. J. Fishman, *East End 1888* (1988), 32.

97 For the development of paediatrics in the 19th cent., see Elizabeth Raine Lomax, 'Advances in pediatrics and in infant care in nineteenth century England', unpublished Ph.D thesis, University of California, Los Angeles (1972).

98 C. Gladstone, *Healthy Nurseries and Bedrooms* (1884), 1. 'Combe on Infancy' was the last published work of the celebrated phrenologist Andrew Combe: *A Treatise on the Physiological and Moral Management of Infancy* (1840).

provide safe guide-lines for their treatment and cure.[99] His *Lectures* on the childhood diseases, first published in 1849, ran to seven editions by 1884, and he became a recognized authority on the subject.[100] His inauguration of the first children's hospital seen in Britain certainly laid an educational foundation for parents in the care of sick children, which should not be underestimated, even though conditions in the hospital were in the early years far from ideal.[101] From a mere 142 in-patients and 1,250 out-patients in 1852, Great Ormond Street was by 1871 treating 678 in-patients and 11,763 out-patients a year.[102]

West's educational endeavours reached beyond the lecture room and hospital. He early published a small book, *How to Nurse Sick Children*, which was sold in aid of the hospital, and which was aimed specifically at persons engaged in the domestic nursing of sick children;[103] in 1885 he published a companion, this time intended for the education of mothers (middle-class mothers, he admitted), that they might 'wisely second' the efforts of their doctors.[104] The chief principle of West's nursing practice was the comfort, cleanliness, and nourishment of the patient, its guiding thought his sympathetic treatment. Although it is impossible to assess the impact of West's work on domestic practice, there is no doubt that by instituting the Hospital for Sick Children at Great Ormond Street he laid the English foundation of the new medical speciality of paediatrics, and of a new development in the tradition of English hospitals. Within twenty years of the opening of Great Ormond Street there were more than twenty children's hospitals in its vicinity;[105] little, however, is known of their social or domestic impact, or of the part they played in their local communities.[106]

Improvements in domestic nursing may have played a part in the small decline in whooping-cough mortality between 1870 and 1900. The sharper mortality decline in London, where there were more children's hospitals and greater philanthropic activity than in other cities, is perhaps significant here. Other factors were undoubtedly at work, however. Basic sanitary measures of sewage disposal and water improvement are unlikely to have affected incidence or mortality because of the nature of the disease, but improvements in housing could have, if Laing's correlation between overcrowding and whooping-cough mortality is accepted. The increase in London mortality in the 1870s took place mostly in districts which experienced rapid increases in population in that decade, and may reflect housing and domestic pressures. Yet whooping-

[99] West, *Lectures*, vii. [100] *Lancet* (1896), ii. 1583.

[101] Smith, *People's Health*, 152–4.

[102] T. T. Higgins, *Great Ormond Street* (1952), 30.

[103] This appears to have been written in the 1860s; the early editions were published anonymously. The first traceable edition is the reissue of 1908: *How to Nurse Sick Children*.

[104] West, *Mother's Manual*. [105] West, *How to Nurse*, preface to the 1908 edition, p. v.

[106] See e.g. M. Newby, *Sick Childrens' Hospital Nursing in Nineteenth Century Britain*, Occasional Papers in the History of Nursing and Caring, 1 (1987).

cough mortality declined in areas of London where little or no improvement in overcrowding levels occurred before 1900 (Figs. 1.2, 1.3).

The evidence for the influence of social factors on mortality makes it tempting to accept that they were a significant factor in reducing whooping-cough mortality. Among the London districts, it was those that saw the greatest social and structural changes that enjoyed the greatest falls in whooping-cough mortality. In St Giles, Holborn, and the City, slum-clearance and the replacement of dwellings by warehouses and business premises probably let in more light and air; while the replacement of slums by model dwellings also brought in a better class of people. In Whitechapel and St George-in-the-East, the influx of European Jews changed local social behaviour and introduced different domestic practices, although only after the elements that drove declining whooping-cough mortality had begun to take effect. It is also possible that lightening skies in the later years of the century reduced the severity of rickets, and that small changes in child-rearing practices, or small improvements in diet, diminished its severity or even its incidence. Anthony Wohl has concluded grimly that, if Victorian air-pollution legislation had any effect at all, it was only to change the colour of the skies from 'gritty black to a dull grey',[107] while London fogs reached a peak of frequency in the 1890s.[108] Yet evidence from Vienna in the 1920s demonstrates the power of even limited quantities of sunlight in ameliorating rickets.[109] While it is impossible to assess the prevalence of rickets among working-class children in the nineteenth century, it was evidently not an unavoidable feature of a poor urban childhood. Jewish children in particular, among whom mortality from the infectious diseases was said to be low, were frequently observed to be remarkably free of rickets, and there can be no doubt that Jewish dietary habits and family eating practices contributed to this freedom. Poverty and domestic overcrowding were factors in the etiology of both whooping cough and rickets, but so were the diet and social behaviour of the families in which these diseases occurred, and changing domestic practices may have been significant in effecting small reductions in the incidence of rickets and the fatality of whooping-cough.[110]

Yet the possibility of a wider cycle of mortality, uninfluenced by the activities of man, must always be considered. It is possible that greater resistance to the impact of the disease and its sequelae was bred first in those areas which had suffered its worst ravages. The pattern of most rapid decline in the districts which previously experienced the greatest mortality lends weight to this interpretation, as does the fact that this pattern was repeated in Scottish cities. The problem of domestic overcrowding, which seems to have had a critical

[107] Wohl, *Endangered Lives*, 219. [108] P. Brimblecombe, *The Big Smoke* (1987), 111.

[109] Dame Harriette Chick, 'Study of rickets in Vienna, 1919–1922', *Medical History*, 20 (1976), 46–9.

[110] I have developed some of these ideas in 'Rickets and the rest: childcare, diet and the infectious children's diseases', *Social History of Medicine* 5 (1992), 389–412.

influence on the incidence and fatality of whooping cough, did not diminish in inner London during the Victorian period.[111] It is notable, too, that measles, another highly infectious disease with a similar age-incidence to whooping cough, whose mortality is similarly linked to overcrowding, poor nutrition, and lack of care, did not become less fatal in this period. The discrepancy in timing of the mortality-declines of measles and whooping-cough suggests the possible operation of a natural cycle of rising resistance to the latter. There are no firm conclusions to be drawn from London's experience of whooping cough in the nineteenth century; an array of possibilities, and a balance of probabilities, are all that the historian can offer. The only assertion that can be maintained with any certainty is that London's preventive services bore little, if any, direct responsibility for the city's reduced whooping-cough mortality in the years before 1900.

[111] See G. S. Jones, *Outcast London* (1971), 175–8; A. S. Wohl, 'The housing of the working classes in London, 1815–1914', in S. D. Chapman (ed.), *The History of Working-Class Housing* (Newton Abbot, 1971), 24–5; John Burnett, *A Social History of Housing 1815–1985*, 2nd edn. (1986), 144–5.

2
Measles

> Measles may be termed the opprobrium of present-day sanitary science. With the doubtful exception of diphtheria, it is the only zymotic disease which has not proved amenable to preventive discipline.
>
> A. Campbell Munro (1890–1)

> Measles and its death-toll [is a] question of national importance. Its satisfactory solution is one of the greatest problems of latter-day preventive medicine.
>
> Frederick Waldo and David Walsh (1896)

'Measles is known to all mankind', wrote Frederick Waldo and David Walsh in 1896. 'The mere mention of measles suffices to carry one back to the nursery and the schoolroom, when "catching" maladies were looked upon as a necessary part of the game.'[1] There was no question of avoiding measles; it is one of the most infectious diseases known to man; a disease from which almost everyone will suffer, unless protected by immunization. Its ubiquity, and its nature, usually as a mild infection of early childhood, have so moulded the popular perception of the disease across generations that it is generally regarded, in Western Europe at least, as a disease of small account. The roots of this attitude lie far back in the past. In the great Victorian cities and in the countryside, among all social classes, measles was mostly thought to be harmless, an integral part of a child's experience.[2] It is a comprehensible attitude, for ordinary measles is a mild disease, requiring nursing, but little in the way of treatment. In the nineteenth century, nevertheless, it was one of the major killers of children under 5 years old.

Middle-class mothers in the 1860s and 1870s were well aware of the dangers of measles. Isabella Beeton described it as a 'much-dreaded disease' which entailed 'more evils on the health of childhood than any other'.[3] For measles can be one of the most formidable of the infectious diseases of childhood. Mild in itself, it can assume a life-threatening form in certain circumstances, in 'virgin-soil' populations, and in the severely undernourished. It also predisposes sufferers to secondary bacterial infections, which may result in permanent hearing and respiratory injury. Under adverse social conditions, and

[1] F. J. Waldo and D. Walsh, 'Murder by Measles', *Nineteenth Century*, 39 (1896), 957.

[2] F. B. Smith, *The People's Health* (1987), 146; *MOAR* St James's, Westminster (1859), 13; Battersea (1885), 33, 43; Clapham (1891), 114; Bow (Poplar) (1895), 180.

[3] Isabella Beeton, *The Management of Children in Sickness and in Health* (1873), 29.

where nursing care is inadequate, bronchitis and broncho-pneumonia are damaging (and the latter often fatal) sequelae. Despite this, and despite the anxious warnings of some middle-class mothers, measles, like whooping cough, was seen as beyond the scope of the preventive services for most of the Victorian period.[4] The medical officers of health infrequently remarked on the disease in their reports, except on occasion to lament its fatality,[5] and nothing was done in any practical way to reduce the measles death-rate. It was only in the 1880s, against a background of worry about national degeneration,[6] and with a declining scarlet-fever mortality, that public-health officials became concerned about measles; by the mid-1890s anxiety over measles mortality had become one of the major features of English preventive literature.

Nineteenth-century measles was both an endemic and an epidemic disease. It was endemic in large cities like London and Liverpool, but was generally epidemic in rural areas. High epidemic death-rates in the latter were due, according to the registrar-general, to 'either gross carelessness *or* bad sanitary conditions', probably both.[7] Unlike whooping cough, measles mortality did not decline in any consistent way in the nineteenth century. Both nationally and in London, mortality rates among the under-fives were higher in the 1890s than in any decade since figures became available in the 1850s. The disease was generally more fatal in large towns and mining areas, and in the North of England more than the South;[8] death-rates in London were well above the national average (Table 2.1). In these larger populations measles had a double cycle, of roughly biennial epidemics within a longer cycle of about ten years, during which mortality was higher or lower than in the decades on either side (Fig. 2.1, Table 2.1). In the long term, the pattern of the disease in the capital mirrored the wave-like movement of the national curve (Fig. 2.1). In the earlier part of the period, the epidemic years of London and of the rest of the country seldom coincided.[9] This became less true in the closing decades of the century, partly perhaps as measles became established in the wider interplay of epidemic diseases, partly because of the increasing range and speed of communications across the country. However, in London, as in Sunderland (1885) and Glasgow (1889),[10] the epidemic wave of the disease moved across the city over a year or series of years, so that different districts experienced maxima successively rather than all at once (Fig. 2.4).

[4] *Lancet* (1882), i. 657. [5] See n. 2 above; also *MOAR* Shoreditch (1896), 243.

[6] G. S. Jones, *Outcast London* (1972), chap. 6. As Jones observes (p. 286), in the 1880s this theory coloured all social debates on the condition of the casual poor.

[7] RGAR, PP 1893–4, xxi. 11. [8] Ibid. 12.

[9] RGAR, PP 1868–9 xxxii. 54. For the pattern of measles epidemics, see A. Cliff and P. Haggett, 'Island Epidemics', *Scientific American*, 250 (May 1984), 110–17.

[10] Harry Drinkwater, *The Epidemic of Measles Prevalent in Sunderland* (Edinburgh, 1885), 47: the disease was epidemic in Bishopswearmouth North from January to April, then moved on to Bishopswearmouth South; *Glasgow Medical Journal*, 31 (1889), 'Epidemic of measles in Glasgow' 278: here the disease moved from west to east, beginning in the wealthier quarters of the city.

TABLE 2.1. *Measles death-rates per 1,000 living under 5, 1851–1900*

	1851–60	1861–70	1871–80	1881–90	1891–1900
England and Wales	2.80	3.00	2.57	3.13	3.25
London	4.23	4.17	3.65	4.74	4.82

Sources: Decennial reports of the registrar-general; Theodore Thomson, 'Report upon Measles', *MOAR* LGB, PP 1895, li, p. 139.

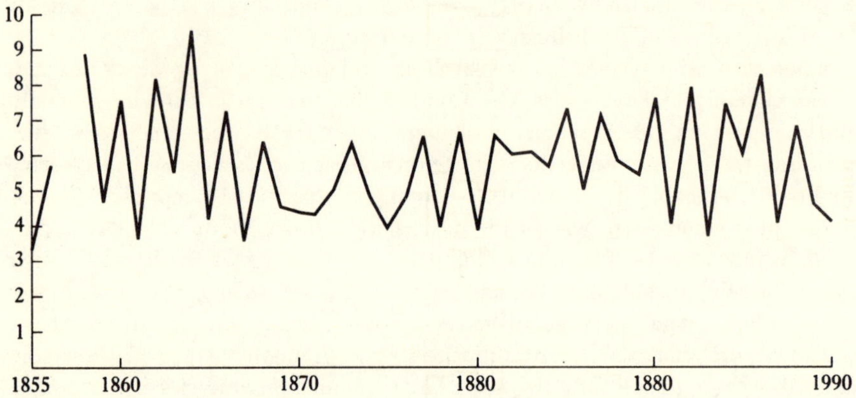

FIG. 2.1. *Measles deaths in London, 1855–1900, per 10,000 population.*

In London, the contrast between falling whooping-cough mortality among the under-fives after 1870, and the rising toll from measles could not be more complete. Nearly all the London districts experienced raised measles mortalities in the 1880s or 1890s (Figs. 2.2, 2.3). There is little obvious pattern to the geography or extent of this raised mortality, although in Hampstead and Hackney, for example, it may be associated with the outward movement of the poorer classes from the centre, and the spread of poor and overcrowded housing into the suburbs. Whatever the factors influencing the decline of whooping cough—better nursing for infants, improved nutrition among older children, diminishing severity of rickets, or the intrinsic cycle of the disease—they had no impact on measles. The virus of measles is extremely stable, so that fatalities are occasioned by external factors. However, whereas whooping cough is most fatal to infants under twelve months old, measles is most fatal to those between twelve and twenty-four months. This age-differential fatality may begin to explain the diverging mortality patterns of the two diseases. The second year of life is that in which true mobility begins, and in which the mother's attention is likely to be distracted by a further pregnancy or the birth of a younger sibling. The nursing of sick and convalescent children and the

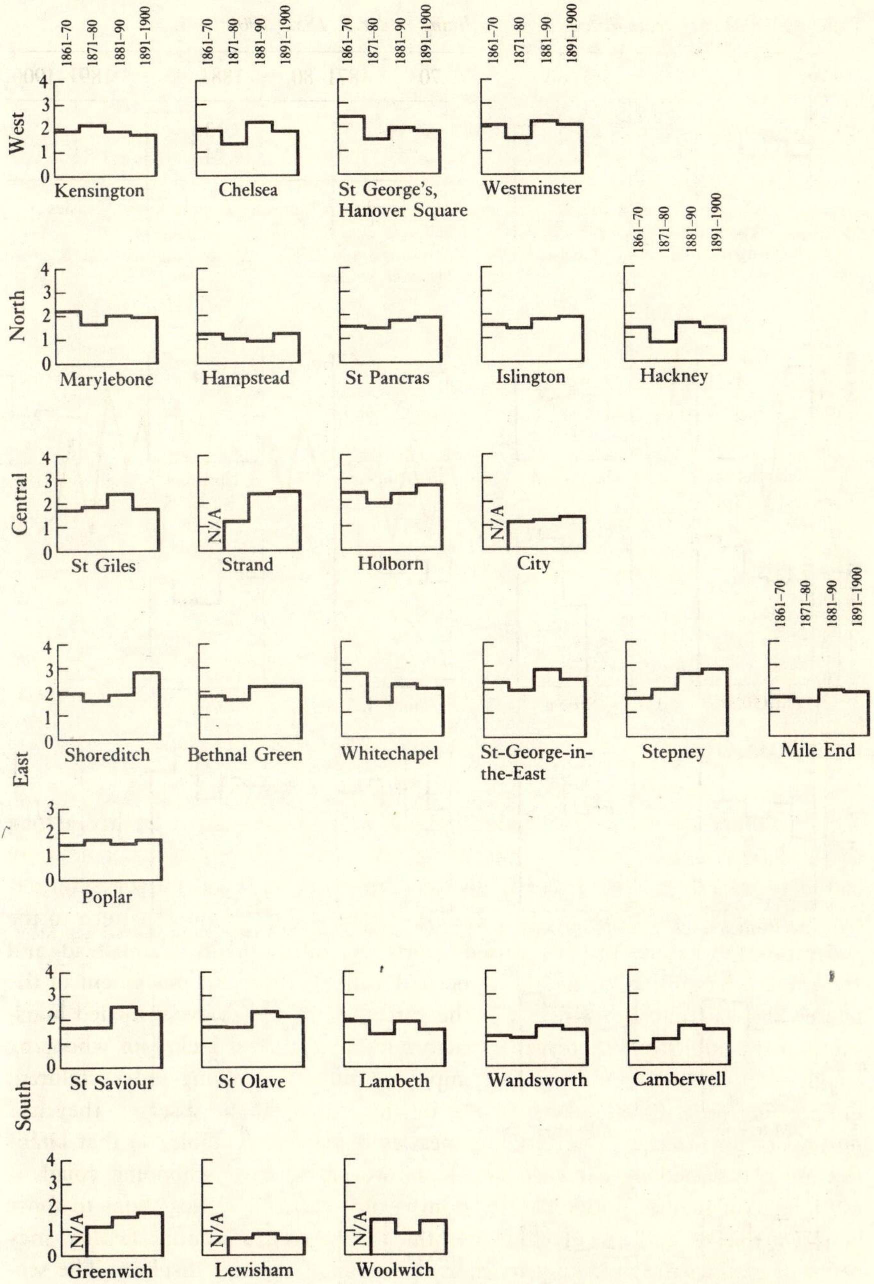

FIG. 2.2. *Measles deaths per 1,000 under 15, London districts; decennial averages, 1861–1900.*

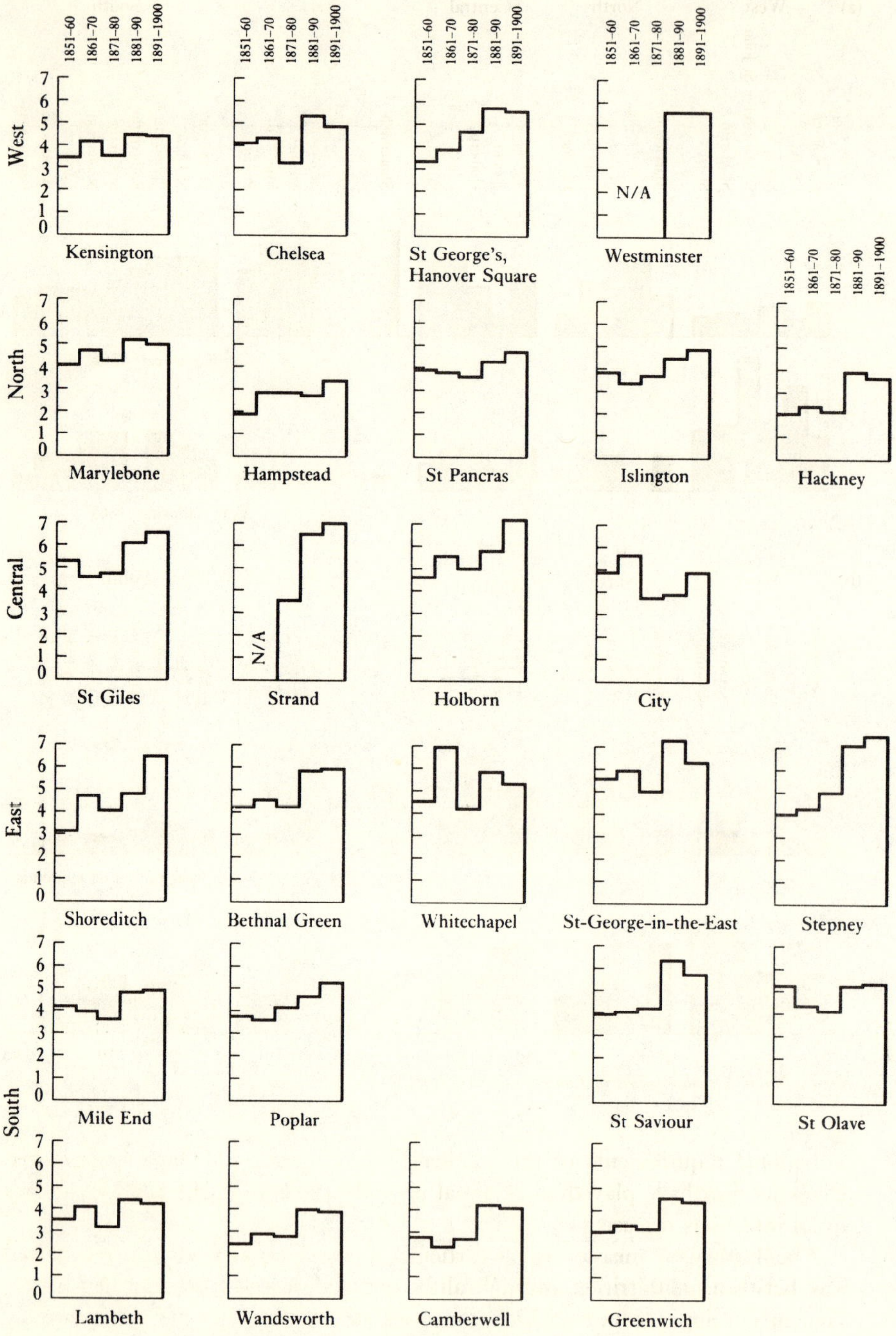

FIG. 2.3. *Measles deaths in London, 1851–1900, per 1,000 under 5.*

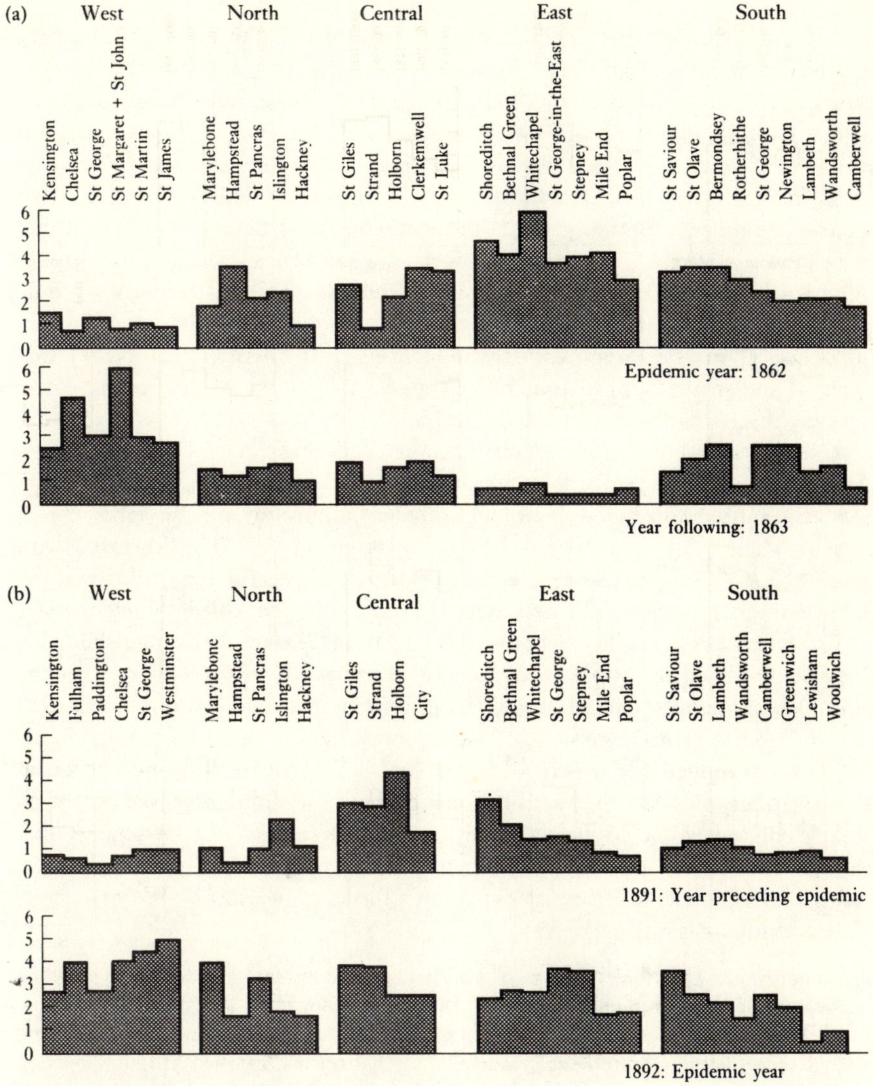

FIG. 2.4.a/b *Measles deaths in London sanitary districts.*

nutritional requirements of the toddler may be neglected. Once again, social elements may have played an essential part in determining the fatality patterns of an infectious disease.

The history of measles is of particular interest because of the recognized link between malnutrition and mortality from the disease. Although it is rarely fatal in developed countries today, measles still causes high mortalities among chronically undernourished children in developing countries. In England and

Wales, the high measles mortalities which characterized the nineteenth century diminished rapidly after 1917. Thomas McKeown, pointing out that 82 per cent of the fall in measles mortality in the post-registration period occurred before specific measures against it became available in the 1930s,[11] argued that two factors were responsible for this remarkable decline in fatality. First, increased industrialization in the early nineteenth century had led to an increased measles mortality, and the subsequent decline owed something to increased resistance to the disease in later generations. Secondly, and more importantly in McKeown's view, rising standards of living reduced chronic malnutrition which had impaired resistance to the disease.[12] McKeown's views on historical measles were strongly influenced by modern Third World evidence,[13] and in the light of the known measles experience of developing countries his thesis sounds attractively plausible.

Recent research by Peter Aaby and his colleagues has, however, drawn attention to the importance of overcrowding as a determinant of early infection and severe disease in measles, although modern authorities on the behaviour of measles have hitherto stressed the relationship of the disease with malnutrition.[14] Aaby's research is of considerable interest in elucidating the behaviour of measles in the nineteenth century, but the link between measles and malnutrition must be considered, since David Morley, a distinguished student of childhood infections in developing countries, is of the opinion that the examples of measles and diarrhoea greatly strengthen McKeown's thesis that the nineteenth-century mortality decline was due to improved nutrition.[15] Morley has applied his expertise to the past, and believes that the change in fatality of measles in the West has come about through improved nutrition among children. When Western children were weaned on to a low-energy diet of high-fibre bread sops, they, like poor African children today, did not have enough energy-reserves to resist the severer forms of measles.[16] 'We may speculate', Morley has written,

> that improvement in the nutrition of children started in the 19th century with the introduction of steel milling of cereals and the removal of more and more dietary fibre from the childrens' diet. At the same time other foods, especially dairy products and refined sugar, became more readily available, so that the mother had little difficulty in providing a high energy diet.[17]

[11] Thomas McKeown, *The Modern Rise of Population* (1976), 97.

[12] Ibid. 85, 135–6.

[13] Ibid. 136.

[14] Peter Aaby *et al.*, 'Overcrowding and intensive exposure as determinants of measles mortality', *American Journal of Epidemiology*, 120 (1984), 49–63; id., 'Severe measles: a reappraisal of the role of nutrition, overcrowding, and virus dose', *Medical Hypotheses*, 18 (1985), 93–112.

[15] D. C. Morley, 'Nutrition and infectious disease', in E. J. Clegg and J. P. Garlick (eds.), *Disease and Urbanisation* (1980), 40.

[16] David C. Morley, 'Severe measles', in N. F. Stanley and R. A. Joske (eds.), *Changing Disease Patterns and Human Behaviour* (1980), 126; id. 'Nutrition', 40.

[17] Morley, 'Nutrition', 40.

Elsewhere, Morley and his colleagues have suggested that the improved condition of children in the West 'owes much to the increase in the consumption of fats and oils over the last 150 years'.[18] General dietary improvements, therefore, as in the consumption of jam and margarine, might be responsible for modern reductions in measles fatality in developed countries.

Closer examination of the nineteenth-century evidence, however, suggests several modifications of McKeown's argument, as well as underlining the dangers of applying recent experience to the epidemiological problems of the past. It should be borne in mind that national measles mortality did not begin to decline in any convincing way until the end of the First World War (Table 2.2); that extensive removal of dietary fibre from wheat began in the 1850s, and that steel-roller mills, introduced from the Continent in 1878, had superseded stone-ground mills by 1910.[19] With regard to fats and oils, consumption of which increased from 12 lb. per person per year in 1880 to 26 lb. in 1909–13 and 44 lb. in 1924–8,[20] aggregate figures conceal the serious downward adjustments which should certainly be made for poverty and family eating patterns among the lower classes.

TABLE 2.2. *Mean average measles mortality per million population, in decennia, 1861–1920*

1861–70	377	1891–1900	399
1871–80	322	1901–10	318
1881–90	392	1911–20	308

Source: *RGDS* (1921), part III, table 12, p. 66.

Measles is an acute infectious and highly communicable disease.[21] It is characterized by catarrhal symptoms in the prodromal stage, by Koplik's spots (tiny bluish-white specks) on the buccal mucal membrane,[22] and by a typical speckled rash. The rash, which first appears on the face and hands, soon spreads across the whole body, so that the patient, as Waldo and Walsh observed, 'in that condition . . . is often likened by the wit of the family to a boiled lobster'.[23] Measles is a near universal infection in societies unprotected

[18] C. Dearden, P. Harman, and D. Morley, 'Eating more fats and oils as a step towards overcoming malnutrition', *Tropical Doctor*, 10 (1980), 138.

[19] D. Burkitt and H. C. Trowell (eds.), *Refined Carbohydrate Foods and Disease* (1975), article by Hugh Trowell on 'Refined Carbohydrate Foods', 44.

[20] J. P. Greaves and D. F. Hollingsworth, 'Trends in food consumption in the United Kingdom', *World Review of Nutrition and Dietetics*, 6 (1964), table 1, p. 38.

[21] F. H. Top and P. H. Wehrle (eds.), *Communicable and Infectious Diseases*, ninth edn. (St Louis, Miss., 1981), 407–8.

[22] Koplik pointed out that these could be detected before the appearance of the rash: *Lancet* (1898), i. 1,205. Although widely accepted elsewhere as a most useful diagnostic tool, the value and reliability of Koplik's spots continued to be debated in Britain in the early years of the 20th cent.: Harold Balme, 'The signs and symptoms of measles in relation to diagnosis and prognosis', *Practitioner*, 73: 2 (1904), 508–9.

[23] Waldo and Walsh, 'Murder', 957.

by immunization programmes, and where it has been absent for any considerable length of time, it is usually highly lethal. It is infectious for the last two-to-four days of its incubation period, before the first symptoms occur; it is also infectious during its initial stage (prodromal period), during which the symptoms are generally similar to those of the common cold, and for the five or six days during which the rash is present. In most cases transmission is direct, by droplet infection from person to person, although it is also likely to be airborne within a small area, and to be transmitted on articles freshly soiled by discharges from the nose and throat. Maternal antibodies protect babies up to the age of six months. Thereafter immunity wanes, and, as with whooping cough, the youngest age-groups are most at risk, mortality being highest in the second year of life.

Although measles has long been known in Europe, being described by Rhazes, Fracastorious, and Sydenham among others, the natural history and etiology of the disease were unknown before the mid-1840s.[24] In 1846, however, the disease broke out in the Faroe Islands, where it had been absent since 1781, and some two-thirds of the 8,000 strong population—all those too young to have acquired immunity in 1781—caught the disease. The Danish government, whose responsibility the Islands were, sent Peter Ludwig Panum to investigate, and to try to alleviate, the epidemic. It was a superb opportunity for epidemiological study, and Panum made the most of it. His *Observations Made During the Epidemic of Measles on the Faroe Islands* is a classic of the genre, and established much of the epidemiology of the disease: the incubation period, the period of communicability, the immunity resulting from a single attack, and its purely contagious nature.[25] Little was added to Panum's work during the rest of the century, although with the advent of bacteriology it became generally accepted by 1900 that the disease was caused by some microscopic *materies morbi*.[26]

Modern research in developing countries has added something to our understanding of measles, beyond the epidemiological characteristics established by Panum. There is little doubt that there is a link between measles mortality and chronic malnutrition: a World Health Organization report of the mid-1970s noted malnutrition as a concomitant factor in 60 per cent of measles deaths in Latin America,[27] and the working of this symbiosis has been amply demonstrated by David Morley among children in the underdeveloped countries of Africa.[28] Morley has described a severe form of measles, whose

[24] Barbara Gastell, 'Measles: a potentially finite history', *Journal of the History of Medicine*, 28 (1973), 34.

[25] Peter Ludwig Panum, '*Observations Made During The Epidemic of Measles on the Faroe Islands in the Year 1846* (New York, 1940).

[26] Gastell, 'Finite history', 37.

[27] M. Behar, 'A deadly combination', *World Health* (Feb.–Mar. 1974), 29. It was this report which deeply influenced McKeown, *Modern Rise*, 136.

[28] David Morley and Margaret Woodland, *See How They Grow: Monitoring Child Health in Developing Countries* (1979), 89–94.

manifestation seems to be the result of poor nutritional status.[29] In this severe measles the rash is much darker than normal, and the spots tend to coalesce; broncho-pneumonia is a frequent and severe complication, and chronic diarrhoea a damaging sequel.[30] Not only are malnourished children more likely to develop this severe form of measles, but measles itself has a deleterious effect on the child's nutritional status: protein-energy malnutrition is more likely to occur than after any other common childhood infection.[31]

Morley has made much use of historical evidence, arguing that the severe measles present in West Africa closely resembles measles in England before the twentieth century.[32] Nevertheless, Morley does not take his argument to the logical historical extreme, and suggest that nutritional standards in nineteenth-century England paralleled those of modern West Africa. Indeed, comparing case-fatality rates in the Metropolitan Asylums Board hospitals (1911–14) with those in a Nigerian hospital (1956–61), Morley notes the much higher fatalities in the 3–5 age-group in Nigeria (in fact fatalities were higher in Nigeria at all ages over 1 year), observing that this is 'perhaps because only serious cases were admitted to the Ilesha hospital and because malnutrition contributes to measles mortality in African children'.[33] Only serious cases were admitted to the MAB hospitals; did malnutrition not play a part in early twentieth-century England? For historians, Morley's historical work on measles raises more questions than it answers. In a different vein, perhaps more usefully to the historian, Morley has also pointed to the importance of existing beliefs as to the nature and domestic treatment of measles as a clue to mortality in some areas.[34]

Morley's work on measles must clearly be taken into account by anyone attempting to unravel the historical puzzle of why the disease began to decline in the second decade of the twentieth century. Given the association between measles and malnutrition which Morley has demonstrated, and which may appear to be a principal prop for McKeown's argument that rising living standards were responsible for declining mortality, it could be assumed that for children, or at least that proportion of the child population which contributed measles fatalities, there was no appreciable rise in nutritional standards before the First World War. On the simple statistical level there are some grounds for associating nineteenth-century measles mortality with living standards or, more exactly, with fluctuations in the national and individual urban economies. Thus the pattern of measles mortality for the period 1850–1900 can be seen to move in waves which roughly correspond to economic fluctuations, both nationally and in London. Lower in the 1850s, when the economy was buoyed

[29] David Morley, *Paediatric Priorities in the Developing World* (1973), chap. 12.

[30] Ibid. 213–17.

[31] Ibid. 207.

[32] D. Morley, M. Woodland, and W. J. Martin, 'Measles in Nigerian children', *Journal of Hygiene, Cambridge*, 61 (1963), 115.

[33] Ibid. 118.

[34] Morley, *Paediatric Priorities*, 212.

by war, measles deaths rose in the 1860s, when both the Lancashire cotton districts and associated ports, and London were enduring local economic crises; they fell in the 1870s, as the economy stabilized, and rose again with the economic troubles of the mid-1880s.[35] These 'waves' of measles were noted by contemporaries, though without being connected to economic conditions.[36] Given, however, the significance of overcrowding to the infectiousness and severity of measles, it may be that changes in social behaviour determined by economic conditions influenced levels of measles fatality, as they influenced the epidemicity of typhus and perhaps the epidemiology of tuberculosis.[37] The social dislocation caused by slum demolitions in East and South London, which produced typhus outbreaks in these districts in the prosperous summer of 1873, may also have been responsible, through increased overcrowding, for an upsurge in measles fatality: in the autumn of 1873 the disease was said to be more fatally present in London than at any time since 1840,[38] and the highest mortalities were recorded in those eastern, northern, and southern districts which were most vulnerable to stress overcrowding.

Beyond the statistics, the picture is more complicated. Throughout the period, measles fatality was heaviest in London and the large towns: those areas where overcrowding, poverty, and malnutrition were concentrated, and where, arguably, economic fluctuations impinged most on ordinary lives. Here, it may be suggested, lies the clue to the distribution of fatalities: as one standard medical text observes: 'Poor nutrition, overcrowding and low economic status predispose to complications and death.'[39] Later nineteenth-century authorities were united in the conviction that measles fatalities occurred principally among the working classes and the poor, where overcrowding, poor nutrition, and low economic status were to be found.[40] Evidence from Glasgow suggests, in line with Aaby's findings, that measles mortality, like whooping cough and lung disease, rose with overcrowding levels: mortality in one-roomed accommodation was twice as high as in two-roomed, diminishing further with the size of lodging (Table 2.3).[41] Poverty and overcrowding were evidently salient factors in nineteenth-century measles deaths; yet it cannot therefore be assumed that 'severe measles', indicating chronic malnutrition, was constantly present during the period.

Measles first came to prominence in England as a serious contributor to childhood mortality in the late eighteenth and early nineteenth century when,

[35] See Fig. 2.1; also McKeown, *Modern Rise*, 96, fig. 5.3.

[36] B. A. Whitelegge, 'Measles epidemics, major and minor', *Transactions of the Epidemiological Society*, 12, (1892–3), 47.

[37] For the changes in social behaviour brought about by economic distress see below, Chap. 7, 'Typhus'; also Chap. 8, 'Tuberculosis'.

[38] *Lancet* (1873), ii. 783.

[39] Top and Wehrle, *Communicable Diseases*, 410.

[40] Charles Creighton, *A History of Epidemics in Britain*, 2 vols. (Cambridge, 1894), ii. 665; *Lancet* (1888), ii. 1,143 and (1896), ii. 201.

[41] A. K. Chalmers, *The Health of Glasgow, 1818–1925* (Glasgow 1930), 343.

TABLE 2.3. *Measles deaths in Glasgow, by house size*

Number of Rooms	Cases	Deaths	Case fatality %
1	3,849	355	9.2
2	14,490	663	4.6
3	2,573	64	2.5
4+	855	13	1.5
Institutions	266	28	10.5
TOTAL	22,033	1,123	5.1

Source: Chalmers, *Health of Glasgow, 1818–1925* (Glasgow, 1930), 343.

with the introduction of smallpox vaccination, more children were spared death from smallpox in infancy.[42] There are some indications that measles was more severe in type in the first half of the century than later. This may have been because of the relative novelty of the disease, but also perhaps because of low nutritional standards. In the great outbreak of 1807–8, for example, as many adults as children were reported to be affected, while many who recovered from the disease were afflicted with 'kwashiorkor-like' symptoms.[43] By the 1850s, however, measles appeared to be settling into an endemic pattern: there had been a shift in mortality towards the first two years of life.[44] By the 1880s Charles West could observe that in its severest manifestations—'the rash presenting from the first a dark, livid hue'[45]—measles was less common than it had been in the 1840s.[46] During the serious outbreak in Sunderland of 1885, at a time when the local population was under severe economic stress, the general practitioner Harry Drinkwater observed the disease to be of a virulence and magnitude that he had not previously encountered in his seven-and-a-half years of practice: in nearly half the cases the rash was exceptionally dark, darker than he had ever seen before.[47] The Sunderland outbreak was exceptional. By the early 1890s Arthur Whitelegge was arguing that there were occasional definite variations in the quality of the disease, which determined its epidemic character. Severe epidemics which killed 10 per cent or more of those attacked were not familiar in Britain: in his view, the key to the epidemiology of measles lay in 'stability of type amid violent fluctuations in quantity'.[48]

The severe measles described by David Morley, characterized by the dark rash and closely associated with malnutrition,[49] does not seem to have been

[42] Smith, *People's Health*, 145–6.

[43] Creighton, *Epidemics*, ii. 650–2; Morley, Woodland, and Martin, 'Measles', 127.

[44] 'Report on district nursing in measles and whooping cough', *Lancet* (1915), ii. 193.

[45] Charles West, *Lectures on the Diseases of Infancy and Childhood*, seventh edn. (1884), 855.

[46] Ibid. [47] Drinkwater, *Measles*, 7, 21. [48] Whitelegge, 'Measles', 43, 53.

[49] Morley, *Paediatric Priorities*, 213–18. Broncho-pneumonia, which Morley also describes as being associated with this condition, clearly developed with great frequency in 19th cent. England in cases without severe rash; the post-measles diarrhoea which Morley describes was often present

commonly present in England by the second half of the nineteenth century. Exceptionally, it appeared in the Sunderland district of Bishopswearmouth North in 1885, at a time when a large proportion of the population had been suffering from semi-starvation for some time, as a result of the almost total stagnation of the shipbuilding and bottle-making trades.[50] In general, however, the nutritional status of English children at this period was good enough to prevent the manifestation of such severe measles. Absence of the dark rash is one indicator, and sequelae suggesting protein-energy deficiency are rarely described in the literature. Creighton's apparently convincing correlations between measles and 'consumption' for 1674 and 1733 cannot be duplicated for the nineteenth century, while his references to measles 'marasmus' are all for the period before 'the age of statistics', as he called his own time.[51] Contemporary terminology, of course, adds confusion to this issue. By the later nineteenth century 'marasmus' was out of favour as a term to describe wasting,[52] and there are indications that the rather less flexible term 'consumption' (which has a principal connotation of respiratory tuberculosis) was in use instead.

Breakdown of a previous primary tuberculosis is a recognized danger of measles, a danger which was also known in the nineteenth century.[53] Charles West's observations on this subject are worth discussing, for they again suggest that, besides true tuberculosis, serious depletion of nutritional status by measles occurred, but to a lesser extent than at an earlier period. Thus West noted that the hazard of 'phthisical disease' as a sequel of measles, 'though perhaps overrated by the older observers, who had not the means we now possess of forming a correct diagnosis', was yet a very real one: the physician should be on his guard against it throughout the whole period of convalescence. Phthisis might develop concurrently with measles, or after it.[54] West goes on to describe a set of circumstances which suggest a modern post-measles pattern described by Morley, in which the child ceases to gain weight after measles, has episodes of diarrhoea and bronchitis, and dies, in this case of whooping cough, a month later.[55] According to West, post-measles phthisis

but was apparently considered curable (see n. 64 below). The 28% cases suffering diarrhoea in the East London outbreak of 1904 suffered it in the prodromal stage; only 10.6% of cases suffered it in the later stages of the disease: Balme, 'Signs', 506, 513.

50 Drinkwater, *Measles*, 8. Peter Aaby and his colleagues have argued that the severity of the Sunderland Epidemic was related to virus dose: see Aaby *et al.*, 'Severe measles in Sunderland, 1885: a European-African comparison of causes of severe infection', *International Journal of Epidemiology*, 15 (1986), 101–7. Following this argument, the severity of the epidemic would hinge not on malnutrition, but on stress overcrowding brought about by economies in rent among unemployed families.

51 Creighton, *Epidemics*, ii. 632–8; Morley, Woodland, and Martin, 'Measles', 126–7.

52 'Marasmus' was thought to be too often used as a shield for neglect, without describing a real condition.

53 Morley, *Paediatric Priorities*, 93; West, *Lectures*, 857.

54 West, *Lectures*, 857.

55 Morley and Woodland, *See How They Grow*, 93.

was more chronic, 'and the child's history is that of an incomplete recovery from measles having been succeeded by progressive failure in health, and by the gradual appearance of consumption, which proves fatal in some months, or a year'.[56] Yet this development of consumption was not apparently common. In Sunderland, where one might have expected a crop of such cases, there were just two (0.6 per cent). Drinkwater observed that one 'will probably recover' (so this may have been a case of depleted nutrition), but that the other had a family history of the disease, and subsequently died.[57] Among Harold Balme's 227 cases in poor East End families, one child died of tuberculous meningitis two months after being attacked by measles.[58]

Charles West's essay on measles makes interesting reading in the light of modern work on the disease. Where relatively recent research has begun to make clear that measles inflicts its more serious damage though disruption of the epithelium,[59] West had been claiming this a century ago. Thus Morley describes how the epithelial disruption produced by measles may both block the narrow bronchi of the infant lung and present as broncho-pnuemonia, and disturb the mucosa of the bowels to present diarrhoea.[60] West similarly describes how the 'extreme susceptibility of the mucous membranes, to which are due the persistence of the cough, the supervention of bronchitis, or the occurrence of ulcerative inflammation of the fauces and larynx on the decline of the rubeloid eruption, very frequently, extends to the intestinal canal and gives rise to diarrhoea'.[61] West observes that this diarrhoea yields readily to treatment in the greater number of cases. In view of Morley's revelation of how this diarrhoea may precipitate children into malnutrition,[62] West's popularly recommended treatment is significant. He described how a child was especially exhausted by diarrhoea, and urged that it must be supported by proper nourishment; even if the child did not seek food, it must not be allowed to remain without it, or it would starve to death.[63] West's advocacy of such treatment may throw some light on the gradual decline that can be detected beneath the terrible peaks of infant-diarrhoea mortality which mark this period, but he goes on to speak revealingly of the popular beliefs that had to be overcome if such mortality was to be reduced. He frequently met with cases of neglected measles diarrhoea among the poor, for they, 'in accordance with the notions of humoral pathology current among the vulgar, generally regard looseness of the bowels after fever as a salutary provision of nature'. In such instances diarrhoea could either seriously threaten life, or, in some cases, destroy it.[64]

The pitfalls of this type of juggling with fragile historical evidence are

56 West, *Lectures*, 857.
57 Drinkwater, *Measles*, 33, 47.
58 Balme, 'Signs', 514.
59 Morley, *Paediatric Priorities*, 216; 'Severe measles', 122.
60 Id., 'Severe measles', 122.
61 West, *Lectures*, 857.
62 Morley, 'Severe measles', 123.
63 Charles West, *How to Nurse Sick Children*, new edn. (1908), 4.
64 West, *Lectures*, 857.

numerous, yet the impression remains that chronic malnutrition was not a considerable contributor to measles mortality in the years after about 1850. This is not to suggest more than that English children were generally above a certain threshold of undernourishment where the dark rash and severe malnutrition manifested themselves as symptom and sequelae in measles. Black measles was not unknown in nineteenth-century England, although middle-class fears of 'malignant measles' may have their roots in the effect of the disease on low-resistance populations in the early years of the century. While doctors acknowledged the existence of severe reactions to measles, they implicitly associated such reactions with poverty. The fictional Mary Norton, who feared to lose her two small children from measles, was reassured by her practitioner: 'Be under no alarm. Your children's blood is sweet and pure—it has not been poisoned by wine or beer'.[65] However, infantile scurvy, present among all social classes,[66] may have had a more specific part to play. William Squire linked 'black measles' more particularly to deficient nutrition and scurvy.[67] Petechial or haemorrhagic blotches in 'cases of considerable intensity' were, he wrote, of 'grave import . . . as indicative of scorbutus, which state ranks next to impaired nutrition in infants, as the most unfavourable concomitant of measles. Black or haemorrhagic measles, without scorbutus, is more rare than haemorrhagic or black small-pox.' Infantile scurvy was at this period a problem among the well-to-do, as well as among London's working class, in whom the disease was also found in adults,[68] yet it is clear that Squire did not consider 'black measles' in any form to be widely current. In his view the great mortality from measles was due to lung diseases, 'not at the height of the fever, but in the second week'.[69] The rarity of black measles by the end of the period was confirmed by J. W. Washbourn (1863–1902), who noted that although the condition was mentioned by his colleague E. W. Goodall, he had never observed it himself.[70] At the same period, Henry Ashby, physician to the Manchester Children's Hospital, stated haemorrhagic measles to be 'extremely rare'.[71]

The cardinal factor in the continuing high mortality from measles in the later nineteenth century seems to have been respiratory complications. Bronchitis and broncho-pneumonia, especially the latter, were the cardinal factors: it has been estimated that over 90 per cent of measles mortality in the past was due to 'pneumonia'.[72] Poor nutritional standards perhaps had a part to play, but not distinguishably from the effects of overcrowding in producing

[65] Eliza Warren, *How I Managed My Children From Infancy to Marriage* (1865), 31.

[66] W. B. Cheadle, *The Artificial Feeding of Infants* (1889), 174–98. Infantile scurvy was none the less an apparently rare disorder, certainly compared to rickets: ibid. 175, 179–80.

[67] William Squire, 'Measles', in R. Quain (ed.), *A Dictionary of Medicine* (1882), 928.

[68] *Lancet* (1859), i. 87; (1889), i. 911.

[69] Squire, 'Measles', 928.

[70] E. W. Goodall and J. W. Washbourn, *A Manual of Infectious Diseases* (1908), 156.

[71] H. Ashby and G. A. Wright, *The Diseases of Children*, fifth edn. (1905), 291.

[72] Top and Wehrle, *Communicable Diseases*, 409.

severer forms of the disease. Ashby, who recognized the far higher measles mortality of the poor, stated explicitly that 'where a number of measles cases are crowded together pneumonia of a malignant type is apt to be rife'.[73] Drinkwater, however, considered broncho-pneumonia to indicate 'a depressed state of health', noting that 'we generally meet with it in its worst form amongst the poorest people'. Eighty per cent of the Sunderland broncho-pneumonia cases were among the children of paupers, and most of the others were children who had been 'delicate' all their lives, or who had recently suffered from bronchitis.[74] Secondary bacterial infections were the principal complications experienced and the primary contributor to continuing high measles mortality up to 1916.[75] Of the 311 cases observed by Drinkwater in 1885, 22.8 per cent developed severe respiratory complications—9.3 per cent bronchitis, 9 per cent broncho-pneumonia, and 4.5 per cent pneumonia. Eighty per cent of the deaths were attributable to respiratory complications. Similarly, of 227 cases observed by Harold Balme in East London, 20 per cent developed broncho-pneumonia, and a further 14 per cent bronchitis.[76]

The causes of this high incidence of respiratory complication did not lie simply in the nutritional status of the children concerned, but in their environment and in the type of care they received. If domestic overcrowding led to high infective doses and maximized the risks of infection for the very young, the overcrowded, poorly ventilated and, probably, warm and damp domestic conditions of the poor and the inadequate nursing received by sick and convalescent children contributed to a high rate of secondary infection. As one inspector of schools noted bluntly: 'They are neglected very much after an illness like measles, and they die at a great rate.'[77] Similarly, Francis Stevens of Camberwell told his vestry in 1898 that the large annual toll of measles deaths was 'almost entirely due to the fact that children are exposed to draughts and chills while still suffering from the disease.'[78]

It was commonly observed that the respiratory complications of measles occurred because children were not coddled sufficiently when ill. As measles was widely accepted as inevitable, and disregarded by parents as something children had to go through, the illness was often completely neglected until the symptoms became severe.[79] Frederick Waldo recorded that, at best, poor children had one or two days in bed 'while the rash is "out"'.[80] Thus, at Cullompton in Devon in the 1890s children were confined to bed, plied with

[73] Ashby and Wright, *Diseases*, 288.

[74] Drinkwater, *Measles*, 28. But note Aaby *et al.*'s analysis of the relative distribution of complications among primary and secondary cases in this outbreak: 'Measles in Sunderland', 101–2.

[75] West, *Lectures*, 854; *Lancet* (1893), i. 21.

[76] Drinkwater, *Measles*, 27; Balme, 'Signs', 513.

[77] *ICPD*, PP 1904 xxxii, q. 8,006.

[78] Camberwell *VM* (30 Nov. 1898); see also *MOAR* St George's, Southwark (1892), 17.

[79] *MOAR* St James's, Westminster (1859), 13; *Public Health*, 2 (1889–90), 508. See also Smith, *People's Health*, 146.

[80] Waldo and Walsh, 'Murder', 960.

hot cider, and covered with heaps of clothes.[81] The survival of the idea that the rash must be brought out was no doubt responsible for this treatment—a lingering folk memory of the belief that measles was the result of the 'bad blood' of menstruation which, unable to escape in pregnancy, entered the foetus and later came out in the form of a rash.[82] It was a sign of the differing public perception of the two diseases that parents were often anxious to have their child's fever described as measles rather than anything else, and that among the poor scarlet fever was universally called measles until a doctor advised otherwise.[83] When in 1889 scarlet fever became a notifiable disease and measles did not, this perception probably became even more widespread.[84]

Lack of nursing was probably most serious for the youngest and most vulnerable age-groups. As do small African children today, small Victorian working-class children led fairly busy lives, shopping and visiting, even the sick, with their mothers, or being minded by siblings, exposed to droplet infection and the elements.[85] The popular underestimate of the seriousness of measles undoubtedly exposed these children to the life-threatening respiratory complications which made the disease so fatal in this period. Malnourished children apparently remain infectious for a longer period than well-nourished children, which, Morley feels, explains why infection occurred at a younger age in the past.[86] However, school-age children were commonly sent to school until the appearance of the rash, and there is ample evidence that the introduction of compulsory school attendance after 1870 caused measles epidemics to spread with unprecedented rapidity in urban areas.[87] As a result, it is possible that infants were more frequently exposed to measles in the pre-school years, at an age when they were especially at risk from secondary infections. Such evidence as there is suggests that measles was more frequently introduced into the home by school-age children than by other sources. Harry Drinkwater, for example, noted that among forty-nine families with three or more children, primary cases occurred in the school-age children in twenty-seven cases (55 per cent), in the youngest child in nine cases (18 per cent), and in intermediate children in thirteen cases (26.5 per cent).[88] In early twentieth-century Willesden, 86 per cent of primary cases were among schoolchildren; in Finsbury, 71 per cent.[89] In a society where there were strong disincentives to keeping a child from school, where infants moved freely among all age-groups, and where the possibilities of infection were disregarded, high infant infection-rates were inevitable. Among the better-off classes, where greater care was taken

[81] *Lancet* (1898), i. 1,079.
[82] Morley, *Paediatric Priorities*, 212.
[83] *Lancet* (1890), i. 176.
[84] Ibid.
[85] Drinkwater, *Measles*, 14.
[86] Morley, 'Severe measles', 120.
[87] *Public Health*, 12 (1899–1900), 244.
[88] Drinkwater. *Measles*, 14. In the extended African family, however, it has been shown that measles usually passes from one pre-school child to another: Morley, 'Severe measles', 121.
[89] *Lancet* (1915), ii. 193.

to remove babies and very young children from the possibilities of infection,[90] it is possible that the risks of complications were further reduced by a higher age at infection.

The seasonal pattern of measles mortality further reinforces the impression that deaths were often due to avoidable secondary respiratory infection. In temperate climates measles exhibits two peaks of seasonal incidence, in early winter and spring, the latter peak being the higher.[91] In nineteenth-century England measles mortality generally matched this pattern, except in London and the industrial towns of Lancashire, where more deaths occurred in the winter season.[92] Creighton attributed this excess winter mortality to 'the injurious effects of London air in winter upon a disease which is largely a trouble of the respiratory organs'.[93] Winter fogs are known to have an adverse effect on bronchitis,[94] and the atmosphere of the Lancashire factory towns, while perhaps not as notoriously fog-laden as that of London, was undoubtedly dense enough to raise mortality from respiratory illness. The MOH for Huddersfield, Dr Cameron, observed that in both the fatal epidemics of 1882 and 1887, occurring in the spring quarter, the weather was warm, close, and damp, without rain, with 'a slight condensation of chill' at night;[95] ideal weather for the aggravating and spread of respiratory conditions. Where these pre-existed in measles victims, it was observed, there was a greater likelihood of respiratory complications, and in these cases measles was more likely to have a fatal outcome.[96] Harry Drinkwater, indeed, observed that while bronchitis was the most frequent complication of measles, it 'seems most frequently to arise from careless nursing, especially where it has not occurred before'.[97] Nursing was not easy in the damp, draughty, and overcrowded homes of the labouring classes; and where adverse weather conditions, and the pressures of the Victorian educational system further hampered the older child's chances of avoiding respiratory complications, high mortalities were the result.

It is thus with some certainty that measles mortality in this period can be ascribed largely to respiratory sequelae, perhaps encouraged by overcrowded housing but also brought about by popular beliefs and practices. Just as if malnutrition amounting to semi-starvation had been the cause of mortality, the children of the working classes and the poor were the most vulnerable. Deaths among the higher social classes were rare because, as the *Lancet* put it, these

90 *Lancet* (1873), ii. 783; Harry Kenwood, 'The notification of measles', *Journal of the Sanitary Institute*, 18 (1897), 176.

91 Top and Wehrle, *Communicable Diseases*, 408; *Lancet* (1893), i. 21; Creighton, *Epidemics*, ii. 664.

92 A. Buchan and A. Mitchell, 'The influence of weather on mortality from different diseases at different ages', *Journal of the Scottish Meteorological Society*, 4 (1875), 194 *RGAR*, PP 1884, xx p. xv; *Lancet* (1893), i. 21.

93 Creighton, *Epidemics*, ii. 664.

94 W. W. C. Topley and G. S. Wilson (eds.), *Principles of Bacteriology, Virology and Immunity*, seventh edn. (1984), iii. 399.

95 *Lancet* (1887), ii. 272. 96 Drinkwater, *Measles*, 25–6. 97 Ibid. 28.

classes took care of their children and were intelligent enough to put them under early treatment.[98] F. B. Smith has noted that the heroic treatment of measles began to be superseded in the 1850s by gentler methods.[99] Certainly Charles West and his successors emphasized that uncomplicated cases of measles required very little in the way of treatment.[100] West, for example, recommended a warm room, spare diet, and 'gentle antiphlogistic remedies'; Drinkwater, tepid baths, a warm room, and whatever food was desired.[101] The fictional Dr Vaughan would recommend only castor oil or a little Gregory's Powder, preferably the former.[102] The emphasis of treatment, and eventually of prevention, was very much on nursing. In 1896 Waldo observed that the death-rate among the well-to-do was due to 'better nursing of the patient, whereby the terribly fatal lung complications are avoided'.[103] In 1909 the *Lancet* was emphatic that the large majority of measles deaths 'are distinctly preventable by careful nursing and after-treatment'.[104] By 1911 the medical officer of the LGB was clear that 'the greatest scope for saving life lies in more complete medical attendance and in skilled nursing and supervision of patients treated at home'.[105]

It could be argued that the contemporary emphasis on nursing care for measles was simply a placebo remedy for a mortality which the preventive service could not acknowledge to be reducible only by resolution of the long-term problem of poverty. The medical officers of health, and the preventive services generally, always preferred environmental explanations for disease problems in this period. The widely different death-rates of well-to-do and poor were thus ascribed to socially acceptable factors. The general measles mortality-rate was estimated by West at 3 per cent of cases.[106] In Sunderland mortality was 8 per cent in 1885; while Sunderland seems to have been an exceptional case, Drinkwater was also exceptional in observing that in nearly every case death was due to the 'impoverished condition of the system beforehand'.[107] This observation was not repeated in other local studies. Frederick Waldo, whose sanitary district was one of the poorest in London, and who drew attention to the sharp contrast between measles death-rates in his area and in that of the wealthy St George's, Hanover Square, resolutely perceived the problem as one of nursing.[108] Death-rates in St George's, Southwark exceeded those for Sunderland, as they were markedly higher than Hanover Square (Table 2.4), but nowhere in Waldo's writings is any explicit consciousness of a nutritional problem expressed.[109]

98 *Lancet* (1898), i. 875; Kenwood, 'Notification', 176.

99 Smith, *People's Health*, 147.

100 West, *Lectures*, 858; Drinkwater, *Measles*, 444; *Lancet* (1871), i. 410; (1874), i. 139.

101 Drinkwater, *Measles*, 444.

102 Warren, *My Children*, 31.

103 Waldo and Walsh, 'Murder', 960.

104 *Lancet* (1909), i. 160.

105 'Memorandum on measles', quoted by the 'Report of district nursing in measles and whooping cough', *Lancet* (1915), ii. 193.

106 West, *Lectures*, 851.

107 Drinkwater, *Measles*, 45, 46.

108 Waldo and Walsh, 'Murder', 960.

109 i.e. in his reports as Medical Officer for St George's, Southwark, 1891–1900.

TABLE 2.4. *Comparative measles death-rates in London districts, 1894*

District	Actual deaths, 1894	Death-rate per 10,000 population	Per 10,000 population 1883–92
Southwark	100	16.6	9.0
Hanover Square	72	5.5	3.7
London	3,293	7.5	6.4

Source: F. J. Waldo and D. Walsh, 'Murder by measles', *Nineteenth Century*, 39 (1896), 958.

In all, the evidence suggests that the preventive authorities were correct to stress the importance of nursing care. Some impression of the significance of nursing quality among cases in a deprived population can be gained from Harold Balme's experience in early twentieth-century London. Balme's 227 cases occurred among children of the poorest class in London,[110] and the very high rate of respiratory complications—34 per cent, with 20 per cent broncho-pneumonia against Drinkwater's 22.8 per cent (98 per cent broncho-pneumonia)—undoubtedly reflects their poor general state of health. Yet Balme, by a dint of intensive nursing care, managed to keep mortality to 3 per cent. He decided to treat all cases, especially if they were aged under 2, from the outset as if they were already seriously ill.[111] Thus a separate cot was improvised (an orange-box, clothes-basket, or tin bath), and this was placed in a corner which could be both screened from draughts and ventilated by an open window. The children were dressed in wool-lined 'pneumonia jackets' provided by the Medical Mission, as well as a bed-gown, and the mother was instructed in daily care. The adoption of these measures before the appearance of serious symptoms was, Balme believed, the key to his success in achieving a 3 per cent mortality-rate, despite the patients' lowly condition in life, and despite the 20 per cent broncho-pneumonia rate—'that fatal complication'.[112] Similarly G. G. Gidley, describing the Cullompton outbreak of November-December 1894, experienced no deaths among the cases which came under his care from their beginning. Those cases left long without 'skilful treatment', however, either died within a few days, or survived only after 'severe hand-to-hand combat': among the lower classes, he noted, cases generally went untreated until broncho-pneumonia made its appearance.[113] In 1914 comparison was

[110] Balme, 'Signs', 504. It is perhaps an indication of their poor nutritional status that this high percentage developed serious respiratory complications in spite of such care from the beginning of their illness. One may speculate that some at least of these cases were of disrupted bronchi presenting as broncho-pneumonia rather than the result of secondary infections.

[111] Ibid. 515.

[112] Ibid.

[113] *Lancet* (1898), i. 1,079. This epidemic was complicated by the presence of lumbricoides (worms) in about 90% of cases, and by the absence of fireplaces in cottage bedrooms. Gidley's observation was that where young children with measles slept in unheated bedrooms on frosty nights, 'broncho-pneumonia usually supervened'.

made between Aberdeen, where there was notification but no further action against the disease, and Willesden, where the medical officer made 'strenuous efforts' to secure the medical supervision and proper nursing of cases. In Aberdeen mortality among the 1–4 age-group was 6.5 per cent, in Willesden, 3 per cent.[114]

Popular attitudes towards measles, continuing high levels of overcrowding, poor facilities for nursing care, and the predisposition of poorly nourished small children with existing respiratory disease to severe respiratory complications, probably explain the failure of the measles death-rates to fall in any real degree before 1916. In the decades after 1870, as other specific infectious death-rates began to fall, this exception among the infectious diseases began to receive greater attention. While local medical officers of health did little actively to stay the ravages of measles and whooping cough in their districts, discussion of this failure, and of ways of limiting the mortality of these diseases, began to fill the pages of preventive literature. Measles, perhaps because deaths were seen to be from preventible complications, figured in these discussions to a far greater extent than whooping cough. As early as 1871 there is evidence that medical men were concerned to achieve special care for such cases: in that year, the year of its opening, the Metropolitan Asylums Board (MAB) hospital at Homerton complained that it was being sent measles cases, although the disease was one that should not be mixed up with other infectious fevers.[115] In 1871, in revising its mission following the advent of the MAB hospitals, the London Fever Hospital began accepting measles cases. The *Lancet* observed on this occasion that the experiment was 'full of interest': measles was one of those diseases whose prevalence might 'undoubtedly' be controlled by hospital *isolation* (my italics).[116] Although the London Fever Hospital continued to accept measles cases, it remained the only London hospital to do so before 1910; the number of cases it accepted was statistically insignificant.

The question of the hospitalization of cases was one of the three great issues of the preventive debates surrounding measles control, the others being notification and school closure. In the early 1870s some doctors evidently already considered measles to be a disease worthy of hospital treatment in certain cases; Shirley Murphy, for example, then assistant medical officer at the London Fever Hospital, was strongly in favour.[117] Homerton Hospital, however, argued that where measles was complicated by pneumonia or diarrhoea, the danger to patients would only be increased by admission to hospitals containing cases of scarlet fever, typhus, and the like. 'Moreover, it would be practically ruinous to provide the hospital accommodation and proper attendance that would be required during an epidemic of measles, even if the mothers would allow their children to be removed.' Further, it was argued,

[114] *Lancet* (1914), i. 549. [115] *Lancet* (1871), i. 410. [116] *Lancet* (1877), ii. 99.
[117] Ibid. 143.

since measles patients were principally very young children, the benefits of hospital admission would be more than outweighed by the absence of the mother's care, and, for infants, of her breast milk.[118] These arguments remained the basis of the case against the hospitalization of measles, just as the high mortality from complications remained the principal argument in favour.[119] When the city of Glasgow tried to introduce the hospital treatment of measles cases between 1872 and 1877, it succeeded in removing only 159 cases, although 1,300 children died of the disease in the city during the same period. James Russell, the MOH, attributed the failure of the experiment to the impossibility of removing young infants from their homes, but added that at the root of both parental opposition to removal and his own reluctance to violate parental sentiment was the parental perception of measles as a process of nature, 'like teething'.[120]

While on the one hand the preventive authorities were acutely aware of the potential expense of hospitalizing cases of a disease as common as measles, the popular apathy towards the disease did little to encourage them to instigate radical measures of prevention. The preventive authorities were further inhibited by the general attitude of their colleagues in the profession, who were inclined to ridicule the idea of treating measles in hospital.[121] Even where attempts at measles control were made, as in Glasgow, time did not always bring results that seemed to justify the expense in money and energy. In Glasgow, Russell had hopefully noted in 1877 that, 'the effect of perseverance and education is very great in sanitary matters'. He instanced the case of scarlet fever, for which hospital treatment had also initially been viewed with disfavour, but which had become generally accepted, to the extent that 'we do not hesitate about compelling removal in fitting circumstances'.[122] Some ten years later, however, Glasgow was no nearer controlling the disease, despite a revolution in attitudes among the working classes.[123] A notable feature of the failure of the Glasgow experiment is perhaps that it was not combined with notification, a measure which did not become an acceptable part of preventive practice until the mid-1880s.

One aspect of the earlier preventive efforts against measles which militated against success was the profession's failure adequately to take account of the extreme infectiousness of the disease. Without vaccination there is no hope of controlling the incidence of measles, as opposed to its mortality. In the 1870s and 1880s, in the absence of hospital beds, notification, and professional treatment, it was the incidence of the disease which the authorities sought to curb.[124] This misguided principle also lay behind the school-closure policy, which became increasingly prominent from the later 1880s, although its value

[118] *Lancet* (1871), i, 410. [119] *Lancet* (1877), ii. 143. [120] Ibid. [121] Ibid.
[122] Ibid.
[123] 'Epidemic of measles in Glasgow', *Glasgow Medical Journal*, 31 (1889), 277–8.
[124] *Lancet* (1877), ii. 99.

was much debated. The danger of epidemic disease in schools had been recognized in the private sector before 1870,[125] but with the opening of the public elementary schools and requirements for attendance after 1870 the problem acquired a new dimension, and preventive anxieties on this score were much aggravated. Already in January 1874 the *Lancet* was warning that in any measles epidemic, 'it is of paramount importance to rigidly examine the conditions of schools and places where children congregate, and as far as possible check the attendance of children coming from infected or suspected neighbourhoods'.[126] The question of 'school influence' became one of the most hotly debated in the preventive literature, not simply with regard to measles, but also for diphtheria, and to a lesser extent (because alternative preventive measures existed), scarlet fever. The rising national incidence of diphtheria in the 1870s, and of measles in the 1880s, were in turn ascribed to the ill effects of increased school attendance. Preventive pressure produced increased powers of action in the early 1880s. In March 1882 the Education Department of the Privy Council issued a new Code, Article 98 of which gave the sanitary authorities power to close schools for a specified period of time, and to exclude individual scholars from school, also for a specific time, with a view to preventing the spread of infectious disease.[127]

The exclusion of particular scholars, either for showing recognizable symptoms of infectious disease or because they came from infected homes, quickly became an established procedure where schools were co-operative. Problems arose, however, because the scholar's performance, and that of the school, were assessed on attendance records; without satisfactory attendance, examination results suffered and state finance was withheld.[128] Thus schools and parents had a positive incentive to burke the preventive regulations, with, in preventive eyes, predictable results. In 1888, for example, the *Lancet* noted that in some districts of London, where measles was epidemic, the 'excessive, and at such times mischievous, energy' of the school-attendance officers was held responsible for 'needless diffusion' of the disease.[129] School-closure, being (as George Buchanan observed) a more serious matter, was even more problematical.[130] Many MOHs were reluctant to order school-closure, and there was much disagreement as to the effectiveness of the measure in respect of measles. Many MOHs appear to have found it admirable,[131] but Louis Parkes (Chelsea) argued that in London the disease spread even faster among children on the streets than it did in the class-room, and Henry Armstrong, the distin-

125 *Lancet* (1871), i. 94.

126 *Lancet* (1874), i. 39.

127 *MOAR*, LGB, PP 1883, xxviii, p. 637; ibid., app. A no. 15., p. 847.

128 *Lancet* (1888), i. 1,037. See also David Rubinstein, *School attendance in London 1870–1904: A Social History*, University of Hull Occasional Papers in Social and Economic History, 1 (1969), 5–7; for the effects of infectious disease on school attendance, see ibid. 75–81.

129 Ibid. 849.

130 *MOAR* LGB, PP 1882, xxviii, p. 849.

131 e.g. Henry Bridgeman, *Lancet* (1889), i. 147; Sydney Marsden (Birkenhead), *Public Health*, (1895–6), 43–4; A. Ashby (Reading), *Public Health*, 9 (1896–7), 293.

guished MOH for Newcastle, had no faith in school-closure as a preventive measure.[132] Indeed, the evidence indicates that health departments had to be alert to make the most of school-closure: Henry Bridgeman of Burton-on-Trent found by experience that the sooner the schools were closed when measles was rife, the sooner the disease could be stamped out and the less the school suffered in the long run.[133] To be effective against measles, schools had to be closed for a minimum of three weeks, usually for four, during which the school visitors were employed to try to discover every house where the disease existed.[134]

One of the strongest proponents of school-closure was the MOH for Jarrow, A. Campbell Munro, author of one of the rare epidemiological studies of measles incidence in this period.[135] Although he described school-closure as 'our sheet-anchor in the case of measles', Munro was insistent that it could not be justified by anything except, 'the precise information as to school attendance which compulsory notification, duly followed up, alone affords'.[136] In Jarrow, where the measles mortality rate had risen alarmingly with the rising school-attendance rate,[137] fatalities had diminished after the introduction in 1885 of voluntary notification supported by the energetic follow-up of notified cases by the sanitary department and by school-closures.[138] Munro's evidence suggests that notification was a critical factor in controlling mortality from measles, but that it was equally critical that it should be followed up by other preventive measures. Evidence from elsewhere seems to confirm this. In Edinburgh, where the notification of measles was practised for ten years up to the early 1890s, no practical benefit could be ascertained from the practice, yet Edinburgh does not seem to have followed up notified cases with any degree of thoroughness.[139] As Alfred Bostock Hill (Sutton Coldfield, later Birmingham) argued, notification by itself did not have much effect in arresting the spread of the disease, but much good could be done in controlling patients through the health inspector's visits, so that exposure to chill and resulting mortality was prevented in many cases.[140] Notification was also supported by the MOH as an important element in the success of the school-closure policy.[141]

Measles was not one of the diseases made compulsorily notifiable under the

[132] *Public Health*, 4 (1891–2), 265. [133] *Lancet* (1889), i. 147. [134] Ibid.

[135] A. Campbell Munro, 'Measles: an epidemiological study', *Trans. Epid. Soc.*, 10 (1890–1), 94–109.

[136] Id. 'The notification of measles', *Public Health*, 4 (1891–2), 263, 265.

[137] Measles mortality in Jarrow rose from 274 per million in 1871–80 to 927 in 1881–9. The average school attendance rate increased from 95 per 1,000 in 1871–80 to 164 per 1,000 in 1881–8. From 68 per 1,000 in 1874, it rose to 162 per 1,000 in 1882, the year preceding the first great measles epidemic of the decade: Munro, 'Measles', 94, 96.

[138] Munro, 'Notification', 262.

[139] T. Orme Dudfield, 'The notification of measles', *Public Health*, 5 (1892–3), 179.

[140] A. Bostock Hill, 'The working of measles notification', *Public Health*, 6 (1893–4), 273.

[141] *Public Health* 8 (1895–6), 44; 10 (1897–8), 292.

Infectious Diseases Notification Act 1889, but the provisions of the Act enabled towns to add it to the list of notifiable diseases if they wished. In the first six months of 1890 only seven towns sought notification powers for measles,[142] although by 1893 this had increased to forty-four urban districts, eighteen rural and one port.[143] Throughout the 1890s, as the debate on the value of measles notification continued,[144] sanitary districts across the country experimentally adopted and sometimes subsequently abandoned the practice.[145] By the end of the decade, a concensus seems to have emerged on the usefulness of notification as part of a package of preventive measures. Even Henry Armstrong of Newcastle became tentatively in favour of school-closure when allied to measles notification (though not of whooping cough) after an experimental year in Newcastle upon Tyne.[146] By 1898 the anxieties of the London School Board on the subject had led the LCC to canvass vestry opinion on the subject. The medical officers' journal, *Public Health*, was led to hope that the LCC would be induced to adopt the notification of measles in London: 'Some reduction in the prevalence and mortality of the disease may confidently be expected.'[147]

Doubts about the practical validity of measles notification, which received prominent attention in the preventive literature, were not the only grounds against its widespread adoption, however. Because of the ubiquity of the disease, the notification of measles was expensive. As early as 1891 Armstrong dismissed the popular argument against notification on the grounds that the disease was infectious for four days before the rash appeared as fallacious, stating bluntly that the expense of measles notification carried more weight than any other objection.[148] Similarly Campbell Munro in 1896, now MOH for Renfrew County, rejected all the professional arguments against measles notification as 'rank nonsense', observing that 'the essence of the opposition to the notification of measles is that notification means money'. He suggested that the notification fee should be payable only for the first case in a household, any further cases occurring within sixteen days to be notified free of charge. In this way, he claimed, expenditure would be reduced by half.[149]

Despite the expense involved, growing preventive pressure in the early years of the twentieth century eventually had its effect. The LCC's initiative on

[142] Munro, 'Measles', 94.

[143] *Public Health*, 5 (1892–3), 208.

[144] The arguments for and against measles notification were set out in detail by John Sykes (St Pancras), reported in *Public Health*, 8 (1895–6), 199.

[145] *Public Health*, 11 (1898–9), 208–9.

[146] *Public Health*, 10 (1897–8), 257.

[147] Ibid.

[148] Henry Armstrong, 'The notification of measles', *Public Health*, 4 (1891–2), 261.

[149] *Public Health*, 9 (1896–7), 169. Munro's expedient evidently appealed to money-conscious government organizations, for when the compulsory notification of measles was introduced in 1915, doctors were obliged to notify only the first case in a household; secondary cases were to be notified by parents or guardians. The expense of notification had further been reduced by the government's wartime expedient of cutting the standard half-crown notification fee; in 1919 the *Lancet* was still agitating for restoration of the full fee: *Lancet* (1919), ii. 1,091–2.

notification having come to nothing in London, the MOHs and the metropolitan Poor Law authorities combined against the Metropolitan Asylums Board policy. In 1910, the MAB hospitals began admitting pauper cases of measles, and non-pauper cases on the recommendation of an MOH.[150] In the three years 1911–13 they admitted 10,858 cases of measles; an average of 3,617 per annum.[151] In London 1914 was a moderate year for measles—the MAB admitted only 770 cases—and so it was elsewhere: the national death-rate stood at a modest 247 per million. However, 1915 proved a sharp contrast. Nationally, deaths soared to 462, a rate unparalleled since 1896 (570). More significantly, perhaps, outbreaks of the disease in military camps attracted public notice.[152] On 27 November 1915 measles became a notifiable disease throughout the country, by order of the Local Government Board, at a time when the registration data showed that the worst of the epidemic was already over.[153]

In the following year, 1916, the death-rate from measles fell substantially, as was to be expected, but the magnitude of the fall surprised everyone. The death-rate of 155 per million was 'by far the lowest' ever recorded for England and Wales.[154] As the registrar-general observed, the relationship between notification and the fall in the death-rate was uncertain—it was improbable that there was a direct relationship in arresting the spread of the disease, but 'very possible' that notification might have had a substantial effect in reducing case mortality: that is, notification had resulted in improved administrative action, which led to better care of the sick, and increased realization by parents of the dangers of the disease.[155] However cautiously one may wish to treat the registrar-general's cautious assessment, it is undeniable that, although measles deaths predictably rose again in 1917, they thereafter entered upon the long fall which McKeown has graphically described.[156] It should be remembered, however, that a decline in the fatality of measles while its incidence still remains high is characteristic of the disease in all developed countries, a fact which one historian of the disease has noted, 'may be attributed . . . to general improvement in housing and education'.[157]

One may speculate that there was rather more to the decline of measles fatality in Western Europe than housing and education, or rising standards of living, or nutritional levels, or preventive effort, taken separately. Some combination of these factors may be discerned at work in England by the first decade of the twentieth century: despite a sharp rise in the fatality of

[150] *MABAR* (Statistical Committee) (1911), 112. [151] *MABAR*.

[152] Chalmers, *Health of Glasgow*, 345. The pattern of measles mortality in the decade 1911–20 is interesting. Young adults experienced a raised mortality from the disease throughout the decade, but the greatest increases were concentrated in the four years of war (1915–18), demonstrating that the concentration of non-immune young men in military camps exposed them to special danger: *RGDS* (1921), part III, p. lxxxvii.

[153] *RGAR*, PP 1917–18 vi, p. 52. [154] Ibid. 51. [155] Ibid. 51–2.

[156] McKeown, *Modern Rise*, 96, table 5.3.

[157] J. D. Rolleston, *The History of Acute Exanthema* (1937), 90.

epidemics in the early 1890s, the retrospective eye could discern a slight fall in crude measles mortality since about 1885.[158] It may be an impossible task to disentangle the various factors contributing to the major decline in measles mortality after the First World War. It can, however, be said with confidence that to attribute this mortality decline to rising living standards, or to reduced dietary fibre in infancy is too simplistic. Living standards were rising from 1870; major reductions in the fibre content of the English wheaten loaf were made around 1850, with further reductions between 1880 and 1910. Measles mortality did not, however, fall substantially until after 1917. If the possible effects of notification and nursing care are discounted as doubtful, it is still evident that something occurred in the years immediately after the First World War that was of special significance in reducing measles mortality.

Two hypotheses present themselves. If we return to Morley's nutritional explanation, it is clear that his thesis has two component parts: reduced dietary fibre, *and* increasing consumption of fats and sugar.[159] While national trends in the supplies of bread and potatoes declined steadily from 1880, and supplies of meat and dairy products (excluding butter) fell slightly between 1909–13 and 1924–8, those of sugar increased noticeably (though less fast between 1909–13 and 1924–8) and fats very markedly. From 12 lb. per annum in *c.* 1880, the quantity of butter, margarine and other fats (excluding lard) available per person per annum increased by 14 lb. up to 1910–13 (26 lb.) and again by 18 lb. up to 1924–8.[160] It is tempting to speculate that it was, therefore, between *c.*1918 and 1924–8 that the significant threshold of fat consumption that made the difference between fatal and mild measles began to be crossed by increasingly large numbers of small children.

In this transition it is unlikely that availability and even purchasing power were the sole factors in operation. The social changes which accompanied the First World War were almost certainly crucial. Jay Winter has argued for the general benefit to the English population of wartime policies, observing that diets were maintained, 'and in some cases actually improved in wartime'. More important, probably, from the measles point of view, were wartime welfare policies, social subsidies, and perhaps especially the redistribution of income and food within the working-class family.[161] As women became primary earners under the pressures of war, it is likely that not only did their own share of the family's food supply increase, but that of children also. School meals for older children, and smaller families, together with renewed emphasis on the national importance of babies were probably also contributing factors.[162] The First World War, according to Winter, achieved what no social policies had previously attempted: the economic transformation of Britain's destitute classes

[158] *Lancet* (1914), i. 549.
[159] Morley, 'Nutrition', 40.
[160] Greaves and Hollingsworth, 'Food consumption', table 1, p. 38.
[161] J. M. Winter, *The Great War and the British People* (1986), chap. 7; p. 244.
[162] Deborah Dwork, *War is Good for Babies and Other Young Children*, (1987), 208 ff.

into a merely deprived class.[163] It was this social transformation which probably produced the beginning of the major measles-mortality decline. Education, spread more widely through the notification policy, and post-war housing improvements made their contribution, but the continued post-war rise in living standards for the poorest sections of society was a salient factor.

Emphasis has earlier been placed on the importance of adequate nursing care in recovery from measles. In trying to assess the relative importance of various factors in reducing measles mortality, it should be remembered that rising living standards imply rising standards of domestic care, including nursing care. The coincidence of the beginnings of the measles decline with the introduction of compulsory notification may be no more than a coincidence; but it cannot be entirely dismissed as a contributing factor. The case of measles gives some support to McKeown's thesis, but not as much as Morley appears to suggest. While the slight decreases in measles mortality in the early twentieth century may indicate a gradual improvement in nutritional standards for the poorest children, they may equally be the result of a reduced measles wave such as occurred in the 1870s. Further, the behaviour of the disease in London in the years 1891–1910 does not suggest that overcrowding levels were the prime determinants of mortality either: in 1891–1900, when measles mortality reached a climax, overcrowding levels decreased throughout London, but over the following decade, when measles fatalities again declined, overcrowding in the central areas increased again.[164] The activities of the preventive authorities were plainly of minimal significance in these years and it seems likely that patterns of measles mortality in the nineteenth and early twentieth centuries, while in some degree determined by levels of resistance in the population, were influenced rather by wider social factors than by living standards, nutritional intake, or even levels of overcrowding.

[163] Winter, *Great War*, 21, and chap. 7.

[164] A. S. Wohl, The housing of the working classes in London, 1815–1914', in S. D. Chapman (ed.), *The History of Working-Class Housing* (Newton Abbot, 1971), 24–5.

3
Scarlet Fever

The deadliest of fevers, continued and exanthemous, often pestilential in its progress, sparing neither the young nor the old, but chiefly infecting the very young, and not unfrequently sweeping off the whole of the children of a family,—its irruption into a household is regarded with dismay.

(*Lancet*, 1865)

Scarlet fever . . . is practically always present in every large community.

(A. B. Whitelegge, 1887)

Scarlet fever was one of the first diseases to have an active preventive policy directed against it, and for some late nineteenth-century observers it came to represent a great triumph of preventive medicine. At the mid-century it accounted for some 10,000 deaths per annum in England and Wales. Its principal incidence was on small children between the ages of 1 and 5; although adults not uncommonly caught it, it was relatively rare in infants. In the 1860s it was 'the most dreaded, yet the least feared, of all familiar diseases',[1] and was considered to be more infectious and deadly than any other disease.[2] It was widespread through all social classes, and was often fatal. The early efforts of London's medical officers in disinfecting and isolating cases where possible had little effect, but the opening of the Metropolitan Asylums Board isolation hospitals in the 1870s was accompanied by a decrease in mortality, more pronounced in London than elsewhere (Table 3.1). By 1884 the registrar-general was suggesting that the MAB hospitals were responsible for this reduction in fatality, drawing attention to the reversal of position in the mortality-rate league between London and England and Wales.[3] Although London was not able to maintain this relative improvement for long (Table 3.1), mortality-rates continued to fall. By the 1890s some medical officers, such as James Niven of Manchester, had come to believe that isolation hospitals helped to reduce the virulence of scarlet fever through the hospitalization of severe cases, which reduced the opportunities for severe strains to propagate themselves.[4] Across the Atlantic, where American epidemiologists were witnessing a similar decline in the virulence of scarlet fever, this argument was also current.[5]

Scarlet fever is, however, a notoriously variable disease. It is caused by Group A haemolytic streptococci, which are responsible for a wide range of afflictions other than scarlet fever, including sore throats of the tonsillitis

[1] *Lancet* (1865), i. 129.
[2] *MOAR* Westminster (1868–9), 15.
[3] RGAR PP 1886 xvii, p. 14.
[4] *Public Health*, 8 (1895–6), 143.
[5] Arthur Newsholme, *Fifty Years in Public Health* (1935), 181.

TABLE 3.1. *Scarlet-fever death-rates per 1,000 living under 5, 1851–1900*

	1851–60	1861–70	1871–80	1881–90	1891–1900
London	5.30	5.80	3.07	1.78	1.00
England and Wales	4.19	4.62	3.49	1.67	0.84

Source: Registrar-general's decennial supplements.

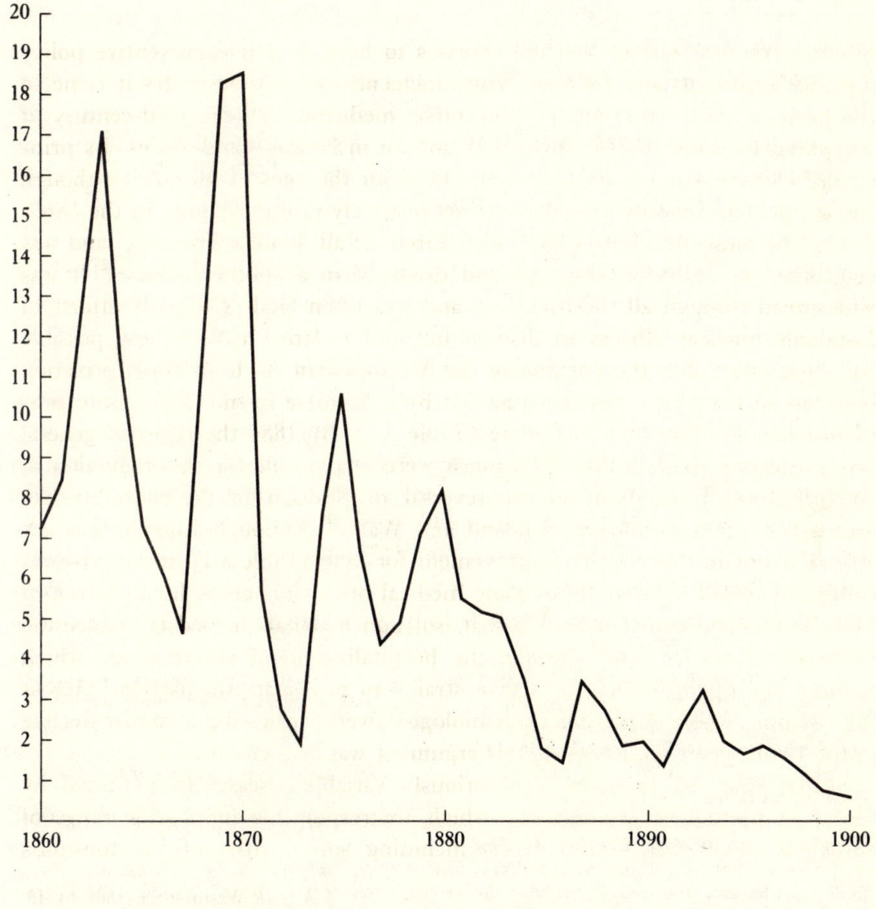

FIG. 3.1. *Scarlet-fever deaths in London, 1860–1900, per 10,000 population.*

type,[6] erysipelas, rheumatic fever, and puerperal fever. Scarlet fever is caused only by certain strains of streptococci which produce a soluble erythrogenic toxin, whose absorption causes the rash characteristic of scarlet fever. One attack confers immunity to the toxin, but not to further streptococcal infections; persons with streptococcal sore throats may thus transmit scarlet fever. Transmission is by intimate contact, but may also occur through contaminated milk. As with all infectious fevers, scarlet-fever patients are more infectious in the acute active stage of the disease, but some may continue to harbour streptococci for months or even years after apparent recovery, and among these are a number of 'dangerous carriers' capable of infecting close associates.[7] While the disease itself now only rarely assumes a septicaemic or toxic form, serious complications may follow, including anaemia, otitis media, rheumatic fever, meningitis, and nephritis. These complications may lead to permanent damage to hearing, heart, or kidneys. There are more than twenty known types and sixty sub-types of Group A haemolytic streptococci, and infection with one confers no immunity to the others. Epidemiologically, scarlet fever is thus a most complicated disease. Although nineteenth-century epidemiologists were actively interested in it, and some came close to explaining its behaviour,[8] it did not begin to be scientifically understood before the work of George and Gladys Dick in the 1920s.[9]

The multiplicity of streptococcal types is partly responsible for the variable virulence and infectiousness of the disease in different epidemics. However, the available evidence suggests that particular strains of scarlet-fever streptococci gain long-term geographical dominance over different areas at different times. Within this broader pattern, different epidemics may vary greatly in severity, depending on the local strain present, with mortality ranging between 0 and 30 per cent. Individual or family resistance may also play a part: as Victorian doctors were aware for scarlet fever, there is a marked familial variation in susceptibility to streptococcal infection.[10] Although in the 1860s and 1870s scarlet fever was so virulent that a family might expect to lose three out of five children to it, and for the health of the remaining two to be seriously impaired,[11] many experienced it only as a mild affliction. As Charles West observed, in some instances it was so trifling as scarcely to interrupt a child's

[6] These are more commonly known as streptococcal sore throats, or, in America, as pharyngitis. The nineteenth-century 'putrid sore throat' almost certainly included streptococcal infections.

[7] For the complex epidemiology of scarlet fever, see B. B. Breese and C. Breese Hall, Beta *Haemolytic Streptococcal Diseases* (Boston, 1978), chaps. 3, 8.

[8] See L. G. Wilson 'The historical riddle of milk-borne scarlet fever', *Bulletin of the History of Medicine*, 60 (1986), 321–42.

[9] For the principal steps towards understanding scarlet fever, see A. L. Bloomfield, *A Bibliography of Internal Medicine: Communicable Diseases* (Chicago, 1958).

[10] *Lancet* (1861), i. 518; Breese and Breese Hall, *Streptococcal Diseases*, 51. This familial susceptibility perpetuated the idea of the 'epidemic constitution': see B. W. Richardson, *The Field of Disease* (1883), 854; D. A. Gresswell, *The Natural History of Scarlet Fever* (Oxford, 1890), 199.

[11] R. J. Reece, 'Scarlet-fever', *West London Medical Journal*, 9 (1904), 263.

cheerfulness for a day, in others 'it is so deadly that medicine is unable to stay its course even for a moment, and then it destroys life in a few days, sometimes even in a few hours'.[12]

In the early decades of the nineteenth century the dominant European strain was very mild, but in the 1830s a more virulent form appeared, and between 1840 and 1875 scarlet fever was a leading cause of death among children under 5. Major epidemics occurred in 1840, 1844, 1848, 1858–9, 1863–4, 1868–70, and 1874. While the disease was widely spread throughout the country, the highest mortalities were experienced in London, the great towns of Lancashire and the West Riding, the Black Country, and the mining districts of Durham and South Wales.[13] The south-western counties also belonged to this group up to 1863–4, but after that date experienced a remarkable diminution in mortality, fifteen years before a comparable decline was observed in the rest of the country.[14]

In the nineteenth century the disease was widely accepted by the medical profession as contagious, and as being little influenced by sanitary conditions.[15] Popularly, however, it was often linked with defective drainage; an idea which one observer claimed to be fostered by sanitarians from interested motives.[16] The evident increase in its fatality during the 1850s and 1860s was a cause of considerable anxiety to the newly formed preventive establishment. In the early years of the new preventive regime little specific was done against scarlet fever. The severe epidemic of 1863–4, however, helped to focus preventive attention on the problem which the disease undoubtedly presented. Scottish hospitals already had separate wards or blocks for fever and smallpox cases, as John Bristowe and Timothy Holmes had reported to the Privy Council in 1863,[17] and by 1864 Dr Morgan of the Manchester and Salford Sanitary Association was advocating the establishment of self-supporting hospitals for scarlet-fever patients.[18] In this he was supported by John Netten Radcliffe of the

[12] Charles West, *Lectures on the Diseases of Infancy and Childhood*, seventh edn. (1884), 862.

[13] Charles Creighton, *A History of Epidemics in Britain*, 2 vols. (Cambridge, 1894), ii. 727.

[14] Ibid.

[15] Charles Murchison, 'The etiology, pathology, and treatment of scarlet fever', *Lancet* (1864), i. 724; (1864), ii. 175; *MOAR* PC, PP 1870 xxxviii, p. 603.

[16] C. E. Prior, 'A contribution to the natural history of scarlatina', *Lancet* (1869), ii. 570. Such was, perhaps, the Medical Department's 1858 investigation into the outbreak of scarlet and other fevers at Conway in North Wales, said to be due to the sanitary condition of the town: PP 1859 xii. p. 266. It may also have been the *Lancet*'s motive when, in 1875, it castigated David Davies, MOH for Bristol, for publicizing his belief that the fatality of scarlet fever was slightly, if at all, dependent on general sanitary conditions: *Lancet* (1875), ii. 746. The theory continued to have a following among a minority of sanitarians. William Budd, for example, believed the disease was spread through the alvine and renal discharges (Budd, *Public Health and Sanitary Review* (1 Feb. 1869), 21; *British Medical Journal*, 2 (1880), 23). The only other significant proponent of the theory seems to have been James Niven of Manchester, who held tenaciously by it into the 1920s (see Woods, n. 40 below, p. 16). For an early account of his views see *Lancet* (1897), i. 54, 66.

[17] Report on the United Kingdom Hospitals', *MOAR* PC, PP 1864 xxviii, app. 15.

[18] J. N. Radcliffe, 'The prevalence, distribution and limitation of scarlet fever in England', *Transactions of the Epidemiological Society*, 2 (1864), 262–77 (see also *Lancet* (1865), i. 129).

Medical Department, who also insisted that a strict system of patient isolation and the disinfection of attendants' clothing would do 'much more to control the spread [of scarlet fever] than is commonly supposed'. Noting that the principal scarlet-fever mortality was located in comparatively few districts—he designated a dozen 'scarlatina fields'—Radcliffe indicated that the local nature of the problem made it a less daunting preventive proposition.[19] By the mid-1860s many leading sanitary reformers were convinced of the need for infectious-disease hospitals, and were urging their case both on the government and on their local authorities.[20]

Where scarlet fever was concerned, however, not all sanitarians shared Radcliffe's optimism. The adoption of the hospital isolation policy was something of a counsel of despair. At the onset of the extremely severe epidemic of 1869, when the MAB hospitals were already in prospect, John Simon, medical officer to the Privy Council, admitted it to be a policy of defeat: 'At the present time, with scientific knowledge limited as it is, and with our very imperfect administrative resources, anyone who is responsible for advising on the requirements of the public health must feel extreme difficulty, and indeed almost humiliation, in having to advise about scarlatina.'[21] In the face of its 'uncontrollable contagiousness', Simon concluded that the isolation of infected individuals was the only known means of limiting the power of the disease.[22] Aware of their own ignorance, of the great infectiousness and terrible fatality of the disease, and of its damaging sequelae, the Medical Department and medical officers accepted the hospital policy for London in the early 1870s as a means perhaps of limiting the spread of the disease, but at least of securing some better form of care for patients than was possible in the overcrowded homes of the poor.

The MAB hospitals were not initially intended as the weapon of a systematic preventive policy, as isolation hospitals came to be perceived in the 1890s.[23] Although managed independently, they were under the control of the Poor Law Board, and in their early years accepted pauper patients only. Entry to the hospitals was arranged through the local relieving officer, and if local-authority employees wished to have patients removed to hospital, they had to go through the relieving officer. In addition, entry to the hospital meant acceptance of Poor Relief, and automatic pauperization for those not already in that condition. From the early 1870s until 1883 the hospitals thus offered the opportunity for professionally isolating only patients from the poorest classes. Although MAB doctors were repeatedly discovered to be covertly admitting

[19] Radcliffe, 'Scarlet fever'.

[20] G. M. Ayers, *England's First State Hospitals* (1969), 12. Bristowe, for example, continued to argue to the case for 'a number of well distributed institutions' in the metropolitan area, to be maintained by rates levied on the public: *MOAR* Camberwell (1864), 28.

[21] *MOAR* PC, PP 1870 xxxviii, p. 602.

[22] Ibid. 603, 605.

[23] For the latter attitude, see J. M. Eyler, 'Scarlet fever and confinement: the Edwardian debate over isolation hospitals', *Bulletin of the History of Medicine*, (Spring 1987), 1–24.

patients who were not paupers, it was not until 1883 that the stigma of pauperism was lifted from admissions, and not before 1887 were the hospitals able to accept all patients of whatever social class.[24] It was not until the late 1880s, therefore, that it became possible realistically to conceive of the MAB hospitals as a practical tool for disease control.

Although the MAB hospitals were initially limited to pauper patients, London's only independent fever hospital revised its admissions policies in step with developments in the Poor Law, to extend hospital provision for fever patients to a broader range of social classes. The London Fever Hospital (LFH) had been treating between 200 and 300 scarlet-fever cases annually in the 1860s, far more in the epidemic years 1868–70 (see Table 3.2). In the years up to 1871 the LFH had treated all classes of patient, but with the advent of the MAB hospitals it ceased to accept pauper patients. Instead, it offered its services free to the artisan classes, continuing to accept fee-paying patients, whether from the servant class or their employers. While the proportion of patients from different social groups accepted by the hospital changed across the remaining thirty years of the century, the LFH continued to make a substantial contribution to London's isolation provision, in terms of the numbers of patients admitted (Table 3.3). The changing social structure of patient admissions can be matched to the changing admissions policy of the MAB hospitals. When, in the early 1890s, the MAB hospitals finally opened their doors to all comers, the LFH adapted itself once again, taking in cases for which the MAB hospitals did not have room, and finding its beds continuously occupied, through the new popularity which hospital accommodation for infectious cases had achieved with the public.[25]

The numbers of scarlet-fever patients coming under hospital isolation and treatment in London grew steadily throughout the later decades of the century; indeed, they formed the bulk of patient admissions to the MAB hospitals. It is impossible to estimate what percentage of total cases was admitted to hospital before notification permitted such calculations to be made, although the *Lancet* suggested in 1887 that admissions must constitute at least one-fifth of the recognized cases.[26] More reliably, perhaps, 7 per cent of fatal scarlet-fever cases occurred in the MAB hospitals in 1878, and by 1894 this had risen to 75 per cent.[27] With the expansion of hospital provision in the 1890s, the opening up of admissions, the introduction of notification, and a greater public readiness to use hospitals, the MAB received an ever-increasing proportion of known scarlet-fever cases. In the early 1890s, when the managers were having problems finding acceptable sites for new hospitals, the system was unable at times to cope with the flood of patients, and the hospitals were often obliged

[24] See Ayers, *State Hospitals*, chaps. 3–7.
[25] *LFHAR* (1890), 11; (1897), 11.
[26] *Lancet* (1887), ii. 1,074.
[27] *Lancet* (1896), i. 258.

TABLE 3.2. *Scarlet-fever admissions to London fever hospitals, 1868–1883*

	London Fever Hospital		Metropolitan Asylums Board	
	Number	% total admissions	Number	% total admissions
1868	399	10.9		
1869	614	18.0		
1870	912	26.2		
1871–2	336	22.3		
1873	45	26.9	92	8.1
1874	207	53.9	804	37.7
1875	525	73.9	1,182	65.1
1876	516	70.7	671	48.2
1877	385	61.2	479	39.7
1878	417	65.7	679	43.4
1879	594	72.7	1,469	70.0
1880	598	67.4	1,949	79.1
1881	667	72.9	1,477	63.6
1882	723	72.2	1,850	64.5
1883	566	60.9	1,920	70.6
1884	440	66.8	1,845	72.4
1885	308	63.4	1,353	72.9
1886	311	59.4	1,780	81.0
1887	762	83.8	5,900	90.3
1888	473	78.4	4,408	85.6
1889	319	67.7	4,518	78.3
1890	454	73.7	6,547	78.4
1891	339	65.8	5,262	67.4
1892	593	79.3	13,093	80.4
1893	764	94.7	14,458	77.4
1894	294	81.2	11,598	69.6
1895	516	74.6	11,271	66.9
1896	637	82.8	15,982	71.8
1897	431	74.4	15,113	66.1
1898	322	53.8	12,125	57.7
1899	448	71.2	13,290	53.0
1900	339	52.7	10,343	47.8

Source: *LFHAR*.

TABLE 3.3. *Scarlet-fever patient admissions to the London Fever Hospital by social class, 1873–1900*

Social class	1873–80	1881–90	1891–1900
Well-to-do	6.9	14.6	14.8
Nurses and servants	22.5	23.2	17.5
Mechanics	20.5	2.2	—
Clerks and employees	17.1	20.4	30.7
Tradesmen	5.3	11.3	26.6
Other institutions	16.1	17.9	8.5
From sanitary authorities	4.2	7.9	—
Average annual admissions, all diseases	620	711	634

Source: *LFHAR*.

to restrict admissions.[28] This caused much annoyance to local MOHs, who pointed to the problems caused to pregnant mothers, and to bread-winners whose work was affected by having patients at home. Some claimed to have evidence that the middle classes were succeeding in getting patients admitted when the hospitals were 'full' to others, and urged that such beds should be given only to patients recommended by the sanitary authorities.[29] Nevertheless, the MAB hospitals received 44 per cent of notified cases of scarlet fever in 1890, rising to 75 per cent by 1900.[30]

The effect of all this preventive hospitalization on the natural history of scarlet fever is, in fact, doubtful. It *may* have encouraged the spread of milder strains of streptococci, but this is unlikely, since most patients probably reached hospital only after they had had ample opportunity to disseminate the disease further. Although some doctors claimed by their precautions never to have had a second case of scarlet fever in a household,[31] such claims must be viewed with detachment, and in any case can only have applied to an insignificant number of households. The problem of the 'return case'—the scarlet-fever patient who was still infectious but without evident symptoms on return from hospital—dogged the hospital service and the sanitary authorities throughout the period.[32] Such 'dangerous cases' were doubtless also produced in the sphere of private practice, but are far from obvious, unless the acknowledged risk of infection during seaside holidays counts as evidence: scarlet-fever

28 e.g. in September–October 1892, and again in June 1893: *MABAR* (1892), 9; (1893), 11–12. The problem was eased with the opening of the Fountain Hospital, Tooting, in October 1893 and later the Brook Hospital, Shooter's Hill (1896).

29 *MOAR* Islington (1893), 63.

30 *MOAR* LCC (1900), 22.

31 William Budd was one of these: *British Medical Journal*, 2 (1880), 23. See also *Lancet* (1863), ii. 131.

32 On return cases, see Eyler, 'Scarlet fever', 4–5; for contemporary expositions of the problem, see *Public Health*, 6 (1893–4), 92; 8 (1895–6), 90.

convalescents from the wealthier classes were commonly sent to recuperate at the seaside.[33] The etiology of scarlet fever is such that the hospitalization policy, as a strategy for controlling the disease, was doomed to failure from the outset. This was certainly true as long as the policy was only partial, but even the introduction of notification for scarlet fever in 1889 and the opening of the MAB hospitals to all comers, could not extend its success in this direction.[34]

Despite hospitalization, and despite the labours of the local medical officers in ensuring disinfection, and in printing and distributing leaflets advising precautions against the spread of the disease,[35] scarlet fever continued to be a most prevalent disease into the closing years of the century, albeit one that was characterized by increasing mildness of type. The failure of the hospital policy to control the disease in any way, and the probability that the declining mortality-rates were due to the autonomously decreasing fatality of the disease, did not go unobserved by contemporaries. A year after commending the MAB hospitals for reducing London's scarlet-fever mortality, the registrar-general admitted that an increased mildness in type of the disease might be the cause.[36] In 1890 Dan Astley Gresswell, a young Oxford graduate who had worked in the MAB's South-Western Hospital during the scarlet-fever epidemic of 1887–8, noted that London and the provinces had experienced concurrently almost the same mortality decline: in view of the much inferior isolation provision available in the latter, Gresswell implied, the role of the MAB hospitals was likely to have been small.[37] By the later 1890s several authorities were arguing forcibly that hospital isolation was immaterial to the reduction in scarlet-fever mortality. John Wilson, MOH for Lanarkshire, suggested that 65 per cent of the reduction in mortality could be ascribed to reduction in fatality, and he was supported by Killick Millard of Burton-on-Trent, in contending that reduced mortality was almost entirely due to a change in type of the disease.[38] At its most vehement and political in the early years of the twentieth century,[39] the debate between those who favoured hospital isolation as the cause of diminished scarlet-fever mortality, and those who maintained it had nothing to do with it, continued into the 1920s.[40]

The continuing ubiquity of scarlet fever, despite its declining fatality-rate, is suggested by the notifications for London, which far outstripped those of diphtheria, its nearest competitor among the notifiable diseases (Table 3.4). None the less, the 1890s marked a turning-point in the behaviour of the dis-

33 *Lancet* (1868), i. 518.
34 Eyler, 'Scarlet fever', 20.
35 See e.g. *MOAR* Camberwell (1869), 49; (1877), 205.
36 *RGAR*, PP 1886 xvii, p. 381.
37 Gresswell, *Natural History*, 194–5.
38 John T. Wilson, 'A contribution to the natural history of scarlet fever', *Public Health*, supplement (Feb. 1897), 18–19; W. Killick Millard, 'The influence of hospital isolation in scarlet fever', *Public Health*, 13 (1900–1), 462–9, 487–92.
39 For the exposition of this debate, see Eyler, 'Scarlet fever', 1–24.
40 H. M. Woods, 'An epidemiological study of scarlet fever in England and Wales since 1900', *MRC* Special Report Series, no. 180 (1933), 16–18.

ease. Previously it had run in epidemic cycles of five years, judging by the mortality peaks. After the epidemic of 1896, however, a seven-year cycle manifested itself, with epidemics occurring in 1901, 1907, 1914, 1921.[41] The hospital fatality-rates fell markedly, from an average of 49.1 per cent in 1895–1904 to 26.2 per cent in 1905–14;[42] and in private practice also, it was clear that fatality-rates were falling.

In 1858 R. Hall Bakewell had found it impossible to obtain reliable case-fatality figures for the disease, while three years later Headlam Greenhow observed how the type of scarlet fever varied greatly in different epidemics.[43] Murchison assumed an average case mortality of 6 per cent in 1864,[44] while in 1888 Arthur Whitelegge suggested 10 per cent to be 'a fair average'. Whitelegge demonstrated the variability of epidemics by contrasting the case-fatality rates for Salford (11 per cent) with those of Nottingham and Leicester (6 per cent). However, he noted that there had recently been several hundred cases in Nottingham where the fatality-rate was less than 4 per cent.[45] Dan Gresswell, however, observed that in Sydenham's time mortality could not have been even 6 per cent.[46] Although the variable fatality of scarlet fever between epidemics, within the larger epidemic cycles, had long been known,[47] it was clear by the mid-1890s that a much milder strain of the disease was becoming dominant than that which had largely prevailed since 1840. In London in 1891

TABLE 3.4. *Notifications of streptococcal disease and diphtheria in London, 1892–1900*

	Scarlet fever	Erysipelas	Puerperal fever	Diphtheria	Scarlet fever % total notifications
1892	27,095	6,934	337	7,781	59.1
1893	36,901	9,700	397	13,026	54.7
1894	18,440	6,080	253	10,655	45.1
1895	19,757	5,660	236	10,772	47.6
1896	25,647	6,436	277	13,362	51.6
1897	22,848	5,794	264	12,803	50.3
1898	16,894	5,169	247	11,543	45.3
1899	18,089	5,606	326	13,345	42.8
1900	13,800	4,762	237	11,776	39.2

Source: MAB Statistical Committee annual reports.

41 Ibid. 21. 42 Ibid. 53. 43 *Lancet* (1858), ii. 565; (1861), i. 346.

44 *Lancet* (1864), i. 695.

45 B. A. Whitelegge, 'Age, sex and season in relation to scarlet fever', *Trans. Epid. Soc.*, NS 7 (1887–8), 153.

46 Gresswell, *Natural History*, 168. 47 See e.g. West, *Lectures*, 862–3.

TABLE 3.5. *Scarlet fever in London, 1891–1900*

Year	Death-rate per 1,000 population	Case-rate per 1,000 population	Case mortality, % notified cases
1891	0.14	2.7	5.1
1892	0.27	6.4	4.3
1893	0.37	8.6	4.3
1894	0.22	4.3	5.2
1895	0.19	4.5	4.2
1896	0.21	5.7	3.7
1897	0.17	5.1	3.0
1898	0.13	3.8	3.4
1899	0.09	4.1	2.2
1900	0.08	3.1	2.6

Source: *MOAR* LCC (1900), 22.

fatality stood at 5 per cent of notified cases, and by 1900 it had fallen to a mere 2.6 per cent (Table 3.5).

The declining fatality of scarlet fever in the later nineteenth century bore no relation to sanitary reform, or to preventive medical strategy. It is doubtful also whether sanitary (or insanitary) conditions had any part to play in the resurgence of the severe form of the disease during the 1840s. The change in the virulence of the disease agent appears to have been autonomous. The pattern of this change is intriguing, for Creighton's observation that scarlet-fever mortality had been declining in the south-west since 1864[48] indicates perhaps that a milder streptococcus had already become dominant there. In Paris, meanwhile, scarlet fever had also acquired milder characteristics by the mid-1860s. Its 'remarkable benignity' was noted particularly because of the virulence which the disease was concurrently displaying in London, Vienna, and Berlin.[49] Remembering the numerous daily communications between London and Paris, the importation of virulent smallpox from France in 1870, and the similar, though more slowly dispersed, importation of diphtheria from France in the late 1850s, it seems possible that this milder streptococcal infection had its origins in France. Entering England, perhaps via London, in the late 1860s, it took between fifteen and twenty-five years to establish itself as the dominant English streptococcal infection: nationally, deaths from scarlet fever fall off noticeably from 1885, but case-fatality rates were still declining in the 1890s.

Meanwhile, against the background of urgent, if fruitless, preventive activity against scarlet fever during the last three decades of the nineteenth century, the popular experience and perception of the disease changed. Even into the

[48] Creighton, *Epidemics*, ii. 727. [49] *Medical Times and Gazette*, 2 (1869), 632.

mid-1880s the great number of scarlet fever cases were nursed at home. By the end of the century hospital treatment for the disease had become a common experience. When the hospital-isolation policy was first introduced, in the 1870s, there had often been considerable resistance to removal. As late as 1881 the MOH for Hampstead noted that it was extremely difficult to overcome parents' dislike of removal of their children, and that in most cases permission was 'obstinately, if not indignantly' refused.[50] Two years earlier, however, the *Lancet* had stated that prejudice against hospitalization was 'slowly but surely' wearing away.[51] By the later 1880s resistance appears largely to have subsided: in 1889 Dr Gayton of the MAB's North-Western Hospital could remark that the admission over the past few years of the children of well-to-do shopkeepers and professional men showed that 'scarcely a vestige' of such prejudice survived even among the socially superior classes.[52]

The increasing acceptance of hospitalization among all social classes was perhaps partly related to the preventive measures forced on families by health authorities and concerned practitioners alike. Even before the advent of the fever hospitals, medical practitioners were as far as possible enforcing quarantines on scarlet-fever patients. C. E. Prior, describing the epidemic of 1853 at Bedford, recommended the isolation of the patient and his nurse within the household as far as practicable, preferably in rooms approached by their own staircase.[53] In common with most nineteenth-century practitioners, Prior insisted that isolation should last until all desquamation had ceased. At the mid-century this was already an established concept.[54] Reinforced by the authority of William Budd in 1869,[55] it was to be extremely influential for the rest of the century. Convalescents from scarlet fever were considered infectious until all peeling of the skin had ceased;[56] it was partly this perception which dictated the monstrously long stays in hospital which were inflicted on scarlatina patients.[57] However, the period of desquamation was also considered dangerous for the patient, since this was the period when kidney damage was deemed likely to occur;[58] for this reason many doctors insisted the patient be kept still until desquamation had ceased. In 1887 Dr Serjeant of the Camberwell Guardians was considered to be 'very brave'—and also to be taking risks—in turning scarlet-fever patients out of the pauper hospital after five to six weeks: an 'old member of the Asylums Board' considered that ten to twelve weeks hospital isolation was 'not too long'.[59]

In view of these practices, it is not surprising that scarlet fever should have

[50] *MOAR* Hampstead (1881), 79.

[51] *Lancet* (1879), ii. 586; *South London Press* (1 Oct. 1887).

[52] *MABAR* (1889), app. 2, p. 27.

[53] *Lancet* (1869), ii. 571.

[54] *Lancet* (1868), ii. 467: 'W.V.R., of Slough noted the popular idea that the period of desquamation was that of greatest infectiousness.

[55] *Lancet* (1870), ii. 653.

[56] *Public Health and Sanitary Record* (1 Feb. 1869), 21.

[57] F. B. Smith, *The People's Health* (1987), 139.

[58] *Lancet* (1887), ii. 672.

[59] *South London Press* (24 Sept. 1887).

been designated 'the most dreaded, if the least feared' of the infectious diseases. The prospect of organizing households to cope with such prolonged isolation, let alone the boredom and frustration suffered by patient and nurses alike must, in the great majority of cases where the disease was not very severe, have far outweighed the anxieties of illness for the protagonists. Parents and schoolmasters alike lamented the difficulties and responsibilities of enforced quarantines in the pages of *The Times*. Mr Bradley of Marlborough College, for example, wrote to demonstrate that the long detention of a boy in the school sick-bay was full of moral and physical evil, yet to send scarlatina convalescents home was not only to inflict an 'unwarrantable peril' upon the community, but also to break the law (that is, Section 38 of the Sanitary Act 1866, which forbade the wilful public exposure of persons suffering from infectious diseases).[60] Small wonder that, where cases occurred in private houses, the well-to-do were often careless in spreading the disease.[61] The working classes and the poor were no better, and it was even more difficult to enforce quarantine among them. As George Millson (Newington) pointed out in 1897, when children were treated at home the services of the medical man were dispensed with after three days on grounds of expense, and the 'isolation' thereafter went unsupervised.[62]

> Before a month has gone by, the patient and nurse are heartily tired of the restrictions of isolation, and the Sanitary Authority is applied to, to have the house disinfected. If the Officers of the Authority refuse after so short a time, the child, after only a few days, is found mixing with other children, or playing at the back of the house with its neighbours. Very often the child is found in the street.

From the preventive officers' point of view, and in the light of contemporary belief, hospital isolation offered the only hope of controlling the incidence of scarlet fever in any way.

The *Lancet* reporter's observation that scarlet fever was the 'least feared' of the infectious diseases indicates rather a mixed general attitude towards the disease itself, which may perhaps be explained by its differing manifestations. Charles West identified three different types of scarlet fever: *scarlatina simplex*, with bright red rash over the whole body and a slight sore throat; *scarlatina anginosa*, with a more intense fever, slower to subside, and severe sore throat; and *scarlatina maligna*, which assumed a typhoid character, often with the sloughing of inflamed tonsils, and in many instances accompanied by severe complications.[63] Mild scarlet fever was evidently common enough to produce a considerable degree of apathy. Yet in a society where the seriousness of any affliction was judged by the external symptoms, attitudes in any one outbreak of the disease were conditioned by the nature of that outbreak, and popular

[60] *The Times* (5 Dec. 1879). See also Budd, *British Medical Journal*, (1880), ii. 23.
[61] *Lancet* (1875), ii. 141.
[62] *MOAR* Newington (1897), 169–70.
[63] West, *Lectures*, 862–3.

reactions to scarlet fever confirm the variability of the disease's manifestations. *Scarlatina maligna*, for example, was presumably dominant in the great outbreak of 1869–70, which Thomas Sarvis, MOH for Bethnal Green, described as 'a fearful epidemic'.[64] In St George's, Southwark, Henry Bateson observed an unusual fear of the disease. It 'evoked a fear and a dread I have never previously witnessed in any other epidemic. Help when most urgently needed could not be had. A house wherein was scarlet fever needed no real cross upon the door to prevent communication. No one would come nigh.'[65] More commonly, however, it was regarded as 'only scarlet fever'.[66] It was an attitude which was difficult to overcome, and it existed not only among the poor. In Hampstead in 1880 the younger son of a private house was sent to a private school as a substitute for his elder brother, who was ill of scarlet fever. It was, Charles Lord wryly remarked, 'an ill-timed piece of economy'.[67] Although well-to-do households could act responsibly in the face of the disease, they were known generally to be 'extremely careless and selfish' when it came to such matters as observing quarantine and endeavouring to limit the spread of disease.[68]

Unlike measles and whooping cough, whose mortality was commonly considered to fall mainly on the lower classes, scarlet fever was also fatal among the well-to-do. Death from scarlet fever was intrinsically less avoidable, since it was caused either by the power of the toxic infection or by complications which were a result of the infection, rather than being due to preventable secondary invasion. As a result, nineteenth-century observers were divided, according to experience, perhaps, between those who thought the disease most virulent and fatal among the well-to-do, and those who considered it to be more destructive among the poor.[69] R. Hall Bakewell, whose 'Statistical inquiry into the causes of epidemics' was published in the *Lancet* in 1858, produced evidence that scarlet-fever mortality always occurred in an inverse ratio to pauperism.[70] Not all the listeners who heard his paper agreed with him: Dr Webster, from Devon, insisted that he had found the disease very fatal among the poor. A. P. Stewart, however, was struck by the gravity and mortality among the 'higher orders' compared with that among the poor.[71] Charles

[64] *MOAR* Bethnal Green (1869-70), 3.

[65] *MOAR* St George's, Southwark (1869–70), 37.

[66] *MOAR* Clerkenwell (1869), 15. See also Smith, *People's Health*, 142.

[67] *MOAR* Hampstead (1880), 72.

[68] *Lancet* (1874), ii. 806; (1875), ii. 141.

[69] Historians likewise have fallen into two camps. According to George Rosen, 'observers at various periods have agreed' that lower-class children were more endangered by scarlet fever, and suffered more malignant complications, than did upper-class children. Rosen suggests that the increase in severity of scarlet fever in the mid-19th cent. was related to the social environment and prevailing social attitudes of the period: in W. R. Bett (ed.), *The History and Conquest of Common Diseases* (Norman, Okla., 1954), 30. F. B. Smith, however, notes the common contemporary belief that the wealthy were harder hit by scarlet fever than the poor, and attributes this phenomenon to contaminated milk supplies, and to the interventionist remedies of private doctors: *People's Health*, 137–9.

[70] *Lancet* (1858), ii. 525; see also Smith, *People's Health*, 137–8.

[71] *Lancet* (1858), ii. 525–6.

Murchison, whose experience was based on the London Fever Hospital, noted in 1864 that scarlet fever was probably as common among the children of the better class as among the poor, contrary to the common impression.[72] Two contrary points of view on the class-incidence of the disease evidently obtained.

The evidence from London leaves no doubt that the disease did manifest itself with great severity among all social classes, but that, on balance, the poorer classes suffered both a higher incidence and an increased mortality. Medical perceptions of the prevalence and severity of the disease among the middle class were probably shaped by personal experience, and by the knowledge that here was one infectious disease whose ravages could not be stayed by vaccination or by scrupulous nursing. Where the disease broke out with malignancy, the *Lancet* noted in 1865, both profession and people were alike possessed by 'an aimless and impractical dread'.[73] The intermittent deadliness of the disease was compounded by the complex mixture of apathy, bravura, indifference, and dread which characterized public reaction to it. The *Lancet*, which gave much space to scarlet fever and its prevention, was frequently driven to the use of strong language to relieve its feelings: 'There is something shocking in the plague-like deadliness of some forms of scarlet fever, especially considered in connection with the uncivilised carelessness with which it is spread.'[74] There is some evidence to suggest, however, that the profession was partly to blame for the mixed public response to the disease, through careless use of terminology. Scarlet fever goes by two names: scarlet fever and scarlatina. Although the profession customarily used the two interchangeably irrespective of the gravity of the case, it was observed that the public considered the term 'scarlatina' to denote a very mild form of the disease, and were very much less inclined to observe medical instructions in instances where 'scarlatina' had been diagnosed.[75] Medical anxiety to publicize the dangers of scarlet fever within their own class may have led to over-emphasis in the literature of its toll on the well-to-do. Thus Charles Murchison, in his June 1864 lectures, made much of the geographical incidence in London in 1863, without stopping to consider the previous or continuing pattern of an epidemic that began in 1862 and ended in 1864. In 1863, 'as often happens', he wrote, deaths in Paddington, Islington, and Marylebone far exceeded those in 'the most crowded and notoriously unhealthy districts', St George-in-the-East, Bermondsey, Rotherhithe, and Lambeth. In the former group scarlet-fever deaths were 1 per 477 population, in the latter 1 per 997.[76] The table which accompanied this statement gave details of various London districts, excluding some of those named in Murchisons's text (Table 3.6). However, if Murchison's table is extended to include other London districts, his selectivity in proof of his point is obvious (Table 3.7). While the experiences of St James's

[72] *Lancet* (1864), i. 725. [73] *Lancet* (1865), i. 129. [74] *Lancet* (1874), ii. 806.
[75] *Lancet* (1887), ii. 635. [76] *Lancet* (1864), i. 725.

and Poplar prove, in a rather different way, Murchison's claim that there was no obvious relation between overcrowding and scarlet-fever mortality, the figures from the well-to-do western districts compared with those of the eastern do suggest that high scarlet-fever mortality was far from being the preserve of the rich. However, it is clear that some 'well-to-do' districts suffered a notable proportionate rise in scarlet-fever mortality in the 1860s over the 1850s (Fig. 3.2). This was certainly the case in Marylebone, where Murchison himself lived and was bringing up his family.

The epidemic of 1868–9 is also instructive in this regard. It began in July 1868, and was initially most severe in the western and central districts of the city. By January 1869 the western districts had suffered a mortality-rate of 122 per 100,000 living and the central, 107; in the north, east, and south, however,

TABLE 3.6. *Scarlet-fever deaths in London, 1863, in districts selected by Charles Murchison*

District	Persons per acre 1861	Scarlet-fever deaths to population
Islington	49	1 : 412
Paddington	59	1 : 587
Hackney	21	1 : 666
St George's, Southwark	196	1 : 638
St George East	201	1 : 652
St Giles	220	1 : 730
St Saviour	144	1 : 804
Strand	247	1 : 955

Source: *Lancet* (1864), i. 724.

TABLE 3.7. *Scarlet-fever deaths in other London districts, 1863*

District	Persons per acre, 1861	Scarlet-fever deaths to population
Kensington	37	1 : 732
Chelsea	80	1 : 1379
St George's, Hanover Square	79	1 : 1488
St James's	218	1 : 1359
Shoreditch	200	1 : 555
Bethnal Green	139	1 : 449
Whitechapel	208	1 : 284
Stepney	121	1 : 333
Poplar	34	1 : 450

Source: *RGAR* PP 1865 xiv, p. 218.

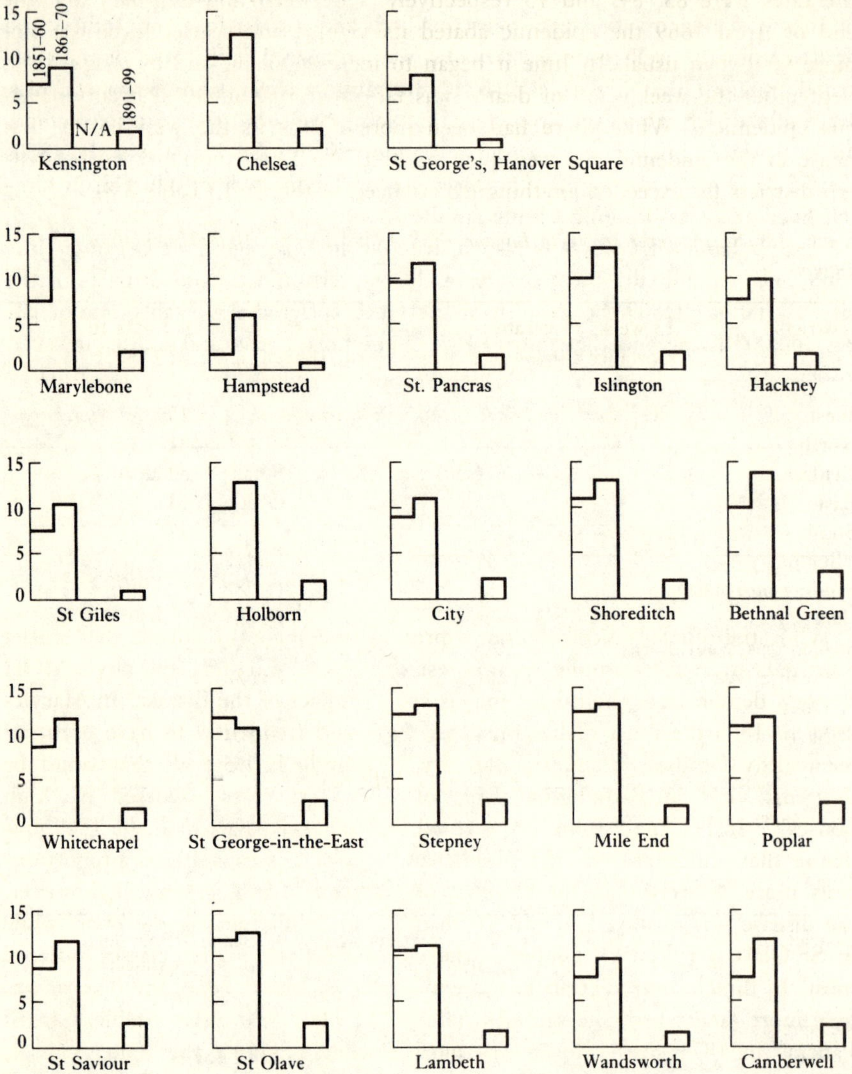

FIG. 3.2. *Scarlet-fever deaths in London districts, per 10,000 population, as available. Source: Registrar-general's decennial supplements; MOAR LCC (1900).*

the rates were 83, 84, and 75 respectively.[77] Between mid-February and the end of April 1869 the epidemic abated its vigour, and scarlet fever was not more fatal than usual. In June it began to increase again, and by August and September the weekly toll of deaths was far above that achieved in any previous epidemic.[78] While there had been more deaths in the west in the first phase of the epidemic, the west now suffered least, and mortality in the eastern districts far exceeded anything experienced in the west (Table 3.8).

TABLE 3.8. *Scarlet-fever deaths in London 1868–1869, rates per 10,000 population per annum*

Districts	13 weeks of greatest mortality 1868–69	13 weeks to 9 Oct. 1869	4 weeks to 23 Oct.
West	28	9	15
North	13	17	21
Central	24	27	42
East	22	41	63
South	14	19	39

Source: *Lancet* (1869), ii. 513, 626.

While the official mortality figures provide unequivocal evidence that scarlet fever was more fatal among the poorest districts of London, the city's MOH Reports demonstrate the miscellaneous social impact of the disease. In Marylebone in 1868 the most malignant cases were said frequently to have occurred in wealthy families, where the sanitary surroundings were all that could be desired;[79] and in Paddington some of the worst cases occurred in 'high houses'.[80] In Hackney, John Tripe noted, it was 'a peculiarity' of the 1869 epidemic that children from the middle and upper classes suffered proportionately more severely than the children of the poor.[81] In Clerkenwell, however, the disease was observed to spread 'readily and fatally' among the poor, while in St Olave Dr Vinen found that the children of the poorer classes suffered most. In direct contradiction to the experience of Marylebone, the disease was here more fatal where the sanitary state of the place was unfavourable.[82] In St Pancras in 1874 scarlet fever was more prevalent among the upper classes, while in Battersea in June 1875 the epidemic broke out in the St John's Hill district, which contained the best houses in the parish, with wide and well-cleansed streets, no overcrowding, and inhabitants all of the better class.[83] In 1882, however, the disease was 'raging over the whole district' of Battersea

[77] *Lancet* (1869), i. 94. [78] *Lancet* (1869), ii. 513. [79] *Lancet* (1868), ii. 558.
[80] Ibid. 711. [81] *MOAR* Hackney (1869), 3.
[82] *MOAR* Clerkenwell (1869), 14; *MOAR* St Olave (1869–70), 17.
[83] *MOAR* St Pancras (1874), 2; *MOAR* Battersea West (1875), 36.

West.[84] In Islington in 1893 fewer cases occurred in the wealthier districts, and the highest proportion of cases occurred in Number Nine sub-district, where the housing was mostly in tenements.[85] For the 1890s as a whole the figures provided by Shirley Murphy show clearly that there was both less scarlet fever and a lower mortality in the districts west of the City of London than in those to the east and north-east, and the south (Fig. 3.3). Despite the medical officers' individual observations, and the evidently quite frequent occurrence of fatalities among the better classes, the underlying reality throughout the second half of the century was of greater scarlet-fever mortality for London's poor.

Modern research suggests that the severity of scarlet fever may be related not merely to the virulence of the streptococcal strain, but also to the infective dose of these agents received by the individual.[86] Thus, greater fatality among the poor might be explained by overcrowding, while severe cases among the better-off could be associated with the overcrowded conditions which prevailed in many nurseries and schoolrooms. Charles West, for instance, condemned the practice of setting aside small rooms at the top of private houses for the children: one for the day nursery and one for the night nursery, in which two or three children would live and sleep with their nurse, without the minimum air requirement of 500 cubic feet each.[87] By the 1880s the movement for the improvement of domestic standards and of child-care within the middle class may have begun to tilt the burden of mortality further towards the poor. Mrs Gladstone's *Healthy Nurseries and Bedrooms*,[88] a Health Exhibition handbook recommended by West, was only one of a series of pamphlets and public lectures on such subjects which appeared during this decade. A growing awareness of domestic health, combined with fairly prompt domestic isolation or hospital removal, may just possibly have had some influence in reducing the severity of streptococcal infections.

Changing medical practices may also have contributed to lower mortalities, as the heroic treatments of the mid-century were replaced by a more non-interventionist type of therapy. The gentle approach of Charles West, with its emphasis on cleanliness, rest, and nourishment, is clearly reflected in the practices of the MAB's South-Western Hospital, as described by Dan Gresswell in 1890—a rare insight into the realities of an MAB hospital ward. On arrival, patients were clothed in two bed-gowns, cotton underneath, flannel on top, and put to bed. The temperature of the wards was maintained as nearly as possible at 60 degrees Fahrenheit—sometimes difficult to keep up when it was freezing outside, since ample ventilation was also a priority, with the upper quarter of each alternate window being open all the time. The beds were of

84 *MOAR* Battersea West (1882), 39.

85 *MOAR* Islington (1893), 63.

86 Breese and Breese Hall, *Streptococcal Disease*, 41–3.

87 Charles West, *The Mother's Manual of Children's Diseases* (1885), 3–4.

88 Catherine Gladstone, *Healthy Nurseries and Bedrooms* (1884).

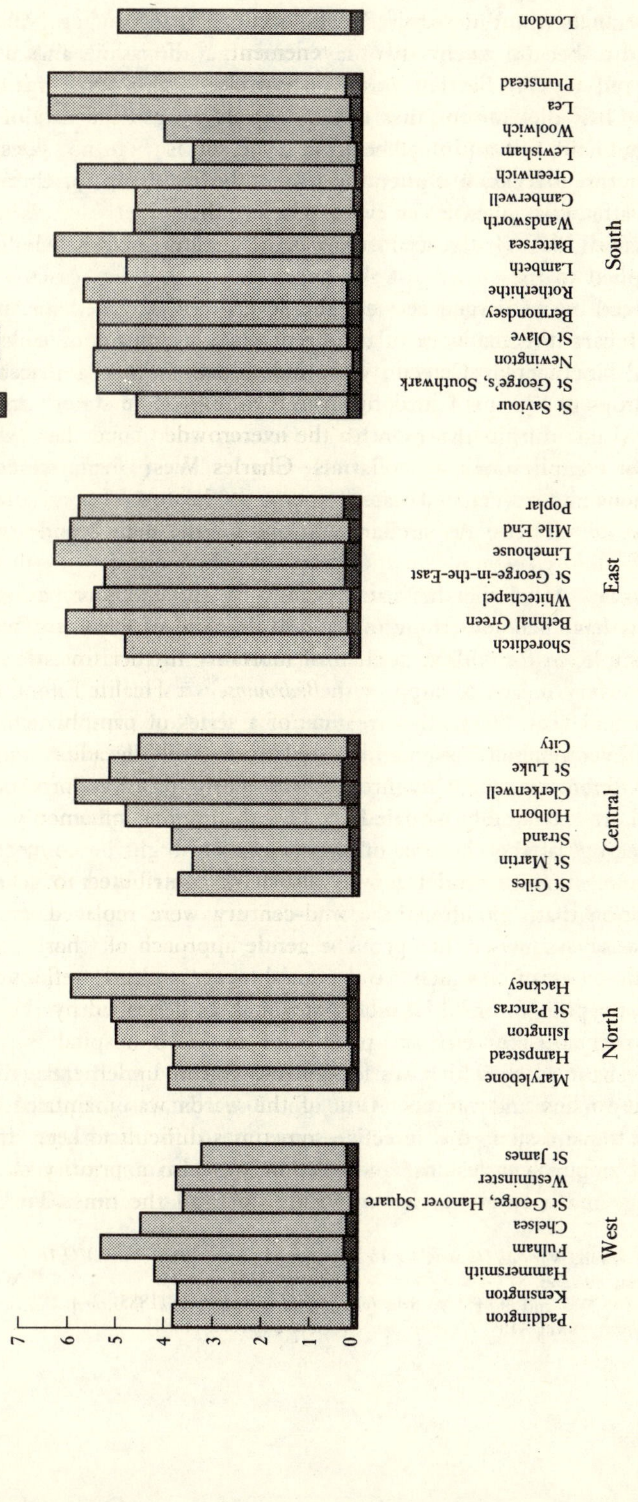

FIG. 3.3. *Scarlet-fever case- and mortality-rates in London districts per 1,000 living, 1891–1900 (fully corrected). Source: MOAR LCC (1900).*

iron, with a feather mattress, blanket, and sheet under the patient, and a sheet, three blankets (more if required), and a counterpane on top. All patients were confined to bed for twenty-two days following admission, and all except those transferred to convalescent hospitals remained in hospital for at least eight weeks. Their diet for the first twenty-two days was milk in almost any quantity, eggs, and half-a-pint of beef tea daily; baths were not generally given in the first three weeks, but after the patient had been up for three or four days warm baths were given every evening before bed.[89]

Gresswell was very restrained in his use of medicines. Medicaments were not applied to the surface of the body, except in a few cases where mustard was placed over enlarged cervical glands. Otherwise: 'Medicinal treatment was in chief part directed to regulating the bowls by means of Colocynth, Castor oil, and tinctures of Catechu and Kino.' Occasionally a placebo of 'two or three drops of Spiritus Chloroformi to three ounces of water' was given during the day, and during the months of October and November (when the incidence of complications was relatively high) a few patients were given oxygen inhalations and oxygenated water. In cases of heart weakness, softness of pulse, 'lividity of surface', or similar conditions, port and brandy were administered.[90]

Gresswell noted that his patients came from very poor backgrounds,[91] and this may have had something to do with the type of treatment accorded. West, for example, in forbidding depletion (blood-letting) and insisting on the adoption of 'every means to support the feeble powers of life', none the less noted that he had been led to this treatment by the 'low type' which a disease like scarlet fever generally assumed among the overcrowded poor, and that a somewhat different treatment might be advantageously pursued 'in the case of children more favourably situated'.[92] Indeed, it was commonly felt that the 'overfeeding' of the children of the well-to-do might be connected with their adverse reaction to scarlet fever.[93] None the less, West concluded with the observation that: 'Children in whom the local affection is severe, or in whom the disease assumes a malignant character, require all those stimulants, and that nutritious diet, which we are accustomed to give to patients in certain stages of typhus fever.'[94] In such cases, it seems, there was to be no distinction in treatment between rich and poor.

The channels by which scarlet fever distributed itself through the community were many and various. Although close contact is required for person-to-person transmission, the infective agent is in the discharges from nose and throat, or purulent lesions, and may be in contaminated dust, lint, or even clothing, and may be carried in milk.[95] All these routes were known or sus-

[89] Gresswell, *Natural History*, 15–16. [90] Ibid. 1617. [91] Ibid. 11.
[92] West, *Lectures*, 875–6. [93] *Lancet* (1858), ii. 525. [94] West, *Lectures*, 877.
[95] F. H. Top and P. H. Wehrle (eds.), *Communicable and Infectious Diseases*, ninth edn. (St Louis, Miss., 1981), 618.

pected by the 1880s.[96] Although scarlet fever was recognized to be 'the very type of a contagious and infectious malady',[97] its continuing severity and ubiquity in the 1860s and 1870s encouraged medical interest in its behaviour. In 1863 the registrar-general remarked that: 'It is an infectious disease, still requiring further study, as all its modes of propagation are not yet known.'[98] In 1897, similarly, the *Lancet* observed that there were considerable differences of opinion within the profession as to the exact channels of infection, as well as a dearth of reliable evidence on the same. 'In a word,' reported the journal, 'the evidence upon which beliefs are founded is somewhat scanty and unsatisfactory.'[99] It was a situation which continued until the work of the Dicks began to unravel the mystery of streptococci and their behaviour in the 1920s.

As so often, medical sources stress the links through which disease might be transmitted from poor to rich, if not vice versa. The *Lancet* warned that there was 'practically no limit' to the various ways that 'subtle poison' of scarlet fever might enter the middle-class home. Clothes which were made or washed outside the home were especially suspect, and large houses which employed outdoor milliners were warned to take pains to ascertain the conditions under which employees worked.[100] Charles Kingsley's *Alton Locke* (1850) highlighted for many the 'fearful risk' of tailors putting out work: there was no telling when a garment would come back impregnated with scarlet fever.[101] Instances were also publicized of the disease being transmitted through the post.[102]

The wide acceptance of the infectiousness of scarlet-fever patients while peeling, and of the products of desquamation produced many anxieties. The autumn rise in prevalence (as indicated by mortality) was attributed to latent infection being activated when children's winter clothes came back into circulation, after having been put away during the summer months.[103] The schools themselves were implicated when Shirley Murphy discovered a striking reduction in scarlet fever among children of school-age in London during August.[104] The seaside holidays traditional for scarlet-fever convalescents were often thought to disseminate the disease further afield.[105] Edward Seaton, then LGB medical officer, in his *Memorandum on Precautions against Scarlatina* (1878), warned particularly against the infectiousness of the dust particles from the skin, and stressed the importance of a final thorough disinfection of the convalescent and his clothes—three times over at least with soap and water—before he returned to the company of those susceptible to scarlet fever. Neglect of this precaution after slight cases of the disease was, he observed, a principal

[96] A. Hirsch, *Handbook of Geographical and Historical Pathology* (1886) 194–5.
[97] *Lancet* (1864), ii. 175.
[98] *RGAR*, PP 1865 xiv, p. 44.
[99] *Lancet* (1897), i. 54.
[100] *Lancet* (1874), ii. 566.
[101] *Lancet* (1875), ii. 638; in Charles Kingsley's *Alton Locke* (1850), the hero contracts typhus after visiting a tailor's sweatshop.
[102] *Lancet* (1875), i. 110.
[103] *Lancet* (1870), ii. 653.
[104] *Public Health*, 7 (1894–5), 350.
[105] *Lancet* (1868), i. 518.

source of infection.[106] Although by the end of the period medical emphasis on the infectiousness of desquamation had diminished, the infectiousness of the patient as long as it lasted was still accepted in the early twentieth century.[107]

The dissemination of scarlet fever through milk, which was first described by Michael Taylor of Penrith in 1867, became generally recognized in the early 1870s when Ballard traced a serious outbreak in Islington to this source.[108] Thereafter singular outbreaks of the disease were regularly tracked down to milk or cream supplies. Ernest Hart listed fifteen such epidemics in 1881, and in 1903 George Newman counted a total of sixty-nine British outbreaks between 1867 and 1903.[109] In London, at least ten milk-borne outbreaks occurred between 1870 and 1901: Islington, 1870; South Kensington, 1875; Paddington, 1880; Russell Square, 1882; Marylebone, 1885; Charlton, 1892; Upper Clapton, 1892; St Pancras, 1893; Blackheath, 1893; north-east London, 1901.[110] Until William Power's investigation of the 1882 Russell Square epidemic, it was assumed that such outbreaks derived from the contamination of milk by human agency; possibly through the medium of the products of desquamation.[111] Power, however, supported by the researches of Edward Klein, indicated that the fault lay in 'the very system of the animal furnishing the milk'.[112]

Whether the source of contamination was human or animal, milk became a suspect item wherever there was a sudden outbreak of scarlet fever from the early 1870s. Milk-borne outbreaks were, however, not the leading source of scarlet fever, even among the milk-drinking well-to-do. Such outbreaks were distinct and individual, apart from the general pattern of the endemic disease, in which the origin of infection was seldom traced beyond a few immediate preceding cases.[113] After 1871 the local authorities became vigilant over the dissemination of scarlet fever through milk, and the disruption of a tradesman's business by such vigilance added to the reasons for concealing the disease from the authorities.[114] Some responsible authorities, however, anxious to prevent both pauperism and the spread of disease, instituted compensation

[106] *MOAR* LGB, PP 1878 xxxvii pt ii, pp. 386–9.

[107] Reece, 'Scarlet fever', 264.

[108] For a contemporary account of these developments, see *MOAR* LGB, PP 1878 xxxvii, p. 418; for a full historical account, see Wilson, 'Historical riddle', 321–42. The implication in Smith, *People's Health*, 138, that the transmission of scarlet fever through milk only became known in 1885 is misleading.

[109] Ernest Hart, 'The influence of milk in spreading zymotic disease', *Transactions*, International Medical Congress (1881), iv. 491–544; H. Swithinbank and G. Newman, *The Bacteriology of Milk* (1903), 279–504.

[110] For these and further references see Hart, 'Influence of Milk'; id., *Report on the Influence of Milk in Spreading Zymotic Disease* (1897); Swithinbank and Newman, *Bacteriology of Milk*, 279–504. I have omitted the outbreaks at Wimbledon and Merton in 1886–7 and Richmond, 1894, from this list, as these districts were not at the time in metropolitan London.

[111] *MOAR* LGB, PP 1878 xxvii, pt ii, p. 389.

[112] *MOAR* LGB, PP 1883 xxviii, 633; also ibid, app. 9, 709–17. For the subsequent history of Klein's researches, see Wilson, 'Historical riddle'.

[113] Whitelegge, 'Age, sex and season', 154.

[114] Smith, *People's Health*, 141.

schemes: in Camberwell in 1887, for example, Mrs Sharp, who had been prevented from carrying on her milk-shop business at a loss of 12 shillings a week during the period she had scarlet fever in the house, received £2 compensation for her lost business from the vestry.[115]

Yet despite the advances in understanding the transmission of scarlet fever, the advent of the MAB hospitals, compulsory notification of the disease after 1889, and an increasing public acceptance of the hospital policy, the London preventive authorities made little headway in controlling the incidence of scarlet fever in the later decades of the century. If fatality declined, the disease itself was as rampant as ever in the closing years of the century. The apparent failure of the isolation policy, obvious to some, was disregarded by the preventive establishment, which continued to advertise the decline in the virulence of scarlet fever as an outcome of isolation, and to argue the case for measles isolation on the basis of the scarlet-fever experience.[116] Increasingly also, as with measles, isolation was justified as a means of raising the age-incidence of the disease, so that children might catch it when they were older and less susceptible to its worst complications.[117]

The history of scarlet fever in the later nineteenth century cannot convincingly be related to any of the preventive measures taken against it. It is possible that greater awareness of the 'sore throat', assisted by rising diphtheria incidence, led to cases being isolated earlier, thus reducing their infective impact. But the continuing high incidence of the disease, the medical profession's ignorance of its cause and true etiology, the beginning of its decline before notification and systematic hospitalization, the statistical evidence of declining case-fatality, and impressionistic evidence of a milder type all contribute to the judgement that preventive measures were largely irrelevant to the declining fatality of the disease after 1870.

[115] 'Camberwell sewers and sanitary committee minutes' (15 Nov. 1887).
[116] *Lancet* (1914), i. 549.
[117] Reece, 'Scarlet fever', 266.

4
Diphtheria

Diphtheria puzzles and embarrasses health officers more, perhaps, than any other 'preventible' disease.

(*Public Health* 1891–2)

This disease seems to be passing out of control.

(*Lancet* 1895)

Diphtheria was first clinically recognized in England in the late 1850s. Although evidence for its presence can be adduced for the 1780s, and for the early 1800s,[1] it was only identified and named as a separate clinical syndrome by Bretonneau in 1821.[2] It was active in France and various European countries in the 1830s and 1840s, but sporadic outbreaks were first (retrospectively) identified in England from around 1845.[3] Membraneous croup, later recognized as a mild form of diphtheria, was known in England in the first half of the century, but the more severe form which had drawn Bretonneau's attention did not become regularly established in the country until the later 1850s, when it was apparently imported from France: 366 deaths occurred at Boulogne in the autumn of 1855–6, several of which were among English visitors.[4] Following this outbreak, which received considerable attention in the English press, cases began to be recorded in south-east England, and the disease eventually spread through the country. By the autumn of 1857 it was being reported from places as far apart as Teignmouth (Devon), Chatham (Kent), and Bolton-le-Moors (Lancashire), and by March 1858 it was prevalent in London.[5]

Although the British, unlike the French, did not consider diphtheria a new disease but rather, in the words of the registrar-general, 'only a more intense form of an old disease',[6] its reappearance in more virulent form generated a

[1] R. Thorne Thorne, *Diphtheria: Its Natural History and Prevention* (1891), 11–112.

[2] P. Bretonneau, *Des Inflammations spéciales du tissu muqueux, et en particulier de la dipthérite* (Paris, 1826).

[3] Thorne, *Diphtheria*, 14.

[4] Ibid. 14–15. As Thorne points out, it is none the less clear from the investigations of the Privy Council Medical Department that diphtheria had been prevalent in England for at least two years before this, and before there was any public knowledge of the fact: see *MOAR* PC, 2, PP 1860 xxix, pp. 363, 369–477. According to W. N. Thursfield (*Lancet* (1878), ii. 145), the disease had prevailed sporadically in various parts of England since before 1837, under such names as cynanche maligna, angina membranea, etc. It may be noted also that Sir William Jenner stated in 1861 that he had seen cases of diphtheria every now and then as long as he had practised medicine: 'Diphtheria', in *Lectures and Essays on Fever and Diphtheria* (1893), 498.

[5] *Lancet* (1858), i. 125, 250.

[6] *RGAR*, PP 1860 xxix, p. 566.

considerable public response. 'Of its novelty to nearly the whole British medical profession, familiar as they were with the angina of scarlet fever, there can be no question', wrote Charles Creighton in 1891.[7] As a result, there was intense medical and popular interest. From 1858 into the early 1860s the medical journals covered the disease extensively, and the *Lancet* ordered a 'Special Sanitary Commission' on the disease by Ernest Hart, editor of the *British Medical Journal*.[8] The registrar-general fulminated against the insanitary habits of the French, notably the 'inscrutable *cabinet*, where the light of French refinement never comes', which he held responsible for the recrudescence of the disease.[9] The excitement surrounding the 'novelty' of diphtheria was taken up by the popular press, and journals such as *The Times* and the *Builder* asked how far the disease was dependent on insanitary conditions, how far on infection, and what precautions should be taken to avoid it.[10] All this publicity woke a 'strong alarm' in the general public, to the extent that the popular response in the first few months of 1859 was said to be akin to that excited by cholera.[11]

This type of public response does not seem to be immediately justified by the behaviour of the disease in the 1850s, which was by no means that of a widespread and fatal national epidemic, or by its mortality relative to that of the other major children's diseases. Diphtheria was classed with scarlet fever in the registrar-general's returns until 1860, and with cynanche maligna until 1869, but in the 1860s its mortality rates were 171 per million living against 391 for measles, 467 for whooping cough, and 890 for scarlet fever.[12] A closer examination of the evidence shows, however, that the initial impact of the disease was much more impressive. As Arthur Newsholme discovered in the 1890s, the General Register Office had actually recorded 'diphtheria' deaths separately on their ticking sheets from 1858.[13] Using this information, Newsholme was able to give an instructive quinquennial breakdown of the mortality statistics (Table 4.1), which revealed a serious epidemic outbreak in the years 1858–65, during which London suffered an especially severe mortality.[14]

The mortality figures for the first epidemic prevalence of diphtheria in 1858–65 may go some way to explaining public alarm, even though they by no means matched those for scarlet fever, and the disease was far less widespread in the community than any of the other infectious children's diseases. The clue to public alarm lay perhaps partly in the perception of the disease as new,

[7] Charles Creighton, *A History of Epidemics in Britain*, 2 vols. (Cambridge, 1894), ii. 736.
[8] *Lancet* (1859), i. 65, 89, 115, 140, 169. This report was also published separately.
[9] *RGAR*, PP 1860 xxix, p. 566.
[10] *The Times*, 29 June 1859.
[11] *Lancet* (1859), i. 27, 563. See also *The Times*, 4–6 Jan. 1859. By mid-May this 'extreme alarm' had subsided with the first vigour of the epidemic: *Lancet* (1859), i. 490.
[12] *RGDS*, PP 1905 xviii, table 5.
[13] Arthur Newsholme, *Epidemic Diphtheria* (1898), 29.
[14] Even so, registered diphtheria deaths were certainly an underestimate of the total due to the disease at this period.

TABLE 4.1. *Annual death-rates per million living of croup and diphtheria in England and Wales, and in London*

	England and Wales			London
Period	Diphtheria	Croup	Diphtheria and croup	Diphtheria
1858–60	372	274	647	458 (1859–60)
1861–65	248	288	535	224
1866–70	127	208	335	133
1871–75	121	184	305	114
1876–80	122	154	276	130
1881–85	156	163	320	221
1886–90	170	126	295	298
1891–94	251	74	325	548

Source: A. Newsholme *Epidemic Diphtheria* (1898), 31, 32.

but it was also fuelled by its random impact, distressing symptoms, and fatality. In many families, it was reported, child after child was carried off, while practitioners found themselves helpless in the face of the 'insurmountable difficulties which too often oppose themselves to their treatment'.[15] Like scarlet fever, it was a disease which did not confine itself to the poor, and it had the unpleasant habit of descending on small communities—a hamlet, a school, a numerous family—and inflicting terrible losses there, without ever passing beyond that community into the immediate neighbourhood.[16] It thus had all the characteristics of a new type of plague, and it generated, initially, a similar panic response.[17]

Diphtheria is caused by the organism *Corynebacterium diphtheriae*. Three types of this bacillus have been identified: *gravis*, *intermedia*, and *mitis*. The two former are generally associated with high case-fatality rates, and it is not clear that there is any consistent difference in severity between them; *mitis* is milder. Each type has its own complications: paralysis in *gravis*; haemorrhage and albuminaria are far more common in *gravis* and *intermedia*; obstructive lesions in the air passages characterize *mitis*. However, all three types vary in virulence, and at its most favourable *gravis* corresponds to *mitis* at its least favourable.[18] The disease is spread by droplet infection, close contact, infected

[15] *Lancet* (1859), i. 27.

[16] Ibid. 62; *The Times*, Dec. 1858. This pattern of behaviour has become an established fact; according to Topley and Wilson, diphtheria is typically a disease of households, schools, and institutions where children are herded together at susceptible ages. A particular school or institution may constitute an endemic centre for months or even years: *Principles of Bacteriology, Virology and Immunity*, seventh edn. (1984), iii. 76–7.

[17] See n. 11 above.

[18] Clinical information is derived from Topley and Wilson, *Principles*, iii. 53.

TABLE 4.2. *Diphtheria death-rates per 1,000 living under 5, 1851–1900*

	1851–60	1861–70	1871–80	1881–90	1891–1900
England and Wales	0.43	0.77	0.47	0.69	1.36
London	0.43	0.92	0.57	1.37	2.98

Source: *RGDS*.

dust, and contaminated milk. The bacillus lodges in the throat of its host and remains there, producing or stimulating a potent toxin which results in the recognized symptoms of the disease. Diphtheria in man is probably a toxaemia in which individual resistance or susceptibility to infection, and recovery or death are largely determined by the presence or rapid production of anti-toxin.[19] Although the development of the whitish-grey membrane over the back of the throat is the most widely recognized characteristic of the disease, and although the membrane may be so extensive that, with the swelling of the throat, it may stop swallowing or breathing, it is none the less the diphtheria toxin which causes death, and it is the toxin which may cause permanent damage to heart and nerves. The bacillus may be carried in the throat for up to and beyond six weeks; cases in which it persists for more than twelve weeks are regarded as carriers. The bacilli disappear more quickly in older than younger children, and most slowly in the *gravis* type. However, bacilli may often be detected in the throat during the incubation period, and it is possible that precocious carriers are as dangerous as convalescent carriers or subclinical cases.[20]

The etiology of diphtheria goes some way towards explaining its historical behaviour. Severe epidemics with high mortality seem to be due to bacilli of the *gravis* and *intermedia* strains, while *mitis* is generally responsible for endemic diphtheria. Fatalities with *mitis* are nearly always due to obstruction of the larynx or trachea, rather than to the effects of diphtheria toxin.[21] When diphtheria was prevalent, the commonest cause of 'croup' was laryngeal diphtheria.[22] Because of the mild nature of the *mitis* strain, however, a large number of children became immune as the result of very light infections, and the disease did not appear as a major preventive problem. The introduction of

[19] Ibid. 74. [20] Ibid. 77.

[21] George Rosen, 'Acute communicable diseases', in W. R. Betts (ed.), *The History and Conquest of Common Diseases* (Norman, Okla., 1954), 25.

[22] Sir MacFarlane Burnet and David O. White, *The Natural History of Infectious Disease*, fourth edn. (Cambridge, 1972), 193. Croup and diphtheria are not identical. Croup is a symptom rather than a disease, typified by the 'barking' sound produced by breathing difficulties in very young children. Today it is largely caused by the narrowing of the immature windpipe through inflammation. Its principal incidence and fatality is in children under 2, who may develop it as a consequence of an ordinary cold infection. Before mass immunization, the age-incidence of diphtheria was highest in children between the ages of 2 and 5.

gravis or *intermedia* strains, however, would result in outbreaks of dramatically more severe and fatal cases, occurring mainly in young children who had not had the opportunity to acquire immunity. The pattern of epidemic diphtheria in the nineteenth century may thus be explained by the shifting dominance of severe and mild strains of the diphtheria bacillus.[23] Membraneous croup, with which early nineteenth-century English observers were familiar, can be identified with laryngeal diphtheria, in which the diphtheria bacilli spread into the larynx posing a grave medical problem. From the available evidence it is clear that *mitis* forms of diphtheria were very widely distributed in communities throughout the country, and that until long after the appearance of more severe forms of the disease they were regarded as minor personal inconveniences, of little importance beyond the daily routine of the family concerned. Burnet has estimated that not more than 5 to 10 per cent of children ever suffered from clinical diphtheria, but also that before immunization 2 to 5 per cent apparently healthy children had diphtheria bacilli in their throats at any one time.[24] Before the upsurge of severe strains in the later 1850s, diphtheria, although widely present, was a far from conspicuous disease, and was certainly not viewed as a preventive problem.

The many variations in severity of diphtheria, and the multiplicity of carriers who show no, or very few, outward signs of the disease, were the two principal factors influencing its public-health history between 1858 and 1900. The identity of the disease and the reasons for its peculiar behaviour were central problems for the English medical profession in this period. Because it was a 'new' disease, contemporaries often compared it to cholera.[25] However, the means of cholera's transmission became clear in the later 1860s, well before the discovery of the cholera bacillus in 1884. By contrast, the epidemiology of diphtheria continued to pose a problem even after the discovery of the bacillus in 1883–4. *Corynebacterium diphtheriae* was discovered by Klebs in 1883. Evidence of its part in the etiology of the disease became available in the following year, when Löeffler published his classic paper arguing that diphtheria was a disease with a single bacterial cause. Yet Löeffler was unable to recover diphtheria bacilli from his experimental animals except from tissues in proximity to the injection site, and his conclusion that death was not due to the dissemination of bacilli throughout the body but to some substance elaborated in the local lesion was greeted with scepticism.[26] It was not until Roux and

[23] Burnet and White, *The Natural History of Infectious Disease*, fourth edn. (Cambridge, 1972), 198; Rosen, 'Acute Communicable Diseases', 25.

[24] Burnet and White, *Natural History*, 195.

[25] *RGAR*, PP 1860 xxix, p. 566; E. H. Greenhow, *Diphtheria* (1860), 80.

[26] For a contemporary assessment of the new research on diphtheria, see *Lancet* (1884), ii. 741. The journal noted the very great differences among bacteriologists as to the 'morphology of the diphtherial fungus', and seemed inclined to favour Emmerich's suggestion that diphtheria was essentially a 'house disease' because it was prevalent during the seasons when dwellings were most overcrowded. Historical accounts of the discovery of the morphology of diphtheria and of the development of antitoxin may be found in Rosen, 'Acute Communicable Diseases', and in H. J.

Yersin demonstrated that the bacillus was accompanied by potent extra-cellular toxins in 1888 that the bacteriological explanation of the disease could be confirmed. Even so, the available evidence suggests that in England the bacteriological explanation of the disease was not fully accepted until the results of the Parisian antitoxin trials were published in July 1894.

Until 1894 the identity and nature of diphtheria was a source of confusion and argument within the English medical profession, and of continual frustration to the preventive authorities. While the existence of three types of diphtheria,[27] its contagiousness, and eccentric means of progress were quickly recognized by Victorian observers, there was widespread controversy over the identity of the disease and its relationship with other types of 'sore throat'. This vexed question of nomenclature was compounded by the vagaries of its behaviour—it would suddenly appear locally, when there were no cases for miles around, and no contact could be proven or even suggested—into a considerable preventive problem. Early investigations by the Medical Department and the Epidemiological Society failed to provide any satisfactory answers to the questions of causation and definition.[28] As a result, there was no standardization of diagnosis or nomenclature. In his *Lancet* Sanitary Commission of 1858, Ernest Hart condemned the 'loose wording' which constantly impeded the preventive search for the local prevalence of the disease. Many observers, he recorded, applied the term to all forms of throat affection; others retained such designations as 'throat fever' or classified it as a form of cynanche (croup), refusing to investigate the 'unassailable grounds' on which a specific character was assigned to diphtheria; still others, 'physicians of intelligence', thought that it was closely allied to scarlet fever and should be classed with that disease.[29] Following Hart's report, the registrar-general ceased to class the disease with scarlet fever,[30] but the problem did not end there. Many English physicians were at first doubtful whether there was any distinction between diphtheria and membraneous croup, a disease with which they had long been familiar; this controversy was only settled in 1879 when a specially convened committee of the Medico-Chirurgical Society, with some hesitation, affirmed the identity of the two diseases.[31]

Despite these efforts to whittle down the sources of confusion, that confusion continued, and the profession as a whole was clearly far from unanimous in its diagnostic approach. Practitioners had traditionally adopted a variety of names for the variety of non-specific throat affections which had afflicted their

Parish, *The History of Immunization* (Edinburgh, 1965), 118–31. See also E. M. Tansey, 'The Wellcome Physiological Research Laboratories 1894–1904: the Home Office, pharmaceutical firms, and animal experiments', *Medical History*, 33 (1989), 1–41.

27 *Lancet* (1858), ii. 477; (1859), i. 169.

28 *MOAR* PC, PP 1860 xxix, pp. 365–511; *Lancet* (1859), i. 195; (1860), i. 14.

29 *Lancet* (1859), i. 115.

30 Ibid. 195.

31 Charles West, *Lectures on the Diseases of Infancy and Childhood*, seventh edn. (1884) 409–12; *Medico Chirurgical Transactions*, 62 (1879), 1–33.

patients, and the authorities' insistence that diphtheria was not a new disease may have discouraged its recognition. Equally, diphtheria itself existed in so many forms that uncertainty in diagnosis was not unacceptable. In 1878 W. N. Thursfield, complaining about the non-specific use of the term 'diphtheria', instanced a recent case where two deaths had been registered as 'inflamed glands' during an epidemic of undoubted diphtheria. On inquiry, the medical attendant said he did not consider himself justified in registering any death as diphtheria in which the false membrane was not plainly developed. It was a principle, admitted Thursfield, 'upheld by many with good reason'.[32] The possible absence of the membrane, and the continued association with 'membraneous croup', perpetuated a special confusion of diagnosis between croup and diphtheria. By the later 1880s Edward Ballard of the Local Government Board had come to regard the two as synonymous, noting that in the epidemic at Camelford in Cornwall, which persisted for four years, the local practitioners used both terms interchangeably.[33] Nevertheless, John Sykes was arguing for a statistical transfer of croup to diphtheria by the 1890s,[34] and this was demonstrated by Newsholme in graphic form in 1898.[35]

Yet the question of nomenclature was of considerable importance, not simply from the perspective of the type of treatment accorded the disease,[36] but for the implementation of preventive measures in private and public practice. Thus the *Lancet* noted of the Camelford epidemic that, 'the question of nomenclature has had a large influence, not only on the spread and fatality of this disease diphtheria, but upon the failure to secure any proper administrative action.'[37] At Camelford the designation of most of the cases under 'the somewhat meaningless term of croup' had lulled even the most experienced observers into a false sense of security, so that no measures were taken against the spread of the disease.[38] Five years later the journal again noted its conviction that the failure to contain the disease was due mainly to difficulties of diagnosis.[39] Where cases were named as diphtheria, proper measures of isolation, nursing, and disinfection would be put in train not merely by the preventive authorities, if they learnt of the case, but also by private practitioners and families, whose anxiety to protect their patients or relations against the scourge of diphtheria was often acute.[40]

If confusion over nomenclature delayed preventive measures designed to control the spread of the disease, the continuing debate over the means of the

32 *Lancet* (1878), ii. 147.
33 *MOAR* LGB, PP 1889 xxxvi, app. A no. 12, p. 119.
34 J. F. J. Sykes, 'The causes of the increase of diphtheria mortality in London', *Public Health*, 6 (1893–4), 331–4.
35 Newsholme, *Epidemic Diphtheria*, 30.
36 West, *Lectures*, 410–11. West found, from retrospective inspection of his case-notes, that the type of treatment he was offering began to change around 1850, reflecting change in the nature or type of the disease: ibid. 458–9.
37 *Lancet* (1889), i. 692.
38 Ibid.
39 *Lancet* (1894), ii. 694.
40 *The Times*, 4 Jan. 1859.

disease's transmission led to differing local emphasis on specific preventive policy, even where it was agreed that an outbreak was diphtheria. The early nineteenth-century French authorities considered diphtheria to be eminently contagious, and it was very generally acknowledged in England that it was communicable by direct contagion from person to person. As Ernest Hart pointed out, this explained how the disease so frequently affected a whole family.[41] Additional evidence confirming its contagiousness was soon provided by repeated diphtheria fatalities among doctors practising oral suction while performing tracheotomies to relieve symptoms of the disease.[42] The profession were nevertheless unable to trace antecedent cases or plausible contacts in a good proportion of cases,[43] and inevitably sought other explanations. Several different causes and means of transmission were assigned to diphtheria in the years before the role of the Klebs-Löeffler bacillus was accepted.

The miasmatic link between unhygienic sanitary facilities and diphtheria, as assumed by the registrar-general in 1858, proved enduringly popular, both with the general public and with sanitary reformers. Among the former it was 'universally prevalent' in the 1890s.[44] Although evidence for the link was far from conclusive, and some were decidedly of the opinion that none could be produced,[45] sewer gas was taken very seriously by the profession as a secondary means of diphtheria transmission. As late as 1889 J. F. J. Sykes, the able MOH for St Pancras, elicited very general agreement from the Society of Medical Officers when he argued for a link between sewer gas and diphtheria. Reginald Dudfield (Paddington) was the only dissenter, stating bluntly that diphtheria was due to a definite organism, and that proof would probably be forthcoming that it was due only to specific infection derived from a previous case. Sykes then suggested that the diphtheria organism might live in the slime of sewers.[46] The early 1890s saw the resurgence of a major debate among sanitarians on the relationship between diphtheria and insanitary conditions, with a mild digression into whether the disease might be carried in horse manure.[47]

The debate peaked in 1894 when Edward Seaton, in a paper delivered to the International Congress of Hygiene at Budapest, effectively squashed argument by pointing out that, while the general death-rate, the zymotic death-rate, and the typhoid death-rate had all steadily declined since 1871 contemporaneously with the extensive public and private works for improved water supply, drainage, and sewerage which had been undertaken in that period, the diphtheria death-rate alone had continued to increase, and the disease did not appear to be subject to the same laws as the others.[48] At the same

[41] *Lancet* (1859), i. 90.

[42] West, *Lectures*, 416. For an example of such a professional casualty and its impact, see the case of Dr Samuel Rabbeth of the Royal Free Hospital, reported in the *Lancet* (1884), ii. 801, 808, 837, 951.

[43] *Lancet* (1860), i. 14.

[44] *MOAR* Whitechapel (1892), 8–9.

[45] Ibid.

[46] *Public Health*, 1 (1889), 257–60.

[47] *Public Health*, 4 (1890–1), 191, 361; 9 (1896–7), 50–5.

[48] *Public Health*, 7 (1894–5), 8–9.

Congress Roux published the results of the his antitoxin trials,[49] which finally, perhaps, confirmed the central role of the bacillus to most of the English medical profession.[50] Yet the idea that defective drainage was responsible had been long established and widely held; it continued to linger. In 1896, for example, the distinguished MOH for Birmingham, Alfred Hill, could still state that 'closet accommodation cannot be ignored as a very probable source of danger', demonstrating that, 'pan closets favour the introduction of the diphtheria virus a little, and when it is introduced facilitate its spread in a marked degree'.[51] The idea that the inhalation of sewer gas weakened throats and made them more susceptible to diphtheria also survived,[52] perhaps with greater plausibility in the face of the new bacteriology.

During the later 1890s interest in sewer gas as a means of transmitting diphtheria gave way to concern about the role of schools in spreading the disease in the community. This theme was introduced, naturally enough, by Shirley Murphy, who put forward the argument for each of the infectious children's diseases in turn.[53] Edward Seaton's influential 1894 paper also helped to shift the focus of preventive attention in this direction, and in the latter years of the century it is the schools question that dominates the diphtheria literature of the preventive journals. As with the apparent increase in the prevalence and virulence of scarlet fever in the 1870s, so it was easy enough to see in the spread of diphtheria since 1870 the effects of the 1870 Education Act in bringing large numbers of children together in schools. While the precise emphasis of the argument underwent various changes,[54] Shirley Murphy's contention that increased school attendance had 'accentuated' a natural upswing in the cycle of diphtheria prevalence since 1870 came to be very generally accepted.[55]

Murphy's argument was based on his observation that notifications for diphtheria (as for scarlet fever) fell off in London during the August school-holiday period, and part of his preventive policy for London was to coerce the London School Board into closer co-operation with the preventive services.[56] Murphy admitted that the notification system supplied an incomplete record of total diphtheria cases, but used this as a further argument for urging help from the School Board.[57] In fact, the less-complete notification records of the years

[49] *Public Health*, 7 (1894–5), 11; *Lancet* (1894), ii. 152 (11 July).

[50] The sewer-gas debate is best studied in the pages of the medical officers' journal, *Public Health*. The volumes from 1888 to 1895 are especially rich on the subject. Thereafter argument faded away, and although many practitioners continued to take the drainage factor into account when relating outbreaks, the theory was now often referred to in a slightly derogatory fashion, e.g. by Louis Parkes (Chelsea), *Public Health*, 9 (1896–7), 58, and by Francis Stevens (Camberwell), ibid. 406.

[51] *Lancet* (1896), ii. 733.

[52] *Public Health*, 5 (1892–3), 114; *Lancet* (1897), ii. 677-8.

[53] *Public Health*, 5 (1892–3), 114; 7 (1894–5), 141.

[54] *Public Health*, 11 (1898–9), 305.

[55] Ibid. 305–6. For the details of Murphy's argument see *MOAR* LCC (1897), app. 1, 'Diphtheria and Elementary Schools'.

[56] *Public Health*, 11 (1898–9) 306.

[57] Ibid.

1892–6, on which he based his argument, may have been epidemiologically misleading. While local instances of the involvement of schools in disseminating the disease were recorded,[58] an independent statistical study of East London in the years 1895–1914, undertaken by E. W. Goodall and others, subsequently found no evidence to demonstrate a relationship between school-closure and the incidence of either diphtheria or scarlet fever.[59]

While Murphy was wrestling with the London School Board, another of the rising stars of the preventive firmament, Arthur Newsholme, MOH for Brighton, was elaborating a final version of the third great diphtheria-transmission theory to exercise the nineteenth-century preventive establishment. Meteorology had been an active interest of nineteenth-century students of epidemiology and disease-prevention since the field developed in the 1850s. Accordingly, diphtheria had been causally associated by some sanitarians with meteorological conditions and geology, and with local problems such as damp and marshes, for as long as it had been a cause of concern in England.[60] Charles Creighton, meanwhile, in the later 1880s, associated the outbreak of diphtheria in 1858–9 with a succession of dry years. Against this background Newsholme developed an interest in the association between diphtheria and rainfall patterns. It was a more sophisticated argument than those previously put forward, for it was based on a series of international statistical comparisons, and sought to establish the cause of the world pandemic of diphtheria since the 1850s.[61] While some interest was initially expressed in Newsholme's theory, it rapidly sank from sight[62] as the new bacteriology generated more practical means of preventing diphtheria than the prediction of series of dry warm years.[63] Indeed, Newsholme's work was based on figures only as far as 1896; and in that year mortality-rates from diphtheria began to turn down, although the series of warm dry years continued until the end of the century. Twentieth-century research, which by use of the Schick test (1913) and throat swab has obtained a more complete picture of the epidemiology of diphtheria than for any other infectious disease,[64] has concentrated instead on social and bacteriological factors, on herd infection and herd immunity.[65]

While the professional sanitarians balanced the dangers of contagion, drains, and dampness (and eventually dryness) in producing diphtheria, popular theories of the disease were even more catholic. The drainage theory naturally retained a deep impression on the popular consciousness: in 1890, for example,

[58] *Public Health*, 12 (1899–1900), 364.

[59] E. W. Goodall, M. Greenwood and W. T. Russell, *Scarlet Fever, Diphtheria and Enteric Fever, 1895–1914*, Medical Research Council Special Report, no. 137 (1929), 10–11, 31–2.

[60] e.g. *Lancet* (1858), i. 250; (1859), i. 115; (1862), ii. 616; (1886), ii. 350.

[61] Creighton, *Epidemics*, ii. 744.

[62] Newsholme, *Epidemic Diphtheria*.

[63] Arthur Newsholme, *Fifty Years in Public Health* (1935), 194. Newsholme's theory is mentioned by E. W. Goodall and J. W. Washbourn in their *A Manual of Infectious Diseases*, of 1908 (p. 100), but not by, e.g., M. Greenwood, *Epidemics and Crowd Diseases* (1935), pp. 197–209.

[64] Topley and Wilson, *Principles*, iii. 76.

[65] Ibid. 76–8, 415–16.

a clutch of diphtheria cases in Paddington released a flood of correspondence to the daily papers on the subject of offensive smells all over the West End of London.[66] Interestingly, it was also popularly assumed that diphtheria was caused by polluted water supplies, even though this suggestion was far from current in contemporary medical literature. In 1868 the Revd W. Langhorne, senior curate of St Paul's, and C. G. J. Aldis, MOH for St George's, Hanover Square, disputed the causes of a diphtheria outbreak in Wilton Crescent in the columns of *The Times*: Langhorne contended that the water supply was to blame, while Aldis demonstrated the innocence of the supply (even the horses in these mews premises drank filtered water), and argued that the overcrowding of six children in one 'malarious' room amply explained the course of the disease.[67] Similarly, in the outbreak in Paddington in 1890 the parents of the affected children blamed the water supply at the Paddington Recreation Ground.[68]

There is no evidence to suggest that diphtheria can be transmitted in water; it may, however, be transmitted in milk. Even more than with scarlet fever and typhoid, the discovery that the disease could be distributed by infected milk supplies was one of the few positive advances made towards an understanding of the etiology of the disease before the 1890s. The connection was first suspected in 1878, when W. H. Power, the Medical Department's doyen of milk-epidemic studies, was investigating an extensive outbreak among mainly well-to-do families in north London.[69] The early cases were observed to fall in one particular milk-walk, but the later pattern of the outbreak suggested that if there had been such a cause it had been transitory.[70] This was perhaps hardly surprising, for the isolation of *Corynebacterium diphtheriae* from milk later proved most uncommon even where grave suspicions were entertained; the incrimination of the milk supply in almost all instances rests on epidemiological evidence.[71] Other explanations continued to be sought,[72] but Power's eventual account was conclusive. The pattern of the epidemic proved beyond doubt that the distribution of diphtheria in the north London epidemic corresponded to the distribution of milk.[73] Milk-borne transmission for diphtheria became an established consideration after 1878, and Medical Department investigators were able to trace further outbreaks to this source in 1883.[74]

While milk-borne diphtheria almost certainly constituted a greater health-

[66] *Lancet* (1890), ii. 892; *The Times*, 15 Oct. 1890.
[67] *The Times* 7/10 Feb. 1868.
[68] *Lancet* (1890), i. 1,437.
[69] *Lancet* (1878), i. 836.
[70] Ibid. See also W. H. Power, 'Thoughts on the nature of certain observed relations between diphtheria and milk', *Transactions of the Pathological Society*, 30 (1879), 546–51.
[71] Topley and Wilson, *Principles*, iii. 77.
[72] *Lancet* (1878), i. 870, 915.
[73] *Lancet* (1879), i. 53, 94.
[74] *MOAR* LGB (1882), PP 1884–5 xxxiii; ibid. 1884–5 xxxiii, pp. 9, 10; app. A, no. 7, W. H. Power on 'An outbreak of diphtheria in Hendon'; app. A, no. 8, Dr Parsons on 'Diphtheria in Devonport'.

hazard for the better-off classes, it is unlikely to have been the only, or even the principal, source of the disease amongst them.[75] As early as September 1879, for example, the MOH for Lower Norwood was unable to find any links with either the milk or water supply in an outbreak in his district.[76] Milk-related outbreaks were generally conspicuous locally in the distribution of primary cases along milk-walks, and the apparently ephemeral nature of diphtheria infection in milk makes it unlikely that such contamination was responsible for other than episodic outbreaks. Harold Swithinbank and George Newman detailed sixteen milk-borne outbreaks of diphtheria in Britain between 1879 and 1900, and listed thirteen others.[77] Apart from outbreaks in Kilburn and St John's Wood in 1878 and 1879, none of these were in metropolitan London.[78] Endemic diphtheria was evidently spread largely through personal contact and carriers, among all social classes.[79]

The discovery of the milk-transmission of diphtheria did not result in any radical departures in preventive practice towards the disease after 1879. Dependence, as generally towards the infectious diseases in this period, was on isolation and disinfection. Despite all other possible means of distribution, contagion was widely accepted as being one of the disease's primary means of transmission.[80] Ernest Hart was one of the first to insist on this, and to recommend the isolation of patients, observance of strict quarantine, and rigorous cleanliness of domestic utensils and clothing.[81] Twenty years later W. N. Thursfield also noted: 'If isolation, disinfection and cleanliness are neglected, diphtheria will spread.'[82] London's medical officers, under the guidance of the Medical Department,[83] dealt with diphtheria cases as they dealt with other types of infectious disease, but after initial comment in 1858–9, the disease excited little notice among them before the later 1880s.[84] Relatively speaking it was too unimportant, and these were years in which they had their hands full, with epidemic typhus in the 1860s, cholera in 1866, scarlet fever in 1869, and smallpox from 1870 to 1877. In 1877, for example, Camberwell's health department performed disinfections for 741 cases of infectious disease: 541 smallpox, 142 scarlet fever, twenty-nine typhus, and a mere five diphtheria.[85] There were thirteen deaths from diphtheria registered in the district in that year.

[75] As implied by F. B. Smith, *The People's Health* (1987), 150.
[76] *Lancet* (1879), ii. 557.
[77] H. Swithinbank and G. Newman, *The Bacteriology of Milk* (1903), 346–51.
[78] Ibid.
[79] See below, nn. 102–4, 112–17.
[80] This was affirmed by Hart in 1859 (*Lancet* (1859), i. 89); by W. N. Thursfield in 1879 (*Lancet* (1879), ii. 148, 210); by John Bristowe (*MOAR* Camberwell (1893–4), 499); and by Francis Vacher in 1895 (*Public Health*, 7 (1894–5), 260).
[81] *Lancet* (1859), i. 90.
[82] *Lancet* (1878), ii. 148.
[83] Diphtheria appears for the first time in the 'General Memorandum on Proceedings' for places attacked by infectious disease in 1859: *MOAR* PC, PP 1861 xvi app. 1, p. 375.
[84] e.g. John Bristowe noted the arrival of diphtheria and gave a careful clinical description of it in 1859: *MOAR* Camberwell (1858–9), 24–6.
[85] Ibid. (1877–8), 202.

A final piece in the jigsaw of diphtheria distribution fell into place in the early 1890s, as a result of the new bacteriology. This was the role of carriers, which is probably important in the dissemination of diphtheria, and partly explains the sudden and apparently unrelated appearances of the disease. The significance of human carriers had been revealed by Koch's work on cholera in 1892–3, and in 1893 the young American epidemiologist William Hallock Park established the concept of the carrier in diphtheria. Park demonstrated the importance of both convalescent and well carriers for the disease, stressing that all members of an infected household were dangerous, whether or not they had manifested symptoms.[86] In England the implications of this work were not extensively realized in the 1890s, and there is little indication of preventive officers acting on such information. The English authorities were still exploring the possibilities of this means of transmission for themselves. In 1895, for example, Herbert Peck, MOH for Ormskirk, reported on eight cases in four houses which showed the possibilities of transmission by non-sufferers.[87] At the laboratories of the Royal College of Physicians between 1894 and 1896, Sims Woodhead made weekly bacteriological examinations of samples from MAB patients, and found that in 1,532 out of 2,758 cases (55.5 per cent), bacilli were still present thirty-nine days after admission to hospital, and that in 243 cases (8.8 per cent) bacilli could still be found at the end of twelve weeks.[88]

In the years up to 1888 diphtheria seemed to be a minor problem for the metropolis (see Tables 4.1, 4.2). In these years its main epidemic force was felt in the rural districts.[89] Extraordinary outbreaks apart, the London preventive establishment took but a desultory interest in a disease which bulked small in their concerns. Until the later 1880s its control seems very largely to have been left to the discretion of private practitioners, who were far from insensitive to the danger the disease represented to the families of patients. Charles West, for example, not only instructed his students to isolate diphtheria suspects, but also advised them to be honest in their diagnosis to parents, urging tact to prevent needless alarm as well as to avoid 'tying your hands by rash declarations that the illness is of no gravity whatever'.[90] The clientele of private practitioners was not extensive among all social classes, however, and misdiagnoses, wrong nomenclature, differing opinions on the means of transmission of throat diseases, and ignorance of the role of carriers all doubtless contributed to negate the effect of any successful limitation of the disease within private families.

The perception of diphtheria as a mainly rural preventive problem rested on a sound statistical basis. The registrar-general's Annual Report series enabled this view of the disease to be established fairly quickly. By 1878 Thursfield

86 Rosen, 'Acute Communicable Diseases', 22–3.

87 *Lancet* (1895), i. 1,496.

88 Goodall and Washbourn, *Manual*, 116–17.

89 See below, nn. 91–3.

90 West, *Lectures*, 451–2.

was writing of diphtheria as 'emphatically a disease of the country . . . and if the country is indebted to the town for periodical invasions of typhus and typhoid, the country returns the compliment . . . with diphtheria'.[91] Three years later Hubert Airy presented a paper on this phenomenon to the International Medical Congress, which was received with interest.[92] It is, however, Longstaff's investigation of 1887, on behalf of the Medical Department, which has received the greatest historical recognition.[93] From his statistics Charles Creighton constructed a table demonstrating diphtheria's inverse proportion to density of population which has subsequently found its way into the history books (Table 4.3).[94] Yet even at the time Longstaff was writing, the pattern was changing. The registrar-general's figures for the first quinquennium of the 1880s, issued in 1888, sounded the alarm in preventive circles. Not only had diphtheria death-rates risen markedly in England and Wales in that period, but they had bounded forward in London (Tables 4.1, 4.2).[95] By the end of the decade it was clear that diphtheria in England, as already in Europe and America, was becoming an increasingly urban disease. From an annual rate of

TABLE 4.3. *Diphtheria death-rates per million living, according to density of population*

Period	Dense	Medium	Sparse
1855–60	123	182	248
1861–70	163	164	223
1871–80	114	125	132

Source: C. Creighton, *A History of Epidemics in Britain* (Cambridge, 1894), ii. 741.

TABLE 4.4. *Diphtheria death-rates per 1,000 living in twenty-eight large towns, 1881–1889*

Year	Death-rate	Year	Death-rate
1881	0.14	1886	0.16
1882	0.16	1887	0.18
1883	0.16	1888	0.21
1884	0.17	1889	0.26
1885	0.17		

Source: R. Thorne Thorne, *Diphtheria: Its Natural History and Prevention* (1891), 9.

[91] *Lancet* (1878), ii. 145, 180–1.

[92] Hubert Airy, 'Observations on the spread of diphtheria', *Transactions of the International Medical Congress*, 7: 4 (1881), 69–84.

[93] G. B. Longstaff, 'The geographical distribution of diphtheria in England and Wales', PP 1889 xxxv, pp. 171–91.

[94] Creighton, *Epidemics*, ii. 741; Smith, *People's Health*, 150.

[95] *Lancet* (1888), ii. 879.

0.14 per thousand living, the diphtheria death-rates for the twenty-eight large towns of England and Wales had nearly doubled, to 0.26 (Table 4.4). In England and Wales excluding the twenty-eight towns, they stood at 0.16. By 1890 the *Lancet* noted that diphtheria could no longer be regarded as a disease of rural districts.[96]

The changing national pattern of diphtheria mortality in the 1880s was reflected by rising preventive concern in London. The registrar-general called the mortality increases of 1888 and 1889 in London 'alarming', as did Dr Bostock Hill of Birmingham.[97] The *Lancet* considered rising urban diphtheria mortality, especially in London, 'depressing'.[98] John Bristowe (Camberwell) found it 'remarkable and disquieting'.[99] For the first time, diphtheria outbreaks began to be examined in detail in medical officers' reports, as individual officers took up the challenge of unravelling the etiology of the disease. Good examples of such local efforts are to be found in the vestry reports of the southern districts especially, perhaps because here, *rus in urbe*, outbreaks were more identifiable, and the possibilities of success in such investigations more feasible.[100] Richard Thorne Thorne's publication, in 1891, of his collection of extant writings on the etiology of diphtheria undoubtedly stimulated such studies. After reading Thorne's study, John Bristowe's junior colleague Francis Stevens, for example, was endeavouring, in 1894, to discover 'the source of the aggravation of this disease'.[101] It was no easy task, as Bristowe admitted: 'It is almost needless to say that the results of his inquiry are up to the present time of no great value. The subject is exceedingly difficult, and especially for anyone who wishes rather to ascertain the actual truth, than, to support popular theories or to write a sensational report.'

Like their rural contemporaries, the London officers had difficulty in discovering any significant pattern to the disease; indeed, the pattern varied from year to year. Putney, for example, still a largely rural area at this date, experienced three epidemic years in the early 1880s: 1881, 1883, and 1884. In 1881 the disease seemed demonstrably spread by contact. It spread slowly from Gay Street, Putney, within a small district of the more crowded parts of the town, among working people and small tradesmen, and was especially frequent in 'cul-de-sacs and dead ends'. In many cases family or social links were found between households, 'the children being actually brought into contact'.[102] In 1883 the pattern was different. Here the epidemic was concentrated in the first three months of the year, but manifested itself as a series of distinct outbreaks, separated by intervals of time and distinctions of locality, and of the age and

[96] *Lancet* (1890), i. 1,085.
[97] *Lancet* (1890), i. 1085; *Public Health*, (1889–90), 7.
[98] *Lancet* (1894), ii. 88.
[99] *MOAR* Camberwell (1893–4), 499.
[100] Good examples can be found in *MOAR* Putney (Wandsworth)—see below, nn. 102–4; *MOAR* Plumstead (1892–3), 90–6; *MOAR* Wandsworth (1897), 109–14.
[101] *MOAR* Camberwell (1893–4), 499–500.
[102] *MOAR* Wandsworth (Putney) (1881), 64.

social status of victims.[103] The outbreak of 1884 revealed no serious defects in the sewers, and in many cases no fault could be found with the sanitary condition of the house involved. The frequency with which the victim was an individual among those least exposed to the sanitary dangers of the household compelled the MOH to seek constitutional and meteorological explanations for the pattern of incidence.[104]

While such local investigations were going on, however, the new situation prompted more concerted preventive measures in the city. The disease had not hitherto been admissible to the Metropolitan Asylums Board hospitals, although the London Fever Hospital had taken a very small number of cases since 1878,[105] and cases were admitted to the general hospitals.[106] In October 1888, after pressure from the medical officers and the Poor Law guardians, and from within the service, the MAB hospitals were opened to diphtheria cases, and these soon became a substantial item in their admissions list, second only to scarlet fever (Tables 4.5 and 3.4).[107] As with scarlet fever, hospitalization was designed to check the spread of the disease through isolation, rather than by effecting a cure.[108] Fatality rates in the early years of diphtheria

TABLE 4.5. *Diphtheria admissions to the MAB hospitals, 1892–1900*

Year	MAB diphtheria admissions	Diphtheria, % total admissions	Admissions % diphtheria notifications*	Total diphtheria notifications
1888	99	1.9		
1889	722	12.5		
1890	942	11.3		
1891	1,312	16.8		
1892	2,009	12.1	25.8	7,781
1893	2,848	13.5	21.9	13,026
1894	3,666	22.0	32.7	11,190†
1895	3,635	23.4	32.4	11,223†
1896	4,508	21.4	38.6	13,808†
1897	5,673	26.4	51.6	13,252†
1898	6,566	31.2	62.5	11,855†
1899	8,673	34.6	69.7	13,734†
1900	7,873	39.5	72.5	11,985†

* Uncorrected for errors of diagnosis; †Diphtheria and membraneous croup

Source: MAB Statistical Committee annual reports.

103 Ibid. (1883), 63.

104 Ibid. (1884), 72.

105 LFHAR. An average of ten cases per annum were admitted in the first decade, rising to under twenty in the later 1880s and the 1890s.

106 *Lancet* (1886), ii. 414.

107 For the background to this broadening of MAB policy, see G. M. Ayers, *England's First State Hospitals* (1969), 86–7.

108 *Lancet* (1890), i. 1,085.

admission were enormous (Table 4.6), although it was noted that this was 'largely due' to the type of cases being 'decidedly severe'; many were moribund on arrival and died within a few hours of admission.[109] But humane considerations as well as preventive ones were also involved in the hospitalization of diphtheria: in Battersea in 1894, 179 diphtheria cases were removed to hospital, 'many *in extremis*, for the sake of having tracheotomy performed as the only method of averting death from suffocation'.[110]

TABLE 4.6. *Case-fatality rates for diphtheria in the MAB hospitals, 1888–1900*

Year	Hospital								All
	East	North-West	West	South-East	South-West	Fountain	Brook	Park	
1888	74.2	42.5	36.7	51.4					46.5
1889	44.2	31.6	35.8	37.2					40.7
1890	38.0	31.4	21.9	32.0	28.6				33.5
1891	33.3	22.1	38.4	47.5	23.8				30.3
1892	35.7	21.8	32.1	56.6	22.5				33.7
1893	35.2	26.4	38.1	39.9	27.2				30.7
1894	30.3	27.1	34.0	27.6	26.5	31.8			28.2
1895	25.9	n/a	20.0	22.8	22.2	19.5			22.5
1896	17.4	29.8	21.9	20.3	16.4	19.7	21.5		21.2
1897	15.7	18.8	17.5	17.1	17.6	20.8	13.1	17.4	17.4
1898	14.6	19.8	15.0	16.6	12.0	14.4	12.4	13.3	15.1
1899	14.3	13.3	11.8	16.6	12.3	10.2	12.4	12.8	13.6
1900	13.0	14.5	11.6	14.6	11.3	7.6	10.6	13.9	12.5

Source: MAB Statistical Committee annual reports.

Although hospital case-fatality rates were raised by delays in getting patients to hospital, the evidence is conclusive that diphtheria was present in London in a more virulent form than previously from the later 1880s. That the rise in diphtheria deaths shown in the city's mortality figures (Fig. 4.1) was not simply the result of deaths being transferred from the categories of croup and laryngitis was demonstrated by Newsholme in 1898.[111] Observations by the MAB medical superintendents also suggest the presence of the several different diphtheria types and their shifting dominance within the city during the 1890s (Table 4.7).

The interplay of the different strains of diphtheria bacilli and the difficulties this presented in preventive terms cannot be demonstrated from London, but is well illustrated by the outbreak at Halstead, Essex, described by Bruce Low in 1889.[112] Here 'sore throat' had been 'very plentiful for many years', not

[109] *MABAR* (1889), 33. [110] *MOAR* Battersea (1894), 26.
[111] Newsholme, *Epidemic Diphtheria*, 30.
[112] *MOAR* LGB, PP 1890 xxxiv, app. A no. 9: extract from Bruce Low on 'Diphtheria in Halstead Rural District illustrating the nomenclature of throat disease', 97–102.

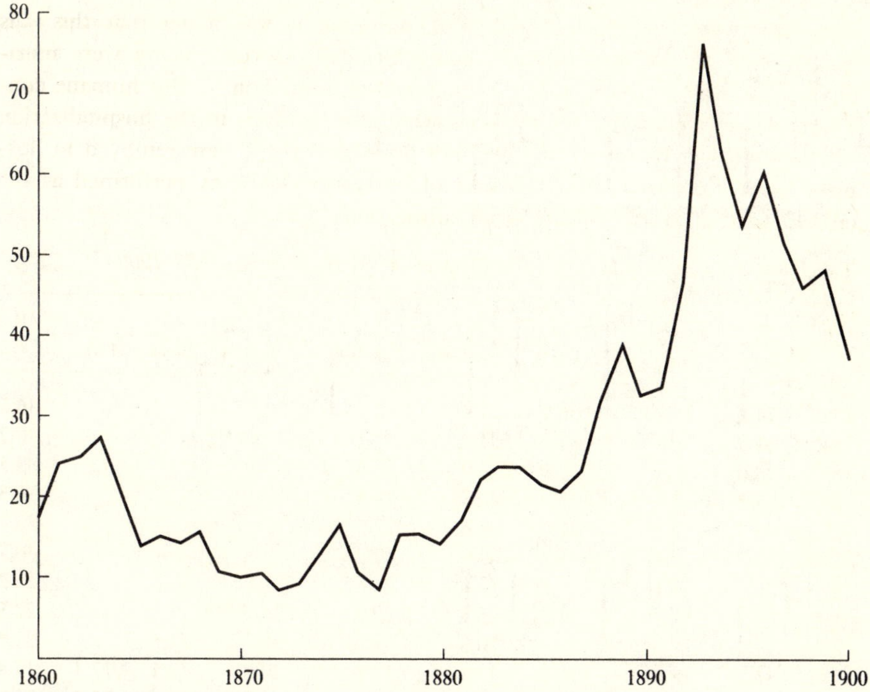

FIG. 4.1. *Diphtheria deaths in London per 100,000 population, 1860–1900.*

only among children, and locally it went under a variety of names: congested sore throat, tonsilitis (*sic*), rheumatic sore throat, follicular tonsilitis (*sic*), and 'Halstead sore throat'. As a rule, Low noted, there did not seem to be any suspicion that this sore throat was in any way related to true diphtheria, even by the local medical men, except in the rare event of a case of undoubted diphtheria occurring in a family.[113] As a result, Low found it impossible to trace the beginnings of local outbreaks, but the enquiries pointed to personal communication as a powerful agent in determining outbreaks. This was hardly surprising, he noted, since in his estimation nine-tenths of the sore throat and fully half of what was really diphtheria had been dealt with 'as of no concern to anyone but the subject of the maladies in question'. It was only when the term 'diphtheria' came into use, applied to a particular case or group of cases, that any preventive precautions had been observed.[114]

Halstead clearly demonstrates the pattern of local diphtheria prevalence, where a *mitis* strain was locally dominant, and suggests the impossibility of getting to grips, preventively, with diphtheria in the urban context. The ubiquity of the disease at Halstead, even allowing for the presence of other types of

[113] Ibid. 102. [114] Ibid.

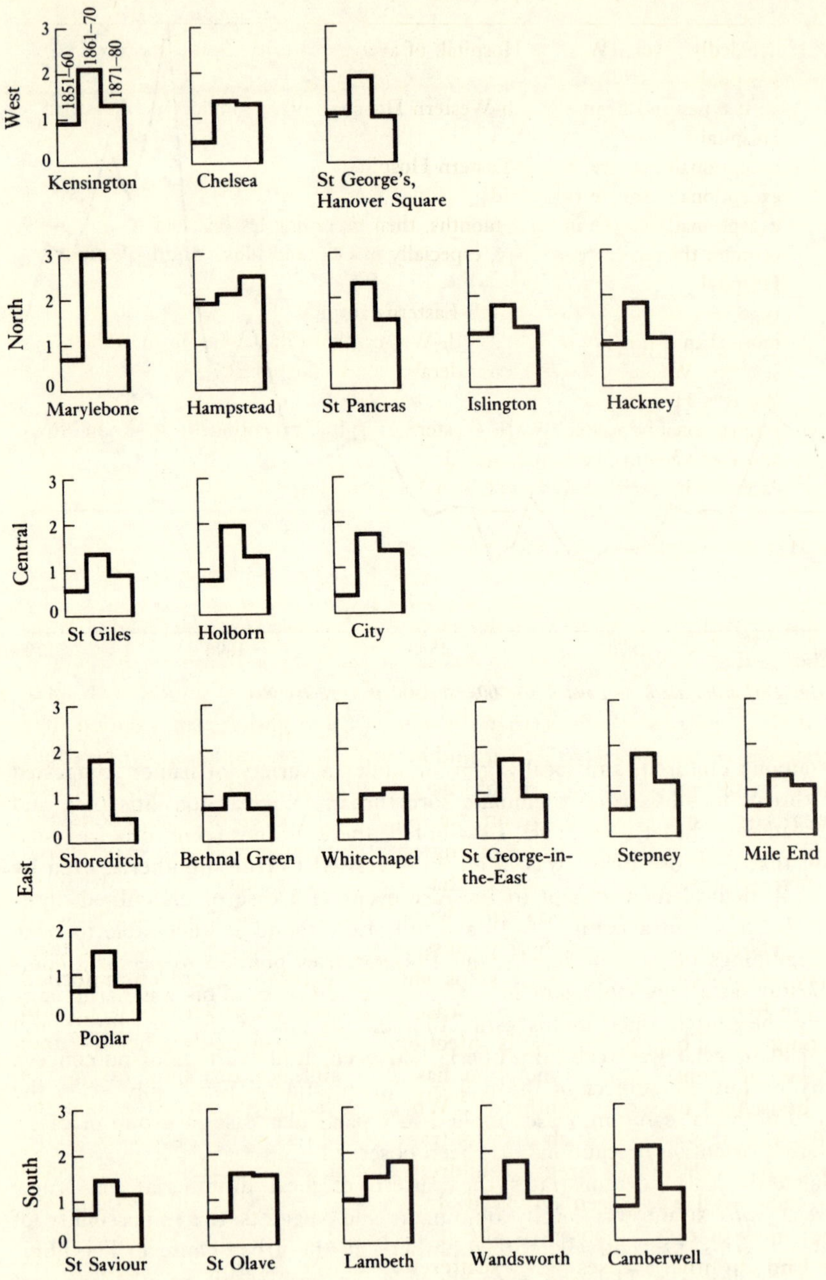

FIG. 4.2. *Diphtheria deaths in London districts, per 10,000 population, 1851–1880.*

TABLE 4.7. *Variations in diphtheria type, MAB hospitals 1889–1900*

1889	decidedly severe: Western Hospital; of average severity: South-Eastern Hospital
1890	all it types and forms: North-Western Hospital; of very mild type: Western Hospital
1891	exceptionally severe: South-Eastern Hospital
1892	exceptionally severe type: ibid
1893	exceptionally severe in early months, then becoming less so: ibid
1894	of more than average severity, especially in Oct. and Nov.: South-Western Hospital
1895	type very similar to 1894: South-Eastern Hospital
1896	more than ordinarily severe: North-Western Hospital; quite up to average severity: Western Hospital; considerably above average severity: South-Western Hospital
1897	unquestionably milder: North-Western Hospital; exceptionally severe in Nov. and Dec.: South-Western Hospital
1900	cases distinctly mild all year: North-Western Hospital

Source: MAB Statistical Committee annual reports.

sore throat, reveals the ease with which it could penetrate even isolated communities and all levels of society. It was far from being a disease of the poor at this period, but, in London at least, it became more so as the century progressed. It is possible, indeed, that the history of diphtheria in London may illustrate the education of the urban middle class in the limitation of infectious diseases. In the epidemic of 1858–65 the greatest impact of the disease fell on the wealthier districts, especially on the northern parishes of Marylebone and Hampstead (Fig. 4.2), although Kensington and Camberwell also experienced above-average mortality. The anxiety that the disease aroused among the well-to-do is well illustrated by a letter written to *The Times* by an 'Afflicted Father', enquiring of the medical profession what precautions should be used by way of prevention, and what steps should be taken to prevent infection from the living and the dead. The disease had 'already thrown thousands into mourning . . . That this disease is infectious no one will doubt who (like me) has taken it from another, and who has seen children dropping off in the same household one after another.'[115] Where such anxiety existed among the middle class, the advice which doctors trained by West and others were giving by the early 1880s, to segregate children and observe strict isolation procedures, may well have been observed. In the early years of the second pandemic, medical officers observed the usual social ubiquity of the disease: in Mile End diphtheria cases were scattered over the district, very general in

[115] *The Times*, 4 Jan. 1859.

incidence on both rich and poor;[116] in Camberwell, John Bristowe observed, diphtheria occurred as frequently among the well-to-do as among the poor.[117] Yet overall, the decennial figures for the 1890s show that in this pandemic the poorest districts of London suffered more than the wealthier (Fig. 4.3).

The pattern of diphtheria incidence in London in the 1890s followed no set path, as far as could be ascertained. Arthur Newsholme's analysis of the years 1888–95 revealed that the disease did not spread steadily across the city, but followed a random pattern. While some localities were suffering severely others were relatively exempt, but later suffered their turn. Again and again he noted this behaviour in contiguous districts, and also that the initial experience of the disease did not exhaust local possibilities: it would return within a few years with renewed virulence.[118] This pattern echoes the experience of Halstead; and Newsholme found it 'impossible to resist the conclusion', that diphtheria was a disease 'which creeps slowly from place to place, in which months or even several years may elapse before it takes firm root and begins actively to propagate itself'. Although the disease manifested itself in every district of the city during these years, in the aggregate none the less, some districts suffered more than others. In the late 1880s a special incidence of diphtheria was observed in Kensington, the East End, Newington, and Lambeth,[119] and eventually the East End was shown to have suffered markedly more than elsewhere. The tabulation of Shirley Murphy's death- and case-rates for the years 1890–9 demonstrates notable inequalities in the local experiences of diphtheria (Fig. 4.3). While death-rates in the western, northern, and central districts were average or below average for the city as a whole, all the seven eastern districts and four of the notably poor southern districts were above average. Poverty, it seems clear, whether through poor resistance or because delays in sending for the doctor delayed treatment, was associated with a higher risk of death from diphtheria. Death-rates for three of the better-off southern districts—Camberwell, Greenwich, and Plumstead—were also above average, indicating local problems. Camberwell, for example, suffered several notable outbreaks which were linked to local schools,[120] while in Plumstead Sidney Davies despaired, after considering all the possibilities, of discovering an answer to the question: 'Why such a healthy place as Plumstead should have so much diphtheria?', and developed a theory that the ventilators on local sewers were to blame.[121]

Sidney Davies's predicament is symbolic. In the early 1890s the English

116 *MOAR* Mile End Old Town (1889), 7.

117 *MOAR* Camberwell (1893–4), 499.

118 Newsholme, *Epidemic Diphtheria*, 56–60.

119 *Lancet* (1889), ii. 800; (1890), i. 1,085.

120 *MOAR* Camberwell (1896), pp. x–xiv; (1899), pp. x–xii.

121 *MOAR* Plumstead (1892–3), 90–5; *Lancet* (1892), ii. 1,199. Manhole ventilators, Davies contended, acted as outlets for sewer gas as well as inlets for fresh air, and it was common to see children playing right over them. If balls or marbles fell down then the owners would press their faces to the manhole ventilators in search of their lost property, with ample opportunity to inhale sewer gas.

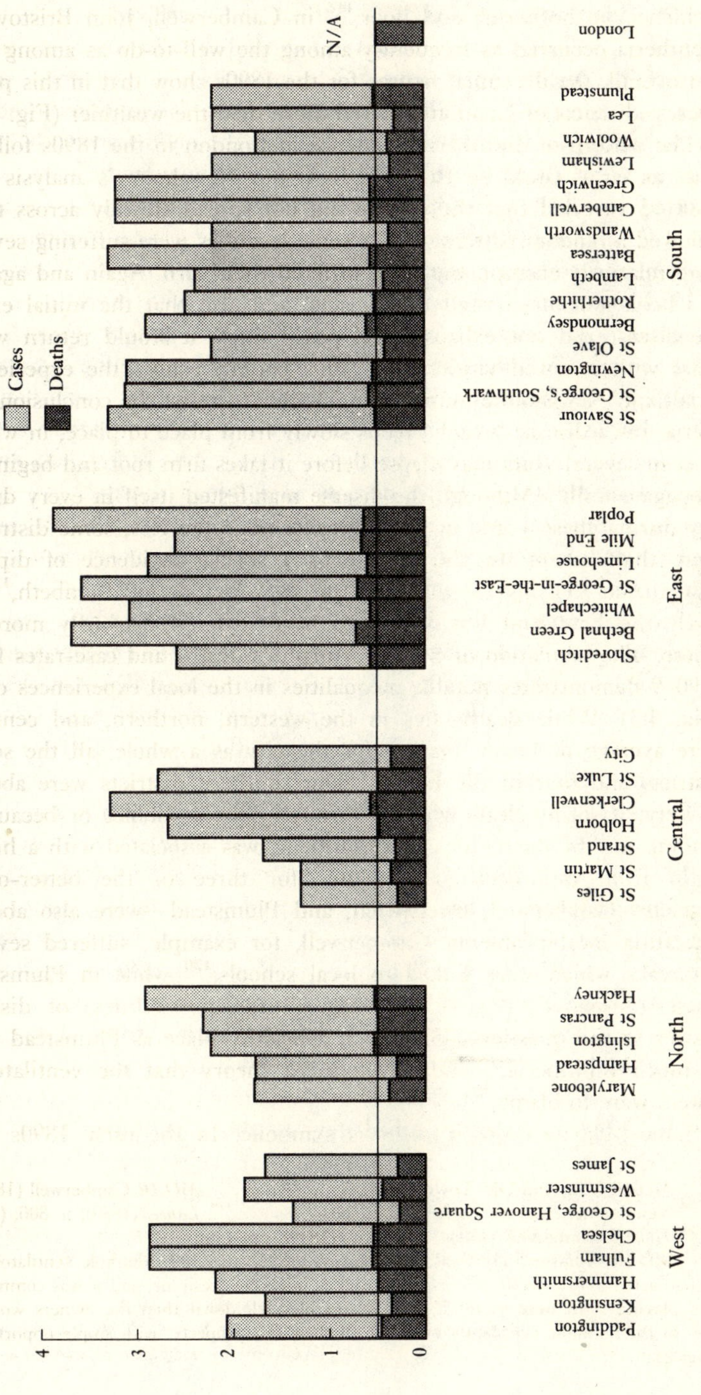

FIG. 4.3. *Diphtheria case- and mortality-rates for London sanitary districts, 1891–1899, per 1,000 population (fully corrected). Source: MOAR LCC (1900).*

sanitary administration was both baffled and dismayed by the behaviour of diphtheria, and by its own inability to control the disease, or modify its effects through treatment. Apart from tracheotomy, which was only permissible in certain circumstances,[122] all that could be done for diphtheria victims was to try to control local symptoms and support the child's strength. According to Charles West, there was by 1884 'a degree of unanimity as to the means be resorted to, such as is of rare occurrence in questions of therapeutics'.[123] Blood-letting, antiphlogistics of all kinds, blisters, and counter-irritants were 'by common consent altogether discontinued'. The merits of particular tonics or local treatments (for example, what to gargle with) were the only points of discussion. There was no remedy, West believed, local or general, which exercised any specific influence over diphtheria, such as quinine did over ague.[124]

Well before Roux and Yersin's demonstration of the toxic nature of diphtheria, English medical men had been aware of the importance of factors other than the local symptoms in the throat. It was these other, unknown elements that led to diphtheria being designated a 'blood disease', like smallpox and typhus.[125] Surgical experience of the disease soon convinced the operators that their patients were more at risk from the 'highly poisoned' state of their blood than from the local complaint relieved by tracheotomy.[126] Nevertheless, tracheotomy offered the only hope in serious cases where the diphtheritic membrane was threatening to suffocate the victim. The operation was often performed in the years after 1858, and was practised in the MAB hospitals from the time when they began to accept diphtheria cases in 1888. As a therapy however, it was not very satisfactory, offering an average recovery-rate of less than 25 per cent.[127]

The outlook for diphtheria patients was thus particularly unpromising when the disease became widely epidemic in urban centres at the close of the 1880s. In 1894, however, diphtheria became the first infectious disease since smallpox to acquire a specific, when the new bacteriology introduced antitoxic serum for the treatment of diphtheria patients. The serum treatment for diphtheria had been developed by Emil von Behring, and was announced in December 1890. Early trials with antitoxin were disappointing, however, and it was not until Roux published the results of his more extensive trials at the Hôpital des Enfants Malades in Paris, in September 1894, that the treatment began to be taken seriously.[128] In England, Roux's report was greeted with immense interest, and English hospitals immediately set about instituting trials of their own. By early October diphtheria patients were being treated with antitoxin at Guy's Hospital, and individual practitioners were also experimenting with

[122] Anne Hardy, 'Tracheotomy versus intubation: surgical intervention in diphtheria in Europe and the United States 1830–1930', *Bulletin of the History of Medicine*, 66 (1992), 536–59.

[123] West, *Lectures*, 452.

[124] Ibid.

[125] *Lancet* (1859), i. 93.

[126] Ibid. (1863), ii. 481.

[127] West, *Lectures*, 465.

[128] For the history of the development of antitoxin, see Rosen, 'Acute Communicable Diseases', 19–22; Parish, *Immunization*, 119–22; Tansey, 'Wellcome Physiological Research Laboratories', 3–5.

Behring's serum.[129] There were difficulties, however, for in these early days supplies of antitoxin were often hard to come by.[130] In October the medical officers of the MAB hospitals reported such difficulties to the managers, arguing that it was their duty to give a fair trial to this new form of treatment, in view of the evidence from Germany, France, and elsewhere.[131] On 8 December the Royal College of Physicians and Surgeons, which had recently been given £1,000 by the Goldsmith's Company for research into antitoxin treatment and for its supply to the poor, offered to supply the MAB with sufficient quantities of serum.[132]

With the introduction of the antitoxin treatment the MAB hospitals entered the age of bacteriology. Bacteriological methods for confirming the diagnosis of diphtheria, already in use in at least two of its hospitals in 1894,[133] were adopted in all hospitals and in all cases of the disease admitted in the first six months of 1895.[134] Once again the Royal College came to the MAB's assistance, and these examinations were performed for the managers by Sims Woodhead and his colleagues at the college's laboratories.[135] In 1895 alone they examined an average of 35.6 specimens from the MAB hospitals daily.[136] Simultaneously, antitoxin treatment came into regular use at the hospitals. In the first year (1895) antitoxin was administered only to those cases which were severe, or threatened to become so at the time of their arrival. Moribund and mild cases alike were not so treated.[137] Even so, the Royal College's laboratories supplied 2,075 doses of antitoxin to the MAB hospitals in the last three months of 1895, and 2,389 between 8 December 1895 and 18 April 1896.[138] In 1895 and 1896 respectively, the hospitals treated 61.8 per cent and 62.2 per cent of diphtheria admissions with antitoxin. By 1898 this had risen to 81.4 per cent.[139] Different hospitals employed different policies, however. In 1896 the North-Western Hospital used it in 71.3 per cent of cases,[140] and perhaps as supplies became easier, increasing numbers of patients were treated with antitoxin every year. At the newly opened Brook Hospital, 80 per cent of diphtheria patients received antitoxin in 1897, and by 1900 this had risen to 92 per cent.[141] In the latter year antitoxin was administered to 84 per cent of cases at the South-Western Hospital, 80 per cent at the Fountain, 96.2 per cent at the Eastern, and 97.7 per cent at the Grove.[142]

The new bacteriology also stimulated the local preventive organizations into new fields of operation. Already in January 1895 medical practitioners in London were considering that the Local Government Board could usefully

[129] *Lancet* (1894), ii. 152. [130] Ibid. 1,106. [131] *MABAR* (1894), 15.

[132] Ibid.; *Lancet* (1894), ii. 1,290.

[133] MABAR (1894), 40, 60. The two hospitals where these methods were definitely in use were the Eastern, under E. W. Goodall, and the Fountain under Dr Caiger.

[134] *Lancet* (1894), ii. 1,290; *MABAR* (1895), part iii, p. 124.

[135] *MABAR* (1895), 66. [136] *Lancet* (1896), i. 190. [137] *MABAR* (1895), part iii, p. 113.

[138] *Lancet* (1896), i. 190, 1,076. [139] *MABAR* (1898), 175. [140] *MABAR* (1896), 178.

[141] *MABAR* (1897), 63. [142] *MABAR* (1900), 51, 59, 60, 61, 64.

establish stations for the bacteriological examination of suspected cases of diphtheria, and by March the board had introduced such a system.[143] The MOHs performed a central role: samples could only be transmitted through them, and it was to them that the results were telegraphed. In this way local outbreaks could be quickly pinpointed, and further preventive measures taken.[144] The British Institute of Preventive Medicine was also offering such a service,[145] and by the end of the century progressive vestries such as Camberwell were appointing their own bacteriologists. In Camberwell, the Bacteriological Department under Dr Bousfield, formerly the vestry analyst, was entirely independent of the MOH, who was dependent on Bousfield's courtesy for information about any of his specimens.[146] Although this particular example demonstrates the possibilities for delay in the distribution of information at even the most local level, in preventive terms the probable benefits of such a local concentration of skills was undeniable.

It is often assumed that the introduction of antitoxin in 1894–5 was responsible for the fall in diphtheria death-rates which occurred almost simultaneously.[147] McKeown remarked that there was nothing in the British experience inconsistent with this interpretation, although the experience of other countries (the United States for example) was less impressive. Influences other than antitoxin may, he suggested, have contributed substantially to diphtheria's decline.[148] Other modern medical authorities doubt that antitoxin played any substantial role in reducing mortality from diphtheria in the 1890s.[149] Evidence from Scandinavia, for example, suggests that the wave of virulent diphtheria was already coming to an end at the time of the introduction of antitoxin.[150] In Stockholm, diphtheria mortality fell markedly in 1894, before the introduction of the serum. In Norway, case fatality remained unchanged at 22–5 per cent in the quinquennium 1890–4, but fell dramatically to 13 per cent in 1895, at a time when serum was only in limited use outside Oslo. In Oslo, a fall in mortality was already noticeable from 1892.[151] Newsholme, in 1898, described similar patterns in other European countries and in many American cities. In Paris, for example, diphtheria mortality had been declining since 1875, while in Baltimore, Pittsburgh, New York, and Brooklyn it had been declining since the early 1880s.[152] The dramatic intrusion of graver diphtheria types on the western epidemiological scene was clearly fading before the introduction of serum therapy; the re-emergence of a dominant strain of *mitis*

[143] *Lancet* (1895), i. 96, 768. [144] Ibid. 768.

[145] Dame Harriette Chick, Margaret Hume, and Marjorie MacFarlane, *War on Disease: A History of the Lister Institute* (1971), 54–5.

[146] *MOAR* Camberwell (1899), pp. xv–xvi.

[147] Smith, *People's Health*, 151; Parish, *Immunisation*, 129.

[148] Thomas McKeown, *The Modern Rise of Population* (1976), 98.

[149] Topley and Wilson, *Principles*, iii. 91.

[150] T. and S. Madsen, 'Diphtheria in Denmark', *Danish Medical Bulletin*, 3 (1956), 112–21.

[151] Ibid. 113. [152] Newsholme, *Epidemic Diphtheria*, 14–17.

type simply coincided with the general introduction of antitoxin therapy in some European countries.

A closer examination of London's experience, as well as suggestive evidence from elsewhere, support the latter argument. In London death-rates rose from 1891 to a climax in 1893, and then declined unevenly to 1900. The decline in 1894 is unlikely to be the result of antitoxin, since its use was only introduced late in the year. As reflected in the case rates, the incidence of the disease did not diminish, but case-fatality rates declined steadily from 1894, after the introduction of antitoxin treatment in the MAB hospitals (Table 4.8). Since antitoxin was only sparingly used outside the hospitals in these years,[153] hospital experience in the use of the serum may put the general figures in perspective. Between 1888 and 1894 MAB diphtheria mortality averaged around 30 per cent.[154] In 1894 it fell and thereafter continued to fall to 1900 (Table 4.9). In the last five years of the century hospital fatality rates fell below those for London as a whole, for the first time (Table 4.10).

TABLE 4.8. *Diphtheria in London in the 1890s*

Period	Death-rate per 1,000 population	Case-rate per 1,000 population	Case mortality %
1861–70	0.18		
1871–80	0.12		
1881–90	0.26		
1891	0.36	1.5	22.5
1892	0.44	2.0	22.2
1893	0.74	3.2	23.3
1894	0.61	2.6	23.6
1895	0.52	2.6	20.4
1896	0.59	3.1	19.3
1897	0.50	3.0	17.0
1898	0.39	2.7	14.8
1899	0.43	3.1	14.2
1900	0.34	2.7	12.8

Source: *MOAR* LCC (1900), 25.

The impact of antitoxin on diphtheria mortality in England in the early years of its introduction was disappointing to contemporaries. In January 1895 the *Lancet* published a survey of international results with antitoxin in the treatment of diphtheria, which gave a total case mortality of 16 per cent.[155]

[153] *MOAR* LCC (1898), 32; *MABAR* (1899), 52. [154] Goodall and Washbourn, *Manual*, 131.
[155] *Lancet* (1895), i. 259.

TABLE 4.9. *Hospital fatality-rates and the use of antitoxin, MAB Hospitals, 1888–1900*

Year	Mortality % of cases treated with antitoxin	Mortality % all cases
1888–94		30.00
1894	n/a	28.23
1895	n/a	22.5
1896	25.9	20.8
1897	20.4	17.5
1898	17.5	15.5
1899	15.4	14.1
1900	12.9	12.0

Source: MAB Statistical Committee annual reports.

This figure was so far below that being achieved in Britain that the journal launched an inquiry into the circumstances of antitoxin administration in England. The *Lancet* Special Commission on the relative strengths of diphtheria antitoxic serums reported on 18 July 1896,[156] causing consternation to English drug companies and concern to practitioners; for the commission discovered that the potency of serums produced in England was small, that their quality was variable, that many doctors thought the quantity of serum represented its antitoxic value (which was far from the case), and that all too often it was used only in severe cases and as a last resort.[157] Despite swift defensive reaction from the drug companies (notably from Burroughs Wellcome, whose antitoxin the commission particularly criticized),[158] this adverse publicity, combined with improvements made by Behring himself in the preparation of serum, resulted within a year in a marked rise in the antitoxic value of serum being put on the market in England.[159] Although the government, as represented by the Local Government Board and the Home Office, resolutely refused to consider the possibility of central provision of, or supervision for, antitoxin production,[160] the Royal College of Physicians undertook in 1897 to test any antitoxic serum sent to them, and return it with a certificate of its strength and purity.[161]

156 *Lancet* (1896), ii. 182.

157 Ibid.; see also p. 196.

158 Ibid. 271, 272, 489. For discussion of the Lancet Special Commission and Burroughs Wellcome's reaction, see Tansey, 'The Wellcome Physiological Research Laboratories', 11–16.

159 *Lancet* (1897), i. 213; ii. 1,677.

160 *Lancet* (1896), ii. 418, 548; (1897), ii. 395. Further improvements were later made in the standardization and value of sera by Paul Ehrlich: see Parish, *Immunization*, 125–9.

161 *Lancet* (1897), ii. 395. The college had since February 1896 been supplying the MAB with serums of a much higher potency than previously. From this date no dose of less than 1,000 Behring units was sent out, normally in 10 cc or less. Towards the end of 1896, doses of 4,000 units in 10 cc were being supplied for the treatment of more severe cases: *Lancet* (1896), ii. 1,103.

It is evident from the reports of the time in the *Lancet* that the use of antitoxin in private practice varied considerably, and that it was probably not used effectively in most instances, even where practitioners attributed recovery to its use. James Samuel from Devonport, for example, gave only one injection of 10 cc of British Institute of Preventive Medicine serum per case, while H. C. Beasley from Middlesex used 1,500 units of Burroughs Wellcome serum.[162] W. J. Nicholls of Chipping Norton used up to three doses of Burroughs Wellcome; that is, a maximum of 4,500 units.[163] These were very small doses, even then. In 1896 the MAB hospitals were giving 'ordinary mild cases' 2,000 units on the first day of illness, but between 8,000 and 12,000 units to severe cases.[164] In 1908 E. W. Goodall advised 1,000 units on the first day as sufficient, except where the patient had fulminating diphtheria; where cases had been ill longer, Goodall recommended 10,000 to 12,000 units or more: 'It is safer to give too much than too little; an overdose will do the patient no harm.'[165] Indeed, 'H.E.G.', writing to the *Lancet* in 1898, stated that when he worked at the MAB, 8,000–16,000 units was no uncommon dosage for a single case.[166] That such dosages should be uncommon in private practice was not surprising. Parke Davis and Co.'s serum cost 17*s*. 3*d*. per 2,000 units at this time; the cost of 16,000 units was thus the astronomical sum of £6 18*s*.[167] Although it has been speculated that the wealthy were those who benefited from the advent of antitoxin,[168] the evidence suggests that there was in fact greater benefit to the London poor, who received treatment not from private practitioners but from the MAB hospitals. Many private practitioners made no use of the serum at all.[169]

Among the deficiencies of early serum therapy small doses and weak sera were critical, but so was the administration of the dose. Antitoxin is most effective if injected intravenously, intraperitoneally, or intramuscularly. It should never be given subcutaneously, as absorption from the subcutaneous tissues is relatively slow, and defeats the main objective: the rapid dispersal of antitoxin throughout the patient's system.[170] In the later nineteenth and early twentieth centuries, however, subcutaneous injection was the method commonly used, as far as can be ascertained. Goodall (1908) recommended that serum be injected with a syringe, subcutaneously into the lateral region of the abdomen.[171] While the site of the injection varied, subcutaneous injection seems to have been the standard practice. Samuel placed his injections into the subcutaneous tissue of the abdomen; Nicholls, in the tissues of the back below the scapula; Beasley, in the lumbar region of the back close to the spine.[172] In these early experimental years there was little standardization of practice.

[162] *Lancet* (1898), ii. 1,733, 1,734.
[163] Ibid. 1,734.
[164] *MABAR* (1896), 190–1.
[165] Goodall and Washbourn, *Manual*, 136.
[166] *Lancet* (1898), ii. 1,734.
[167] Ibid.
[168] Smith, *People's Health*, 151.
[169] *Lancet* (1898), ii. 1,544; and n. 149 above.
[170] Topley and Wilson, *Principles*, iii. 90.
[171] Goodall and Washbourn, *Manual*, 136.
[172] *Lancet* (1898), ii. 1,733, 1,734.

While the MAB continually emphasized the importance of giving antitoxin as soon as possible, and of giving large doses in severe cases, the administration of antitoxin in private practice, where it occurred, was almost certainly inadequately performed.

The limited, and often (it may be suggested) ineffective, use of the serum in England in the later 1890s tends to confirm the view that antitoxin was largely irrelevant to falling diphtheria mortality. In London, case-fatality rates among patients treated at home were falling slowly but steadily from 1895, in parallel with the fall in hospital fatality rates. A noticeable feature of these rates at this time was their reversal of position: up to 1895 hospital cases suffered a higher mortality than patients treated at home; from 1895 mortality among them was lower (Table 4.11). E. W. Goodall argued that the introduction of antitoxin treatment was the only factor which would explain this change (which had not occurred in scarlet-fever fatality).[173] His colleague, F. M. Turner, was more cautious, pointing to the reduced virulence of the disease, to the less impressive results with antitoxin in tracheotomy and laryngeal cases (Table 4.12), and to

TABLE 4.10. *Diphtheria fatality in London, 1892–1898: mortality % notified cases*

	1892	1893	1894	1895	1896	1897	1898
Hospital mortality	24.8	27.1	25.0	18.3	17.7	14.9	13.4
Home mortality	21.5	23.7	24.5	23.3	21.3	20.1	17.1
Hospital admissions % notifications	30.1	24.5	38.8	41.5	39.9	51.4	62.4

Source: *MAB Statistical Committee Annual Report* (1899), ii. 52.

TABLE 4.11. *Hospital mortality in laryngeal and tracheotomy cases, 1894–1900*

Year	Laryngeal Cases		Tracheotomies	
	Numbers	Mortality %	Numbers	Mortality %
1894	466	62.0	261	70.4
1895	468	46.2	219	49.3
1896	516	29.6	212	41.0
1897	491	30.9	264	40.5
1898	654	34.4	313	38.0
1899	687	29.3	382	39.1
1900	799	24.6	390	34.3

Source: MAB Statistical Committee annual reports.

173 *MABAR* (1899), part ii, p. 52–3.

TABLE 4.12. *Severe cases % MAB diphtheria admissions, 1894–1900*

Year	Laryngeal cases % admissions	Tracheotomies, % admissions
1894	12.7	7.1
1895	12.9	6.0
1896	11.4	4.7
1897	8.7	4.7
1898	10.0	4.8
1899	7.9	4.4
1900	10.1	5.0

Source: MAB Statistical Committee annual reports.

the statistical effect of the increasing numbers of mild cases admitted to hospital.[174] The publicity surrounding the introduction of antitoxin, combined with the introduction of bacteriological methods of diagnosis at the hospitals, may indeed have resulted in the admission of a greater proportion of mild cases in these years. The percentage of severe admissions where the larynx was involved, and the percentage of cases needing tracheotomy both declined slightly, if unevenly, between 1894 and 1900 (Table 4.12). This may have been partly the result, as Dr Matthews of the Fountain Hospital claimed, of cases reaching hospital at an earlier stage, when they were more likely to benefit from antitoxin treatment.[175] Although antitoxin may have given the concurrent decline in diphtheria fatality an added edge, there can be little doubt that the increasing dominance of less-virulent types of the disease played a central part in declining English diphtheria mortality in the later years of the nineteenth century.

By the end of the century diphtheria, alone among the preventible diseases, had become the object of a fully coherent preventive effort based on the new bacteriology. The cause of the disease was known, as was most of its etiology; the preventive mechanism of notification, hospitalization, and disinfection was in place; and there was a moderately effective therapy. The ultimate preventive dream, a specific preventive such as had been available for smallpox over the past century, became a reality in the new century. Yet it cannot be doubted that the preventive campaign had little substantial relevance to the reduction in mortality from diphtheria which occurred in England after 1894, and that the myth of the miracle of antitoxin treatment has distracted historical attention from the epidemiological reality. If antitoxin serum assisted a natural decline in the virulence of the disease, the eventual disappearance of diphtheria as a serious threat to the lives of children in the twentieth century was due to the immunization campaigns launched in the years after 1923.[176]

174 *MABAR* (1898), part ii, p. 175; (1899), part ii, p. 57.
175 *MABAR* (1899), part ii, p. 57.
176 Burnet, *Natural History*, 198.

5

Smallpox

This most loathsome but most controllable malady.

(*Lancet*, 1863)

Under the peculiar circumstances of the government of the metropolis, small-pox is undesignedly cultivated in a fashion from which smaller communities appear to be free, and which is a scandal equally to the Central Government and to the Local Government.

(*Lancet*, 1880)

SMALLPOX VIRULENCE AND THE FAILURE OF VACCINATION POLICY

Smallpox has an ancient history; alone of the communicable diseases, it also has a finite one. It was first accurately described by the Arab physician Rhazes, who died *c.*AD 923 or 930. It seems to have been unknown to ancient Greece and Rome, but apparently existed in ancient Egypt (*c.*1160 BC) and China (*c.*1122 BC).[1] Into modern times it was a persistent scourge of human populations, but the last known case of smallpox was recorded in Somalia in 1977, and in 1980 the World Health Organization declared the disease to have been eradicated.[2] Smallpox was also the first of the infectious diseases for which a specific preventive was developed. Inoculation, an apparently ancient practice in China and the Near East, began to be practised in Europe in the eighteenth century, and the practice probably became widespread in England during this period.[3] Inoculation has its drawbacks, however, since it protects by inducing mild cases of the disease, which may in fact turn out not to be mild at all, and are in any case fully capable of infecting other persons.[4] It was only after the development of vaccination by Edward Jenner in the 1790s that control and elimination of the disease became a real possibility, and European states began to mount official anti-smallpox campaigns.[5] The nineteenth-century history of smallpox has been largely neglected by historians in favour of that of cholera, yet it was in this period that the techniques were developed by which the dis-

[1] Cyril Dixon, *Smallpox* (1962), 187–8. The history of the disease is described by Dixon in chap. 10. See also H. J. Parish, *A History of Immunization* (Edinburgh, 1965), 20–4.

[2] F. H. Top and P. H. Wehrle (eds.), *Communicable and Infectious Diseases*, ninth edn. (St Louis, Miss., 1981), 577.

[3] Parish, *Immunization*, 21–4; P. E. Razzell, *The Conquest of Smallpox* (Firle, Sussex, 1977).

[4] See A. J. Mercer, 'Smallpox and epidemiological-demographic change in Europe: the role of vaccination', *Population Studies*, 39 (1985), 287–307.

[5] For an insight into 18th cent. inoculation, and the fears and precautions it aroused among the middle classes, see Donald Gibson (ed.), *A Parson in the Vale of the White Horse* (Gloucester, 1982), 103–4.

ease was eventually to be eliminated. It is often assumed that vaccination measures were the means by which the disease was brought under control.[6] This assumption is founded on ignorance of the real limitations of vaccination measures, and undervalues the crucial contribution of associated preventive practices in reducing the incidence and mortality of the disease. Although vaccination was the tool which permitted the eradication of smallpox, the simple availability of vaccination would never have resulted in the eradication of the disease. In the evolution of the methods by which vaccination was made effective, the British smallpox experience, and that of London in particular, is of central importance.

The history of smallpox in later nineteenth-century England presents perhaps the most successful face of the new preventive medicine. During the first sixty years of the century, which coincided with the introduction of vaccination, the disease declined. It resurged in the 1860s but had become a relatively rare epidemic by 1900. Although Cyril Dixon considered that smallpox control in Britain was 'not very effective' at this time,[7] it is clear that, given existing limitations, smallpox control in Britain was impressively and increasingly effective from the mid-1870s. There were, of course, failures—the most notable being the outbreaks of variola major in London, Liverpool, and Scotland in the early years of the twentieth century—but in all smallpox mortality in the later nineteenth century underwent a convincing decline.[8]

TABLE 5.1. *Smallpox mortality per million living, London and the provinces, 1838–1900*

	1838–42	1847–9	1851–60	1861–70	1871–80	1881–90	1891–1900
London	755	460	280	276	457	145	10
Provinces	547	274	222	162	245	46	13

Source: *MOAR* LGB PP 1886 xxxi, p. 485; 1901 xv, p. civ, table 24, p. cv table 25.

The smallpox experience of London was, however, distinctive (see Table 5.1). Viewed from the national perspective, it clearly demonstrates the critical importance of the preventive services in reducing the incidence and mortality of the disease. London had long been a national endemic focus of smallpox, and the disease persisted longer here than elsewhere, remaining a source of preventive anxiety throughout the Victorian period. Although it went through various cycles of virulence, determined partly by the presence of different

[6] e.g. H. J. Parish, *Victory with Vaccines* (Edinburgh, 1968), 57–8; Mercer, 'Smallpox', 307. F. B. Smith, *The People's Health* (1987), 170, is more perceptive, suggesting a multi-causal approach to the question of why smallpox declined which is similar to the argument presented here.

[7] Dixon, *Smallpox*, 364.

[8] Thomas McKeown, *The Modern Rise of Population* (1976), 99.

strains of the virus, smallpox was rarely entirely absent from London in the years up to 1900. The great epidemic of 1871–2, while it affected the entire country, was most serious in London, and appeared to renew the endemic status of the disease in the city. Thus, while seven of the other eighteen great towns had a higher smallpox mortality than London in the decennium 1871–80, mortality in these was concentrated in the earlier years of the decade, when the epidemic was in progress, while that of London was continuous.[9]

The greater impact of smallpox in London had been observed since the 1860s,[10] but the apparent acceleration of the disease in the city during the 1870s, despite new preventive measures, generated great anxiety. Already in 1877 the 'great and continued' presence of the disease in the capital as compared with the other large centres of population had aroused the concern not only of the Metropolitan Asylums Board and the local preventive authorities, but also of Parliament.[11] By 1878 the MAB was appealing to the Local Government Board to investigate the causes of smallpox fatality in London since 1871, but the LGB evaded the issue on the grounds that the most recent epidemic, that of 1876–8, had recently subsided.[12] It was only after considerable local agitation, and growing disquiet among the medical profession, that government confronted the problem in the early 1880s. The revisions of preventive policy which followed the Commission on Smallpox and Fever Hospitals (1882) were of central importance in bringing about the decline in smallpox which can be observed from 1885. The difficulty of controlling a highly infectious disease in a metropolitan context, and the necessity of developing a range of preventive techniques to supplement vaccination if the disease was to be brought under control, are amply demonstrated by the history of smallpox in Victorian London.

Smallpox was one of the most unpleasant diseases ever to have afflicted mankind. It was caused by a brick-shaped virus, morphologically indistinguishable from the viruses of vaccinia, cowpox, and monkeypox. After an incubation period of ten to twelve days, classical smallpox began abruptly, with a high temperature accompanied by severe muscular pains, often with severe backache, nausea, and vomiting. These symptoms lasted for two to four days, after which period the typical smallpox eruption would appear. There were several different clinical types of smallpox, with differing prognoses; most generally they were divided into two groups, variola major, which predominated in the fearsome outbreaks of the eighteenth and nineteenth centuries, and variola minor (alastrim) which continued as the dominant, possibly indigenous, strain in Britain after 1901.[13]

[9] *RGAR*, PP 1882 xix, p. 20, table 52.

[10] *CSFH*, PP 1882 xxix. p. ix.

[11] *MOAR* LGB, PP 1882 xxx pt 2, p. 584.

[12] *Lancet* (1878), ii. 635.

[13] Anne Hardy, 'Smallpox in London: factors in the decline of the disease in the nineteenth century', *Medical History*, 27 (1983), 111–38.

The principal difference between smallpox types lay in the varying density of the lesions: the more dense and confluent the eruption, the more severe the illness and the greater the likelihood of a fatal outcome. In its more severe manifestations smallpox rivalled the horror of cholera, for the rash was so dense that the spots appeared almost to coalesce, and was accompanied by bleeding. Survivors were recognizable by their facial scarring; many were also blinded. In 'ordinary' smallpox, fatality rates in the unvaccinated were between 20 and 40 per cent, but in the most severe type—haemorrhagic smallpox—fatality was nearly 100 per cent. The disease was not, in fact, highly infectious since transmission did not occur during the incubation period, and was mainly by droplet infection to very close contacts, but it could occur through the medium of clothes and persons, and on occasion was clearly airborne.[14] The virus was also present in the crusts which formed on the 'pocks', and could remain viable there for several weeks: a case was considered infectious until the crusts had dropped off. Throughout the nineteenth century there was no dispute about the infectiousness of smallpox and its transmission by personal contact and in soiled clothing. There was no suggestion that it had a miasmatic origin, although drains and sewers were standardly disinfected during smallpox-prevention operations.[15] Contemporaries were well aware, as were more modern authorities,[16] that its infectiousness was in a large degree dependent on social conditions. Wynter Blyth, for example, stressed the importance of night overcrowding in spreading the disease: 'When points of human contact are multiplied, the chances of absorbing infection are also multiplied.'[17] Unprotected by a previous infection or by vaccination, everyone was susceptible to smallpox, nor did nutritional status offer any protection against its severest manifestations; it was a disease that was universally feared. In the words of Thomas Orme Dudfield, it was 'the most loathsome of all diseases, and the most dreaded'.[18] None the less, much of its dread could be removed by the simple expedient of vaccination.

The principle of vaccination, as introduced by Jenner, was the taking of lymph, the nearly clear exudate, from the vesicles of cowpox lesions, and inoculating it into the skin of the arm.[19] During the nineteenth century both liquid lymph, taken directly from the vesicles of a recently vaccinated child, and dried calf-lymph, provided from the National Vaccine Establishment, were routinely used. There were drawbacks to both these methods, and levels of successful vaccination were locally variable.[20] The accepted standard of

[14] Top and Wehrle, *Communicable Diseases*, 578.

[15] *CSFH*, PP 1882 xxix. p. ix; A. Wynter Blyth, 'The prevention of smallpox in the metropolis', *Journal of the Sanitary Institute* 23 (1902), 14–15.

[16] W. W. C. Topley and G. S. Wilson (eds.), *Principles of Bacteriology, Virology and Immunity*, seventh edn. (1984), iv. 173.

[17] Blyth, 'Prevention', 13.

[18] T. O. Dudfield, *Two Sanitary Addresses* (1889), 31.

[19] Dixon, *Smallpox*, 18. See his chap. 7 for the clinical practice of vaccination.

[20] These are ably described by Smith, *People's Health*, 161–4.

successful vaccination at this period was four good puncture scars.[21] By 1862 it was assumed proved 'beyond all doubt' that the number and typical quality of the vaccine scar were the elements which denoted the efficiency of the protection afforded against smallpox.[22] From the time of the introduction of vaccination, and especially after the principle of state provision for the operation was established, the vision of a world free of smallpox danced alluringly before the eyes of those concerned with preventive medicine. 'Smallpox', observed John Syer Bristowe in 1858, 'is wholly preventable; and were vaccination universally adopted, as it ought to be, throughout the country, would become for this land a disease of the past.'[23]

The vaccination of infants before they reached the age of four months became compulsory under the Vaccination Act 1853, with the added incentive that the operation would be entirely financed by the state.[24] It was hoped by the most sanguine supporters of the Act that its provisions would lead to the stamping out of smallpox,[25] but it quickly became clear that infant vaccination under the Act would not alone lead to the eradication of the disease. Smallpox was a preventive objective from the first establishment of a secure national public-health department in 1858. One of the first tasks which John Simon undertook as medical officer to the Privy Council was the reorganization of the National Vaccine Establishment to provide a more secure lymph supply.[26] For the first ten years or so after the establishment of the new preventive organization in London, however, smallpox remained constantly present in the country and in the capital, although its mortality remained fairly low. The registrar-general, noting in the mid-1860s the disappointed hopes of the Vaccination Act, observed that, although there had been a diminution in smallpox mortality, which might be fairly ascribed to vaccination, the disease as yet showed no signs of extinction.[27]

It seems probable, however, that smallpox was undergoing a period of diminished virulence in the first half of the nineteenth century.[28] Except during the epidemic of 1837–40, the smallpox mortality-rate per thousand living fell steadily from the late eighteenth century (Table 5.2).

Although the experience of the London Smallpox Hospital suggested that case-fatality rates were rising in these years—Dr Munk of the LSH told the

[21] This standard much modified in the 20th cent.: one or two punctures were recommended in primary vaccination. Where the multiple-pressure technique was used, six to ten punctures were recommended in primary vaccination: Top and Wehrle, *Communicable Diseases*, 584.

[22] *MOAR* PC, PP 1863 xxv, app. 1, p. 88.

[23] *MOAR* Camberwell (1857–8), 30.

[24] Dixon, *Smallpox*, 278–81; see also R. S. Lambert, 'A Victorian national health service: state vaccination, 1855–71', *Historical Journal*, 5 (1962), 1–18.

[25] *RGAR*, PP 1867 xvii, p. 38.

[26] *MOAR* PC, PP 1859 xii, pp. 261–6. The National Vaccine Establishment had been founded in 1808 to promote the general adoption of vaccination. Its principal function since the 1820s had been to maintain for general use, and to distribute as required, a trustworthy supply of vaccine lymph.

[27] *RGAR*, PP 1867 xvii, p. 38.

[28] Hardy, 'Smallpox', 113–14.

TABLE 5.2. *Smallpox mortality-rate, 1771–1880*

Period	Deaths per 1,000 living
1771–80	5
1801–10	2
1811–35	0.83
1837–40	2.3
1841–50	0.4
1851–60	0.28
1861–70	0.28
1871–80	0.46

Source: *CSFH*, PP 1882 xxix, pp. vii, 320. The Commission gives no source for these figures, which should be regarded as interesting but suspect, especially for the pre-registration period.

1882 Commission on Smallpox and Fever Hospitals that each successive smallpox epidemic in the nineteenth century had been more severe, the case-mortality greater—commentators in the 1860s looked back to the relative mildness of the disease in these years.[29] A change in the character of the disease appears to have occurred around 1860. In 1858, for example, John Bristowe stated smallpox to be a 'comparatively rare and mild disorder'.[30] In 1861, however, the MOH for St James's, Westminster, recorded 'one of the greatest attacks of smallpox that has been known since the days of Jenner'.[31] His colleague at Mile End observed that the disease had been 'so long in abeyance that we had almost ceased to look upon its existence as a matter of moment'.[32] These reactions may have been based on the fact that in this epidemic the eruption was generally semi-confluent; the case-mortality was apparently low.[33] However, the disease was epidemic in London again in 1862–3, and this outbreak was stated by the LSH to be the 'severest in the memory of the present generation' in respect of both numbers of cases and their severity and fatality-rate. In 1866 the number of cases admitted was even higher.[34] The available figures from the LSH reflect something of the epidemic pattern of the disease

[29] *CSFH*, PP 1882 xxix, p. 261. Dr Munk's views may have been influenced by his experience of hospital mortality, which was not representative at this period, the worst cases only generally finding their way to hospital.

[30] *MOAR* Camberwell (1857–8), 30.

[31] *MOAR* St James's, Westminster (1860–1), 12.

[32] *MOAR* Mile End Old Town (1859), 7.

[33] *MOAR* Lambeth (1859), 12; the published mortality figures bear out this statement.

[34] *MOAR* Whitechapel (1864), app., fn. to table vii; *Lancet* (1867), i. 466.

Table 5.3. *Smallpox at the London Smallpox Hospital*

Period	Admissions	Mortality %	Vaccinated cases % admissions
16 years to Dec. 1851		21	53.0
1851–2			66.7
1854–6			71.2
1859–60			78.0
1863	1,537	17	
1864	836		
1865	1,249		
1866	2,069	13	
1863–6			81.0
1868	1,026	11	

Source: *Lancet* (1867), i. 466; (1869), i. 237.

in these years, and of the extent to which mortality may have been influenced by vaccination (Table 5.3).[35]

Towards a 'Stamping-out Policy': Smallpox in London in the 1860s

It was thus only in the early 1860s that the new London preventive organization began to come to grips with the problem of smallpox, and to realize the inadequacies of compulsory vaccination, and of the arrangements made for its implementation. Compulsory infant vaccination was a flawed tool for smallpox eradication in any case, since vaccination, contrary to the teaching of Jenner (a teaching not accepted elsewhere in Europe), does not confer lifelong immunity to the disease.[36] It was some time, however, before the need for subsequent revaccination came to be widely accepted by the English preventive authorities. Although revaccination was being used in epidemic periods from at least 1860,[37] John Simon was still insisting in 1857 that infant vaccination 'properly

[35] The London Smallpox Hospital is something of an enigma. Founded in 1788 for the relief of poor persons suffering from smallpox, it was first located on the site of King's Cross Station, but in 1846 moved to Highgate Hill. Its annual reports were lodged with the British Library, but have now been lost. A history of the hospital by one of its Medical Officers, Herbert Goude, seems to have been published in the mid-19th cent., but I have been unable to trace a copy. It was taken over by the LCC in 1929, and survives as part of the Whittington Hospital. See Ben Weinrab and Christopher Hibbert (eds.), *The London Encyclopaedia* (1983), 380, 962.

[36] See Dixon, *Smallpox*, 285–93, 342–3. In recent times the international vaccination certificate was valid for only three years.

[37] *MOAR* Mile End Old Town (1860), 14; *MOAR* Islington (1863), 13.

performed', conferred lifelong immunity,[38] and in 1881 the registrar-general assumed the same when he stated that the main cause of continued smallpox outbreaks was the neglect of vaccination, in a context where it was clear that he meant infant vaccination.[39] In his report for the following year, however, he reported the current situation: 'It is pretty generally recognized, and this on good grounds, that the immunity derived from vaccination is both less perfect and less permanent than that conferred by smallpox itself: its efficacy diminishing with the lapse of time, while the protective influence of smallpox remains practically unaltered.'[40] None the less, he noted that this 'difficulty' was not universally admitted, but that the best authorities accepted it.[41] In practical terms, those who wished to avoid or to modify the disease must submit to revaccination in later life.[42]

The realization that the arrangements for public vaccination were essentially inadequate for the purpose for which they had been established came with the resurgence of epidemic smallpox in the early 1860s. Under the 1853 Act the provision of vaccination was in the hands of the Poor Law authorities. The thirty-nine Poor Law unions in the metropolis each made independent arrangements for public vaccination; the efficiency of local arrangements depended on the good faith of the local guardians. It was they who appointed the vaccination stations and regulated their services. The system was frequently inconvenient: it was found that children often had to be taken some distance to reach their parish vaccination station, when the station of a neighbouring parish was closer to their homes. Many thousands of families were said to be affected by this discrepancy,[43] and in some areas it constituted a serious hindrance to acceptance of the legislation: persons living in north Woolwich, for example, had to cross the Thames to get to the vaccinating station in their own union of Woolwich proper.[44] There were 232 public vaccinators with 260 stations among the thirty-nine unions in 1863, and little uniformity of organization or of practice. In almost all cases the stations were private residences or surgeries, but in only five districts (St George's, Hanover Square; Paddington; St James's, Westminster; Hampstead; and Clerkenwell) were the vaccination arrangements independent of the Poor Law medical facility. In many others the Poor Law medical officers appointed the vaccinators, and in nearly half of all unions they were the only public vaccinators. At their surgeries vaccination was generally offered in the same place, and at the same time, as attendance on pauper sickness cases. As a result, the performance of the operation was often very imperfectly disassociated from the receipt of

[38] John Simon, *Papers Relating to the History and Practice of Vaccination*, PP 1857 xxxv, p. xxix.

[39] *RGAR*, PP 1881 xxvii, p. 28.

[40] *RGAR*, PP 1882 xix, p. 24.

[41] The authority he cited was Dr Marson of the LSH in Reynolds' *System of Medicine*: see J. F. Marson, 'Smallpox', in Sir J. R. Reynolds (ed.), *A System of Medicine*, second edn. (1870), i. 269; see also entry by Edward Cator Seaton, on 'Vaccination', in the same work, 299.

[42] *RGAR*, PP 1882 xix, p. 26.

[43] *MOAR* PC, PP 1864 xxviii, app. 1, p. 92.

[44] Ibid.

parish relief.[45] In Deptford and Woolwich it was plain that this confusion was resented by the public, who almost universally took their children to the surgery of the vaccinator who held no parish appointment. In St George-in-the-East many parents refused the services of the vaccinator, who was the workhouse surgeon, but made no difficulty about consulting his deputy, who had no parish appointment. The most extreme example of the effect of this association was observed in St Giles, where the only vaccinating stations were the workhouse and some neighbouring premises used for parish purposes: the guardians had considered it desirable to dissuade people from obtaining vaccination at the public expense if they could be shamed into paying to have it done privately.[46]

The lack of planning in the siting of vaccination stations across London combined with the relief association to diminish the appeal of public vaccination: the average attendance at each station each vaccinating day was less than half a child, at a time when it was estimated that an annual total of 500 vaccinations performed on one day each week was the minimum necessary to secure an effective station.[47] This was because vaccination was largely performed arm-to-arm at this time, and a regular adequate turnover was necessary to secure satisfactory lymph supplies. The arm-to-arm method was also that preferred by parents. As a result of the generous provision of vaccinating stations in the metropolis, only nineteen of the total of 232 vaccinators consistently obtained the requisite number of annual vaccinations for an effective station. Sixty-six performed 200–500 operations a year; fifty-one performed between 100 and 200; forty-three performed 50–100; and thirty-one performed less than fifty. Of the 221 vaccinators whose practice was enquired into, 123 maintained their own supply of lymph, while ninety-eight were dependent on outside sources. Even so, those who maintained their own supply were generally forced to resort to some method of storage. Thirty-four of these did attempt to keep their lymph moist as long as possible (the rate of failure with dry lymph was higher), but twenty-three of them were unmindful of the time limits within which such lymph should be used.[48] In all, the situation was far from satisfactory. Only one station could be described as 'model' (the Pimlico station of St George's, Hanover Square), and only seven were rated as 'good'.[49]

It was evident from the Medical Department's enquiries that vaccination was a most difficult weapon to use satisfactorily in combating smallpox. In the 1860s, however, the London preventive establishment had little idea of how to combat smallpox other than by renewed and re-emphasized public insistence

[45] See Smith, *People's Health*, 161.

[46] *MOAR* PC, PP 1864 xxviii, app. 1, p. 94.

[47] Ibid. 95.

[48] Ibid. 102.

[49] They were at King Street, Woolwich; 39 Bethnal Green Road; 337 Hackney Road; 46 Marsham Street, Westminster; 10 Lisson Grove; 16 Upper Berkeley Street, Marylebone; and 162 Caledonian Road.

on vaccination. When the more fatal form of the disease made its appearance in 1859, John Simon instructed Edward Seaton to investigate the vaccination condition of the worst-affected London parishes,[50] of which there were seventeen, lying in the northern, central, and west-central parts of the city.[51] The handling of preventive measures in the city during this outbreak reflects clearly both the limitations of contemporary preventive action, and the influence of certain social stimuli to action. The epidemic had begun in the eastern and southern parts of the city in the last quarter of 1858. In the first three quarters of 1859 it was felt 'strongly and very fatally' in the eastern, southern, and east-central districts; and comparatively little in other parts of London. In the last quarter of the year, however, it became more widely diffused, spreading into most of the western, northern, and west-central districts; those chiefly affected were Paddington, Westminster, Marylebone, St Pancras, Islington, and St Giles (see Table 5.4).

TABLE 5.4. *Numbers of smallpox deaths in London, 1859–1860*

Period	District					
	Western	Northern	West-central	East-central	Eastern	Southern
Quarterly average, 1856–8	5	9.5	4	6	6.5	7
Quarter ending						
31. 12. 58	3	18.0	8	14	35.0	19
31. 3. 59	8	11.0	11	32	83.0	29
30. 6. 59	13	20.0	5	14	96.0	57
30. 9. 59	20	20.0	8	47	91.0	73
31. 12. 59	46	42.0	29	44	86.0	120
31. 3. 60	45	63.0	35	43	65.0	158
30. 6. 60	31	16.0	11	18	43.0	87
30. 9. 60	20	13.0	3	9	19.0	18

Source: *MOAR* PC PP 1861 xvi, p. 382.

It was only the apparent increase in the disease in the more affluent west and west-central districts in the December quarter of 1859 that spurred John Simon's department into action. During the twelve months that the disease had been established in the less fashionable areas of the city, the central

[50] *MOAR* PC, PP 1861 xvi, app. 3.

[51] They were: Paddington; Kensington; Fulham; Chelsea; St George's, Hanover Square; Westminster; St Martin-in-the-Fields; St James's, Westminster; Marylebone; Hampstead; St Pancras; Islington; Hackney; St Giles; Holborn; Strand; and Clerkenwell.

authority had taken no action. The memory of London's last smallpox epidemic, which had lasted two-and-three-quarter years, roused the fear that if the disease became localized in the west, a 'very serious amount' of preventable deaths would ensue there,[52] and Seaton was directed to lead and organize a thorough local preventive effort, employing the weapon of vaccination to the full.

Seaton found the local MOHs already fully engaged in preventive measures,[53] but the extent of the measures taken in the different districts varied greatly. In St George's, Hanover Square, for instance, the vaccination condition of children in the parochial and charitable schools had already been enquired into during a smallpox alarm the preceding summer; in Westminster, where the disease had long been present, and had made 'considerable progress', no preventive steps had been taken at all. Seaton, accompanied in each instance by the local MOH, visited each Board of Guardians in turn with a list of preventive proposals. This strategy was successful: in every union measures based on their recommendations were put into practice. Notices were issued advertising the risks run by neglect of infant vaccination, and reminding parents and guardians of the legal penalty incurred by such neglect; in each district the MOH was personally involved in the inspection of children in the national, parochial, and other charitable schools. Enquiries on the Register of Vaccinations, aimed at detecting children born within the previous twelve months who had not yet been submitted to the operation, and house-to-house visitation in infected localities to detect unvaccinated cases were more partially adopted. Nevertheless, Seaton estimated that the number of vaccinations performed in the six weeks following the introduction of these measures was some 12,000; in twelve months the operators concerned normally vaccinated above 20,000.[54]

The measures instigated by Seaton in the early months of 1860 were judged a success. Begun in January, it was not until March that their effect could begin to be properly assessed. The total number of deaths registered in the western, northern, and west-central districts from 1 February to the end of the epidemic in September was 187, of which seventy-three occurred before 17 March (there were also forty-nine deaths in the London Smallpox Hospital of persons belonging to these districts). Further, as Seaton pointed out, the period when these measures were carried out was that in which 'the epidemic force was culminating' in the affected districts, and mortality should therefore have gone on increasing, as it had done in the southern and eastern districts which had felt the force of the epidemic earlier. In some parishes, such as Chelsea, the period of coherent preventive activity coincided almost exactly with the period during which they were affected by the epidemic. From the beginning of the epidemic in London in November 1858 to its close in September 1860,

52 *MOAR* PC, PP 1861 xvi, p. 383.

53 Ibid. See also *Lancet* (1863), i. 510.

54 *MOAR* PC, PP 1861 xvi, p. 390.

2,063 persons died of smallpox. In the southern, eastern, and east-central districts the death-rate was 11.2 per 10,000 population. In the northern, western, and west-central districts, however, the death-rate was only 5.7 per 10,000, of which only 2 per 10,000 took place after the introduction of active measures in January 1860. For Seaton the success of the operation was clear, but so also was the lesson: 'the hopelessness of being free from fatal epidemics of smallpox while unvaccinated children are allowed thus to accumulate.'[55]

The extensive neglect of vaccination was one lesson learned from the 1858–60 epidemic; another was that the London population was in many instances reluctant to have preventive action thrust upon it. In districts where house-to-house visitation was undertaken, considerable difficulty was experienced in discovering infected localities. In many cases, even of the severe forms of the disease, medical assistance was not sought until the case was far advanced, and sometimes not until a death certificate was likely to be required; in other cases, which were medically attended, no intimation of the occurrence of the disease reached the MOH. Unvaccinated children were very frequently found in houses contiguous to infected houses, and sometimes even in infected houses themselves, some time after the outbreak of the disease. Several MOHs circularized practitioners in their areas specially requesting information of any outbreak of the disease; in some areas cases were brought to their knowledge, but the request was often disregarded. Similarly many smallpox cases came under the care of the charitable dispensaries of the city, and while the medical officers of some of these took great pains about vaccination and gave early notice of outbreaks, others did not.[56]

This pattern was to be experienced again and again in smallpox outbreaks in the metropolis. Throughout the 1860s the MOHs and the Medical Department of the Privy Council struggled to extend vaccination protection in the city. The registers of successful vaccination were soon found to be wholly inadequate as an indicator of the proportion of London-born children operated upon.[57] They were based on the returns of registered births, and a considerable proportion of births were never registered at all; a large number of operations were never registered (almost all those performed by private vaccinators, and some of those done by the public vaccinators); children born in one district were frequently vaccinated in another; and finally, because of the constant immigration into the city, large numbers of children were now resident there neither whose birth nor vaccinations appeared in the city's registers.[58] After the next smallpox epidemic, in 1863, Drs Seaton and Buchanan investigated

[55] Ibid. 396.

[56] Ibid. 387. See also *MOAR* Islington (1860), 4; *MOAR* Shoreditch (1862), 18; *MOAR* Chelsea (1863–4), 72.

[57] PP 1864 xxviii, app. 1, p. 85.

[58] See also *MOAR* Holborn (1859–60), 28 and (1866), 55; *MOQR* Whitechapel (1, 1859), 6; *MOAR* Islington (1868), 9; *MOAR* St James's, Westminster (1868), 43.

the vaccination condition of London on behalf of the Privy Council, and found 'conclusive proof' that the vaccination of children was postponed and neglected to a 'dangerous extent'.[59] The extent of this neglect varied greatly between different areas, however. St George's, Hanover Square, St James's, Westminster, and St Martin-in-the-Fields were all examples of well vaccinated districts; St Olave, St George's, Southwark, and St Margaret's, Westminster were the opposite. But the two doctors found no data for accurate comparison and classification of the unions in this matter; they could only say that, 'whenever we had proof of the exercise of unusual vigilance by the local authority, or by medical officers of health, or by the local administrators of vaccination, we were sure to find a relatively small number of unvaccinated.'[60] They observed that in districts where the disease had long been absent, such as Lewisham, there was generally a high proportion of unvaccinated; a finding which tallied with the 'uniform testimony' of those acquainted with the localities, that the cause of so much postponement and neglect was in the main parental apathy and indifference.[61] Their conclusion was optimistic:

> We found a very strong impression existing in the mind of Registrars and others who had the best opportunities of being acquainted with the dispositions of the people with regard to vaccination, that, with proper arrangement, a very moderate amount of systematic supervision would suffice to ensure a general observation of the vaccination laws.

It was an optimism that was to prove ill-founded.

In 1862–3 epidemic smallpox again underlined the inadequacy of the capital's defences against the disease. In spite of the activity of the preventive organization in 1860, some 2,280 deaths occurred from smallpox between the middle of 1862 and the end of 1863.[62] The case-fatality was estimated at 10 per cent.[63] Spurred by the Privy Council, the local authorities issued countless placards and notices warning against the approach of the disease, and recommending vaccination and revaccination. However, the efficiency of the various authorities differed greatly. St Pancras, for example, was said to be insufficiently placarded, while in Shoreditch and St Saviour bills of warning were to be seen on the corner of every street. Schools were inspected and street-and-house enquiries instituted to urge vaccination in districts where the disease was present. Twelve unions appointed special smallpox committees to watch the progress of the epidemic, and Islington and Clerkenwell appointed extra public vaccinators. Nevertheless, when Seaton and Buchanan came to examine the circumstances of preventive action in the metropolis, they found still further inadequacies in the preventive arrangements.

The shortcomings now detected in the preventive system centred principally on the hospital provision for smallpox patients. With few exceptions, all the

[59] *MOAR* PC, PP 1864 xxviii, app. i, p. 86. [60] Ibid. 87. [61] Ibid. 88.
[62] Ibid. 105. [63] Ibid. 108.

London unions in ordinary times customarily sent such smallpox cases as recommended by the district medical officers to the Smallpox Hospital at Highgate. In times of epidemic the hospital rapidly became full (although in 1862–3 Islington and Clerkenwell secured the admission of all their cases by agreeing to pay three times the normal admission fee). When this happened, the guardians were accustomed reluctantly to receive smallpox patients into their workhouses, or into a parochial or hired building fitted up for the purpose. (In 1862, only two unions met the problem in this fashion.) The extent to which smallpox patients were isolated from other workhouse or infirmary inmates was found to be 'most various'. In general, isolation was said to be 'usually fairly complete', but in St Giles smallpox patients were customarily received into the ordinary wards of the parish infirmary, and this had also happened in Paddington at the height of the epidemic. In ten workhouses where smallpox patients had been taken in, smallpox cases subsequently appeared among other inmates; the worst such outbreak was in the Wandsworth workhouse, where fourteen outside cases were admitted, resulting in eighteen inside. Further, although all but two or three unions kept a special vehicle for the removal of smallpox patients, only Islington and St Pancras kept a vehicle exclusively for this purpose, and street-cabs were often used, even for parish cases. It was evident that, while the hospital arrangements might spread the disease further within a limited area, the ambulance arrangements, or lack of them, could spread it widely outside.[64]

As a result of Seaton and Buchanan's investigations, preventive concern began to focus around two points on the smallpox issue: vaccination and hospital provision. The importance of the latter was soon to be given greater significance. In 1864 Seaton and Buchanan forecast that the next smallpox epidemic would strike the capital in 1866 in keeping with the London pattern of an epidemic every two years.[65] In fact neither of the epidemics which struck London in 1866 was of smallpox; one was cholera, the other cattle plague. It was the latter epidemic which, however, inspired Sir James Young Simpson to recommend the application of the stamping-out principle to smallpox; a further instance of the continuing preoccupation of the wider medical profession with the problem of smallpox in these years.[66]

Simpson's proposals for smallpox control were not strictly-speaking original, since he suggested a return to the isolation policies which had prevailed in the eighteenth century, but it was widely accepted by contemporaries that his work was crucial in reintroducing the idea of isolation to the nineteenth-century preventive world.[67] Simpson's inspiration sprang from a recognition of

[64] Ibid. 110–11. [65] Ibid. 110.

[66] For the history and details of Simpson's proposal see Hardy, 'Smallpox'.

[67] *RCV*, PP 1896 xlvii, p. 207; J. C. McVail, *Half a Century of Smallpox and Vaccination* (Edinburgh, 1919), 56; see also Edgar M. Crookshank, *The Prevention of Smallpox, with Special Reference to the Origin and Development of the Stamping-Out System* (1894).

the shortcomings of the vaccination policy. He pointed out that, although a stricter enforcement of the new compulsory vaccination law and a greater attention to the proper performance of the operation with proper matter[68] would no doubt in time diminish the susceptible group, in the meantime, smallpox 'still revels with fatal power among our population'. Reliance on vaccination alone would not arrest the progress of the disease, but vaccination supplemented by other measures might. He pointed out that in the 'last two or three years' the public mind had become familiarized with the idea of 'stamping out' disease—the policy which had been employed in eliminating the scourge of rinderpest. This was not to imply that the destruction of affected individuals should be used to eliminate smallpox: in the human context the parallel demonstrated that 'isolation is the chief and leading measure required to stamp out smallpox'. The rules for stamping out which Simpson propounded were elementary in their simplicity; deceptively so in view of the difficulty of implementing them in a Victorian city.[69] None the less, they were quickly accepted, with the additional precaution of vaccinating contacts; a measure which Simpson had not mentioned, perhaps because it was not a measure which could be enforced in the existing state of the law, but which quickly came into practice as part of the preventive package, so that vaccination or revaccination was offered to contacts.[70] In essence, Simpson's system was that which became the basis of the so-called 'Leicester system'—Leicester's only originality lying in the fact that this package was not used in conjunction with an infant vaccination policy, but to replace it.[71]

The effect of Simpson's pamphlet can clearly be seen in the changed tactics of the London medical officers between 1863 and the next major smallpox epidemic in 1871. In the epidemic years 1859–64 their efforts had been chiefly directed towards publicizing vaccination, as described by Seaton and Buchanan in their reports. By 1871, however, the concentration on vaccination had substantially diminished. Although posters and handbills were still issued in quantity (as they were in every major epidemic of communicable disease), the principal efforts of the sanitary departments focused on the tracing of victims and on preventive measures taken in response to identified cases. These consisted of the isolation of the patient, or his removal to hospital where possible; the tracing and vaccination of contacts; and the cleansing and disinfection as necessary of all rooms, furniture, clothes, and bedding. Many London authorities had established disinfecting arrangements during the 1860s, and where this was not the case, arrangements were hastily made as the scale of the 1871 epidemic became clear. In only one respect was Simpson's system not fully

[68] The incorrect performance of vaccination was blamed for many of the operation's supposed inadequacies at this time.

[69] As seen above.

[70] This was in fact already established practice: PP 1864 xxvii, p. 110.

[71] For the Leicester system, see Stuart Fraser, 'Leicester and the smallpox', *Medical History*, 24 (1980), 315–32.

adopted: the notification of cases did not become a legal requirement until 1889, and in the absence of compulsion was exceedingly difficult to achieve.[72]

The provision of adequate isolation facilities was a crucial feature of the stamping-out policy for smallpox, and the establishment of the Metropolitan Asylums Board in 1867 seemed fortunate in contemporary preventive terms in relation to the disease history of the capital. The scarlet-fever epidemic of 1869 was the most severe scarlet fever of recent years, and during the autumn of 1870 it became clear that a major smallpox epidemic could not be long delayed: the disease was severely epidemic in France, and was already beginning to appear in coastal towns with foreign connections. Despite the experience of the 1860s, the smallpox epidemic of 1871 surprised even experienced observers by its ferocity. The surprise was perhaps the sharper since in the previous four years the disease had been very much in abeyance; John Simon had attributed this in the first place to climatic conditions,[73] but stated with some complacence that 'the efforts made since 1863 to render the vaccination of our population more complete and perfect have probably saved us, during 1866 and 1867, from an epidemic more serious even than that of 1863'.[74] Whatever the tributes to the increased virulence of the disease in the early 1860s, the epidemic of 1871 surpassed all previous experience of epidemic smallpox.

In spite of the epidemics of the earlier 1860s, the preventive authorities were in some respects unprepared for a serious outbreak of smallpox. In some quarters at least the disease had made no impact for some considerable time. In Southwark, for example, Dr Bateson had noted in 1869 that 'smallpox is now rare, and its repulsive appearance almost forgotten'.[75] The *South London Press* observed retrospectively that 'up to 1870 . . . [smallpox] had become so rare that it is not to be wondered that people grew neglectful of vaccination'.[76] It is well known that the physical horrors of severe epidemic disease fade swiftly from the public mind, but Dr Evans of the Strand recorded that the last few months of 1870 were marked by the outbreak and rapid spread of smallpox for the first time since 1856.[77] Although Dr Seaton might have foreseen an epidemic of the disease in 1870, basing his calculation on the observed epidemic cycle, few of his colleagues had been so perspicacious, and the epidemic certainly took the public by surprise: local newspapers did not consider it misplaced to warn their readers of the symptoms of the disease, and to advise on its treatment.[78]

[72] See Chap. 9.

[73] 'Smallpox is . . . clearly a disease the extension of which is promoted by cold weather and checked by hot weather.' *MOAR* LGB, PP 1868–9 xxxii, p. 72.

[74] Ibid.

[75] *MOAR* St George-the-Martyr (1868–9), 12.

[76] *South London Press*, 8 July 1876.

[77] That is, since the London MOHs took office. *MOAR* Strand (1870–1), 15.

[78] e.g. *South London Press*, 11 Apr. 1871. The paper warned against the 'fatal error' of resorting to alcoholic stimulants, and recommended the generous use of disinfectant, and a milk diet and doses of castor oil for the patient. It also emphasized the value of vaccination.

The epidemic of 1870–2 was the worst of the century: there were some 44,500 smallpox deaths, nearly 8,000 in London alone. World-wide the epidemic was, according to Seaton, 'marked wherever it occurred by an intensity and malignancy unequalled by any previous epidemic of the disease within living memory'.[79] The disease was very widely diffused, attacked a high proportion of those who would otherwise have been considered protected (that is, the vaccinated), and malignant or haemorrhagic cases occurred with 'quite remarkable frequency'.[80] The ordinary case-mortality of the disease observed at the London Smallpox Hospital was 35 per cent, and in epidemics up to 47 per cent. No previous experience had led doctors there to expect anything like the mortality-rates of 66.2 per cent and 77 per cent which were achieved in 1871 and 1872 respectively.[81]

The epidemic of 1871 was a watershed in the history of smallpox in London, both because it saw the establishment of the stamping-out policy against the disease, and because it marked the beginning of the metropolitan preventive effort to come to grips with the problem of smallpox in the capital. The Vaccination and Local Government Acts of that year finally established a satisfactory framework for the monitoring and administration of the vaccination procedure.[82] The vaccinating stations were reorganized on the lines suggested by Seaton and Buchanan, and vaccination officers were appointed to enforce the law in the localities. For the first time it became possible to evaluate accurately the amount of successful vaccination in the districts of the capital, and to compare the efficiency of the local arrangements. The years 1871–83, it has been said, marked the consummation of the state vaccination programme.[83] After 1883, with the gradual disappearance of smallpox, and with the rise of the anti-vaccinationist lobby, the effectiveness of the vaccination service began to diminish. Nationally, the numbers of children annually accounted for remained at over 90 per cent until 1890, but then fell to 77.1 per cent in 1896, of which only 66 per cent were vaccinated.[84] The effectiveness of the service, and of the legal sanctions against parents who refused to comply with the law, are well illustrated by these figures. It was only after the appointment of the Royal Commission on Vaccination in 1890, with the hope of revision of the compulsory vaccination laws, that compliance with the law began to fall off markedly.[85]

There were, none the less, notable local variations in the extent of the

[79] *MOAR* LGB, PP 1875 xl, app. 5, p. 51. [80] Ibid. [81] Ibid. 53.

[82] Local Government Board Act, 34 & 35 Vict., c. 70; Vaccination Act 1871, 34 & 35 Vict., c. 98.

[83] Lambert, 'Victorian National Health Service', 1.

[84] Ibid. 13. For the anti-vaccinationists, see R. M. MacLeod, 'Law, medicine and public opinion: the resistance to compulsory health legislation, 1870–1907', *Public Law* (Summer 1967), 106–28, 188–211; D. and R. Porter, 'The politics of prevention: anti-vaccinationism and public health in nineteenth-century England', *Medical History*, 32 (1988), 231–52.

[85] *MOAR* Whitechapel (1892), 7.

TABLE 5.5. *Infant smallpox deaths and infant vaccination in London, 1870–1900*

Union	Deaths under 5 % deaths at all ages	Number of infants not finally accounted for % of births		
	1871 + 1872	1873–9	1880–9	1890–1900
Chelsea	28.6	6.3	5.7	12.4
Fulham	—	5.9	4.9	8.7
Paddington	30.4	8.3	9.4	11.5
Kensington	—	5.5	5.6	10.4
St George's, Hanover Square	40.0	8.0	4.0	5.2
Westminster	29.4	4.3	6.8	18.2
Marylebone	34.4	10.4	6.0	15.5
Hampstead	14.8	5.6	4.3	8.3
Islington	30.4	8.1	8.5	18.5
St Pancras	33.2	7.3	7.5	19.8
Hackney	30.8	8.0	6.0	58.6
St Giles	35.8	11.5	13.2	21.3
Holborn	28.9	7.0	8.5	21.0
Strand	32.2	9.0	8.5	15.6
City	32.6	6.5	5.7	12.9
Shoreditch	41.8	12.9	7.5	36.0
Bethnal Green	55.7	7.3	10.6	56.2
Whitechapel	42.6	8.8	1.8	6.4
Stepney	31.5	8.3	5.7	31.8
St George-in-the-East	36.0	12.0	5.5	20.0
Mile End	35.2	8.3	9.3	55.8
Poplar	37.9	4.2	5.0	33.3
St Olave	37.5	4.3	8.6	20.7
St Saviour	43.4	8.3	10.6	19.5
Lambeth	30.3	9.9	10.0	22.7
Camberwell	33.0	8.8	7.7	25.2
Greenwich	37.8	5.8	9.5	12.8
Lewisham	18.4	2.2	4.9	16.0
Wandsworth	39.9	4.3	8.8	19.4
Woolwich	38.2	5.8	2.5	4.5

Sources: *MOAR* LGB PP 1875 xl, App. 5, p. 78; Annual Reports of the Local Government Board.

falling off in infant vaccination, as the London experience shows (Table 5.5), and these variations reflect not simply levels of local prejudice against vaccination, but the attitude of the local guardians, many of whom ceased to administer the law with any enthusiasm once the prospect of change came into view.[86]

[86] Ibid.

Thus the recorded levels of infant vaccination were more a reflection of the efficiency of the local bureaucracy, and of local social attitudes, than of local protection against smallpox: in England as a whole, smallpox incidence showed no correlation with the infant-vaccination rate.[87] Indeed, the anxiety which the disease caused, and the attention which it received from the preventive organization were little diminished by the apparent success of the infant-vaccination programme in terms of infants vaccinated up to the 1890s. The 'pabulum' of unvaccinated persons remaining was known to be sufficient to keep the disease alive in the city, while revaccination remained unenforced and widely unacceptable.[88] Although the available smallpox statistics for this period are difficult to use in establishing a behaviour pattern for the disease, the figures given by the MAB for notifications in the 1890s make it clear that infant vaccination did indeed have little effect on local smallpox incidence in London at this time (Table 5.6). The immigration of adults with an unknown vaccination history could, for instance, critically affect local events. In the eastern group of districts, for example, Whitechapel experienced the highest level of smallpox notifications in 1893 and 1895, despite its admirable infant-vaccination record: population mobility and the absence of revaccination left ample opportunity for the spread of the disease in the district. In fact, in the epidemic of 1893, a notable change was remarked in the age and sex incidence of smallpox: once a disease of women and children, it now fell very largely upon adult males,[89] and these were nearly all males of the casual class. The incidence of the disease in Whitechapel was largely determined by the existence there of 'residential' facilities for such men.

SMALLPOX IN ITS SOCIAL CONTEXT

Vaccination, although vital to the success of the 'stamping-out' policy, was, therefore, only one element in the preventive equation, despite the relative efficiency of the infant-vaccination campaign of the 1870s. Nor could vaccination and hospital isolation, the twin pillars of the system, function effectively without an intermediary. In the absence of notification, this function devolved upon the city's medical officers of health, who played a crucial part in the reduction and eventual elimination of smallpox from London. The difficulties which confronted the MOHs in the attempt to contain smallpox in the 1870s

[87] Dixon, *Smallpox*, 293–4. He noted: 'The vaccinial state of a population is only one factor affecting the incidence and mortality of smallpox.'

[88] There was a considerable class differential in levels of revaccination. By the 1890s it was recognized that people who gained a living by working with their arms avoided revaccination outside epidemic periods, because it was liable to interfere with their work for at least a week: Blyth, 'Prevention', 13.

[89] *Camberwell VAR* (1892–3), 251. Hitherto the proportion of the victims among women and children against males had been 3 : 2; in 1893 it was 1 : 3.

TABLE 5.6. *Smallpox notifications in London, 1892–1900*

District	Number of cases notified in:								
	1892	1893	1894	1895	1896	1897	1898	1899	1900
Kensington	3	102	18	9	13	—	—	—	6
Fulham	4	47	50	2	2	—	—	1	11
Paddington	3	68	28	10	4	1	—	—	5
Chelsea	4	43	14	4	2	—	—	—	2
St George's, Hanover Square	1	23	11	4	1	1	1	—	2
Westminster	2	47	1	6	2	—	1	—	—
St James	4	52	3	1	3	3	—	—	—
Marylebone	11	179	308	106	4	4	1	2	5
Hampstead	1	14	18	2	—	—	—	—	—
St Pancras	34	120	97	15	6	3	2	—	7
Islington	42	122	84	25	51	3	—	3	2
Hackney	27	65	36	14	10	5	2	2	16
St Giles	7	73	7	13	—	3	—	—	—
St Martin	—	11	1	3	1	1	—	—	—
Strand	7	32	5	5	—	8	—	—	—
Holborn	3	30	8	31	1	—	1	—	—
Clerkenwell	3	17	7	11	5	—	—	—	—
St Luke	9	16	16	3	2	—	—	—	—
City	5	27	1	6	2	2	1	—	—
Shoreditch	83	28	29	16	1	1	—	1	3
Bethnal Green	36	79	85	94	2	2	—	—	4
Whitechapel	23	99	11	102	4	—	2	3	1
St George-in-the-East	4	53	5	21	2	1	—	1	7
Limehouse	7	80	9	21	7	—	—	2	1
Mile End	10	115	45	54	2	—	—	—	1
Poplar	5	217	112	28	9	9	4	2	2
St Saviour	—	18	2	4	4	—	—	—	—
St George's, Southwark	2	80	7	48	3	1	—	1	—
Newington	—	64	15	20	3	—	—	—	1
St Olave	1	11	—	1	—	1	—	—	—
Bermondsey	2	55	8	8	4	1	1	—	—
Rotherhithe	—	90	7	38	5	—	—	—	—
Lambeth	24	103	26	54	18	2	1	1	—
Battersea	4	116	12	22	8	5	4	—	—
Wandsworth	—	34	3	15	2	1	1	—	4
Camberwell	16	143	16	86	13	32	5	3	3
Greenwich	11	183	25	42	14	1	—	1	—
Lewisham	—	26	7	1	1	—	—	1	—
Woolwich	2	61	14	1	1	2	—	1	2
Plumstead	19	60	22	18	4	—	—	—	—
Lee	—	—	9	5	1	1	3	—	—
Port	4	10	7	2	5	10	2	4	2
TOTAL	423	2,813	1,192	979	225	104	32	29	87

were legion. More than with any of the other indigenous diseases, their reports give an insight into the social context in which smallpox operated, and of the social responses it evoked. The disease was much feared; it was known to be preventable; and while it was recognized as highly contagious, it was also known that prompt measures could do much to limit its spread. For these reasons medical officers gave it detailed attention when it occurred, and incidents connected with the disease were more frequently reported.

Although smallpox at this period is commonly seen as a disease of the poor which occasionally made incursions into the wealthier classes,[90] the evidence suggests a more complex picture. The anxiety which the disease created was an important factor in determining both public and private responses to its appearance. Smallpox never appeared without causing considerable alarm,[91] and even the most experienced MOHs were filled with revulsion on coming across severe cases.[92] Dr Collier of Fulham related in 1878:[93]

> I once went to a house in Dawes' Lane, where I heard that some cases of smallpox were tried to be concealed. The parents were out; so I asked if anyone was there, when two living masses of corruption raised themselves from off a heap of rags on the floor. It was impossible to discern that they were human beings: they appeared mere masses of blood and corruption.

The horrible nature of the disease and the fear which it aroused gave it a powerful social stigma. Families did not like it known that the disease was present among them.[94] Tradesmen feared loss of custom; many feared hospital removal, even before the inauguration of the MAB institutions.[95] As late as 1895 it was observed that a medical man notifying a case of smallpox might find himself the recipient of an action for damages.[96]

To the fear which the disease itself aroused, there was added the knowledge, after 1856, of the consequences should cases come to the knowledge of the preventive authorities. Isolation of cases and contacts curtailed the normal activities of the entire household; both business and social life came to an end, often with dire financial consequences for poorer families.[97] The disinfection procedure which the sanitary authorities insisted upon was not only tiresome,

[90] Smith, *People's Health*, 157.

[91] *MOAR* Islington (1881), 45. It was, said Dr Ballard, the most dreaded of diseases: 'In perhaps no other disease and upon no other hypothesis would 522 out of 797 persons (or 65.5%) have been prevailed upon to go to hospital.'

[92] Readers with strong stomachs are advised to consult Dixon for photographic experience.

[93] *MOAR* Fulham (1878), 48.

[94] *MOAR* Bethnal Green (1871–2), 4; *MOAR* St Martin-in-the-Fields (1870), 20.

[95] In September 1859, for example, Dr Gibbon failed to persuade a family in Bull Yard Holborn to send two children to the Smallpox Hospital: *MOAR* Holborn (1859–60), 31.

[96] *Lancet* (1895), ii. 145.

[97] Occasionally this might be relieved by individual charity. William Iliff, MOH of Newington, found that the occupants of houses affected by smallpox willingly gave up their work for as long as was necessary, but he offered such cases financial assistance from his own pocket: *South London Press*, 8 Apr. 1871.

but usually resulted in the desecration of at least one room in the house: the local authority was under no obligation to make good the damage which corrosive sublimate and the fumes of burning sulphur caused to decorations and internal fittings. Then there was the fear of removal to hospital, a fear which became particularly prevalent after 1871, with the extension of isolation facilities provided by the MAB. It was partly due to possible pauperization through use of a Poor Law medical service, but also stemmed from family solidarity and fear of the unknown, from the fear of a pauper's death, and from prejudice.[98] It was, for example, only after complaints had been made of the management of the Hampstead Smallpox Hospital in 1871 that people became alarmed and refused to allow sick friends to be moved there.[99]

This package of apprehensions instigated widespread efforts to conceal the existence of smallpox cases from the preventive authorities. In this effort the wealthier classes were better placed to achieve success. Financial security was crucial: it bought the services of a private practitioner who, in treating the victim, also assisted in concealing the existence of the disease from the local authority. Those who could not afford private treatment were vulnerable to exposure if they sought help: the Poor Law medical service worked in close co-operation with the local sanitary departments, and so, frequently, did the dispensary practices. Smallpox cases coming to the attention of these would invariably be reported to the MOH.[100]

The concealment of smallpox cases was a major thorn in the side of the medical officers, for each concealed case represented a serious source of infection. It is clear that concealment was widely practised, probably with particular success among the wealthier classes; the MOHs had their own channels of information, and were convinced that this was the case, at least until the 1880s when the disease began to die away. Thus the disease was known to be widespread among both rich and poor in St Pancras in 1869, and in Newington and Paddington in 1871.[101] In this year Dr Ballard learnt 'enough from private sources to satisfy him that small-pox is widely sown amongst all classes of the community; but that the upper classes are very generally protecting themselves by re-vaccination'.[102] Dr Puckle of Lambeth was also of the opinion that the

[98] For the makings of the popular fear and distrust of Poor Law institutions, and especially for their association with the transgression of traditional funerary beliefs and practices, see Ruth Richardson, *Death, Dissection and the Destitute* (1988), p. xvi and chap. 1.

[99] *MOAR* St Giles (1871), 7. The nature and justice of these complaints are difficult to evaluate; however, I have found one instance in which a child, Eliza Knoll aged 10, was said to have been 'lost' by the Hampstead Hospital, although she was later retrieved: Camberwell *VM*, 29 Dec. 1871, 17 Jan. 1872.

[100] Thus, in 1863 Dr Barclay was able to assess the incidence of smallpox in Chelsea as falling probably chiefly upon the poor: there were many fewer cases in the dispensary practice than among those seeking poor relief: *MOAR* Chelsea (1863–4), 72.

[101] *MOAR* St Pancras (1869), 6; *South London Press*, 14 Jan. 1871; *MOAR* Paddington (1870–1), 6.

[102] *Lancet* (1871), i. 284.

disease was widely prevalent among all classes.[103] In Bethnal Green information was easily obtained about cases attended by the parochial surgeons, but not about cases in private families. Indeed, the MOH found it 'utterly impracticable' to get exact knowledge of such cases: in some no medical man attended, in others he would not make a return even though stamped forms were supplied.[104] In many cases whole families were attacked who would not accept regular medical attendance for fear that some of them should be sent to hospital, and in many cases death took place before the preventive authorities became aware of what was going on.[105] In Dr Sarvis's experience there was more concealment with smallpox than with any other disease.[106] Indeed, during the 1871 epidemic the *Lancet* reported that the MOHs 'without exception' expressed entire ignorance of the cases attended by private practitioners.[107]

Although it was reported from St Giles in 1871 that private practitioners co-operated with the sanitary department 'in the most frank and liberal manner',[108] it cannot be doubted that the concealment of smallpox cases was practised on a wide scale. John Tripe estimated on the basis of 241 notified deaths, and a case fatality rate of 1:6, that more than 1,200 cases of smallpox had occurred in Hackney in 1871 of which the sanitary authority was ignorant.[109] In Mile End, Dr Corner sent out forty-eight letters to medical men in the district requesting information about smallpox cases. He received twenty-three replies, reporting some sixty cases. A subsequent special inquiry revealed 108 cases under treatment in private practice over a period of fourteen days.[110] In Bethnal Green, through the efforts of a few private practitioners, the clergy, the Sisters of Charity, the district visitors, parochial medical officers, and house-to-house visits by the sanitary inspectors (who visited every known case, no matter from what station in life), 2,469 cases were brought to light in 1870–1, and 1,477 in 1871–2 (total 3,946).[111] Since the number of smallpox deaths registered in the district in the years 1870–2 amounted to 563, indicating some 3,378 cases on Tripe's calculation, either Dr Sarvis's system was most efficient, or substantial numbers of Bethnal Green deaths were registered elsewhere.

Fear and concealment explain some of the apparent behavioural patterns of the disease. The great majority of cases reported in the better-class areas were servants.[112] Dr Barclay of Chelsea, however, was clear that if any members of upper-class families suffered, the fact was carefully concealed from the preventive authorities.[113] Servants usually fell ill on or very near a Sunday, generally

[103] *South London Press*, 14 Jan. 1871.
[104] *MOAR* Bethnal Green (1870–1), app., p. vii.
[105] Ibid. (1871–2), 4.
[106] Ibid.
[107] *Lancet* (1871), i. 284.
[108] *MOAR* St Giles (1871), 16.
[109] *MOAR* Hackney (1871), 10.
[110] *MOAR* Mile End Old Town (1871–2), 5–6.
[111] *MOAR* Bethnal Green (1870–1), app. p. vii; (1871–2), 5.
[112] *MOAR* Kensington (1875), 33; (1878), 18; *MOAR* Chelsea (1879–80), 113; *MOAR* Hackney (1882), 17.
[113] *MOAR* Chelsea (1879–80), 113.

indicating infection on a previous 'Sunday out'.[114] If infection was introduced into upper-class households in this way, prompt removal of the victim to hospital would clear the house of sanitary interference before the disease made any appearance among the family proper: in 1871, for instance, St George's, Hanover Square began to feel the epidemic force of the disease in January, but it was not until March that Dr Corfield received information that it had begun to extend to the upper classes.[115] As long as further cases occurring within the family itself did so after the local-authority service had done its work, the family practitioner could be usually be relied on to prevent any further interference.

Even where the sanitary authorities did receive information of smallpox cases in better-class housing, they were often obstructed in attempts to take preventive measures. In 1884, for example, Dr Millson of Newington, investigating an outbreak of smallpox in a 'roomy and airy' house on the well-to-do Surrey Gardens Estate, found that 'we were misled at every turn, wilfully, and our efforts to check the spread of the disease thwarted'.[116] Edmund Gwynn reported from Hampstead in 1881 that householders were only too anxious to be rid of smallpox cases, and to seek the aid of the sanitary authority in disinfecting rooms,[117] but this seems likely to have been in connection with servant cases: Dr Tripe had similarly found three years earlier that a large proportion of the adult cases removed to hospital from Hackney were servants.[118] Servants with smallpox were often treated ruthlessly by their employers. In Camberwell in 1881, in two separate and almost identical instances, a 'lady' was summonsed for exposing her servant while suffering from smallpox. The servant, being unwell, had been sent by the mistress to a local doctor, who recognized smallpox and told the servant to return to her mistress. The mistress in each case refused to receive the servant, but gave her her dirty linen and sent her off to her own home, whither she travelled by public transport. In one of the cases the servant came from one of the poorest parts of Camberwell, the infamous Sultan Street.[119]

The well-protected privacy of the better classes emphasized smallpox outbreaks in poorer areas more vulnerable to preventive surveillance. Nevertheless it does seem that the disease fell more heavily on poor localities. Dr Tripe analysed the social composition of 912 smallpox deaths occurring between 1871 and 1880 for which the addresses were available. The population divided into two groups: the poor and the better-off class. The former lived in small houses, chiefly occupied by more than one working-class family, most of them 'decidedly poor'; the remainder lived in better-class houses and belonged, 'at

[114] *MOAR* Kensington (1878), 18.
[115] *MOAR* St George's, Hanover Square (1870–1), 55.
[116] *MOAR* Newington (1884–5), 123.
[117] *MOAR* Hampstead (1881), 74.
[118] *MOAR* Hackney (1877), 4.
[119] *MOAR* Camberwell (1881–2), 106. For Sultan Street, see H. J. Dyos, 'The slums of Victorian London', *Victorian Studies*, 11 (1967).

any rate the largest number', to those possessing 'all the necessary comforts of life'. There was a very striking contrast between the smallpox death-rates of the two groups, especially since the deaths of servants and employees living-in at linen-drapers and other large establishments were included among those of better-off class. Among the better-class group, the death-rate was 0.2 per 1,000 living, among the poor, 1.76. Among the population as a whole, mortality corrected for 'foreigners' was 0.64 per 1,000 population.[120] Tripe noted that this greater mortality among the poor was to some extent to be expected, 'as the poor before 1874 were not properly vaccinated in the same proportion as the others; have not the means of isolation in their homes; visit one another indiscriminately; and do not avoid infected houses and persons like the better classes'. Tripe's analysis provides a quantitative element which is not matched elsewhere, although many MOHs echo his observations. Dr Ballard, for example, found that the disease tended to fall where the population was 'crowded, ignorant and careless, and where other zymotic maladies flourish and extend': in the 1860 epidemic which he was discussing, the worst-affected area of Islington was the Thornhill district.[121] Similarly, John Burdon Sanderson found for Paddington in 1862 that smallpox 'like every other [disease] of a like nature', manifested itself chiefly in the area of the Canal Basin, the poorest part of the district.[122]

The social and domestic habits of the poor were repeatedly singled out as a principal factor in spreading smallpox, and thus in raising the mortality of this section of the population. In 1877, according to John Syer Bristowe, smallpox spread from the East End across London, attacking mainly the poorer classes in the most overcrowded areas, 'where there is the freest intercourse between neighbours, and where it is most difficult to enforce vaccination and ensure isolation of the sick'.[123] William Odling found that smallpox spread with great speed in culs-de-sac in Lambeth.[124] Culs-de-sac were the habitats *par excellence* of the poorest, and in them the community solidarity and community life of this class were at their closest. Dr Barclay, surveying Chelsea streets with exceptional smallpox incidence in 1879, described the worst affected, Slaidburn Street (forty cases), a cul-de-sac in which nearly half the houses had been infected at different times. The inhabitants were of the migrant class, therefore most likely to escape vaccination, and in this constantly changing population fresh arrivals either brought the disease from elsewhere or encountered the contagion among their new neighbours. As a cul-de-sac, and free from traffic, the street was a common playground for poor children, facilitating the exchange of infection between households.[125] Dr Tripe similarly described a series of smallpox outbreaks in a group of streets inhabited by very poor people 'with a large number of children who play with each other indiscrimi-

[120] *MOAR* Hackney (1880), 9.
[121] *MOAR* Islington (1860), 6.
[122] *MOAR* Paddington (1862–3), 18.
[123] *MOAR* Camberwell (1877–8), 197.
[124] *MOAR* Lambeth (1876–7), 22.
[125] *MOAR* Chelsea (1879–80), 118–27.

nately in the streets'.[126] But proximity and social intercourse were a hazard not only among the very poorest: Dr Griffin observed that more than 11 per cent of known smallpox cases in Clerkenwell in 1878 occurred in model dwellings; a high proportion considering that they contained by no means 10 per cent of the population.[127]

Fearsome as it was, and despite the fear it provoked, smallpox demonstrates clearly the indifference of the poor to the realities of infection. Dr Iliff observed how the daily occupations of the people were continued despite the presence of serious infectious disease, 'the sick and the sound, children and adults, mingling indiscriminately'.[128] Dr Bateson recounted in even greater detail:[129]

> We have known underclothing taken from a person suffering from small-pox and pawned or sold; we have seen mangling done where a small-pox patient lay in an adjoining room; and where dressmaking was going on in the same room; we have seen men walking in the streets with the disease full upon them; we have seen the contents of a costermonger's barrow under a bed upon which lay a small-pox patient; we have known a child go out to work in the day, and sleep at night with a sister suffering from small-pox; and in two or three instances we have met with schools in houses where there were cases of small-pox present. I need not mention the going out and coming in of persons where small-pox was present, and who must have carried the poison in every direction.

In 1879 the medical superintendent of the Fulham Hospital listed the elements chiefly contributing to the dissemination of smallpox in London, which were, he considered:

> inadequate isolation of cases treated at home, particularly in shops; the concealment of cases; the migration of infected families; the visiting of servants and friends in infected localities; laundries; neglect of vaccination and re-vaccination in the household of occurrence of a case; and the outdoor departments of hospitals and dispensaries.[130]

The dangers of infection were everywhere present in a Victorian city, and infection not infrequently ignored social niceties. In Clerkenwell in 1877 the northern and least-crowded parts of the parish had nearly double the number of smallpox cases that occurred in the southern and most densely populated wards: the disease was prevalent in Islington 'to an enormous extent', and the northern districts were more open to infection.[131] It was observed that Fulham, in the days before the smallpox hospital, was more susceptible to smallpox than neighbouring Hammersmith: 'probably from its closer contact with the more thickly peopled parts of Chelsea and greater intermingling of the population, and probably by its easier river communication with infected parts'.[132]

126 *MOAR* Hackney (1881), 21.
127 *MOAR* Clerkenwell (1878), 18.
128 *MOAR* Newington (1871–2), 112.
129 *MOAR* St George's, Southwark (1871–2), 15.
130 *Lancet* (1879), ii. 434.
131 *MOAR* Clerkenwell (1877), 21.
132 *MOAR* Fulham (1872), 9.

The means by which the disease was transmitted through the city was, of course, a source of continuous interest to MOHs. In 1889, for example, Dr Birdwood of the MAB's Hospital Ships recounted one series of cases which may be taken as typical. On the morning of 5 January 1889 a young female servant left her place at Tilbury and came to her uncle's house there, bringing her clothes with her. She complained of feeling ill, and her aunt told her to go and rest on the children's bed. That evening the girl was ill and feverish. Her mother was a widow at Grays, and the uncle thought she had better be ill at his house. As the girl could not stand, he lifted her off the children's bed and put her on his own. As the disease developed, they thought it was chickenpox; but a fortnight later two of the children fell ill, and the disease was recognized as smallpox. The father shut himself up in a room with the sick children, and nursed them until they were removed to hospital. The niece remained for three weeks, and returned to Grays before she was quite well, on about 23 January. Her brother was admitted to hospital on 7 February, and a neighbour living next door but one, who had helped attend the child, fell ill of smallpox on 18 February. On 14 February the family's new sister-in-law, who had visited them in late January, was ill of smallpox at her lodgings in London, and subsequently her landlady and landlady's son also caught the disease.[133]

A similarly colourful example of how smallpox infection travelled across the country comes from Camberwell, where in 1895 a woman living in Beckett Street had not been feeling very well when she set off for the hop-picking at Waterbury on 5 August. Five days later, not feeling any better, she travelled home by train. Her case was initially diagnosed as chickenpox, and the result was what threatened to be a local epidemic in Beckett Street.[134] No doubt many of the woman's contacts, who must have numbered several hundred, dispersed to transmit the disease to other parts of the country. In Camberwell the disease subsequently spread to neighbouring Toulon Street, on one side of which were houses inhabited by fish-curers, on the other tenements housing the 'poorest of the poor'.[135] The business of the fish-curers probably helped to spread the disease further afield in London.

The medical officers' anxiety about the spread of smallpox meant that the minutiae of city-wide and cross-class infection through the medium of servants, laundries, dressmakers, and public contacts were repeatedly observed.[136] Even religious events could be dangerous: in April 1884 cases were traced to a religious service held in a tent in Agincourt Road, Hampstead.[137] Financial incentives to disregard illness, apathy, and social custom all had their part to

[133] *Public Health*, 2 (1889), 94.
[134] *MOAR* Camberwell (1895–6), 417–8.
[135] Ibid. The return of the hop-pickers from Kent and Sussex towards the end of September was a recognized danger-period in the preventive calendar: *RGAR*, PP 1870 xxxviii, p. 659.
[136] See, for the 1890s, J. F. J. Sykes, *Smallpox in London in 1901* (1901), 1–3.
[137] *MOAR* Hampstead (1884) 25.

play. Yet custom was perhaps the most intractable of practices to dislodge. That of visiting the sick was a recognized and persistent problem: friends and neighbours were said to flock around patients, 'some from kindness, others from curiosity, and many from mere bravado'.[138] Smallpox patients were often treated as a curiosity; William Iliff was outraged by kinks in the sensibility of the poor that could allow the exhibition, as a spectacle, of the corpse of a smallpox victim.[139] The rites connected with death, especially in the context of crowded housing conditions, were a cause of continuous concern. Smallpox corpses were considered to be highly infectious so that bodies kept in one-roomed tenements until the funds for burial were forthcoming, wakes held in honour of the deceased at which the body officiated, and delayed interment for sentimental reasons, were all thought decidedly dangerous.[140] While smallpox was more-or-less endemic in the settled population of the city, MOHs fought a losing battle against such social traditions. It was only with the decline in the virulence and prevalence of the disease after 1885 that they ceased to be a major concern.

SMALLPOX HOSPITALS: A SOCIAL AND PREVENTIVE PROBLEM

If vaccination and the local achievement of control policies were problematic for the preventive organization, the isolation hospitals, that vital third element in stamping out, proved hardly less so. In the years between 1871 and 1885 the attention of the local medical officers was directed increasingly to the location and organization of the MAB's hospitals in the city. Already in 1860 Dr Ballard had noticed that the part of his district earliest and most severely attacked by smallpox was that in the neighbourhood of the London Smallpox Hospital.[141] In the years 1860–70 a connection between smallpox hospitals and increased smallpox incidence was not a preventive issue, even in Islington, but it rapidly became so with the establishment of the MAB hospitals in the early 1870s. Shortly after its opening in 1871, Dr Tripe raised the question whether the Homerton Hospital was a focus of the disease in Hackney: he believed that 'careful examination of the facts' showed that it was.[142] Tripe calculated that the smallpox case-rate in the streets about the hospital was 73 per 1,000 population. In other streets examined for sanitary purposes, of a similar or nearly similar character, the rate was 19 per 1,000. When all the streets in which the disease had prevailed most severely were grouped together, some of which had the poorest residents and the worst conditions in the district, their case-rate was found to be 45 per 1,000.[143] Tripe's observations launched the preventive world into one of its most agonized debates: what precisely were smallpox's

[138] *MOAR* Greenwich (1884–5), 13.
[139] *MOAR* Newington (1871–2), 112–13.
[140] *MOQR* Whitechapel (1, 1871), 10.
[141] *MOAR* Islington (1860), 6.
[142] *MOAR* Hackney (1871), 10.
[143] Ibid.

powers of aerial convection, and what, if any, role did the smallpox hospitals play in maintaining the disease in the city? Both issues rapidly became the subject of a prominent, and occasionally vituperative, debate.

The medical officers principally concerned in the smallpox hospital debate were Tripe of Hackney and Bristowe of Camberwell, while the medical officers of Fulham, Lambeth, and Greenwich were less deeply involved. Nicholas Collier of Fulham and William Odling of Lambeth were less convinced than Tripe and Bristowe that the hospitals played a critical role in determining smallpox incidence in their districts. Collier, who was MOH for both Fulham and Hammersmith, expected a larger number of smallpox cases in the former because it contained a large poor population.[144] He could find no direct evidence that the hospital caused the disease to spread in the parish, but thought it certain that it did so to some extent.[145] Odling may similarly have expected a larger number of smallpox cases because of his district's poor population; but he did observe that the severity of smallpox epidemics had greatly increased since the opening of the Stockwell Hospital.[146] Henry Pink of Greenwich, however, was positive that the hospital ships moored in the Thames alongside his district were not connected with outbreaks of smallpox there.[147] While medical officers whose districts did not contain, or abut upon, a smallpox hospital took little part in the debate, they probably followed it with interest, since its outcome would have implications for the city as a whole. As Dr Rygate of St George-in-the-East noted, those districts were worst off that had neither hospitals of their own nor made use of hospitals outside, while those which had no hospitals of their own but made full use of those elsewhere enjoyed the greatest immunity from the disease.[148]

The greater anxiety of Tripe and Bristowe over the smallpox hospitals may well have been due to the character of the districts for which they were responsible. Both Hackney and Camberwell were still largely suburban and essentially middle class in their social composition. So far as their sanitary condition was concerned they, and their MOHs, had been fortunate in the timing of the Metropolis Local Management Act and subsequent improvement activity, which saved them from the worst encroachments of urban deterioration. Suburban in character, with relatively small populations and only localized patches of extreme poverty, their local authorities were engaged in a sanitary holding operation and reacted sharply to threats to their comparative salubrity. The MOHs played a crucial role in such reaction: as resident sanitary experts their opinions carried weight with outside authorities, and their professional pride was involved in maintaining the superior sanitary standing

[144] *MOAR* Fulham (1882), 83.

[145] *MOAR* Fulham (1879), 62–4. By the time of the Commission on Smallpox and Fever Hospitals, Collier had become converted to the idea of hospital influence: *CSFH*, 124–9.

[146] *MOAR* Lambeth (1880), 28.

[147] *CSFH*, 293–6.

[148] *MOAR* St George-in-the-East (1884), 45.

of their districts. Both Tripe and Bristowe expended much ink and argument in the later 1870s and early 1880s in demonstrating the dangers of the smallpox hospitals.

In their campaign against the location of smallpox hospitals within the city, Tripe and Bristowe had the full support of local opinion. Londoners in general, even in the poorer areas in which infectious disease hospitals tended to be sited, had no wish to live in their vicinity. Powerful middle-class opposition succeeded in closing the MAB smallpox hospital at Hampstead in the early 1870s, and for the rest of the century each new hospital proposal had to run the gauntlet of strenuous local opposition. Indeed, the difficulties which the managers experienced in the 1890s when searching for sites to accommodate the greatly increased patient numbers which the opening of their hospitals had brought, prompted one observer to remark that the task of the managers was a hard and thankless one: they were bound to provide accommodation for all infectious-disease cases in London, and were severely condemned for both their attempts and their failure to do so.[149]

Given the nature of smallpox and the fear which it generated, it is hardly surprising that local reaction to smallpox hospitals was intensely hostile. When the new MAB hospital was opened at Stockwell in January 1871 the immediate neighbourhood emptied: houses in the area were deserted, there was a 'perfect exodus' of outside residents, pupils were withdrawn from local schools, and trade was extensively disrupted.[150] A proposed smallpox hospital in Battersea was fiercely opposed by local residents: it would keep visitors from the park, and would damage the trading interests of York Road, then the principal shopping street in Battersea, and crowded nightly with working men and their wives.[151] In Camberwell there was considerable local agitation in the district closest to the Deptford Smallpox Hospital.[152] In Fulham, well after the smallpox hospital was built, Nicholas Collier recorded that most of the inhabitants would not accept the hospital in the interests of humanity.[153] Indeed, there was nearly a riot when the local authority established its own temporary hospital for non-pauper smallpox cases in 1881: 120 policemen had to be called on to protect the hospital tent, which lay on an isolated piece of ground at the end of Imperial Road, on the bank of the Thames. In fact a heavy shower of rain fell at the time appointed for a mass protest and effectively cooled tempers, but the Gas Light and Coke Company were not so easily satisfied, and took Fulham District Board to court for an injunction to prevent their using the site.[154]

[149] *South London Press*, 12 Aug. 1893; for details of this opposition, see Ayers, *State Hospitals*, chap. 8.

[150] Ibid. 4 Feb. 1871; 24 June 1871.

[151] Ibid. 11 Mar. 1871.

[152] Camberwell *VM*, 28 May 1879; 23 Feb. 1881; *MOAR* Camberwell (1881–2), 90.

[153] *MOAR* Fulham (1881), 69.

[154] Ibid. 89–90. The action failed, after the board had given an undertaking to take no more than nineteen patients at any one time. There were seventeen at the time of the hearing.

Such local feelings only strengthened the determination of the local authorities concerned to indite the MAB hospitals as foci of infection. Tripe and Bristowe examined the incidence and distribution of the disease in their districts minutely. Tripe's annual reports between 1871 and 1885 repeatedly chronicle his observations on the effects of the hospital. In 1871 the area about the hospital had the highest smallpox case-rate; in 1876 the focus of the disease was soon concentrated in Homerton—although the epidemic did not begin there, it was clear from the distribution of cases that 'infective smallpox matter' must have been extensively spread in Homerton on or about 14 October; in 1881 he noted the persistence of smallpox in the vicinity of the hospital, 'where we can never stamp out the disease'.[155] Tripe was convinced that the hospital was too close to the neighbouring residential area, allowing the aerial spread of infection; he also pointed to more-immediate channels of infection: the hospital ambulances had not been disinfected until he had suggested it; the drivers frequently stopped at pubs for refreshment on the way home; when the vehicles stopped outside the hospital grounds, children crowded round them; tradespeople were admitted into the grounds and even the corridors of the hospital; visitors were allowed into the sick wards; a footpath ran close by the hospital laundry.[156] By 1884, in which year a severe epidemic in the vicinity of the hospital persuaded the MAB both to reduce permanently the number of cases at the hospital, and to limit the hospital's catchment area, Tripe was observing patient movement at the hospital: in one week in May 224 persons were brought in and taken away, very few of whom counted as patients, because they did not even spend a night there. This 'incessant carrying about of smallpox patients' was, he thought, decidedly injurious in infecting the neighbourhood.[157]

Like Tripe, Bristowe found over a period of years that the district close to the Deptford hospital was never free of smallpox; and at times the incidence of the disease was 'appalling'.[158] The representations which Tripe and Bristowe made over the years had their effect, and towards the end of 1880 the Local Government Board asked William Power to investigate the circumstances surrounding smallpox incidence in the area around the Fulham hospital,where there had been little smallpox for some years.[159] The results of Power's inquiry were dramatic, for it so happened that a sudden outbreak of smallpox occurred around the hospital just after he began his investigation in January 1881, enabling him to study the phenomenon with 'very notable exactness'.[160]

155 *MOAR* Hackney (1871), 10; (1876), 4; (1881), 21.

156 Ibid. (1880), 16–17.

157 Ibid. (1884), 15.

158 *MOAR* Camberwell (1881–2), 94.

159 *MOAR* LGB, 10, PP 1882 xxx, pt 2: supplement containing the report and papers submitted by the Board's Medical Officer on the use and influence of hospitals for infectious disease, pp. viii–ix.

160 Ibid., app. 2, pp. 302–32. The local outbreak in Fulham, within a limited area around the hospital, occurred after cases had been admitted to the hospital from the East End, where smallpox was then epidemic.

When finally, in June 1881, following intense alarm in the affected district, Camberwell Vestry went in deputation to the Local Government Board, armed with maps of local smallpox distribution prepared by Bristowe and the vestry clerk, and requesting a government inquiry similar to that just concluded on the influence of the Fulham hospital, they learnt that a Commission would shortly be appointed to inquire into the whole subject of smallpox hospitals in the metropolis.[161]

The *Report of the Commission on Smallpox and Fever Hospitals* resulted in a final, and finally successful, reorganization of London's smallpox facilities. It was clear from the evidence before them that the smallpox hospitals, either because of aerial transmission, or because of the opportunities for personal infection through visitors, tradesmen, staff, ambulances, sightseers, and so on, were helping to sustain smallpox as an endemic disease within the city. It was equally clear that the efficiency of the capital's smallpox-limitation provisions was being compromised by the diversity of authorities involved in their execution; it was strongly argued by informed witnesses that the lack of cohesion in prevention arrangements was a salient factor in maintaining the disease in the metropolis. This argument was evidently a powerful one. Without being able to reach any conclusion as to whether the hospitals were indeed centres of infection or not, the commissioners recommended that the existing hospitals should become the main fever hospitals, and that provision for smallpox cases should be made in hospitals situated on river-banks or floating on the river itself, away from residential areas.[162] For the managers of the Metropolitan Asylums Board they had nothing but praise; an attitude justified by the subsequent history of the hospitals.[163] Among their other recommendations, designed to achieve a maximum degree of efficiency by the MAB, were the complete disassociation of the hospital authority from the Poor Law; the compulsory notification of infectious disease; and wider responsibilities for the local MOHs in securing the isolation and disinfection of patients. They also suggested that the hospital authority should have entire control over the ambulance service, and that personal communications should be strictly regulated.[164] With the single exception of notification, which was delayed a further four years, the programme outlined by the commission came into being in July 1884.

With the implementing of the commission's principal recommendations

[161] *MOAR* Camberwell (1881), 92–3. The maps were submitted to the Commission as part of Bristowe's evidence: *CSFH*, 39–47.

[162] *CSFH*, pp. xxii, xxxii.

[163] Although fever hospitals within the city continued to be unpopular, and the managers experienced great difficulties securing sites for new ones in the 1890s, complaints about the smallpox services disappear from the literature after 1885, to be replaced by tributes to their efficiency. See e.g. J. F. J. Sykes, *Public Health Problems* (1892), 218–19; Charles Augustus Scovell, 'The isolation of cases of infectious disease in the metropolis', *Journal of the Sanitary Institute* 17 (1896), 43–9.

[164] *CSFH*, pp. xxxi, xxxiii.

through the removal of the smallpox hospitals from their city-centre sites, and the reorganization of the ambulance service, the cycle of indigenous smallpox in London appears to have been broken. Although the city's plummeting smallpox death-rates are misleading (since deaths now occurred in the hospital ships at Long Reach, and were registered at Dartford in Kent), the incidence of the disease apparently also underwent a remarkable decline in the years after 1885. The sharp decrease in smallpox incidence was confidently ascribed by contemporaries to the revised policy; and the efficiency of the ambulance service, which the MAB also instituted at this time, was accorded a great deal of the credit for this success.[165] Although the simultaneous decline of smallpox throughout the country may on this model have been caused by the elimination of the endemic focus of the disease in London, it seems likely, in the absence of compulsory notification, and in view of the later history of the disease in the city, that other factors contributed to its diminished virulence in this period. One critical development was almost certainly the introduction of more stringent regulations by the port sanitary authorities in 1885. In operation since 1872, these authorities were concerned to prevent the introduction of dangerous infectious diseases into the country, and, where they failed in this, quickly to trace introduced cases and limit the spread of disease. In national terms, the port sanitary authorities formed a vital part in a stamping-out policy with regard to both smallpox and cholera.[166] The coincidence in timing of the introduction of the revised port sanitary regulations and the removal of the isolation hospitals from central London may have been fortunate for the history of smallpox in the city.

SMALLPOX AS AN IMPORTED DISEASE

The awareness of smallpox as an imported disease developed with the 1871 epidemic, whose origins seemed clearly to lie in France.[167] Although it is not possible to trace the London smallpox epidemics of 1876, 1881, and 1884 with any certainty to infection from abroad,[168] and neither the registrar-general nor the medical officer of the LGB suggest foreign sources for these outbreaks, it may be that the 1881 epidemic at least had its origins abroad. The beginnings of this epidemic lay in the East End: on 4 December 1880 the *Lancet* reported that another smallpox epidemic threatened London: the disease was 'very

[165] *Lancet* (1892), i. 1,258. See also *MABAR* (1887), 15: 'It may . . . be fairly assumed that the spread of Smallpox has been in a great measure checked by the rapid system of removal organised by the Ambulance Committee, and by the more perfect isolation which is now obtainable in the Floating Hospitals at Long Reach.' For the procedures of the ambulance system, see Sykes, *Problems*, 218–19; Scovell, 'Isolation', 43–9.

[166] For the formation of the port sanitary authorities and their work in respect of smallpox, see Hardy, 'Smallpox', 125–33.

[167] *RGAR*, PP 1873 xx, p. 31.

[168] Hardy, 'Smallpox', 132.

active' in the eastern districts.[169] The East End, with its proximity to the docks, was especially vulnerable to imported disease, whether imported by infected individuals, or by goods destined to service its local industries. Significantly, Dr Corner of Mile End found that a very large proportion of the cases occurring in the early stages of this epidemic originated in houses occupied by custom-house officials, dock labourers, and persons engaged in cleaning and making up imported articles such as feathers. In Corner's view, the epidemic was sustained or even originated through such channels,[170] and it seems more than likely that he was correct in his view of the case.

In the years after 1885, with the relaxation of the MAB's admissions policy, evidence of imported smallpox becomes more frequent. In 1887, for example, the superintendent of the MAB hospital ships, Dr Birdwood, showed that the disease had been imported into London from Port Said, Seville, Lisbon, Portsmouth, Stockton-on-Tees, and Sheffield.[171] The four known foreign importations were: two British sailors coming from Spain and from Sydney via Port Said respectively, the latter causing at least seven further cases among relations living in Woolwich; a Spanish ship's steward coming from Seville, where smallpox was known to be epidemic; and a British ship's steward's boy coming from Lisbon and causing a further sixteen cases among friends and relations in Whitechapel.[172] In 1888 there were again at least five cases imported from abroad, from Barcelona and Madrid, and at least six from the provinces; from Tilbury, Grimsby, Hopton, Spalding, and Hull.[173] The records of the medical officer of the Port of London sanitary authority provide further instances of such introductions; indeed, it is clear that smallpox introductions were a continuous concern of the port sanitary authorities generally at this period.[174]

The efficiency of the port sanitary authorities, and their constant vigilance for epidemics abroad that might enter Britain by shipping and passenger traffic, meant that foreign importations of smallpox were not a wider preventive issue. Provincial importations were another matter, however, and as the capital became increasingly free of indigenous smallpox in the years after 1885, these importations became more noticeable. Provincial importations fell into two categories: those that were imported by coastal shipping traffic, and thus came under the aegis of the port sanitary authority, and those that entered by land. The latter were the least easy to trace, in that they usually occurred among the 'unsettled' population, among visitors or transients through London. As early as 1871 it had been observed that persons in public occupations—barmaids, shopmen and women, bus and cab drivers, waiters, and so on—were among those most vulnerable to smallpox infection.[175] Such contacts remained a problem into the last decade of the century. In 1892, for example,

169 *Lancet* (1880), ii. 900.
170 *MOAR* Mile End Old Town (1880–1), 5.
171 *MABAR* (1887), 14.
172 Ibid., app. 8, p. 8.
173 *MABAR* (1888), 18.
174 Hardy, 'Smallpox', 129–31.
175 *Lancet* (1871), i. 372.

there were seven cases among the settled population of Camberwell which were mostly unconnected, and whose origins were quite unknown.[176] Earlier in the year the disease broke out among a colony of Swiss waiters, one of whom, employed in a large London hotel, contracted it in a very mild form.[177] Such examples serve to underline the continuing difficulties which highly infectious diseases like smallpox posed for the preventive organization, as well as illustrating the dangers involved in daily life in a Victorian city.

The introduction of the disease into the city from outside constituted only one aspect of London's continuing smallpox problem in the later decades of the century. A more worrying feature was the persistence of the disease among the vagrant population. It was only during the course of 1893 that the preventive organization became aware of the existence of a reservoir of smallpox among the city's vagrants—a reservoir which appeared difficult to eliminate, and which would constitute a continuous threat to the settled population. After the Swiss-waiter epidemic died away in August 1892 the city was free of the disease for a while, but cases began to be reported again during September. The first was that of a tramp, who had probably been infected outside London. It was not until October that indigenous cases began to appear in the city, but by the end of the month the disease was epidemic, and by the new year the focus of the epidemic was beginning to become clear. Between December 1892 and July 1893 the infection of 325 smallpox patients was traced to various free shelters in the city.[178] The shelters most heavily implicated were three belonging to the Salvation Army, in Blackfriars, Lisson Street, and Horseferry Road. Another 179 cases were traced to common lodging houses, and twenty to casual wards. Only nine cases were traced to definite casual wards, although at least thirty-five cases were admitted to hospital direct from them. According to Dr Lang of the MAB, this showed that casual wards played 'the part of filters in removing vagrant infection rather than that they assisted in the spread of the disease'.[179] Once again the epidemic began in the East End: by the end of January 1893 there were 'centres of infection everywhere' east of a line drawn north—south through Euston Station, and before long the disease had appeared in the rest of the city, although it was rather slower to establish itself south of the river.[180] Major outbreaks occurred in Spitalfields (February–October), Stepney (March), Bloomsbury (January), Tottenham Court Road (March–July), and Edgware Road (April–June); lesser ones in Poplar, Mile End, and Kensington. South of the river, thirteen areas were affected in all: Peckham (December 1892–February 1893 and again in May), Bermondsey and East Greenwich (February); Deptford, Woolwich,

[176] *MABAR* (1892), app. 9, 72.

[177] Ibid. Dr Lovett of St Giles suspected that the disease had been imported from Switzerland, where it was very prevalent at the time: *MOAR* St Giles (1892), 71.

[178] *MABAR* (1893), part 3, p. 161. [179] Ibid. 163, 166. [180] Ibid. 166.

Plumstead, Camberwell, and Stockwell (March); Rotherhithe, Southwark, and Wandsworth (April); Battersea (late April), and Vauxhall (May).[181]

The two main features of the epidemic were its link with the vagrant population, and its focus on the poor quarters of the capital; there was no evidence that more people were attacked in high-density areas: in the West End and the suburbs, the disease selected islands of poor people.[182] Even so, the MAB were defeated in their attempts to analyse the structure of the epidemic. In general terms, Dr Lang was certain that the epidemic had been 'brought in from outside', but 'when one tries to trace it in, one can find hardly any evidence whatsoever'.[183] The failure was not for want of trying: fifty-eight people had contracted the disease outside London, and of these it had been ascertained that thirty-five did not infect others; four probably did not; six had infected one or two people each, and eight might have done so. The remaining five were all casuals, and had infected various shelters in January, February, and March. The great difficulties were in tracing the connections between the various outbreaks and between the vagrant and other classes: as Lang observed, outbreaks were hardly ever caused by people who could trace their infection. In such cases the smallpox attack did not come as a surprise: the disease was recognized and precautions were taken. It seemed likely that a very large number of cases had escaped detection during the year. Further, the curve of attacks among the population as a whole followed that of attacks among the vagrants. Areas which continually produced cases in the spring and summer of 1893 were not infected until the disease had appeared among the vagrants, and since the disease had been stamped out among the latter, it had 'only smouldered' among the rest of the community. Such small outbreaks as did occur (in the Portobello Road, for example) were promptly stamped out.[184] Not in one instance, however: 'in Marylebone a case nursed at home in a community where there was little vaccination produced an outbreak of 'almost unprecedented character' in Portland Town. Over 250 cases were traced to this one in the second half of 1893.[185]

The smallpox outbreak of 1893 produced some alarm among the preventive authorities, and in July 1894 the LCC organized a well-attended conference at County Hall to discuss the problem of smallpox among vagrants. Here the London authorities discovered that the vagrant problem was widespread: in thirty-seven out of sixty-three urban districts (59 per cent) smallpox was known to have been first introduced by vagrants, and in forty-six (73 per cent) the disease was known to have been so introduced sooner or later.[186] Nine

[181] Ibid. [182] Ibid. 163. [183] Ibid. 171. [184] Ibid. 171–2.

[185] *MOAR* Marylebone (1894), 11; (1895), 11. Dr Wynter Blyth reported that subsequent events showed that the disease had never been completely stamped out in the district: *MOAR* (1894), 13. The MAB reported that the disease was finally stamped out here after nine months in March 1895: (1895), 152. From Wynter Blyth's description, however, it seems that the epidemic lasted twenty-one months, from July 1893 to March 1895.

[186] *LCC Public Health and Housing Committee* (1894–5), 102.

resolutions were adopted for the prevention of the spread of smallpox by vagrants. These were soon put to the test, for in June 1895 there was a sharp resurgence of the disease in London: 440 cases from every union in the city were notified in July and August. Once again, the vagrant population proved the centre of infection. Of thirty-five cases admitted to the MAB hospitals in June, only half-a-dozen possessed a fixed address.[187]

The pattern of the epidemic closely followed that of 1893.[188] When the disease appeared among the vagrant population it was in abeyance in the settled population. It was introduced by unknown means into the vagrant class, and obtained some hold before its presence was known. Once again there were cases where the infection had clearly been acquired in the provinces, but there was no evidence to show the extent to which these played a part in spreading the disease in London.[189] As far as could be ascertained, the agencies by which the disease was spread in the city were the common lodging houses and Salvation Army shelters: between June and August infection was traced in fifty cases to the former, and to the latter in sixty-four cases, with four cases which might have been acquired in either. No particular common lodging house was involved, but seventeen cases were traced to the Salvation Army shelter in Blackfriars Road, and twenty-seven to that in the Whitechapel Road. Following the vagrant outbreak the disease spread into the settled population, and after the end of August was practically confined to the latter. 'Coincidentally', the number of admissions to the MAB hospitals began to decline. By the later months of 1895 the disease was almost confined to the south and east of the city.[190]

The experiences of 1893 and 1895 awoke the preventive organization to the difficulties of controlling smallpox infection in the vagrant population, and to the unsatisfactory arrangements, in preventive terms, of the accommodation available for this class. Dr Norton of Westminster, for example, investigated a common lodging house in Great Peter Street and the Salvation Army shelter in Horseferry Road, which had registered sixteen and fourteen smallpox cases respectively. There were more than 600 beds in the lodging house, and over 200 in the shelter. The beds were not marked or numbered, and there was no record of which man had slept in which bed.[191] In all these cases the great difficulty was to trace where the patients from these shelters had slept in the days before and after noticing the smallpox rash: one man had slept in five different beds after noticing it.[192] Additional problems were the difficulty in getting this class to accept vaccination or revaccination, and the monitoring of contacts not yet manifesting signs of the disease. Such problems left the pre-

[187] *MABAR* (1895), app. 10, 152.

[188] Ibid. 153–4.

[189] One of these cases was that of a Hereford solicitor, who had been in contact with 'some dirty tramps' while out shooting: *MOAR* St Giles (1895), 82.

[190] *MABAR* (1895), app. 10, p. 152.

[191] *MOAR* Westminster (1893), 26.

[192] Ibid. (1895), 44.

ventive organization with a lingering anxiety about the vagrant class in its relations to smallpox. When variola major was imported into England for the last time in 1901, the LCC immediately turned a vigilant eye on the common lodging houses.[193]

TOWARDS ERADICATION: SMALLPOX IN THE 1890S

If smallpox introductions still constituted a preventive problem in the 1890s, the London preventive organization had by this time achieved a largely efficient method of detecting and controlling them. Constant vigilance was necessary, for the danger of a major outbreak was always present, as the epidemic of 1901–2 was to prove. On this occasion the disease was again introduced from abroad. Virulent strains had been threatening the country for some years from India and the Near East, but it is probable that the infection finally came from France, where the disease was particularly severe in Paris in the early years of the new century.[194] While the cornerstone of English smallpox prevention was still, as it had been since 1871, the detailed isolation of the sick, the refinements subsequently made to the system, in the way of hospital relocation, ambulance provision, notification, and modifications to local practice, on this occasion demonstrated their worth.[195] The 1901 epidemic in many ways proved the efficiency of the system. Smallpox had been repeatedly introduced in the summer of 1901, and detected and limited before gaining a hold in the city in August. By August 1902 it had been virtually eliminated, without having spread seriously into the provinces, and without having affected all districts of the metropolis.[196] In preventive terms this was a considerable

[193] *MOAR* LCC (1902), app. 1.

[194] Hardy, 'Smallpox', 137; *MOAR* LGB, PP 1902 xxxvii, p. 435.

[195] In 1896 Dr Rygate enumerated the steps of the 'stamping out' policy as it was then practised locally: *MOAR* St George-in-the-East (1896), 36. On notification, the patient was immediately removed to isolation hospital. The MOH personally inspected the infected premises and its inhabitants. Vaccination and revaccination were strongly urged, and the importance of calling in medical aid if any further sickness occurred insisted on. The schools were notified, and information was passed to the vaccination officer and the public vaccinators as each case arose, and also to the MOH concerned if the victim had worked outside the parish. Premises were cleaned and limewashed after the patient's removal to hospital, and all bedding and clothing burnt. A circular letter was addressed to the keepers of all common lodging houses in the parish informing them of the outbreak of smallpox, and urging them to seek medical assistance in the event of sickness among their inmates. Handbills containing all necessary information on vaccination, disinfection, and medical assistance were issued to affected households.

[196] The epidemic was effectively over by June 1902, but more than 6,000 cases were notified between August 1901 and the end of March 1902. The outbreak was initially concentrated in St Pancras, Holborn, and St Giles, but moved into the East End in January 1902, reaching its climax there in March, when the disease was waning in most other areas. In that month 2,000 cases were admitted to the MAB hospitals. Poplar supplied the highest total of cases (547); the seven Eastern unions together supplied very nearly 60% of all smallpox cases admitted by the MAB in 1902: *MOAR* LGB, PP 1902 xxxvii, p. 435–6; *MABAR* (1902), 243–4.

achievement: William Power, then MOH of the Local Government Board, felt that there 'could be no doubt at all' that the efficiency of the MAB hospital and ambulance service had contributed largely to this unprecedented success in dealing with a London epidemic;[197] yet the efficiency of the local preventive services was equally crucial to the outcome.

The virtual absence of smallpox from London during the later 1890s did not mean that outbreaks did not occur. The disease repeatedly broke out in Camberwell in these years, and there were also outbreaks in Kensington, Islington, Lambeth, and Greenwich in 1896, and in the Strand in 1897.[198] The Camberwell outbreaks regularly occurred in the slum area around Beckett Street.[199] The residual power of smallpox is well illustrated by the pattern of the disease in London in these years. In 1898 Francis Stevens was driven to observe that there was 'little variation from the monotonous history of the beginning in an unvaccinated person, and spreading to those that are either unprotected or in whom the protective power of vaccination has waned'.[200] The city's freedom from smallpox was not due to the vaccination state of her population, although vaccination alone made fully effective the elaborate preventive mechanism which in fact protected the city from the disease.

With the increasing rarity of smallpox in the closing decades of the century, the identification of cases became more problematic. In mild cases of the disease there had always been some difficulty of identification, and such cases were often diagnosed as chickenpox.[201] In 1885, indeed, the registrar-general went so far as to assume that the hundred or so deaths registered annually from chickenpox were in fact due to smallpox, since the former 'is usually so trifling an ailment and so rarely fatal'.[202] On the other hand, it could also be assumed that since the number of deaths ascribed to chickenpox varied little from year to year, and did not move with the epidemic curve of smallpox, they were in fact due to chickenpox. In one instance Dr Tidy recorded two smallpox deaths registered as chickenpox and subsequently so tabled in the official figures 'in accordance with the practice of the Registrar-General'.[203] The level of smallpox mis-diagnosis in the nineteenth century cannot be accurately assessed, but the evidence suggests that the problem increased in the last decades of the century, as the disease became increasingly rare (see Table 5.7). From at least 1887 the medical superintendent of the MAB's smallpox ships, Dr Birdwood, was urging the managers to open the hospitals for clinical

[197] *MOAR* LGB, PP 1902 xxxvii, p. 439.

[198] *MABAR* (1896), 12; *MOAR* Strand (1897), 135. Eight cases occurred in Strand, all men living at a lodging house in Vere Street. They were all regular lodgers, not vagrants who might have carried the disease into the country. It is significant that the first victim carried a sandwich board in Bond Street.

[199] *Camberwell VAR* (1895–6), 415–20; *MOAR* Camberwell (1896–7), 8–9; (1897–8), 10.

[200] *MOAR* Camberwell (1897–8), 8.

[201] *MOAR* Kensington (1880), 30.

[202] *RGAR*, PP 1884–5 xvii, p. 15.

[203] *MOAR* Islington (1887), 73.

observation, that medical students might learn to recognize the disease.[204] By 1889 the MAB, LGB, and Royal College of Physicians were preparing to implement such a scheme.[205] As late as 1896, however, Dr Harris of Islington, about to castigate local doctors for diagnosing three cases of smallpox as chickenpox, 'recollected that very few medical men when students ever see, or have the opportunity of seeing, cases of Small Pox', and felt obliged to view the error in a more lenient light.[206] Two years later, Dr Birdwood deduced from the high percentage of mis-diagnosed cases arriving at the MAB wharves that 'the ordinary practitioner in London practically never sees . . . smallpox'.[207] Such mistakes perhaps also suggest a salutary caution in the diagnoses of at least some of London's general practitioners.[208]

TABLE 5.7. *Mis-diagnosed smallpox cases as % of smallpox admissions at MAB hospitals, 1886–1900*

1886	1893	1894	1895	1896	1897	1898	1899	1900
26.1	3.3	12.2	10.8	28.7	42.9	83.3	64.3	32.0

Source: *MABAR*.

The literature of nineteenth-century smallpox is a vast and fascinating one, through which the historian may obtain access to forgotten fears, forgotten practices, and the ways by which infectious diseases moved through communities in the past. Less spectacular than cholera because long familiar, smallpox was at least as terrible; yet it has vanished so completely from recent European experience that its central position in Victorian public-health concern may easily be overlooked. It was from smallpox, and not from cholera, that the English preventive services learnt the lesson of detailed preventive action—of minute attention to the local circumstances of individual cases of infectious disease—that became the dominant ethos of local prevention in the years before 1914. London's smallpox history in this period demonstrates not only the difficulties of prevention, but also the gradual process by which measures were evolved to meet the varied challenge posed by the disease. The decline of smallpox in the nineteenth century was perhaps the major achievement of the public-health organization. If vaccination was the principal feature of

204 *MABAR* (1887), app. 6, p. 35; ibid. (1888), app. 7, p. 49.
205 Ibid. (1889), 16.
206 *MOAR* Islington (1896), 77.
207 *MABAR* (1898), 31.
208 The principal sources of confusion were chickenpox, measles, and skin affections such as acne and eczema: *MABAR* (1887), app. 6, p. 35; ibid. (1889), 16. More spectacular examples were known to occur, however. In 1879 a smallpox scare in Battersea was dispelled when the supposed victims were examined by 'more skilled doctors': the patients were suffering from severe mosquito bites, a plague of the insects being said to have been released by a cargo of cedar-wood at Messrs Woolf's pencil factory in York Road: *South London Press*, 16 Aug. 1879. The paper observed, however, that cedar-wood was known not to be a healthy harbour for mosquitoes, while Mr Woolf said none had ever been seen on his premises.

preventive policy up to the later 1860s, control of the disease after 1885 was maintained through the vigilance of the local preventive departments, and the limitation of such epidemics as inevitably occurred to episodes of modest proportions is evidence of the effectiveness of those services in circumstances where a complete preventive package could be devised to deal with a specific disease.

6
Typhoid

The endemic fever of England.

(Charles Murchison, 1868)

Typhoid mortality . . . 'that sensitive but trustworthy test of sanitary condition'.

(*Lancet*, 1888)

Typhoid we have always with us.

(E. Ray Lankester, 1900)

TYPHOID AND WATER QUALITY: A NEW URBAN PROBLEM IN THE NINETEENTH CENTURY

Typhoid was the common fever of the nineteenth century; insidious in its onset, often mysterious in its origin, endemic, familiar, without respect to social class or locational exclusivity. It was perhaps the most democratic of the preventable diseases, common among the poor, but attacking the aristocracy and the well-to-do with equal frequency.[1] In contrast to cholera, with which it epidemiologically had much in common, typhoid was a local and domestic problem.[2] In the early years of sanitary reform preventive efforts were generally directed, on a broadly miasmatic assumption, towards clearing cesspools and manure heaps, closing wells, extending piped-water supplies, and ventilating and repairing sewers and drains. In the early 1870s, however, just as the specific identity of typhoid, and the likelihood of its having a specific cause were becoming widely accepted by the medical profession, a series of typhoid outbreaks among the better classes in London and elsewhere,[3] together with the much-publicized illness of several high-ranking individuals—of the Prince of Wales (1871); in the household of the Earl of Cadogan at St James's (1874); and of Prince Leopold (1875)—made typhoid the subject of generalized public concern. The public discovery of typhoid as an independent disease at this

[1] *LFHAR* (1861), 6.

[2] Perhaps for this reason it has been largely neglected by historians, with the honourable exception of Bill Luckin. The current chapter should be read in conjunction with his two essays: 'Typhus and typhoid in London', in R. I. Woods and J. Woodward (eds.), *Urban Disease and Mortality* (1984), 102–19; and 'Typhoid fever', in his *Pollution and Control: A Social History of the Thames* (Bristol, 1986), 118–38. See also F. B. Smith, *The People's Health* (1979), 244–9; A. S. Wohl, *Endangered Lives: Public Health in Victorian Britain* (1983), 127–8.

[3] The most notable of these were those at Islington (1870), later famous because Edward Ballard was able to trace its origins to the milk supply, and at Marylebone, where the family of Charles Murchison, London's leading expert on fevers, was among those affected: see *MOAR* Islington (1870), 9; *LFHAR* (1872), 7–8.

time was to have important preventive repercussions, and may be said to have begun the process by which modern standards of personal and domestic hygiene were eventually achieved; within a very few years it resulted in an upsurge of sanitary awareness and private sanitary effort among nearly all social groups that was unparalleled both as a response to a particular disease, and in the annals of sanitary reform. Individual observation of the basic laws of hygiene was one of the chief prerequisites for the reduction and eventual elimination of typhoid mortality, along with satisfactory water supplies and sewage disposal. In the case of typhoid, alone among the communicable diseases, private efforts at disease control ran in tandem with those of the preventive organization in the final decades of the nineteenth century.

TABLE 6.1. *Typhoid death-rates per 100,000 population, 1870–1900*

	1871–80	1881–90	1891–1900
England and Wales	32	20	17
London	24	19	14

Sources: *RGDS* PP 1905 xviii, table 5; *MOAR* LCC (1900), 35.

The history of typhoid before the 1870s is obscure. Until 1869, it was not distinguished from typhus and simple continued fever in the statistics of the registrar-general. According to Creighton and others, typhoid only became a disease of any significance in England in the later 1820s: it was identified as a new fever and studied by physicians at Guy's and St George's hospitals in the years between 1826 and 1830, having made its appearance in the autumn of the former year, after the 'driest and hottest summer of the century'.[4] In the 1830s and 1840s, the identity of typhoid was submerged by the resurgence of epidemic typhus, which dominated British medical concern in these years.[5] Contemporary disagreement with French physicians over the nature and treatment of fever was founded in the predominance of typhoid rather than typhus on the Continent at this time. The use of the term 'typhus' as a generic to cover all kinds of fever added further to the confusion. It was not until William Jenner, physician to the London Fever Hospital, delivered his careful analysis of the clinical characteristics of the different fevers to the Royal Medical and Chirurgical Society in December 1849 that the English medical profession came to distinguish clearly between typhoid, typhus, and relapsing fever.[6] Even so, confusion still lingered. Although recognized as clinically distinct, disagreement continued about the nature and relationship of the differ-

[4] Charles Creighton, *A History of Epidemics in Britain*, 2 vols. (Cambridge, 1891), ii. 185–6, 217.
[5] Ibid. 188, 199–200; *LFHAR* (1851), 9.
[6] Sir William Jenner, *Lectures and Essays on Fevers and Diphtheria* (1893); *LFHAR* (1848), 9.

ent fevers.[7] Wunderlich's discovery, published in 1868, that the temperature of typhoid victims followed a characteristic pattern, finally established the separate identity of the disease, and it was after this that the English registrar-general began to distinguish between the different forms of fever. None the less, there were still doctors in the 1870s who used the term 'typhus' to describe all types of fever. The similarity of the terms 'typhoid' and 'typhus' was thought to lie behind some of this confusion, and for this reason the term enteric was frequently employed to designate typhoid from the mid-1870s.[8]

In spite of the doubt which must surround some of the use of the terms 'typhoid', 'typhus', and 'fever' up until about 1880, it is still possible to speak of typhoid and typhus as unified diseases in the London context from the date of William Jenner's seminal analysis.[9] The London Fever Hospital differentiated between the two diseases from 1848, and their diagnoses and statistics were accepted by the registrar-general as reliable indicators (indeed the only indicators) of the relative prevalence of these diseases in London. The LFH records for the years 1848–70 show clearly that typhoid, while endemic in London, remained on the whole stable in incidence during the 1850s, but began to rise during the 1860s (Fig. 6.1); annual variations in typhoid incidence in the 1860s could generally be attributed to extraordinary climactic conditions.[10] Mountainous peaks in annual admissions figures were dictated by the epidemic manifestations of typhus. By the 1870s, as the Metropolitan Asylums Board hospital figures show, while typhus continued to be an anxiety, the bulk of continued fever cases were of typhoid (Table 6.2). Although typhoid now took the proportionate lead among these fevers, the aggregate continued fever mortality fell fairly steadily to 1900 and beyond (Fig. 6.2). Comparison of the LFH records for the years 1848–70 with the mortality curve of the registrar-general's post-1870 figures suggests that typhoid deaths rose to a peak around 1870, and declined thereafter.[11]

It was not, however, a decline without problems.[12] Major Greenwood, one of the most notable early twentieth-century historical epidemiologists, distinguished three phases in the decline of the disease in England and Wales: a rapid fall between 1875 and 1885, due mainly to improvements in water supplies and drainage; a period of stagnation, 1885–95; and further decline after 1900, when the role of carriers was recognized and greater attention was paid to the rapid hospitalization of patients.[13] Within Greenwood's framework a

[7] *Lancet* (1856), i. 159. For the general background, see Margaret Pelling, *Cholera, Fever and English Medicine 1825–1865* (Oxford, 1978).

[8] *Lancet* (1878), ii. 414.

[9] Luckin, 'Typhus and typhoid', 119–21; 'Typhoid fever', 118–19, 121, 122.

[10] *LFHAR* (1861), 7; (1865), 7.

[11] See the discussion of these figures in Luckin, 'Typhus and typhoid', 106–7.

[12] Luckin, 'Typhoid fever', 121.

[13] M. Greenwood, *Epidemics and Crowd Diseases* (1935), 157–8; this pattern was also noted, with minor differences of detail, by the RGDS, 1919, part III, p. lviii. See also Luckin, 'Typhoid Fever', 121.

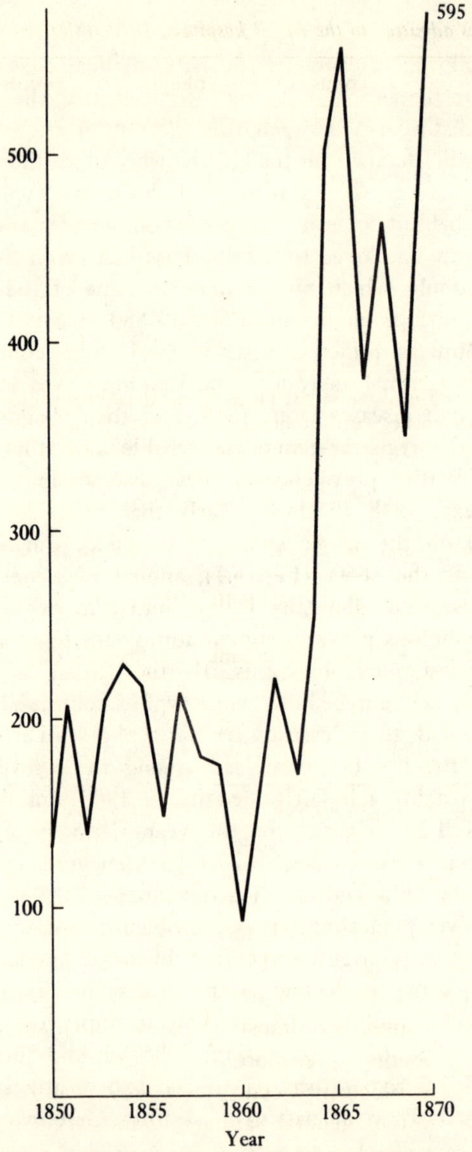

FIG. 6.1. *Typhoid admissions to the London Fever Hospital, 1850–1870.*

good deal remains to be discovered about the way in which typhoid operated in the local context, which may contribute to our understanding of the overall pattern of the rise and decline of the disease. Among the notable features of the post-1870 decline, for example, was the greater reduction in deaths among women than among men (Table 6.3), and this was parallelled by a greater

TABLE 6.2. *Fever cases admitted to the MAB hospitals, 1872–1880*

Year	Typhus	Typhoid	Simple continued fever
1872	82	183	
1873	160	233	
1874	536	258	
1875	65	299	102
1876	21	134	
1877	175	372	
1878	168	484	
1879	48	249	
1880	10	164	

Source: Minutes of proceedings of the MAB. These figures should be treated with some caution, as the hospitals' admissions policy varied from year to year depending on the pressure of smallpox and scarlet-fever cases, but they may be taken to indicate the comparative prevalence of typhus and typhoid.

TABLE 6.3. *Typhoid in England and Wales: decrease % of mortality in each sex*

Sex	1881–90	1891–1900	1901–1910	1881–90	1891–1900	1901–10
	Compared with previous decennium			Compared with 1871–80		
M	-33.6	-6.0	-46.0	-33.6	-37.7	-66.4
F	-42.3	-17.9	-51.0	-42.3	-52.7	-76.8
Persons	-38.0	-12.1	-48.0	-38.0	-45.5	-71.7

Source: *RGDS*, 1919, part III, p. lix, table 23.

reduction of deaths among the very young and the old, than in the middle years of life. By the decade 1901–10, indeed, excess female typhoid mortality had contracted to the age-group 5–15 (the years at which female mortality generally exceeded male), from the more extended range 0–20 in 1871–80. Whereas typhoid had caused an almost equal mortality among both sexes in 1870, by 1910 it had become much more fatal to men.[14]

Throughout the later nineteenth century, typhoid was regarded as a sensitive and trustworthy test of general sanitary conditions,[15] and the clear epidemiology of typhoid certainly admits this interpretation.[16] The only source of typhoid bacilli (*Salmonella typhi*) is an infected person; one attack confers immunity, except in some 5 per cent of cases which experience relapse. There are three chief means of transmission: through infected water or food, or by

14 *RGDS*, 1919, part III, p. lx.

15 *Lancet* (1888), i. 785.

16 Epidemiological information is taken from W. W. C. Topley and G. S. Wilson (eds.), *Principles of Bacteriology, Viroloy and Immunity*, seventh edn. (1984), iii. chap. 68; F. H. Top and P. H. Wehrle (eds.), *Communicable and Infectious Diseases*, ninth edn. (St Louis, Miss., 1981), 736–42.

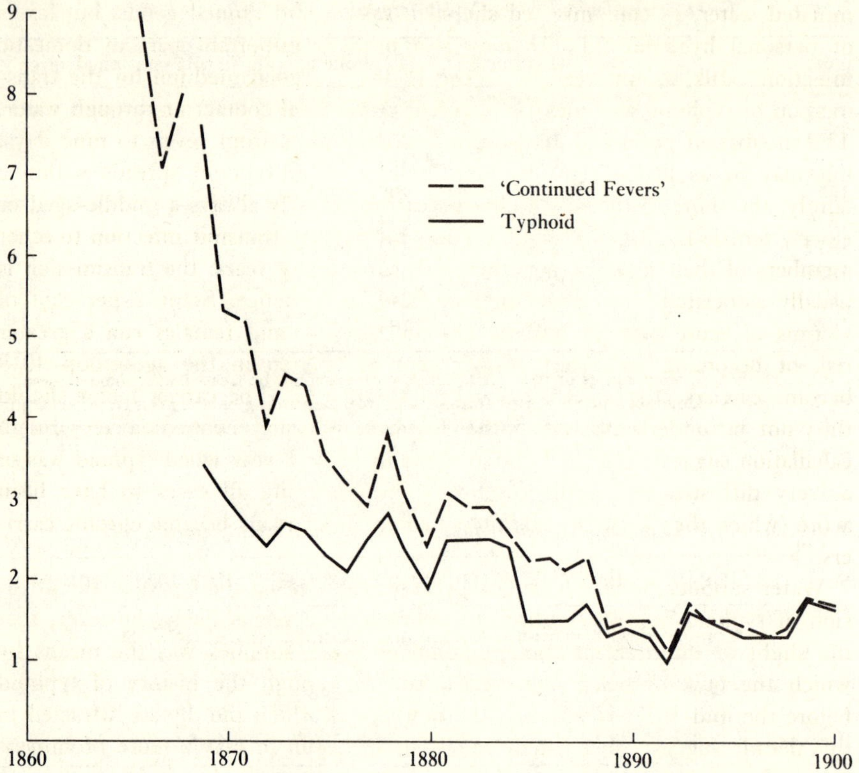

FIG. 6.2. *Deaths from typhoid and 'continued fever' in London, 1869–1900, per 10,000 population.*

carrier. The disease is most frequently spread by contaminated water, but infected food may be responsible for a considerable proportion of cases where domestic hygiene practices are poor. Infective doses of *Salmonella typhi* may be very small, and it is an elusive bacillus, whose presence in water, for example, is often transitory. Water-borne typhoid occurs in two forms, either as an explosive outbreak where a normally safe water supply is contaminated, or as a series of single cases or small groups of cases appearing over a considerable period of time and affecting only a small proportion of consumers, when the infection of water is slight or intermittent. The incubation period of water-borne typhoid is generally long—from eighteen to twenty-one days—and the attack-rate is usually lower than in food-borne outbreaks.

Water-borne typhoid has received the lion's share of attention from historians, and was certainly an important source of infection in the nineteenth century. Other types of infection were probably nearly as significant, however, and may bear much of the responsibility for the slowing-up of the reduction in typhoid mortality after 1885. Food-borne infection is often conveyed via contaminated water, in contaminated shellfish, salads, and canned goods, but levels of personal hygiene and flies may also play an important part in domestic infection. Milk, as was realized in the 1870s, is a good medium for the transmission of typhoid, and may be infected by personal contact or through water. The incubation period of food-borne typhoid varies from seven to nine days, but may be as little as twenty-four hours. Where typhoid spreads within a family, the source is usually a chronic carrier ('nearly always a middle-aged or elderly female').[17] Many chronic carriers only rarely transmit infection to other members of their families, and then only after many years: the transmission is usually associated with lapses in food-handling practice. Some 2 per cent of victims of acute typhoid become chronic carriers, and females run a greater risk of becoming so: about 16 per cent of women in the age-group 40–9 become carriers after an acute attack of the disease. The carrier factor should thus not be underestimated in the nineteenth-century context: a very rough calculation suggests that in London alone in 1894, a year when typhoid was of a 'very diffusive and virulent type',[18] and assuming all cases to have been acute (which they probably were not), some 500 persons became chronic carriers.[19]

Water supplies, infected food, and carriers all played their part in the diffusion of typhoid in nineteenth-century London. It seems likely, however, that the slight or intermittent contamination of water supplies was the means by which the bulk of cases was contracted.[20] Although the history of typhoid before the mid-1820s is obscure, the new notice which the disease attracted in this decade suggests that it may indeed have begun to play a more prominent role in London's morbidity. In terms of the upsurge in the city's population-size and density, and of the nature of its water supply and sewage arrangements in the early decades of the century, it would not be surprising if there was a significant upsurge in the level of typhoid endemicity beginning in this decade. The years between 1815 and 1830 saw both a marked deterioration in the condition of the Thames,[21] and, with the commercial expansion of the London water companies, an extension of the area and population supplied from the river.[22] The water closet also became increasingly widespread after 1800, and from 1815 house drains were permitted to empty into the sewers and from thence into the river.[23] At about this time the old night-soil system,

[17] Topley and Wilson, *Principles*, iii. 414.

[18] *MOAR* Lambeth (1894), 4.

[19] This doubtful calculation is based on an estimated mortality of 20%, and the registrar-general's figure of 4,781 typhoid deaths in London. Mortality in the MAB hospitals stood at 15.9%, but because of a shortage of beds many acute cases were treated in the general hospitals, and this figure was regarded as conservative: *MABAR* (1894), 12.

[20] This was agreed by contemporaries: W. H. Corfield, *The Etiology of Typhoid Fever and its Prevention* (1902), 34–5.

[21] Leslie Wood, *The Restoration of the Tidal Thames* (1981), 19.

[22] Anne Hardy, 'London's water supply in the ninteenth century', in W. F. Bynum and R. Porter (eds.), *Living and Dying in London*, *Medical History* supplement, no. 11 (1991).

[23] Anne Hardy, 'Water and the Search for Public Health in London in the xvii and xix centuries', *Medical History* (1984), p. 263.

by which solid wastes were removed from the city regularly, came to an end. Meanwhile increasing pressure of population put an unprecedented strain on the city's wells and cesspools. New ones were continually being dug, and in ever-closer proximity to each other. By the 1830s the contamination of wells by cesspool soakage was becoming a regular and recognized problem.[24] When chemical assessment of sewage pollution became possible in the 1860s and 1870s many of the wells most popular with Londoners for the flavour of their water were found to be highly contaminated with sewage. The infamous Broad Street well is a case in point, but there were many others, among them the Billingsgate well, whose waters were commonly drawn to supply the casks of seagoing Thames shipping.[25]

There can be little doubt that channels for the transmission of typhoid became much more numerous from the 1820s on. Before the 1840s the water companies rarely filtered supplies before distribution, and it is clear that the early filtration systems were frequently inadequate.[26] Water from private and public shallow wells was never filtered at all. The relationship between typhoid and London's supplies of piped drinking water have been examined in some detail by Bill Luckin,[27] and while these certainly played an important part in the distribution of typhoid through the city, and probably contributed to rising typhoid mortality from the 1830s, the significance of the city's well waters should not be forgotten. There can be no doubt that these constituted an important water source for private households until the 1870s, nor that they were becoming increasingly and profoundly polluted from the 1820s at least.[28] While the numbers and distribution of private wells in London remains unknown, Robert Woods has demonstrated a clear connection between high typhoid mortality and the distribution of private wells in Birmingham during the 1880s.[29] While the removal of water-company intakes from the lower Thames during the 1850s, the spread of resting and filtration practices, and more especially the introduction of official monitoring of water quality in the 1870s, all resulted in improvements in the quality of supplies distributed by London's water companies, the efforts of the London sanitary departments in abolishing cesspools and closing local wells wherever possible during the 1860s and 1870s probably made a substantial contribution in reducing typhoid mortality. The introduction of Sunday supplies of piped water after 1870, and the increasing availability of constant supply from the later 1860s, facilitated the abolition of wells; local evidence suggests that the medical officers instigated an

[24] Hardy, 'Water supply'.

[25] Return of . . . surface wells within the metropolis', PP 1872 xlix, p. 851.

[26] H. W. Dickinson, *A History of Water Supply* (1954), 120–1. The Lambeth Water Company Act 1838 was the first to make statutory provision for filtration.

[27] Luckin, 'Typhoid Fever'.

[28] Hardy, 'Water supply'.

[29] R. I. Woods, 'Mortality and sanitary conditions in late nineteenth-century Birmingham', in Woods and Woodward (eds.), *Urban Disease and Mortality*, 197–8.

energetic closure programme in the early 1870s,[30] around the time when the down-swing in typhoid mortality apparently began.

Explosive outbreaks of water-borne typhoid were relatively rare in the second half of the century, and furnished a minority of cases. Towards the end of the century Ernest Hart published the details of 205 water-borne typhoid epidemics recorded in England and Ireland between 1858 and 1893: of these only three were reported from London.[31] None of these London outbreaks was caused by the pollution of drinking-water supplies: in all three the vehicle of infection was milk, which had been contaminated with infected water.[32] The deaths linked to these outbreaks represented only a fraction of the city's total typhoid mortality during this period.[33] Explosive outbreaks in London were more commonly associated with milk, as at Islington and Marylebone in the early 1870s and Plumstead in 1895,[34] and in the closing years of the century with shellfish and food distribution.[35] Most water-related typhoid throughout the period was of the scattered or intermittent type, and therefore difficult to disentangle from other domestic sources of the disease, such as food contaminated by flies or accidental infection through insanitary plumbing or food-handling practices. Most typhoid cases seem to have occurred singly or in small groups; they seemed usually to be unrelated; and only rarely could the source of the infection be traced. This was, for example, clearly the case in St James's, Westminster, in the years 1879 to 1900, during which the MOH published a detailed list of cases of infectious disease coming to the notice of his department.[36]

THE IMPORTANCE OF DOMESTIC WATER SUPPLIES: WATER-CLOSET TECHNOLOGY

The improvement in both quality and quantity of domestic water supply which took place in London in the years after 1870 was of undoubted

[30] *MOAR* St George's, Southwark (1871–2), 4; *MOAR* Kensington (1875), 30.

[31] Ernest Hart, *Waterborne Typhoid* (1897).

[32] Ibid., table analysing the epidemics. The three outbreaks in question were those at Marylebone (July–Aug. 1873), St Pancras and Islington (Mar. 1877), and Clapham (June–July 1882).

[33] Ibid. Of the three, the Marylebone outbreak was the largest, numbering 244 cases with 26 deaths; there were 34 cases with 2 deaths at St Pancras and 22 cases and 3 deaths in Clapham.

[34] Hart listed five milk-borne typhoid epidemics in London in the years after 1882. They were at Clapham (as in n. 33 above), St Pancras (July–Sept. 1883), Greenwich and Rotherhithe (Sept.–Nov. 1892), Lambeth (Mar.–Apr. 1894), and Plumstead (May–June 1895): Ernest Hart, Report on the Influence of Milk in Spreading Zymotic Disease (1897), 19–24. The scale of these outbreaks was as follows: Clapham, 22 cases and 3 deaths; St Pancras, 431 cases, 30 deaths; Greenwich, 551 cases (no deaths reported); Lambeth, 59 cases, 10 deaths; Plumstead, 177 cases, 23 deaths. See also H. Swithinbank and G. Newman, *The Bacteriology of Milk* (1903), 316–36.

[35] For milk and shellfish infection see Luckin, 'Typhoid fever', 125–6; for the dissemination of the disease (probably by carrier infection) through fried-fish shops in the 1890s, see *MOAR* LCC (1900), app. 1.

[36] The details of the known St James's typhoid cases appear in the MOH's annual reports.

importance in diminishing typhoid incidence. The extension of constant water supplies throughout the poorer districts of London from the early 1870s meant that reliance on surface well water virtually disappeared, as well as facilitating cleanliness and other domestic chores. Although by the 1890s there were still poor areas of London supplied by the intermittent system, this prevailed widely only in the better class of housing.[37] Despite continuing intermittent problems with the purity of London's water supply, extension of constant water supply to the poor areas of East London in the 1870s probably contributed to the reduction in incidence of both typhoid and typhus, as observed by contemporaries.[38] Although the London water companies had been prohibited from drawing supplies within the limits of London's self-pollution of the Thames after 1855, and were required by the Metropolis Water Act 1852 to rest and filter their water before distribution, aberrations did occur, and filtration technology was still progressing. Thus, the brief distribution by the East London Company of unfiltered water in 1866 resulted in the East London cholera epidemic of that year, while as late as 1868 the Southwark Company's Battersea reservoir was still connected with the tidal Thames by an old conduit to Battersea Reach, and in certain instances tidal Thames water reached the Battersea reservoirs by soakage, leakage, or by direct inflow.[39] In 1871 Edward Frankland reported that only the West Middlesex and New River Companies (apart from the Kent Company, which drew all water from deep chalk wells), exhibited efficient filtration, and in January 1872 the Southwark Company confirmed this by delivering unacceptably turbid water because of heavy floods and hurried filtration.[40]

From the early 1870s, however, the quality of water generally delivered in London improved steadily and markedly. In part this was due to the regular official monitoring of water quality instituted by the Board of Trade, but it was also dependent on technological advances. It is, for example, highly important to the success of the filtration process that it should be conducted slowly and regularly. To achieve a constant rate of discharge and uniformity in the condition of the filtered water, the filter head has to be regulated. Before the 1870s, these regulators were worked by hand: the earliest regulator, that installed by the Chelsea Company at their works in 1839, consisted of no more than a couple of valves worked by hand on the inlet and outlet pipes of the filter bed. This type of measure was essentially a rough-and-ready one, which did not uniformly prevent such sudden variations of the head as could disturb the surface film of the filter bed and so produce great increases in the number of bacteria in the filtered water. The deficiencies of the system were first pointed out in 1869, after which the use of automatic regulators became wide-

[37] *RCMWS*, PP 1893–4, xl (part ii), app. c no. 65, p. 485.
[38] *Lancet* (1875), i. 486.
[39] *RCMWS*, PP 1872 xlix, p. 805; PP 1872 xxxviii, app. 5, pp. 767–93.
[40] *RCMWS*, PP 1872 xlix, p. 827; ibid. 790–1.

spread.[41] Increasingly, however, problems of intermittent pollution were due to extraordinary pressures of, for example, weather conditions, on an increasingly stressed water-delivery system; and these achieved recognition and concern in the 1890s.[42]

The infection of domestic water supplies before distribution was a problem which was being overcome during the second half of the nineteenth century, and which could be tackled in the traditional way of sanitary reform: by legislation to ensure certain standards, by the new device of official monitoring, and by pressure from local medical officers. Other channels of infection were less amenable to direct preventive action. Contamination of company water supplies within the household, for example, probably occurred frequently through faulty domestic plumbing arrangements, where domestic water supply and house-drainage pipes were inadequately separated.[43] More seriously, domestic sanitary facilities were also an important vehicle for the transmission of infection. In 1892, indeed, Louis Parkes, MOH for Chelsea, vouchsafed the opinion that the decline in typhoid mortality since 1870 was no less due to better domestic sanitation, especially among the poor, as to improved water supply and sewage.[44] In the mid-1890s studies by Philip Boobyer, MOH for Nottingham, were demonstrating a clear connection between the prevalence of typhoid and conservancy systems of sewage disposal,[45] and by the end of the century local observation had confirmed the role of these in spreading typhoid, in sharp contrast to the safer water-carriage method.[46] In Manchester, for example, between 1891 and 1898, 7.3 per cent of typhoid cases occurred in the 19.3 per cent of Manchester houses with water closets, compared with 69.8 per cent and 22.9 per cent in the 62.3 per cent houses operating the pail system, and the 18.4 per cent of houses with privies.[47] In Leicester, where the transfer from pail system to water closet was finally completed in the 1890s, the death-rate from typhoid fell by 49 per cent between 1889–93 and 1899–1903; in Nottingham, where 84 per cent of houses remained on the pail system throughout this period, typhoid mortality rose by 15 per cent.[48]

The experience of these northern manufacturing towns with conservancy systems holds some lessons for the history of typhoid in London, despite the fact that housing throughout the capital was generally provided with water closets by 1870.[49] Indeed, the spread of the water closet probably increased the

[41] R. Baldwin Wiseman, 'Statistical and experimental data on filtration', *Minutes of Proceedings, Institute of Civil Engineers*, 181, (1909–10), part iii, p. 40.

[42] Luckin, *Pollution*, chap. 2.

[43] Luckin, 'Typhoid fever', 127.

[44] *Lancet* (1892), i. 1,423.

[45] Philip Boobyer, 'Typhoid in midden towns', *Public Health*, 9 (1896–7), 380–3; ibid., 'Enteric fever and conservancy methods', 402–3.

[46] See Martin Daunton, *House and Home* (1983), 252–5.

[47] Ibid. 253.

[48] Ibid. 254–5.

[49] Baldwin Latham, *Sanitary Engineering* (1873), 38, table 5; William Pole, 'Report on constant water supply', PP 1872 xlix, p. 730.

incidence of typhoid in more direct ways. On the one hand, housing in the poorer areas of the city was not generously provided with closets, several families frequently having to share one facility. Secondly, the early closets were frequently defective in design and operation, leaving pedestals insufficiently cleansed. About one-third of faecal matter by weight consists of bacteria, and although the vast majority of these are dead, several, including the organisms of dysentery and typhoid, are alive when excreted. While the normal two-gallon flush of a modern cistern leaves only a few-score bacteria per cubic centimetre of water in the pedestal, a defective or even slightly reduced flush leaves up to a million more per cc. The volume of water discharged in the flush is crucial. An inadequately flushed closet may have a bacterial population of over ten million organisms per cubic centimetre, presenting a serious health risk since the splashing of contaminated water in the closet pedestal during excretion constitutes one of the highest risks of cross-infection.[50] This risk must have been maximized with the early closets, whose operation, despite a flush of at least two gallons,[51] was in very many instances defective.

In the poorer districts of London, the danger of typhoid infection via the closet was probably particularly great, for up to the 1870s the vast majority of closets had no water laid on, but had to be flushed by the use of handpails. Although it is impossible to estimate the number or proportion of closets in these areas, they were probably, from the 1860s at least, the commonest form of disposal. The engineer William Pole, during his investigation for the Board of Trade in 1870–1, was impressed by the general standard of closet cleanliness in the poor districts, notwithstanding the handpail flush, and found only a few cases of gross filthiness.[52] Nevertheless, the handpail flush, discharging something less than a gallon of water, cannot have been a bacteriologically effective form of disposal.

The earthenware pan-closets initially used in poorer property also left much to be desired: their internal parts quickly became besmeared and offensive, and quite probably hindered effective flushing.[53] The 'hopper', or valve-closet, which largely replaced the pan in working-class housing after 1870, was something of an improvement, but still had serious drawbacks: it was said to be flushed by an inadequate dribble of water which was generally enough to wet the basin but not to clean it; the faeces fell on the sides of the pan, and these

[50] Information in this paragraph is drawn from Alan Mill, 'Flush it or fester', *New Scientist* (3 Jan. 1985), 39–40.

[51] There was a very ardent sanitary debate about the amount of water necessary to obtain an effective flush. The quantity allowed by the water companies, and legalized in the Metropolis Water Act 1871, was two gallons, an amount far from adequate in the view of many sanitarians. S. S. Hellyer felt strongly that four or even six gallons was not too little; Francis Vacher recommended a three-gallon flush: S. S. Hellyer, *The Plumber and Sanitary Houses*, fourth edn. (1884), 309–10; Francis Vacher, *A Healthy Home* (1894), 142.

[52] Pole, 'Report on water supply', PP 1872, xlix, p. 730.

[53] Roy Palmer, *The Water Closet* (1973), 33; Daunton, *House*, 256–8 is also enlightening on this subject.

being dry, a 'fixture' was left.[54] By the 1890s further improvements to the valve-closet had made it almost acceptable, but even so, it needed 'the help of a good flush and a little attention'.[55] It was not until this decade that the modern type of closet, with basin and trap all in one piece, finally emerged in a cheap and reliable form.[56]

The domestic sanitary arrangements of middle- and upper-class housing also left something to be desired at this period. Different types of closet were generally in use for servants and their masters; and by the 1880s, in all households but the smallest, two closets were the norm, one for the family, a second for the servants.[57] The defects of this system were pointed out as early as 1862 by a builder named Rigby, who considered them to be the cause of the 'ordinary fever which has lately so often and so unexpectedly broken out in the houses of the rich'.[58] Rigby noted that the two closets were generally positioned one above the other within the house, and were connected by the soil-pipe; their cisterns were similarly connected, 'the overflow of water being brought into the lead-trap and into the soil-pipe by a waste pipe'. The lower closet was generally supplied with water from a cistern in the kitchen, whose waste-pipes, sinks, and so on were all connected to the drains of the upper closet. Water from the cistern was used for domestic purposes, supplying water for the breakfast and tea tables, and for cooking generally. In a remark which casts an interesting light on the domestic and hygienic practices of Victorian households, Rigby further observed that: 'In some cases water is even drunk without being submitted to the process of boiling'.[59] In addition, Rigby condemned the condition of cisterns in many of the well-to-do houses with which he was familiar; it was a condemnation frequently echoed by medical officers of health: dirty cisterns were not a health hazard among the poor alone.[60] Routes for the dissemination of typhoid evidently existed in plenty in wealthier households, quite apart from the condition of the closets themselves.

Problems of water-closet cleanliness were not the preserve of the poor either. In better-class housing various types of closet, with differing degrees of efficiency, were used within a single household. The classier valve-closets, as invented by Sir John Harrington in the sixteenth century and produced by Bramah and his imitators, and the later wash-out and wash-down closets (the former available from the 1870s, the latter developed by the London firm of Humpherson's in 1885) were considered too expensive and too fragile for

[54] Hellyer, *The Plumber*, 192–3.
[55] Vacher, *Healthy Home*, 141.
[56] Ibid.; Daunton, *House*, 258.
[57] S. F. Murphy (ed.), *Our Homes and How to Make Them Healthy* (1882), 90.
[58] *Lancet* (1862), i. 439. The information in this paragraph comes from the *Lancet* leader, stimulated by the publication of Rigby's book on this subject, noted in the same issue of the journal (p. 587). I have, however, been unable to trace a copy of Rigby.
[59] Ibid.
[60] *MOAR* Wandsworth (1870), 8; *MOAR* Lambeth (1878–9), 20–3; *MOAR* Kensington (1897), 166. Luckin notes the cleanliness of cisterns as a problem in working-class housing ('Typhoid Fever', 126), but it was quite clearly a problem among all social classes.

general domestic use; the closet most commonly installed in the servants' quarters was the hopper, which cost a mere 2*s*. 6*d*.[61] The urgings of sanitary literature also suggest that the cleanliness of water closets may have been commonly neglected: S. S. Hellyer, for example, noted that servants were seldom instructed to wash down closets, and recommended that every home invest in a turks-head brush for the purpose.[62] Countess de Viesca spoke of closets as 'the housekeeper's *bête Noire*', and found it necessary to stress that disinfectant powder should be kept at hand and used regularly, and that ladies should provide proper brushes for cleaning the closet, and make sure that they were used daily.[63] Francis Vacher, similarly, noted that although closets should be as far as possible self-cleaning, they should have daily attention and be kept clean.[64] One French visitor, in London specifically to observe the city's sanitary arrangements, remarked that while conveniences in public buildings and working-class housing were admirably kept, this was not the case in better-class housing, the 'logements de la petite bourgeoisie', where the sanitary inspectors were reluctant to trangress domestic privacy.[65] How far the 'clean middle classes of England' were a Victorian myth is difficult to assess, but their standards of domestic hygiene were plainly not fully up to the expectations of their sanitary mentors.[66]

The interpretation which links typhoid to the spread of water-based sanitation was commonly made during the nineteenth century. Most generally, defects in house drains and sewers were held responsible, including, as Creighton noted, the partial adoption of the system, the 'transition state from the older system', tardy extension to new streets, and cheap and faulty construction.[67] Thus Charles Murchison's observation that the increased prevalence of typhoid in London in the later 1860s coincided with the completion of the main drainage system[68] was not incompatible with the claims of, for example, Alfred Carpenter, MOH for Croyden, effectively to have banished typhoid by the systematic overhaul and surveillence of his district's entire sewerage and drainage system.[69] In view of the problems which can be discovered in the domestic sanitary arrangements of all types of Victorian housing, it seems likely that contemporary observers were correct in their assessment that

[61] Palmer, *Closet*, 33. [62] Hellyer, *The Plumber*, 311.

[63] Countess Dolores de Viesca, 'Sanitary house management', *Transactions of the Sanitary Institute*, 7 (1885–6), 133.

[64] Vacher, *Healthy Home*, 142.

[65] E. Vallin, 'L'Hygiène de Londres', *Revue d'hygiène*, 5 (1883), 365–8.

[66] The phrase 'clean middle classes of England' was used by David Davies, medical officer for Bristol, in his *Typhoid Fever in Bristol* (Bristol, 1879), 3. In 1851 the medical officer of the London Fever Hospital noted that typhoid was chiefly to be found in the classes occupying better-quality dwellings and above want, for example, lower-class shopkeepers, labourers in receipt of wages, and domestic servants: *LFHAR* (1851), 11–12.

[67] Creighton, *Epidemics*, ii. 220. See also Andrew Fergus, 'On the sanitary aspects of the sewage question', *Edinburgh Medical Journal*, 17 (1871–2), 717–33.

[68] C. Murchison, *Continued Fevers of Great Britain*, fourth edn. (1884), 442.

[69] Alfred Carpenter, *Hints on House Drainage*, third edn. (1866), 3–4.

the initial development of water-based sanitation in London led to an increase in levels of endemic typhoid, not only through increased infection of domestic water supplies, but directly through incorrect closet maintenance and poor personal hygiene.

The down-turn in typhoid mortality from around 1870 was probably due to a complex interaction of improvements both in the quality of drinking water and in domestic sanitation. In the early 1870s there existed three main theories on the causation of typhoid. The English medical profession was generally agreed that typhoid was due to air or drinking water polluted by sewage:[70] opinions differed only on how the infection occurred. William Budd's contention that typhoid was always derived from the excreta of individuals already suffering from the disease was contested by Murchison, who believed that decomposition was always the factor determining the generation of infection.[71] Whereas Budd's theory emphasized the importance of individual hygiene, Murchison's pythogenic theory stressed not simply the danger of faecal effluvia, but the specific danger of such effluvia in confined spaces: 'A stinking privy outside a house is not so dangerous as a badly appointed water-closet within.'[72] Finally, there was Max von Pettenkofer's theory that the prevalence of typhoid was related solely to the amount of water present in the soil.[73] Although Creighton subscribed to this view as late as the 1890s, it was never widely accepted in England.[74]

THE ROYAL IMPETUS

Although progressive medical men were moving towards a view of typhoid as a disease caused by specific infection by the end of the 1870s,[75] Murchison's pythogenic theory died hard. As early as 1859, Budd had observed that Murchison's theory precisely expressed the popular view of typhoid;[76] and once popularly established, such ideas are difficult to eradicate. Even after Eberth's discovery of the typhoid bacillus in 1880, the elusive characteristics of the bacillus contributed to prolonging the life of the pythogenic theory.[77] In

[70] Murchison, *Continued Fevers*, 483.

[71] Ibid. 483–7. See also *Lancet* (1859), i. 337.

[72] Murchison, *Continued Fevers*, 494–5.

[73] For Pettenkofer's theory see ibid. 449–50; Creighton, *Epidemics*, ii. 218; C. E. A. Winslow, *The Conquest of Epidemic Disease* (Princeton, NJ, 1943), chap. 15.

[74] Creighton, *Epidemics*, ii. 222. George Buchanan observed inconsistencies in Pettenkofer's evidence: *Medical Times and Gazette*, 12 Mar. 1870. Murchison thought the theory too exclusive, failing to account for the frequent British observation of a connection between typhoid and defective house drainage or impure drinking water irrespective of any variations in subsoil water: Murchison, *Continued Fevers*, 450. See also *Lancet* (1885), ii. 214.

[75] Davies, *Typhoid in Bristol*, 3–5. This acceptance had been generated by Budd's publication of *Typhoid Fever* in 1873, and by strong support of his arguments by Professor Tyndall in a letter to *The Times*, 6 Nov. 1874: Corfield, *Typhoid*, 30–1.

[76] *Lancet* (1859), ii. 4.

[77] Corfield, *Typhoid*, 29.

terms of sanitary improvement, the pythogenic theory was certainly more influential than any other until at least the turn of the century. As a development of the miasmatic theory which had launched the sanitary-reform movement in the public consciousness, pythogenic theory had the advantage of continuity. It had become largely discredited among the profession by the later 1880s,[78] but its popular acceptance, and its value as a spur to local sanitary improvement, ensured that it continued in active use. When, in August 1889, there was a limited outbreak of mild, scattered typhoid cases in Mayfair and elsewhere in the West End, there were abundant complaints of the bad smells arising from local sewers and drains, although, as the *Lancet* remarked, it was 'not at all probable' that these were the cause of the outbreak.[79]

Specific preventive concern with typhoid appears to date from the death of Prince Albert in December 1861. The character of the disease as an endemic, as well as the general confusion over the continued fevers, meant that it had little independent treatment before this date. In the early 1860s, however, typhoid began to attract more specific attention. The experiences of the newly established Medical Department of the Privy Council had much to do with this development. The department's investigations into typhoid outbreaks at Bedford, Bath, Kingston-Deveril (Wiltshire) and Dronfield (Derbyshire) in 1860, for example, followed the traditional pattern of establishing no more than that any or all of the air, soil, or water of the place was contaminated with excrement.[80] However, the etiological arguments of Budd and Murchison, which figured so prominently in the medical press at the turn of the decade, both pointed to the origin of the disease in specific sanitary defects or habits. Budd, for example, although now praised by the profession for his insistence on contagion, on the excretion of infective material in the faeces, on the spread of the disease by family habits, and on the role of water and milk,[81] nevertheless also emphasized the role of sewer air, and the way in which its issue through defects in sewers and closet or privy traps would spread the disease to the healthy. It was, he wrote, essential to a true view of the disease 'to understand that when the poison issues into the air, the atmosphere generated is immeasurably more infectious than that which immediately surrounds the fever patients. The sewer may be looked upon, in fact, as a direct continuation of the diseased intestine.'[82] Thus, while the imprecise auras of sewer gas remained a cause for preventive concern, specific directions were suggested for preventive action.

[78] By the early 20th cent., a pythogenic cause—sewer gas—was still believed to be responsible for diarrhoea, though not for typhoid: Corfield, *Typhoid*, 803.

[79] *Lancet* (1889), ii. 652; see also *The Times*, 4, 6, 7, 10, 11, 16 Sept. 1889.

[80] *MOAR* PC, PP 1861 xvi. See also *MOAR* PC, PP 1863 xxviii, app. 18; and *MOAR* PC, PP 1864 xxvi, app. 9.

[81] Topley and Wilson, *Principles*, iii. 407.

[82] William Budd, 'Fever at the Orphan Clergy Asylum', *Lancet* (1856), ii. 618. See also id., *Typhoid Fever* (1861), 8.

The death of Prince Albert helped to focus public and preventive attention on specific local causes, although it is a reflection of how much public consciousness of preventive disease increased during the 1860s that the response to the Prince Consort's death was by no means as immediate, in sanitary terms, as that to the illness of the Prince of Wales ten years later. In the early 1860s it seemed to be the sanitarians alone who observed (and that indirectly) a preventive lesson. In January 1862 the *Lancet* reported in some alarm that 'fever' had retreated from the houses of the poor to the homes of the rich: the work of the metropolitan MOHs had driven fever from the former, but 'the houses of the rich have not had the intelligent care and supervision which by law are given to the dwellings of the poor . . . the middle classes of the metropolis are now suffering from typhoid fever—the fever of filth, of sewage gas, and of tainted water'.[83] It was from about this time that George Buchanan and other inspectors of the Medical Department, under the guidance of John Simon, began to look for specific rather than general origins for typhoid. By 1866 Buchanan, surveying the results of public-health works in England and Wales, could produce an individual analysis for typhoid. The drying of town soils and reduction in overcrowding had been generally, but not consistently, followed by a reduction in the fever. Much more important, however, appeared to be the replacement of scanty and impure water supplies by ample supplies of good water; but the purification of the atmosphere from decomposing organic matter by the removal of cesspools and middens and the introduction of drainage had been most uniformly followed by a reduced typhoid incidence.[84] Three years later John Simon noted that the consumption of polluted water was the factor most frequently associated with typhoid outbreaks.[85]

The methodology of detection of local sources of typhoid received several further boosts in the early 1870s. In 1870 Edward Ballard, MOH for Islington, traced a severe outbreak of typhoid in his district to the distribution of contaminated milk.[86] Although this method of disseminating typhoid had been observed as early as 1858,[87] it was only through Ballard's work and in the context of developments during the 1860s that this factor came to be fully appreciated. From 1870 on, milk supply was always checked in typhoid investigations. Yet although milk epidemics were spectacular in their manifestations, they were of relatively rare occurrence. As with the spread of typhoid by consumption of contaminated shellfish, first observed in 1827,[88] such outbreaks were of limited importance compared to the great bulk of endemic typhoid cases attributable to contaminated water, defective drains, carriers, and poor personal hygiene. The sensation which Ballard's investigation caused in

[83] *Lancet* (1862), i. 106.
[84] *MOAR* PC, PP 1867 xxxvii, app. 2, p. 44.
[85] *MOAR* PC, PP 1870 xxxviii, p. 621.
[86] *MOAR* Islington (1870), 7.
[87] By Michael Taylor of Penrith: id., 'On the communication of fever by ingesta', *Edinburgh Monthly Medical Journal* (May 1858).
[88] *Lancet* (1873), i. 247.

preventive circles did not long distract from the fundamentals of drains and water supplies, for typhoid's next appearance on the public stage directed attention straight back to them. In December 1871, exactly ten years after his father's death, Edward, Prince of Wales, contracted typhoid while staying at Londesborough Lodge, Scarborough.

The events at Londesborough Lodge constitute a significant episode in the history of typhoid, as well as in that of the Royal family and of the English country house. The Prince of Wales was not the only victim: Lord Chesterfield and a groom died. In common with general popular beliefs, sewer air was assumed to be to blame. Lord Londesborough called in expert opinion: William Henry Corfield, Professor of Hygiene at University College London. Corfield did not immediately confirm the popular diagnosis, for his epidemiological skills could not overlook one salient fact: the only persons to contract the disease were visitors; none of the regular inmates of the house were affected. His initial, reluctant conclusion that sewer air could not be to blame[89] was overset by caution; although he could find no serious sanitary defects in the house, nor in the water closet used by the prince, there was a defect in another closet and Corfield was 'unable to say positively' that the disease was not contracted there.[90] Rereading his notes on the case at the turn of the century, Corfield suspected that the vehicle of infection had been contaminated food partaken of by the male guests on their shooting party; in 1872, however, his location of one defective closet provided a generally acceptable, and generally accepted, explanation of the outbreak.

The repercussions of Londesborough Lodge were far-reaching. Corfield was established in a flourishing practice as a specialist on the sanitary facilities of country houses; at his death he was said to have remodelled the sanitary arrangements of hundreds.[91] More importantly, perhaps, he was recognized as an authority on sanitary arrangements in general, and embarked upon a successful career as the author of popular works on this subject.[92] Together with his friend, the engineer Rogers Field, he was the pioneer of house sanitation and the first exponent of the 'true principles of a healthy home'.[93] Within a few years healthy-house sanitation had become a rapidly expanding industry, generating a large literature of popular works, and stimulating private sanitary reform on a scale previously unknown.[94] It created a new profession, that of the sanitary engineer. As S. S. Hellyer later remarked, the illness of the Prince

89 *The Times*, 22 Jan. 1872.

90 Corfield, *Typhoid*, 109.

91 *British Medical Journal*, (1902), ii. 628.

92 Among Corfield's publications were: *Foul Air in Houses* (1884); *The History of House Sanitation* (1885); *Dwelling Houses and Their Sanitary Construction* (second edn., 1885); *The Laws of Health* (1896); *Disease and Defective House Sanitation* (1896).

93 *Lancet* (1902), ii. 778.

94 Hellyer, e.g., claimed in his second edition that the plumbing of Marlborough House, Buckingham House, and of a score of gentlemen's residences had been reconstructed on the principles laid down in the first edition (1877) of his book, *The Plumber and Sanitary Houses*: Hellyer, *The Plumber*, p. xv.

of Wales had done more than anything else for the advancement of knowledge of the principles of healthy plumbing: since then architects, civil engineers, medical men, sanitary engineers, and the general public had turned their attention to house drainage and plumbing: 'Suddenly a host of "sanitary engineers" have sprung up, like the 500 Clan Alpine of Roderick Dhu, at a moment's notice.'[95]

THE PROFESSIONALIZATION OF PLUMBING AND LEGAL RESPONSIBILITY FOR DOMESTIC SANITATION

The involvement of private enterprise in sanitary reform on the scale generated by Corfield's work at Londesborough Lodge was something unprecedented in the history of public health, which had hitherto been largely the preserve of philanthropists and public servants, pursued within a framework of laws and by-laws and their enforcement. The reform of the plumber's trade which resulted is one of the unrecognized milestones of public health history. Until the 1870s plumbers were trained on the apprentice system. This involved no formal training: there was generally no attempt to instruct the apprentice systematically in his trade—he was expected to pick up 'whatever crumbs and scraps' of information came his way.[96] There can be little doubt that work standards were in general very low. When William Pole reported on the domestic technology of a constant water supply for London in 1871, he stressed the need for control over the immense amount of plumbing work that would need to be done. The experiences of Manchester and Liverpool in this area had shown how badly this was generally done when uncontrolled: 'and I may here add that I should think in no town in the world do plumbers' work and the plumbing trade stand lower than in London.' In Pole's estimation it would be 'injudicious in the extreme' to trust the implementation of the constant system to the small London plumbers without regulation and control, and he strongly recommended that if necessary, legislation be put through to ensure that this was done.[97] As late as 1885 it was still said that, although more good plumbing work was being done that at any former period, 'most householders can, from sad experience, testify to the fact that inferior or "scamped" plumbers' work prevails to a very considerable extent'.[98] Right up until the end of the century the flow of popular works detailing the plumbing defects commonly found in English housing continued unabated.

The 1870s, however, marked the beginning of an educational revolution in

[95] Ibid., p. xiv.

[96] *Lancet* (1893), ii. 442. Review of J. Wright Clark, *Lectures to Plumbers*: this work has not been traced.

[97] Pole, 'Report on water supply', PP 1872 xlix, p. 732.

[98] Frederick Scott, 'Plumbing and plumbers' work', *Transactions of the Sanitary Institute*, 7 (1885–6), 241.

the plumbing trade. Informally, works such as Hellyer's *The Plumber and Sanitary Houses*, first published in 1877, were aimed specifically at both 'head-workers and hand-workers', that is, at both architects and builders and the ordinary plumber.[99] The 1870s also saw the foundation of the Sanitary Institute of Great Britain, which aimed at disseminating information and guiding public opinion on sanitary matters. Contributors to the institute's congresses, held annually from 1877, included medical officers, sanitary inspectors, civil engineers, sanitary engineers, and plumbers, individuals distinguished in preventive medicine and as well as those who never rose above obscurity. More importantly, perhaps, formal training courses in plumbing began to appear in the curricula of educational institutions attended by working men. By the early 1880s such courses were being offered by the London Polytechnic, and in 1885 the Worshipful Company of Plumbers of London took action, instituting a registration system dependent on training certificates.

By the 1890s the training of plumbers was proceeding on a scientific basis. J. Wright Clark, for example, himself a plumber trained in the old school, was giving lectures at the Polytechnic (now the Central London Polytechnic) to student classes in building and construction work, as well as to architecture and engineering students, and to sanitary officers at the Sanitary Institute. Clark stressed not only the achievement of manual dexterity, but also the understanding of the scientific principles on which the work was based: plumbers must be conversant with elementary chemistry, physics, and mathematics. His course included lectures on the chemical and physical properties of the materials which plumbers handled in their daily work, on the manipulation of metals, and on geometry as applied to plumbing; throughout, he emphasized the importance of planning the work.[100]

The publicity given to the importance of plumbing and the link (albeit erroneously based on sewer air) with disease, had by the 1890s come to involve the general public in paying greater attention to the nature and quality of domestic sanitary facilities. There were signs of active individual attempts to regulate domestic conditions. Several court cases in the later 1880s demonstrated that owners of houses were liable for proper drainage and water supply; and that of *Charley* v. *Jones* showed that lessors could be held responsible for typhoid deemed to have been contracted through faulty house drains.[101] The *Lancet* took up this issue,[102] and made it something of a sanitary crusade. In November 1893, for example, the journal recorded a group of court cases in which three different individuals attempted to win compensation from landlords for death or other inconvenience supposedly caused by defective drains.[103] At the

[99] Hellyer, *The Plumber*, preface to second edn., p. xiii.

[100] *Lancet* (1893), ii. 442

[101] *Public Health* 1 (1888–9), 82, 91, 123; 2 (1889–90), 29.

[102] *Lancet* (1892), ii. 440: *Lancet* Special Commission in relation to the Law and Practice of House-letting, ibid. 490, 667.

[103] *Lancet* (1893), ii. 1,202–3.

West London Police Court a lady wished to know whether she could be compelled to pay rent for an insanitary house. She claimed that, although the landlord had represented the house drains as in perfect order, there had been typhoid fever in the house, and her daughter had died of it. Another lady wanted compensation for being obliged to move out of her house so that the landlord could make sanitary repairs which he had declared done when she took the house. More interestingly, perhaps, and recorded in greater detail, was the case of Samuel Steggall before Islington County Court.

Steggall was a shoemaker who, with his wife and eight children, had moved into the basement flat in Ebenezer Buildings, Rotherfield Street, the previous autumn. Soon after moving in his wife had a sore throat;[104] in November she had rheumatic fever, in February typhoid, and in April diphtheria. In February also five of the children caught typhoid, and two died. The engineer of the Sanitary Protection Society testified that the main soil-pipe of the tenement was laid inside the building (by the standards of the 1890s it should have been outside), was of light cast iron (it should have been of lead), was so badly made that it could not be properly jointed, and was unventilated (the most heinous of plumbing crimes). On these grounds the house was unfit for human habitation. It was further testified that the stench was abominable, and that leakage from the roof descended to the kitchen. Some of this leakage fell into the cistern—which cistern supplied both the water closet and the drinking water (another cardinal sin). On this evidence the jury recorded a verdict in the plaintiff's favour, although allowing only £28 of the £50 claimed in damages.[105] It was against this background that the *Lancet* began to agitate for greater legal definition of a landlord's sanitary responsibilities towards his tenants.[106]

Although it is impossible to quantify the amount or effects of the improvements in domestic plumbing which took place in the later years of the nineteenth century, it is likely that these played their part in the reduction in typhoid incidence. The emphasis placed on the dangers of sewer air, while certainly contributing to the quality of life, meant that large numbers of improvements, such as the taking of soil-pipe ventilator exits away from windows up to the eaves, were of little direct relevance to disease transmission, but the general overhaul of domestic sanitary arrangements also remedied such real defects as mains water-pipes discharging directly into water closets, and the general intercommunication of domestic water supply and drainage pipes, and may have led to the installation of more efficient and hygienic sanitary ware.[107] Further, as contemporaries were aware, the monitoring of house

[104] According to Corfield, sore throats were 'perhaps the commonest manifestations of foul air of any kind': *Disease and Defective House Drainage* (1896), 8.

[105] *Lancet* (1893), ii. 1,202–3.

[106] *Lancet* (1893), ii. 1,203.

[107] For the most up-to-date system of house-sanitation and drainage available in the 1890s, see the description of the arrangements of 5 Queen's Gate, home of the editor of the *Lancet*, in *Public Health*, 2 (1889–90), 124.

drains and water pipes, and the abolition of cesspools and wells, reduced the likelihood of local contamination of household water supplies. The prominent position which house drains came to occupy in the mind of the health-conscious householder possibly also reflects a growing consciousness of domestic hygiene—that greater attention to the cleanliness of closets and to the washing of hands which was of paramount importance in reducing the opportunities for the spread of typhoid within households.[108]

THE DECLINE OF TYPHOID AND LOCAL SANITARY MEASURES: THE EVIDENCE FROM LONDON

The impact of improvements in sanitation and water supply on typhoid incidence and mortality can be broadly gauged by the aggregate mortality figures for London (Table 6.1). The assessment of district mortality figures is more than usually complicated in the case of typhoid after 1871, for not only were cases accepted into the MAB hospitals, but into the large metropolitan teaching hospitals as well.[109] Thus calculations based on the correlation of the registrar-general's figures and those of the MAB, as made by Bill Luckin (Table 6.5),[110] still do not allow for what may have been a considerable mortality in the London hospitals. High typhoid mortalities in Westminster, the City, Marylebone, St Pancras, and Lambeth may simply reflect hospital deaths not belonging to the district. Similarly, death-rates for Islington are more slightly affected by the presence of the smaller London Fever Hospital, which after its pauper service was superseded by the MAB hospitals, took in patients from higher social classes, although after 1888 it virtually stopped taking typhoid cases in order better to meet the demand for scarlet-fever beds (the latter, as a recognized infectious fever, was not treated in the general hospitals). Despite these reservations, Luckin's figures seem likely to be substantially accurate, and are largely supported by Shirley Murphy's corrected data for typhoid deaths by district for the years 1890–9 (Table 6.5).

The Luckin figures being accepted as essentially correct, some interesting correlations may be made at district level when they are set against the background of known local conditions and advances. Charles Murchison recorded in 1858 that typhus and relapsing fever only prevailed to any extent in certain districts, while typhoid was confined to none, and was met with in the most favoured areas of the city. Proceeding from the centre to the suburbs, the proportion of typhus and relapsing fever to typhoid diminished, until the former

108 Evidence of developments in personal hygiene are, however, difficult to come by.

109 e.g. in November 1877 the eight general hospitals had sixty-seven typhoid cases under treatment between them: *Lancet* (1877), ii. 668.

110 Luckin, 'Typhus and typhoid', 108–9; 'Typhoid Fever', 124.

TABLE 6.4. *Typhoid mortality in London registration districts, 1851–1900, per 100,000 population*

District	1851–60	1861–70	1871–80	1881–90	1891–1900
	(Typhoid and typhus)				
Kensington	61	54	21	22	10
Chelsea	77	70	29	16	13
Westminster*	87	81	32	23	27
Marylebone	68	61	27	18	13
Hampstead	65	31	20	19	11
St Pancras	72	67	29	23	16
Islington	77	76	32	24	13
Hackney	83	71	33	27	13
St Giles	93	100	23	19	13
Holborn	78	100	30	19	16
City	104	136	48	29	18
Shoreditch	132	120	34	20	16
Bethnal Green	102	119	36	21	19
Whitechapel	116	135	42	39	13
St George-in-the-East	100	152	35	17	17
Stepney and Mile End	101	123	32	25	18
Poplar	70	113	32	24	19
St Saviour†	92	98	32	15	17
St Olave‡	103	101	34	20	17
Lambeth	76	85	35	25	12
Wandsworth	66	60	27	16	12
Camberwell	56	64	32	15	10
Greenwich	91	104	41	30	20
Lewisham	57	56	25	12	8
Woolwich	—	—	34	12	4
TOTAL	87	89	30	18	12

Notes:
* includes St George's, Hanover Square, Westminster, St Martin, St James's, and Strand; † includes St Saviour, St George and Newington; ‡ includes St Olave, Bermondsey and Rotherhithe.

Source: W. Luckin, 'Typhus and typhoid', in Woods and Woodward (eds.), *Urban Disease and Mortality* (1986), table 5.1, pp. 108–9.

vanished altogether.[111] During the years *c*.1850–65 there was no unusual prevalence of typhoid in London, judging by the steady LFH admissions and contemporary observation. Fever mortality in the outer and the wealthier districts at this time was probably very largely from typhoid. The decreases in

[111] Murchison, 'The etiology of continued fever', *Medico-Chirurgical Transactions*, 41 (1858), 251.

TABLE 6.5. *Typhoid and diarrhoea in London sanitary districts, 1890–1900, fully corrected death-rates*

	Typhoid				Diarrhoea	
	Case-rate per 1,000		Death-rate per 1,000		Death-rate per 1,000	
District	1891–9	1900	1891-9	1900	1891-9	1900
Paddington	0.5	0.4	0.11	0.06	0.61	0.75
Kensington	0.6	0.6	0.11	0.1	0.53	0.62
Fulham	0.5	0.7	0.11	0.14	1.18	1.09
Hammersmith	0.6	0.9	0.12	0.15	0.86	0.86
Chelsea	0.7	0.9	0.13	0.2	0.69	0.8
St George's, Hanover Square	0.6	0.7	0.12	0.14	0.32	0.22
Westminster	0.6	0.6	0.11	0.17	0.64	0.42
St James's	0.7	0.6	0.17	0.14	0.36	0.34
Marylebone	0.7	0.6	0.14	0.09	0.58	0.66
Hampstead	0.6	0.6	0.09	0.11	0.29	0.27
St Pancras	0.8	1.5	0.14	0.27	0.73	0.86
Islington	0.7	0.8	0.12	0.15	0.61	0.53
Hackney	1.0	1.0	0.17	0.19	0.7	0.69
St Giles	0.7	0.9	0.16	0.14	0.53	0.54
St Martin	0.8	0.8	0.11	0.25	0.3	0.34
Strand	0.6	0.5	0.15	0.19	0.54	0.39
Holborn	1.0	0.8	0.18	0.13	0.74	0.8
Clerkenwell	0.9	0.9	0.17	0.09	0.97	0.84
St Luke	0.7	0.8	0.12	0.16	1.13	1.21
City	1.0	1.1	0.2	0.07	0.22	0.15
Shoreditch	0.9	1.1	0.15	0.12	1.17	1.29
Bethnal Green	1.0	1.2	0.18	0.14	0.89	0.81
Whitechapel	0.7	1.0	0.13	0.11	0.68	0.62
St George-in-the-East	1.0	1.3	0.15	0.21	1.37	1.03
Limehouse	1.1	1.3	0.17	0.12	0.95	1.12
Mile End	0.9	1.1	0.17	0.2	0.87	0.95
Poplar	1.3	1.6	0.21	0.28	0.9	1.29
St Saviour	0.5	1.2	0.08	0.26	0.79	1.15
St George's, Southwark	0.6	3.0	0.12	0.2	1.15	1.45
Newington	0.7	0.8	0.12	0.17	0.95	0.97
St Olave	0.6	0.6	0.14	n/a	0.86	0.28
Bermondsey	0.7	1.5	0.13	0.33	0.8	0.95
Rotherhithe	1.1	2.0	0.17	0.26	0.79	0.93
Lambeth	0.6	0.9	0.1	0.18	0.73	0.59
Battersea	0.7	1.2	0.13	0.19	0.78	0.91
Wandsworth	0.6	0.7	0.1	0.12	0.63	0.65
Camberwell	0.6	0.7	0.11	0.13	0.72	0.76

	Typhoid				Diarrhoea	
	Case-rate per 1,000		Death-rate per 1,000		Death-rate per 1,000	
District	1891–9	1900	1891–9	1900	1891–9	1900
Greenwich	1.1	1.0	0.17	0.13	0.78	0.8
Lewisham	0.5	0.6	0.08	0.12	0.57	0.64
Woolwich	0.6	0.6	0.14	0.07	0.75	1.33
Lee	0.7	0.4	0.09	0.09	0.42	0.44
Plumstead	0.7	0.6	0.11	0.13	0.6	0.52
TOTAL	0.8	1.0	0.13	0.16	0.74	0.78

Source: *MOAR* LCC (1900), 36, 39.

mortality registered in all the western and northern districts (Table 6.5),[112] and in the two most rural southern districts, Wandsworth and Lewisham, in the decade 1861–70 against 1851–60, probably reflect a reduction in typhoid incidence and mortality, stemming from sanitary improvements, and, less certainly for the latter, from improved water supplies.[113] Except for Hampstead, where the decrease amounted to 52.3 per cent, the gains were modest—an average of only 8.0 per cent in the ten districts concerned. In two, Islington and Lewisham, the decrease was less than 2 per cent.

Some indication of the type of sanitary progress made in these years can be ascertained from the experience of the district of St Olave, a poor and long-inhabited parish immediately to the south of the river.[114] Here the medical officer, Dr Vinen, described the sanitary changes effected in the district in the twenty years since he had taken office (1855–6 to 1875–6).[115] Viewed in the historical perspective, it may be considered that, on balance, the drainage improvements may have been more significant than those of water supply. With regard to the latter in 1856, many courts and streets had only obtained a supply from a small iron pipe leading from the main. There had never been more than two or three pipes to a court (containing perhaps twenty houses),

[112] Kensington, Chelsea, Westminster, Marylebone, Hampstead, St Pancras, Islington, and Hackney.

[113] In 1858 the medical officer for Wandsworth recorded that water had been laid on to only one house in that year: great numbers of the poor residents took their drinking supplies straight from the Thames and Wandle, which were little but dilute sewage: *MOAR* Wandsworth (1858), 8–9. By 1865 things had perhaps progressed sufficiently for him to note that the water-company supply was still intermittent and partial: *MOAR* Wandsworth (1865), 15–16.

[114] According to Luckin's calculations, mortality in the *registration district* of St Olave (that is, in that parish, Bermondsey, and Rotherhithe), fell from 103 per 100,000 in 1851–60 (for typhus and typhoid) to 34 per 100,000 in 1871–80 (typhoid only): Luckin, 'Typhus and typhoid', 108–9.

[115] *MOAR* St Olave (1875–6), 20–2.

and the water had been turned on for only half or three-quarters of an hour daily. People had flocked to these stand-pipes, and their scanty supplies had been stored in open tubs, pans, and the like; even in houses with a separate supply, the 'most objectionable receptacles'—pans and butter firkins—'uncovered and decaying' had been in constant use. By 1876 the stand-pipes had been 'long abolished'; every house not separately supplied received water from one or more large cisterns which supplied the whole court; water was turned on daily, including Sundays; and the unsuitable receptacles were gradually giving way to closely covered cisterns of galvanized iron.[116] If far from ideal, the provision of water supplies in St Olave had certainly been improved in the first twenty years of Vinen's administration.

It was a similar story with the drainage of St Olave. In 1856 large open privies and cesspools had proliferated in the small backyards of the small terraced houses, and the need to empty these had from time to time caused an 'intolerable nuisance' to the whole neighbourhood.[117] In the twenty years that followed some 700 cesspools had been abolished; and by 1876 Vinen was not aware of a single cesspool extant in the district. During this time water closets had been widely provided, and pans, traps, and water scrupulously supplied to every closet. In addition, 'immense numbers' of house drains had been constructed, and Vinen evidently felt that the sanitary condition of the district had been entirely, and satisfactorily, reconstituted. While other medical officers did not feel obliged to provide similar retrospective vignettes of sanitary improvement at this period, it is evident from their listings of achievements in this quarter that a very great deal of such mundane but significant work was achieved during these first twenty years of their responsibility.

If St Olave provides an example of the effects of steady sanitary effort by medical officer and staff, a more dramatic case is furnished by the East End parish of Shoreditch. Shoreditch was the one exception to the general London pattern of decreased fever mortality in wealthy and rural areas and increased (probably on account of epidemic typhus) fever mortality in the central southern and eastern districts in the 1860s. Here fever mortality decreased by 9 per cent, despite the presence of epidemic typhus. Slum-clearances for the railways in this decade, and their replacement by model dwellings with improved sanitary facilities and piped water, may have contributed to this result.[118] More important, perhaps, was the work of the parish sanitary department. When this was established in the mid-1850s Shoreditch was notorious for the prevalence of typhoid.[119] The medical officer, Dr Barnes, reported that the whole surface soil of the district was sodden with faecal matter, the soakage of cesspools; this layer of foul earth was from one to sixteen feet deep, and undoubtedly contaminated the wells.[120] As a result, the sanitary department's programme largely featured the building of drains, the closing of wells, and the extension of piped

[116] *MOAR* St Olave (1875–6), 20–1. [117] Ibid. 21. [118] *MOAR* Shoreditch (1863), 13.
[119] Murchison, 'Etiology', 254. [120] Ibid. 274.

water supplies. By 1863 Barnes was able to report considerable improvements in drainage and the condition of dwellings in the parish.[121] The presence of the Regent's Canal was almost certainly a further factor contributing to a high typhoid mortality, as at this period the London canals were used for both drainage and water-supply purposes by local inhabitants. The records of St Mary's Hospital, for example, show that typhoid was very common in those streets which were in the immediate vicinity of the Paddington Canal Basin;[122] while, no doubt for similar reasons, Dr Orton of Limehouse in 1866 recorded 300 cholera deaths within 200 yards of the Regent's Canal.[123]

The decline of typhoid in Shoreditch during the 1860s must have been due very largely to the efforts of the sanitary department, but the impact of improved water supplies is difficult to assess. The district was served by both the East London and the New River companies. With the passing of the Metropolis Water Act 1854, both these companies were obliged to adopt improved standards of water storage and filtration, although their sources of supply remained unchanged. As the East London cholera epidemic of 1866 proved, the arrangements of the East London Company at least were fallible, and before Frankland's regular monitoring of the companies' services in the later 1860s was recorded, there is no means of telling how often such 'accidents' occurred. Unlike cholera, the distribution of typhoid bacilli through water supply would result in scattered and apparently disconnected cases over a wide area and with no marked time-sequence; in a city where the disease was in any case endemic, this type of distribution is difficult to pin-point. Further, until the later 1860s company water was not widely distributed to London's poor, who often relied on the local surface wells, as well as on rivers and canals, for their domestic supplies. The apparent decline of typhoid in Shoreditch during the 1860s is likely to have been in response to the sanitary department's attempts to cope with the linked problems of surface-soil pollution, drainage, and polluted wells—problems which had been recognized by sanitarians since the 1840s.[124]

During the 1880s Shoreditch shared in the general London pattern of a sharp decline in typhoid mortality. In this decade the death-rate in the eastern and central districts fell by 31.5 per cent against 1871–80, compared with 21.4 per cent for the western and northern districts (to which Kensington proved a remarkable exception, with an increase of 4.7 per cent), and 45.5 per cent for the southern districts. This general fall across London was probably much more closely linked to the improving quality of company water, and to its increasingly wide distribution through the poorer areas of the city. By 1874 constant company water was generally supplied in the northern part of Whitechapel, and by 1879 the whole of Shoreditch was similarly supplied.[125]

[121] *MOAR* Shoreditch (1863), 13.
[122] Murchison, 'Etiology', 274.
[123] *MOAR* Limehouse (1866), 5.
[124] Hardy, 'Water supply'.
[125] *MOQR* Whitechapel (2, 1874), 9; *MOAR* Shoreditch (1877–8), 32.

By 1884 the entire metropolitan area of the East London Company was on constant service, and progress in this direction was being made by nearly all the London companies.[126] Despite this progress in supplying greater quantities of better-quality water to the East End, the comparative experiences of Shoreditch and Whitechapel in these years demonstrate the balance between water and drainage systems in the causation of typhoid, and the necessity of improving both to a sanitary standard if levels of typhoid mortality were to be reduced.

Whitechapel, according to Bill Luckin's calculations, was the singular exception to the pattern of marked improvement in typhoid death-rates in the East End in the 1880s. In this district a fall of only 7.1 per cent over the 1870s was registered. For this slower improvement, the district's social structure and environmental problems were perhaps partly responsible. It was in this decade that the district became in effect the reception centre for poor Jewish immigrants from Russia and Poland. Although few settled permanently in Whitechapel, the ever-increasing stream of these immigrants, especially after 1881, completely changed the character of the district by the end of the century.[127] As a riverside parish containing St Katharine's Dock, Whitechapel had always had a migratory population, and had long been notorious for its insanitary conditions. John Liddle observed in 1864 that conditions had greatly improved compared with 1846,[128] but the general condition of the district remained far from satisfactory.[129] The district had long contained an established Jewish community; it was also well placed to take in immigrants arriving at the London docks. Already from the 1860s a steady stream of Russian and Polish Jews were entering the country through Whitechapel, and many of them settled in the district.[130] When, following the assassination of Tsar Alexander II in 1881, successive waves of terror affected Jews throughout Eastern Europe,[131] the district became the focus of large-scale immigrant arrivals: it has been estimated that 100,000 Jews arrived in Britain during the years 1881–1905, and that between 2,000 and 5,000 per annum were added to the total of London Jewry.[132] The influx of newly arrived, short-stay immigrants aggravated existing sanitary problems in Whitechapel in particular, notably in the years before 1884 when the Jewish Board of Guardians took up sanitary work in earnest.

Death-rates from typhoid in Whitechapel in the 1870s and 1880s were the

[126] Hardy, 'Water supply'.

[127] *MOAR* Whitechapel (1894), 3. See also V. D. Lipman, *A Social History of the Jews in England* (1954), 66, 94–9, 105.

[128] *MOAR* Whitechapel (1862), 8.

[129] The district was described in Charles Booth (ed.), *Life and Labour of the People* (1892 edn.), i. 63–70.

[130] Lipman, *Social History*, 66.

[131] Ibid. 85–6.

[132] Ibid. 86–8, 94. The transformation of Whitechapel and of neighbouring Mile End and St George-in-the-East are described in detail on pp. 95–8.

highest in London. The influx of poor Jewish migrants was almost certainly a factor in this.[133] On arrival, the immigrants were weary, travel-stained, and confused. Most probably possessed little experience of urban life; and sanitary facilities of the London type (water-closets) were strange to them. At night they crowded into tenement houses whose basic sanitary facilities were strained to the utmost by over-use.[134] Contemporary observers stressed the initial difficulties which the immigrants had in adjusting to English urban conditions,[135] while the difficulty of maintaining sanitary standards in housing occupied by the migratory class was well known.[136] Although piped drinking-water supplies were becoming common in the East End in these years, water was not automatically laid on to water-closets, and while William Pole had been impressed by the domestic routine of flushing closets among London's poor, the need for this elementary chore was not immediately obvious to immigrants used to earth closets and old-fashioned privies. In these circumstances, it is likely that the influx of Jewish migrants sustained typhoid infection in Whitechapel through the 1870s. The vulnerability of city immigrants to the disease is well attested,[137] and although the Jews were said to be unusually immune to attacks of cholera and typhus, neither of these immunities precludes vulnerability to typhoid.[138]

In sharp contrast with the 1880s, typhoid mortality in Whitechapel fell by a remarkable 66.6 per cent in the 1890s. Since the immigration rate increased rather than diminished in these years, the achievement is the more surprising, and reflects considerable credit on the Jewish Board of Guardians, which had adopted a broad-ranging policy of sanitary improvement among its people after 1884.[139] Throughout the 1870s and early 1880s Whitechapel's sanitary problems had been compounded by the limited manpower of its sanitary department,[140] by vestry indifference, and by problems of communication between Russian and Polish immigrants and the English health officials.[141] Although the Jewish Board of Guardians appointed its own inspector to supervise its

[133] Recent American research has thrown considerable light on the health problems caused by immigrant populations. See R. Higgs and D. Booth, 'Mortality differentials within large American cities in 1890', *Human Ecology*, 7 (1979), 353–69; R. A. Meckel, 'Immigration, mortality and population growth in Boston, 1840–1880', *Journal of Interdisciplinary History*, 15 : 3 (Winter 1985), 393–417.

[134] *MOQR* Whitechapel (3, 1879), 9.

[135] *MOAR* St George-in-the-East (1887), 57; *MOAR* Mile End Old Town (1888–9), 69; *MOAR* Bethnal Green (1893), 6.

[136] *Lancet* (1893), ii. 1,312.

[137] Murchison, 'Etiology', 282 and *Continued Fevers*, 455.

[138] Such claims for cholera were disputed by Edward Headlam Greenhow: *Lancet* (1855), i. 50. Cholera was certainly not unknown among London Jews: between 28 July and 11 August 1866 the Jewish Board of Guardians relieved 391 cholera victims and their families, giving an approximate case-rate of 12 per 1,000 persons: *Lancet* (1866), ii. 223.

[139] Lipman, *Social History*, 105–6; id., *A Century of Social Service 1859–1959: The Jewish Board of Guardians* (1959), 66.

[140] One medical officer and two inspectors for a population of the poorest type.

[141] *Lancet* (1869), i. 265, noted that the peculiarity of the Polish Jews' dialect made it equally incomprehensible to both English and German speakers. See also *MOAR* Bethnal Green (1893), 6.

poor from 1874, and claimed in the 1880s a gradual but distinct improvement in conditions,[142] it is significant of the problems posed by an immigrant and mobile population that it was not until the later 1880s, when the Jewish Guardians undertook a programme of rebuilding and population dispersal, that typhoid mortality began to decline. As late as 1891 the *Lancet*, while congratulating the board on its efforts, stressed the need not merely for inspection but for education, suggesting the distribution of leaflets and exertion of the rabbis' influence towards inculcating an understanding of the importance of cleanliness and the dangers of unwholesome surroundings.[143]

The Whitechapel experience, when taken in conjunction with that of Shoreditch, may also illustrate the importance of local sanitary policies in relation to typhoid death-rates. Although Whitechapel had an able, articulate and dedicated MOH in John Liddle,[144] and although company water for drinking purposes became generally available in the district in the 1870s, parish policy towards domestic sanitary arrangements was of the traditional kind, based on the assumption that the poorest classes were too hard on domestic sanitary ware to be trusted with the most modern type of conveniences. Evidence of ignorance about the true uses and treatment of water-closets certainly exists. In 1865, for example, Dr Beale of St Martin-in-the-Fields stressed the bad habits of tenement families in this respect. They used vessels in their rooms in preference to the water closet, and these were emptied into the closet once a day, so carelessly, wrote Beale, that the seat was made unfit for use, while the closet itself was often virtually inaccessible from the variety of rubbish dumped there: the general state of closets in tenement houses was one of the greatest difficulties of sanitary work, and the fault lay with the tenants, not the landlords.[145] It seems clear, however, that there was only one closet per house: although Beale insisted that even if there were half-a-dozen, bad habits would still have to be overcome, it seems likely that a shorter journey to the closet might have helped the process of education considerably. Nevertheless, problems of closet maintenance evidently existed, and continued to be a thorn in the side of MOHs and landlords for many years: in 1884 Bristowe of Camberwell was adamant about the difficulty of maintaining sanitary facilities in the poorest class of housing.[146]

In the light of such evidence, the policies of Whitechapel's sanitary department are more comprehensible. Although Liddle regarded it as essential that

142 Lipman, *A Century*, 125–6.

143 *Lancet* (1891), i. 732. In this year also the MOH for Mile End praised the board's educational efforts: *MOAR* Mile End Old Town (1891), 11.

144 *Lancet* (1879), i. 750. The journal observed that the twenty-three years of Liddle's service as MOH had seen the transformation of Whitechapel; Liddle thoroughly appreciated the functions of a medical officer of health, and considering the peculiarities of the district, the *Lancet* marvelled that so much had been achieved.

145 *MOAR* St Martin-in-the-Fields (1865), 20–1.

146 *MOAR* Camberwell (1883–4), 160–3.

privies in poor localities be furnished with pans and traps, water was not commonly supplied to these closets as it was in better-class housing with only one family per house. Liddle did not think this form of closet-hygiene desirable, thinking it 'infinitely preferable' that the pans should be pail-flushed a couple of times a day. He claimed, in 1880, that this plan had been practised satisfactorily in Whitechapel for many years: the ordinary water-supply apparatus of closets frequently broke down, causing a disgusting and dangerous nuisance. It was therefore an ineligible system for those unlikely to take proper care of it, or unable to afford to have it properly repaired.[147] Thus it was that the Jewish Board of Guardians was appalled to find, in 1884, that 1,621 houses out of 1,747 (92.8 per cent) visited were unprovided with any arrangement for flushing the drains. Under pressure from the Jewish community vestry policy eventually changed, and by 1890 only 2 per cent of the closets inspected were without flush.[148] The later 1880s thus seem to have been marked in Whitechapel by a considerable improvement in the general level of domestic hygiene, whose nature is possibly reflected in the dramatic percentage decline in the typhoid death-rate of the 1890s.

THE FINAL ERADICATION OF TYPHOID, 1890–1914

The 1890s witnessed a continuing decline in aggregate typhoid mortality for London as a whole. Nevertheless, problems remained, as the rising death-rate in the last years of the century suggests (Fig. 6.2). In the 1890s London's health authorities returned to the question of water-related typhoid distribution,[149] at least in part as a result of the political agitation against the London water companies which the creation of the LCC had brought to a head. London experienced three years of above-average typhoid mortality in the decade 1891–1900: 1893, 1899, and 1900. In 1894 also a change was observed in the seasonal pattern of the disease: instead of the heaviest mortality falling in the three autumn months (August–October), it occurred in the winter months of November and December.[150] In a paper to the Royal Commission on Water Supply, Shirley Murphy, medical officer of the newly created LCC, had suggested that the Lea water, rather than poverty, was responsible for the higher typhoid mortalities experienced by East London in the years 1885–92.[151] In his calculations for these years, Murphy found that, on average, the districts served by the Lea companies, the East London and the New River, experienced a far higher typhoid case-rate than those served by other London companies (Table 6.7). This was equally the case in 1894 (Table 6.8);

[147] *MOQR* Whitechapel (3, 1880), 10–11.
[148] *Lancet* (1891), i. 732.
[149] Luckin, 'Typhus and typhoid', 116–17; 'Typhoid fever', 129–134.
[150] Corfield, *Typhoid*, 73.
[151] RCMWS, PP 1893–4, xl (part ii), app. C 17, pp. 212–16; app. C 18, pp. 216–23.

TABLE 6.6. *Water supply and typhoid fever in London, 1885–1892*

Water company	Mean population, 1885–92	Typhoid death-rate per million	Comparative mortality (London = 100)
Kent	122,533	89	65
Thames	1,683,617	119	88
Kent and Thames	487,287	135	99
New River and Thames	366,555	137	101
New River	496,909	147	108
New River and East London	458,723	155	114
East London	504,063	179	132

Source: *RCMWS*, PP 1893–4 xl, part II, app. C.18, table A, p. 221.

TABLE 6.7. *Average weekly typhoid cases occurring in London water-company districts, 1894*

New River	14.7	Middlesex	6.7
East London	13.9	Kent	4.8
Southwark	9.8	Chelsea	4.1
Lambeth	6.7	Grand Junction	2.8

Source: *MOAR* LCC (1894), 34.

nevertheless, in the crucial weeks 46–52 of 1894, when cases occurring in all other districts were way above average, notifications in the East London, as well as in the Kent, district were relatively low.[152]

Shirley Murphy's work, taken in conjunction with the various annual district-mortality figures for the 1890s, confirmed that complex environmental factors were more important than mere poverty in determining the distribution of typhoid: the increased case-rate observed in the winter months was associated with exceptional river flooding, which overburdened the company filtration systems.[153] The correspondence between the curve of London typhoid mortality and the national curve reveals that this was more than a local metropolitan problem (Fig. 6.1), and suggests the extent to which contemporary waterworks were in need of further technical refinement,[154] but perhaps also the importance of meteorological factors such as were indicated in the LFH reports during the 1860s. Meanwhile the variations in mortality at district level in London during the 1890s suggest that water supply alone was not the most critical of environmental factors involved in typhoid distribution at this period

[152] *MOAR* LCC (1894), 34, app. 1.

[153] Luckin, 'Typhus and typhoid', 116–17.

[154] The revelations of the Tyne-Tees Typhoid Inquiry in respect of this particular subject led the *Lancet* to draw this conclusion from the increased typhoid mortality of 1893: *Lancet* (1893), ii. 1,198; F. W. Barry, 'Report on enteric fever in the Tees valley'. *MOAR* LGB, PP 1893–4 xlii, pp. 261–528.

(Table 6.5). Although aggregate case and fatality rates within the East London and New River districts indicate a role for water supply, a closer inspection of district rates indicates the importance of other factors, for the annual rise and fall of rates is not consistent within water-company areas. Thus, in 1900 the typhoid death-rate of Islington was above its average for the years 1890–9, while that of Holborn was below (Table 6.4); both were exclusively served with water by the New River Company. Although the City, which received water from the Lea and had a poverty ratio of 31.5 per cent, suffered severely from typhoid throughout the 1890s, achieving one of the highest average typhoid death-rates for the years 1890–9 (20 per 100,000), Islington, which also received Lea water and had a very similar level of poverty (31.2 per cent), experienced no more than a moderate excess over the London average in 1892 and 1896, and achieved a decennial score below the London average (12 per 100,000). The districts served entirely by the East London Company (Bethnal Green, St George-in-the-East, Mile End, Limehouse, and Poplar) did have a mortality almost consistently above average in these years, but Whitechapel and Shoreditch, which were shared by the New River and East London, only experienced marked excess mortality in 1899, and achieved low overall averages (Table 6.4). Water supply, which was a factor of importance, was not the only element determining the incidence and mortality of typhoid.

The case for continuing intermittent slight infection of piped drinking-water supplies has been convincingly argued by Bill Luckin,[155] but the vagaries of district typhoid and diarrhoea incidence during the 1890s, and the downward trends of both from the early years of the twentieth century, suggests the continuing importance of other factors in determining the prevalence of the enteric group of diseases. Local factors relating to drainage and refuse-disposal were probably notably important in determining levels of local infection, although the likelihood of imported cases must always confuse such evaluations. In the years just after 1900, however, a number of different factors came into play which may have affected the incidence of typhoid more generally, bringing about a sharp down-turn in mortality. While contemporary propagandists related the decline of typhoid in London from 1902 to the provisions of the Metropolis Water Act of that year (Fig. 6.3), by which the ownership of the city's water companies was transferred to the Metropolitan Water Board,[156] it is plain that the transfer of the water-supply undertakings had nothing to do with the case: the Act was passed in 1902, but its provisions did not come into force until 1904.[157] Among other factors for consideration, the seasonal incidence which was so marked a feature of typhoid, as of diarrhoea (Fig. 6.4), indicates the possibly considerable role of flies as a source of

[155] Luckin, 'Typhoid fever', 134–5.

[156] *Morning Post*, 9 Dec. 1935.

[157] Metropolis Water Act 1902, 2 Edw. VII, c. 41. The 'appointed day' for the Metropolitan Water Board to take over the companies was 24 June 1904: ibid., sec. 37.

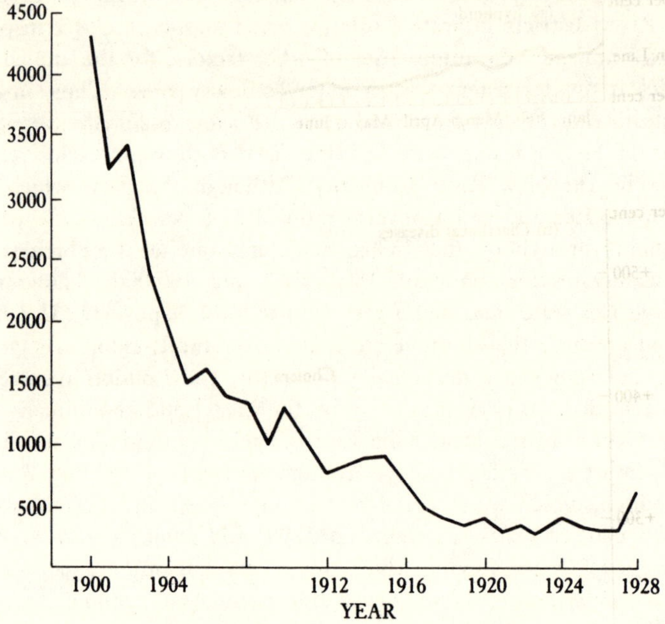

FIG. 6.3. *Typhoid cases in London, 1900–1928.*

infection, while changes in preventive and hospital practice were perhaps of crucial significance.

Flies were ubiquitous in the Victorian city: the horse population alone ensured that;[158] and the seasonal peak of the annual typhoid curve coincided with that of greatest fly activity, at the time of year when harvesting and fruit-cropping meant that farmers were often too busy regularly to relieve the city of its manure.[159] Following the discovery that the granular opthalmia of Egypt was transmitted by flies in the region of the Nile, the English medical profession became increasingly aware of flies as a possible source of disease during the 1880s. As early as 1871, indeed, the *Lancet* was drawing attention to errors in an elementary school-book, which asserted that the fly kept the air 'pure and wholesome by its zig-zag flight'; there could be no doubt, warned the journal, that flies were frequent carriers of impurities and unwholesomeness;

[158] The British horse population peaked in 1902 at some three-and-a-half million animals; each of these was estimated to produce between six and seven-and-a-half tons of droppings annually: F. M. L. Thompson, *Victorian England: The Horsedrawn Society* (1970), 10, 19.

[159] *Lancet* (1861), ii. 382. In the colder months, farmers brought hay and other produce into London in their carts, and returned with the city's manure. In the summer, being busy elsewhere, they sent the hay by rail; thus the manure, 'which should be removed daily', was left to rot during the hottest months.

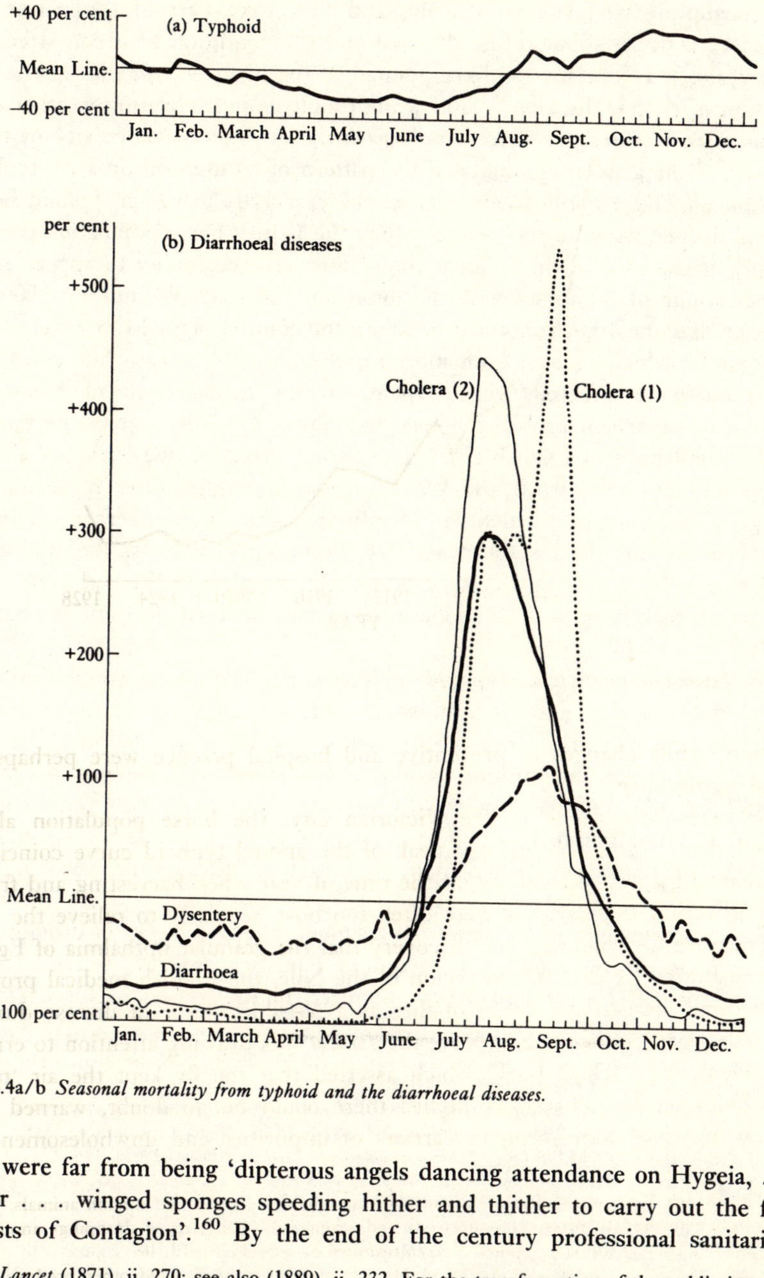

FIG. 6.4a/b *Seasonal mortality from typhoid and the diarrhoeal diseases.*

they were far from being 'dipterous angels dancing attendance on Hygeia, . . . rather . . . . winged sponges speeding hither and thither to carry out the foul behests of Contagion'.[160] By the end of the century professional sanitarians

[160] *Lancet* (1871), ii. 270; see also (1889), ii. 232. For the transformation of the public image of the fly in America, from household friend to household enemy, between 1890 and 1920, see Naomi Rogers, 'Germs with legs: flies, disease and the new public health', *Bulletin of the History of Medicine*, 63 (1989), 599–617.

were beginning to focus on the fly, and flies were part of the reason for increasing concern about refuse-disposal and the condition of urban streets in these years.[161] Historians too have pointed to the likely role of flies in the distribution of enteric diseases,[162] and while problems in correlating weather conditions with disease-prevalence emphasizes the etiological complexity of these diseases,[163] the general reliability of the pattern of autumn maxima for typhoid is significant. By a curious coincidence, the year 1902 in which typhoid began its final decline was also the year in which the British horse population peaked. Already at the turn of the century complaints were beginning to appear about the behaviour of motorists towards horses on the roads,[164] and by 1906 the presence of some 10,000 motor cars across the country signalled a reduction in horse traffic which became even more rapid after 1914. Meanwhile concerned sanitarians were effecting improvements in the management of roads and refuse-disposal which probably helped to reduce, in some degree, the swarming fly populations of English cities. In London, street paving with asphalt was progressing by 1900, while the LCC introduced new by-laws regarding the storage of horse-manure which considerably reduced the number of local complaints about the city's stables; and, as importantly perhaps, the traditional fixed dust-holes which had received household refuse since the eighteenth century began to be replaced by modern, moveable, covered dustbins during the 1890s.[165]

The seasonal pattern of typhoid incidence was something which had long intrigued sanitarians, and correlations had often been made between weather conditions and the prevalence of the disease. In 1860, for example, the cold and rainy summer and autumn produced an 'interesting' decline in typhoid cases.[166] In 1865, however, the opposite was the case: the excess prevalence of typhoid was thought to be in great measure due to the 'exaggerated climatic conditions' favouring its development. The number of cases increased in June, with the arrival of several weeks of hot, dry weather, and its incidence increased as the summer advanced. By October, after six weeks of drought and a mean temperature of 66.5°F, it acquired a further lease of life, and admissions to the LFH were still over a hundred in the month of December.[167]

161 E. Shrapnel Smith, 'Some sanitary and allied advantages attending the introduction and use of motor vehicles', *Journal of the Sanitary Institute*, 20 (1899), 72–6; W. Nisbet Blair, 'The insanitary condition of London streets', ibid., 21 (1900), 304.

162 R. S. Lambert, *Sir John Simon, 1816–1904, and English Social Administration* (Bristol, 1965), 600; Ian Buchanan, 'Infant feeding, sanitation, and diarrhoea in colliery communities, 1880–1911', in D. J. Oddy and D. S. Miller (eds.), *Diet and Health in Modern Britain* (1985), 148–77.

163 L. C. Parkes, 'The common house fly (*Musca Domestica*)', *Journal of the Royal Sanitary Institute*, 32 (1911), 279–80.

164 *The Times*, 27 Aug. 1901. The initial letter was inspired by the report of a 'dangerous accident' involving a carriage and a motor car at Rickerstoke on 24 August. It was followed by a spate of correspondence on the subject; see *The Times*, 28–31 Aug. and 3, 5, 6, 10, 12, 13, 18, 21 Sept. 1901.

165 *MOAR* Kensington (1898), 141; (1899), 190.

166 *LFH Ann. Rep.* (1861), 7.

167 Ibid. (1865), 7.

These examples of climatic influence on typhoid incidence suggest the influence of weather conditions on both drinking-water supplies and fly populations, as do the raised typhoid mortalities of the hot summers of the 1890s. Yet there were—and are—no easy correlations to be made on the relationship between climate and typhoid incidence. Louis Parkes, who attempted a closer examination of the whole question, came to the realistic conclusion that the influence of rainfall and temperature on the seasonal prevalence of typhoid, however real, was obscured by the operation of 'other influences' still to be investigated.[168] These still await fuller historical investigation.

These 'other influences' probably played a central part in the continuing, if declining, incidence of endemic typhoid from the 1890s, and among them personal cleanliness, as Major Greenwood noted, seems likely to have been of paramount importance.[169] The swifter decline in typhoid mortality among women (Table 6.3), who are more open to hygienic education, is suggestive here. In the decade 1871–80, in which elementary education became compulsory, the preventive organization was extended to all urban and rural areas, and the Sanitary Institute launched its hygiene crusade upon the English people, the excess typhoid mortality of men over women stood at 11 per cent. By 1901–10 it was 84 per cent. As the registrar-general observed (and it was an observation that applied to young children as well as to women: 'Conceivably household infection has become a less potent influence in spreading the disease than it was when the methods of transmission were less understood. The effect of such a change would of course be felt mainly by females, as the nursing sex.'[170] The changing age-incidence pattern which accompanied the decline equally indicates that rising standards of personal hygiene were influential: children under 5 are those most amenable to maternal sanitary discipline, while the elderly, for whom life moves at a slower pace, were perhaps more likely to take time and trouble in small matters of personal hygiene than those engaged in an active working life.

While hand-washing and clean food-handling practices were clearly fundamental precautions in preventing the spread of typhoid, social factors also came into play; it was far more difficult to maintain hygienic standards when nursing typhoid victims in overcrowded conditions, where access to lavatory facilities and running water were often distant from the patient. Among the salient features of the decline of typhoid—perhaps more convincingly than diminishing quantities of stored horse manure—was, therefore, the greater awareness among the medical profession of the role of carriers in disseminating

[168] Louis Parkes, 'On the seasonal prevalence of enteric fever', *Transactions of the Epidemiological Society* 11 (1891–2), 110.

[169] Greenwood, *Epidemics*, 158.

[170] *RGDS* (1919), part III, p. lxi. As regards the reduction in child mortality, the registrar-general noted (p. lx): 'It is conceivable that thirty or forty years ago many deaths of children resulted from infection in the home from their elders which would now be prevented by modern methods of nursing and isolation.'

typhoid, and the more stringent hospitalization of typhoid cases.[171] While typhoid cases had been received into the MAB hospitals from their inception, the proportion of admissions to notified cases rose steadily throughout the 1890s; in 1902, for the first time, the proportion of hospitalized cases rose to over 50 per cent, and only once fell slightly below that percentage up to 1911 (Table 6.8). The coincidence of the rise to 50 per cent admissions in 1902 with the decline in incidence of typhoid from that year may be no more than a coincidence, but it is none the less suggestive. Bill Luckin has argued that hospital admissions of typhoid during the 1890s were a possible contributor to declining mortality, contrary to McKeown and Record's pessimistic conclusions about the impact of hospitalization on infectious disease during the nineteenth century.[172] It may be that a threshold of at least 50 per cent of cases hospitalized (and these coming from the poorer classes, among whom hygienic practices may be supposed to be inferior) is necessary for the achievement of a definite impact on typhoid incidence. Typhoid's means of transmission could

TABLE 6.8. *Notifications and MAB hospital admissions of typhoid cases, 1890–1911*

Year	Number of cases notified	Hospital admissions % notifications
1890	n/a	22.5
1891	n/a	27.3
1892	2,465	25.3
1893	3,663	20.0
1894	3,360	20.2
1895	3,506	24.1
1896	3,190	27.0
1897	3,103	30.4
1898	3,024	36.6
1899	4,453	40.8
1900	4,291	47.7
1901	3,194	45.3
1902	3,407	53.2
1903	2,339	51.8
1904	1,896	51.7
1905	1,552	51.4
1906	1,600	55.1
1907	1,394	51.5
1908	1,357	50.4
1909	1,043	49.3
1910	1,284	51.7
1911	1,022	50.6

Source: *MABAR*.

[171] This point was first made by Greenwood in *Epidemics*, 158. See also Luckin, 'Typhus and typhoid', 117.

[172] Luckin, 'Typhus and typhoid', 117.

be a critical factor in this equation; much higher levels of hospitalization for a directly communicable disease like scarlet fever had no discernible impact on incidence.

In the event, the purity and availability of domestic water supplies probably had little to do with the decline of typhoid infection after 1902. At most, the tightening up of filtration requirements and other procedures following the take over by the Metropolitan Water Board in October 1904, and the introduction of chlorination in the years after 1915, reduced and eliminated the possibility of such accidental contamination as might be reflected in large-scale outbreaks of the disease. Although infected water supplies constituted the principal vehicle of infection for endemic typhoid during much of the nineteenth century, their influence had been considerably diminished by the 1890s. Water was not the only vehicle of infection, and the significance of other vectors became increasingly obvious in these years.

While much of the reduction in typhoid incidence after 1870 may be attributed to improving domestic water supplies and to rising standards of domestic hygiene, the contribution of the preventive services should not be overlooked. Individual medical officers, like John Liddle of Whitechapel, played an important part in the achievement of better water both by agitating for constant and purer water supplies, and by supervising the conditions in which these supplies were used. Nor was their contribution to the reduction in typhoid incidence limited to water. Their constant, often unrewarding, struggle to ensure satisfactory domestic sanitary provision in poorer-class housing supplemented middle-class efforts and probably helped to extend an appreciation of higher sanitary standards among the urban working class, while their contribution to the procedures of hospital removal for typhoid victims, and the subsequent processes of domestic disinfection, undoubtedly helped significantly to reduce the foci of typhoid infection. Finally, London's medical officers were constantly concerned with the problems of London dust removal, and were instrumental in effecting the painful transition to modern refuse-collection methods between 1890 and 1915.[173] The significance of this transition in health terms is suggested by the research of Ian Buchanan, whose comparison of infant-mortality experience in eight mining communities indicated that the relative prevalence of infant diarrhoea before 1911–12 was influenced specifically by the relative prevalence and behaviour of house flies, which was in turn

[173] e.g. *MOQR* St George's, Southwark (2, 1858), 7; Camberwell Sewers and Sanitary Committee Minutes, 4 Jan. 1870; *MOAR* Hackney (1883), 16; *MOAR* Kensington (1885), 120–1. Dust-holes became a part of the London refuse system when street paving was first introduced in the 18th cent. The moveable dustbin was introduced to Paris by Eugène René Poubelle, prefect of the Seine, in 1884. Everywhere outside Britain the advantages of Poubelle's system were rapidly recognized, but in London there was considerable resistance to its introduction until the local authorities began to apply pressure for its adoption in the first decade of the 20th cent.: T. H. Lyon Thompson, 'The Collection and Disposal of House and Trade Refuse', *Journal of the Royal Sanitary Institute*, 32, (1911), 57–61.

determined by local-authority policy with respect to the proximity of rubbish tips to residential housing.[174] Given the role of house flies also in transmitting typhoid, it is probable that the abolition of London's dust-holes and their replacement by dustbins after 1890 made a contribution both to the changing incidence of infant diarrhoea, and to the final downward turn of endemic typhoid in the early years of the twentieth century.

TABLE 6.9. *London sanitary districts and their source of water supply, 1850–1900*

Kent Company (deep well water)	
Woolwich	
Plumstead	
Kent and Thames Companies	
Rotherhithe	Lewisham
Camberwell	Greenwich
New River and East London Companies (Lea water)	
Hackney	Shoreditch
City	Whitechapel
Thames Companies	
Paddington	St Saviour
Kensington	St George's, Southwark
Hammersmith	Newington
Fulham	St Olave
Chelsea	Bermondsey
St George's, Hanover Square	Lambeth
Westminster	Battersea
Marylebone	Wandsworth
New River Company (Lea water)	
Islington	Clerkenwell
St Giles	St Luke
Holborn	
New-River and Thames Companies	
Hampstead	St James
St Pancras	Strand
St Martin-in-the-Fields	
East London Company (Lea water)	
Bethnal Green	Poplar
St George-in-the-East	Limehouse
Mile End Old Town	

Source: *RCMWS*, PP 1893–4 xl, app. C.18, p. 218.

174 I. H. Buchanan, 'Infant mortality in British coal mining communities, 1880–1911', unpublished Ph.D thesis, University of London, 1983; see also id., 'Infant feeding, sanitation, and diarrhoea in colliery communities, 1880–1911', in Oddy and Miller (eds.), *Diet and Health*, 148–77.

7
Typhus

> The disease appears to have been prevalent to a greater or less extent in almost every district of the metropolis, but as usual has prevailed principally in a few localities, the same localities whose names are so familiar in the records of this hospital . . . the seed-plots of disease in these districts remain the same from year to year; and from year to year they steadily produce the same fruits . . .
>
> (*LFH Annual Report*, 1853)

> It is evident that the ordinary practitioner in London practically never sees . . . typhus.
>
> (*MAB Annual Report*, 1898)

THE MEDICAL UNDERSTANDING OF TYPHUS

Typhus was the indigenous fever of London for the first thirty years of the nineteenth century. Between 1830 and 1870 it shared the city with typhoid, and thereafter diminished steadily in importance, until by the turn of the century it had virtually vanished from the mortality tables. The shift in emphasis between the two diseases was the result of profound changes in the economy and sanitary structure of the city, which first superimposed the typhoid ecology upon the typhus, and then undermined the latter. Typhus is often known as a famine disease but is in fact more closely associated with social dislocation than with want or starvation. It is more epidemic and less endemic in character than typhoid, and at this period was, in its epidemic form, usually and increasingly associated with local economic problems and resulting social distress.[1] As an endemic disease it flourishes as a very local problem, among very unclean people, and generally goes unnoticed, as the cases are usually children who are only lightly affected by the disease. It is above all an environmental fever, which cannot survive in conditions of personal and household cleanliness, and in this respect it has much in common with tuberculosis, whose transmission is similarly facilitated, and activation of the disease encouraged, where domestic hygiene is poor. Alone of the communicable diseases, typhus and tuberculosis work within a broad environmental ecology, highly dependent on domestic and working conditions, on cleanliness, ventilation, and personal hygiene, and the economic rhythms of society which affect them, whereas smallpox and the children's diseases depend on no more than intimate personal

[1] I have argued this point in Anne Hardy, 'Urban famine or urban crisis? Typhus in the Victorian city', *Medical History* 32 (1988), 401–25.

contact, and cholera and typhoid on contaminated water supplies and unhygienic practices. Declining death-rates from typhus and tuberculosis in the years after 1870 reflect wide social and economic changes in British society more tellingly than any reduction in the rest of the spectrum of preventible diseases.

Typhus is caused by *Rickettsia prowazeki*, one of a distinct genus of organisms, and appears to be invariably louse-borne among human beings. Like dysentery, it appears wherever poverty, crowding, and insanitary conditions prevail, in times of social dislocation, and principally in the winter months. The incubation period of the disease in man is ten to fourteen days; infected lice invariably die, usually within seven to twelve days, and although the infection is not transmitted to their eggs, it can survive in the dust of their faeces for months or even years.[2] The human louse is very sensitive to temperature, preferring that of 29°C which it finds in the folds of clothing worn by a healthy person. Lice therefore tend to leave febrile patients and corpses in favour of those with normal temperatures, but die in a few hours if exposed to room temperature. They are easily killed by common antiseptics, and once a typhus patient has been deloused and bathed, he cannot transmit the infection by contact to others. Case-fatality in man varies from 10 to 40 per cent in untreated cases; the nineteenth-century case-mortality is estimated to have been between 20 and 45 per cent. The disease is principally fatal to adults: mortality among children (except infants) is negligible, and is rarely more than 5 per cent among the under-twenties, but fatality thereafter increases sharply with age. One attack confers immunity on survivors for many years, and in this way the disease may be maintained among the child population of small communities, leaving resident adults unaffected.[3]

Throughout the nineteenth century, however, doctors and public-health officials worked in total ignorance of the true nature and origins of typhus. Only in 1909 did Charles Nicolle and his colleagues at the Institut Pasteur in Tunis show that infection is spread by the body-louse ingesting the infected blood of the typhus patient.[4] After about a week the *rickettsiae* have multiplied in the louse gut and are excreted in the faeces. Infection of normal persons generally takes place through the skin by scratching, and sometimes by the inhalation of dust containing dried but still viable *rickettsiae*. Transmission may thus occur either through individual louse infestation, or by the inhalation of

[2] *British Encyclopedia of Medical Practice*, second edn. (1952), xii. 392.

[3] Medical information on typhus has been drawn principally from W. W. C. Topley and G. S. Wilson (eds.), *Principles of Bacteriology, Virology and Immunity*, seventh edn. (1984), iii. chap. 77; F. H. Top and P. H. Wehrle (eds.), *Communicable and Infections Diseases* (St Louis, Miss., 1981), chap. 57; F. L. Horsfall and I. Tamm, *Viral and Rickettsial Infections of Man* (1965); P. D. Hoeprich (ed.), *Infectious Diseases* (Hayerstown, Md., 1977). The estimate of 19th-cent. case fatality was made by Bill Luckin, in 'Typhus and Typhoid in London', in R. I. Woods and J. Woodward (eds.), *Urban Disease and Mortality* (1986), 104.

[4] Topley and Wilson, *Principles*, 575. See also James Busvine, *Insects, Hygiene and History* (1976), 233–9.

infected dust; the nutritional status of the victim is immaterial in increasing resistance to either infection or to its effects. In the nineteenth century, middle-class victims were generally infected by inhaling contaminated dust: they never caught relapsing fever, in which contact with the body fluid of the louse is required for transmission.[5] Modern treatment of the disease is by the broad-spectrum antibiotics; and prevention is recognized to be mainly by controlling or eliminating the insect vector by reducing louse infestation to a minimum and preventing overcrowding: in 1939–45, for example, long-acting insecticides such as DDT were impregnated into clothing and sprayed over houses and potentially infected areas generally.[6]

It was typhus rather than typhoid which provided the image of the fever-nest which so powerfully provoked middle-class reactions of fear and sanitarian zeal between 1800 and the 1870s. The first site chosen by the London Fever Hospital Committee in 1801 was, significantly, near the notorious St Giles's rookery, and the hospital's records soon established the reality of the 'fever nest': localities in which, despite every effort of whitewash and fumigation applied by the hospital authorities, fever continued month after month, year after year, to claim a succession of victims.[7] By the time Southwood Smith and James Kay-Shuttleworth came to investigate the nature of the metropolitan fever areas more closely in the mid-1830s, the phenomenon was well-recognized;[8] and it was immortalized by Charles Dickens in the great festering slum of Tom-all-Alone's, from whose fever-houses the inhabitants were carried dead and dying 'like sheep with the rot', and from which the winds delivered his revenge on the classes who would not remedy his evil.[9] It was the ability of these fever-nests to spread the disease around them, and the knowledge that 'fever' could not be confined to the poor, that lent potency to the image of these epidemic streets. Although the use of the term 'fever-nest' almost disappeared from preventive literature during the 1870s, the idea of poverty as the source of disease which could not be restrained from spreading to the rich remained latent, and was revived to stimulate the anti-tuberculosis campaign in the early years of the twentieth century.[10]

[5] W. P. MacArthur, 'The medical history of the famine', in R. D. Edwards and T. D. Williams (eds.), *The Great Famine* (Dublin, 1956), 280. For examples of middle-class victims during the 1860s, see Hardy, 'Urban famine', 413.

[6] Topley and Wilson, *Principles*, 578.

[7] W. F. Bynum, 'Hospital, disease and community: the London Fever Hospital 1801–1850', in Charles Rosenberg (ed.), *Healing and History* (1979), 104, 106.

[8] *PLCAR*, PP 1837–8 xxviii, app. A supplement 1, pp. 67–83: N. Arnott and J. P. Kay, 'Report on the prevalence of certain physical causes of fever in the metropolis'; app. A, no. 2, pp. 83–94; T. Southwood Smith, 'Report on some of the physical causes of sickness and mortality to which the poor are particularly exposed'.

[9] Charles Dickens, *Bleak House* (Harmondsworth, 1971), 364, 683; see above, Introduction, n. 1.

[10] See H. Timbrell Bulstrode, 'Report on sanatoria for consumption and certain other aspects of the tuberculosis question', *MOAR* LGB, supplement, PP 1907 xxvii, p. 86.

The lingering confusion between typhus and typhoid and about their etiologies meant that the terminology of the fever-nest was applied to both during the 1850s and 1860s, even though typhoid did not exist in a 'fever-nest' ecology.[11] None the less, Jenner's diagnostical distinction between typhoid and typhus became very generally accepted in these years, and in general, too, there was agreement over the circumstances of typhus transmission: in overcrowded localities and in times of destitution.[12] The disease was broadly accepted as being contagious—hence the dangers of overcrowding—but there continued to be some disagreement over the finer points of its behaviour. In particular, Charles Murchison, the greatest fever expert of the 1860s, believed that typhus might be generated *de novo*, that is, independently in conditions of squalor, overcrowding, and so on.[13] This position was disputed by colleagues, and became gradually discredited in the years after Murchison's death: overcrowding and squalor were in many places constant, whereas typhus was only occasional.[14] By the 1880s those medical men still concerned with typhus were almost certain that it was transmitted exclusively by contagion, but they had no positive means of proving their contention.[15]

The disagreements over spontaneous generation did not compromise the essential consensus on the way in which to deal with typhus. It was a matter of general observation that typhus frequently appeared without warning, and without the contacts on which contagion should depend being in any way traceable. Murchison chose to explain this phenomenon by spontaneous generation; others to assume that the contagion had been imported in a fashion that defied detection.[16] Similarly, observation indicated the role of infected clothes, and suggested that of infected housing.[17] However, until the role of the louse and its faeces as vector and the dangers of infected dust were understood, there could be no clear explanation. Following the distinction of typhoid and typhus, and in the absence of any bacteriological certainty, differing explanations of the observed behaviour of the disease were perhaps inevitable.

Observation, however, provided the foundations for a fundamentally correct preventive approach to the disease, the basis of which was thorough disinfection. From its earliest days, the London Fever Hospital had followed this policy with regard to typhus, and besides removing infected individuals, had attended to the disinfection of apartments, furniture, and clothing of affected localities.[18] For the rest of the century this remained the accepted method of

[11] The *Lancet*, for example, ran three articles on 'Old cholera haunts and modern fever nests' in 1865; the 'fever' concerned is plainly typhus: *Lancet* (1865), ii. 522, 602.

[12] Margaret Pelling, *Cholera, Fever and English Medicine 1825–1865* (1976), 283, notes that medical interest in typhus declined from the second quarter of the 19th cent., as the disease waned in epidemic importance.

[13] Charles Murchison, *Continued Fevers of Great Britain*, fourth edn. (1884), 99–104.

[14] Ibid. 99.

[15] See George Buchanan and J. Spear in *MOAR* LGB, PP 1887 xxxviii, pp. 635, 959–62; Alex Collie, *On Fevers* (1887), 105–7.

[16] Ibid.

[17] *MOAR* St Olave (1867–8), 23.

[18] Bynum, 'Hospital', 101.

dealing with typhus, and was generally found effective, provided it was thoroughly carried out. In St Olave in the 1860s, for example, houses were being disinfected with Calvert's powder, carbolic acid, and chlorine, and infected bedding (a recognized vehicle of typhus) was disinfected before being burnt.[19] This, with (as far as possible) the isolation of patients, was the standard preventive treatment. Even so, the remedy was flawed. Disinfection might be incomplete, and there were often difficulties with contacts. In practice it was not easy to secure the disinfection of persons and their clothes who had been exposed to typhus, and preventive authorities frequently, and generally fruitlessly, urged the necessity of houses of refuge, where personal purification could be carried out.[20] The LFH early found fumigation and whitewash inadequate in certain specific areas.[21] In some cases the final remedy was closure of affected houses. In Orange Street, St Saviour, where eleven typhus cases occurred in January 1887, disinfection proved ineffectual, and the series of cases only came to an end after all the inhabitants had been removed to a temporary shelter, and all the houses in the street closed.[22]

THE INCIDENCE OF TYPHUS IN LONDON: 'FEVER-NESTS' AND EPIDEMICS

The distribution of typhus in London was, up to the 1870s, linked to very specific areas within the central, southern, and eastern registration districts. Within these areas certain localities were possibly never free from fever: the register of admissions to the LFH show that even during non-epidemic years typhus was active in the city (Fig. 7.1). Local medical officers were well aware of such localities within their districts, and others were generally recognized by interested sanitarians as special haunts of typhus.[23] The *Lancet* drew particular attention to the fever-nests of St Giles, St George's, Southwark and Whitechapel in 1865: the latter was the 'nucleus of the metropolitan fever field'.[24] Within these districts certain streets, courts, or alleys, and within them, even, certain houses, played a central part in furnishing victims and maintaining the disease. In St Giles the courts and alleys around Great Wild Street and Drury Lane were especially notorious; in 1879 the medical officer, Dr Lovett, declared that every outbreak of typhus in the district had always been traced to Lincoln Court and Orange Court, Drury Lane.[25] In such localities and others like them it was apparently the case that particular houses constituted the foci of infection. William Rendle, for twenty-four years Poor Law medical officer in St George's, Southwark, and subsequently, if briefly, its

[19] *MOAR* St Olave (1867–8), 23; *MOAR* St Saviour (1871), 7.
[20] Buchanan and Spear, 960.
[21] Bynum, 'Hospital', 106.
[22] *MOAR* St Saviour (1887), 28–9.
[23] *MOAR* St George's, Southwark (1866–7), 6.
[24] *Lancet* (1865), ii. 522, 602, 656.
[25] Ibid. 522; *Lancet* (1879), ii. 793.

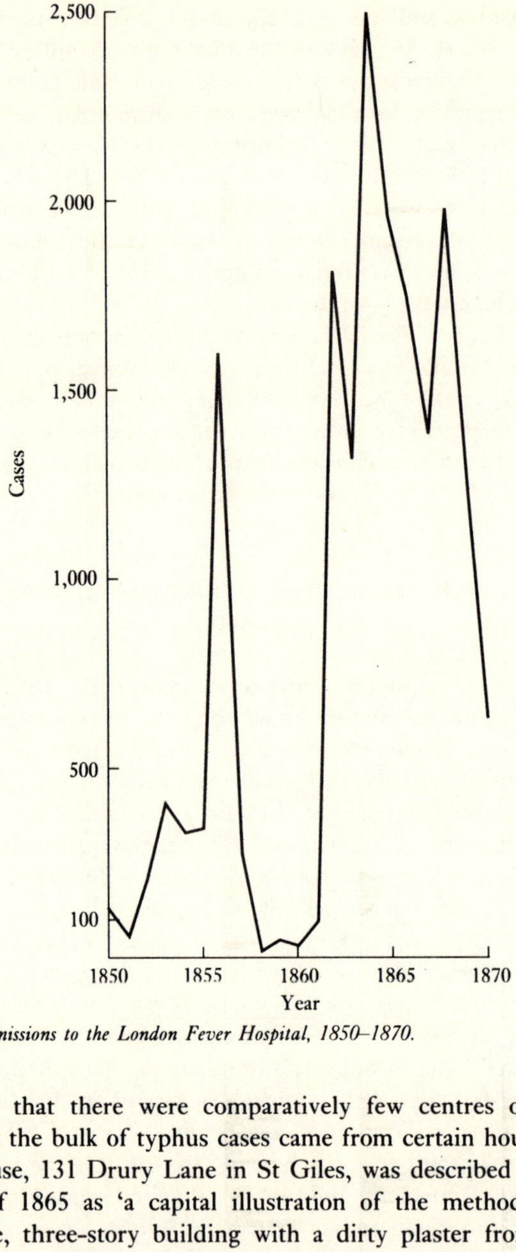

FIG. 7.1. *Typhus admissions to the London Fever Hospital, 1850–1870.*

MOH, declared that there were comparatively few centres of infection for typhus, and that the bulk of typhus cases came from certain houses.[26]

One such house, 131 Drury Lane in St Giles, was described in detail in the *Lancet* report of 1865 as 'a capital illustration of the method of preserving typhus'. A large, three-story building with a dirty plaster front, it housed a second-hand clothes shop in the basement, in whose window hung a notice advertising rooms to let, notwithstanding that the whole house was full of

[26] W. Rendle, *London Vestries and their Sanitary Work* (1865), 11–12; *Lancet* (1869), i. 737.

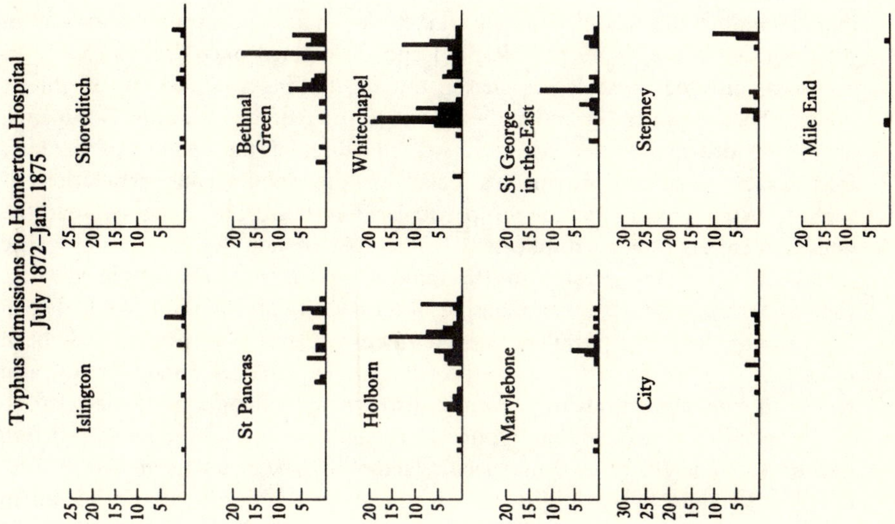

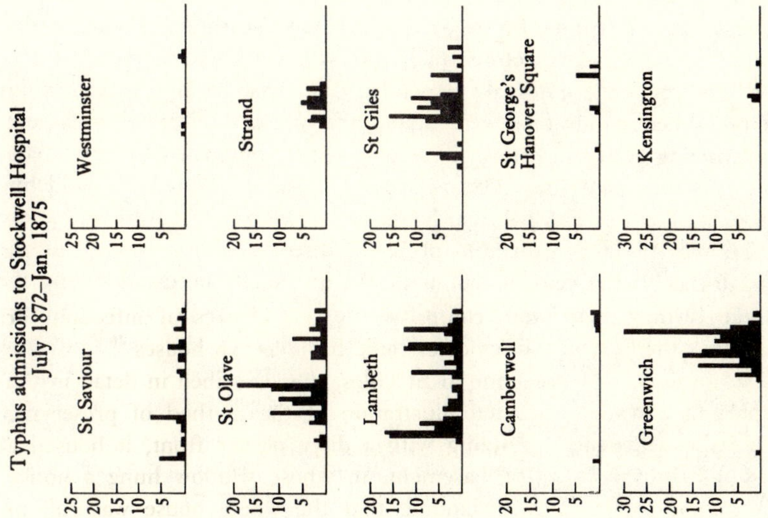

FIG. 7.2. *London hospitals typhus admissions, 1872–1875.*

typhus, and only an infected room vacant. Every room contained two or three people. The disease had begun in a family on the second floor, whose daughter, living in nearby Drury Court, had caught the infection from a fellow-lodger there. Over two months the disease spread from family to family at 131 Drury Lane, but did not interrupt the various occupations pursued under that roof, including the manufacture of trinkets for ladies' heads and dresses.[27] In such houses, if they were not cleansed and disinfected once typhus cases had occurred, infected louse faeces shaken out of clothing and bedding might lie undisturbed for years, awaiting the arrival of further non-immune occupants, or the disturbance caused by increased crowding of the rooms, to generate fresh cases. Charles Murchison's belief in the spontaneous generation of typhus, based on observation of particular instances, also suggests that the houses themselves were implicated.[28] The role of housing in sustaining the disease was probably assisted by the rapid turnover of inhabitants in quarters such as St Giles. In 1861, for example, the London City Mission found that in one month half the families in Monmouth Court, St Giles, had been replaced.[29] Unrecognized cases, especially among children, undoubtedly also served to maintain typhus in particular districts and among a particular class.[30]

The persistence of endemic typhus in particular localities, or its spread into new ones,[31] was determined by specific factors: by the character of the population living there, by their dirt and by the dirty conditions of the houses in which they lived, and especially by overcrowding. Medical officers repeatedly pointed out that overcrowding, lack of ventilation, and want of cleanliness were the chief causes of the disease, and that these characterized the dwellings of the poorer classes.[32] Yet these conditions in themselves do not explain the epidemic upsurges of typhus, which were so marked a feature of London's disease experience in the years before 1870, and which were so markedly absent thereafter. The epidemic outbreaks depended directly on economic conditions in the city. When conditions were stable the disease remained quiescent, though continuing active in certain limited localities; but when the city's economic life was disrupted the resulting social changes permitted the epidemic extension of typhus from its habitual haunts. The MOH for Liverpool, where endemic typhus was a considerable problem, discovered in a survey of the years 1862–6 that 93 per cent of typhus deaths in the city occurred among the weekly-wage earning class, who inhabited courts and alleys 'where sanitary provisions are conspicuously absent'.[33] They were also the class most vulnera-

[27] *Lancet* (1865), ii. 522.
[28] Murchison, *Continued Fevers*, 99–104.
[29] L. H. Lees, *Exiles of Erin* (Manchester 1979), 58.
[30] Collie, *Fevers*, 107.
[31] This was the case in Poplar. See Hardy, 'Urban famine', 413.
[32] *MOAR* Mile End Old Town (1859), 6; *MOAR* Westminster (1864–5), 14; *MOAR* Camberwell (1864–5), 25. For the mechanics of typhus transmission in overcrowded conditions, see MacArthur, 'Medical history', 271–2.
[33] Of the remaining typhus deaths, 5.4% occurred among the small shopkeeping class, and 1.3% (some 100 individuals) among scripture readers, medical men, relieving officers, pawn-

ble to economic dislocation. In London, weekly-wage earners constituted a large proportion of the working class, and most were in occupations that experienced seasonal slackness, with under- or unemployment. Among these people it was a common emergency economy for families and friends to double up in accommodation.[34] Domestic cleanliness almost certainly suffered under such pressure, and if seasonal depression coincided with severe weather, the insanitary effects of this temporary 'stress' overcrowding were aggravated by measures taken to keep warm—sleeping fully dressed, and not washing. It was circumstances like these which offered typhus an ideal opportunity for epidemic escalation, and increased crowding into habitations infested with typhus exposed more people to infection.

The pattern of epidemic typhus in London in the 1850s and 1860s was closely associated with the economic stability of the city. There were two significant epidemic outbreaks of the disease: in 1856, and more seriously in 1861–8. In between these two episodes typhus was so markedly absent from London that there were serious plans to convert the LFH into a hospital for general cases.[35] The epidemic of 1856 occurred, it has been said, at the end of the Crimean War, by implication introduced by returning soldiers.[36] It was, however, unique to London. The escalation of typhus cases began in the city in December 1855, and continued through January to April 1856; peace was signed in the Crimea in February 1856. The proportion of typhus to typhoid in London during these months was noted as 'extraordinary' by the medical officer of the LFH, J. D. Scurrah; in the months of August to November 1856, however, the two diseases returned to their normal ratio.[37] In fact the timing of this epidemic had little to do with returning troops, but was triggered by the temporary dislocation of the London economy. In Murchison's words: 'The disasters of the Crimean campaign had brought mourning into many families of the higher class, and this, conjoined with increased taxation, suspense, and other causes, interrupted the ordinary gaieties of London life.'[38] The winter season of London society was a subdued one in 1855–6, and the working people of London who depended on the luxury trade it generated suffered accordingly. Many were thrown out of work, and at the same time prices rose. The winter months were the ideal time, in the typhus ecology, for these circumstances to induce an epidemic, and an epidemic was the result. With the coming of spring, the restoration of peace and a good harvest in 1856 were sufficient to bring the typhus outbreak to an end.[39]

According to Charles Murchison there was a third factor which influenced the disappearance of epidemic typhus in 1856, and this was 'increased

brokers, and undertakers, all of whom risked in one way or another coming into contact with typhus patients: *Lancet* (1867), ii. 608.

[34] G. S. Jones, *Outcast London* (1972), 117–18.

[35] *LFHAR* (1861), 6.

[36] Charles Creighton, *A History of Epidemics in Britain*, 2 vols. (Cambridge, 1894), ii. 209.

[37] *LFHAR* (1856), 7–8.

[38] Murchison, *Continued Fevers*, 52.

[39] Ibid.

attention to sanitary arrangements among the poor'.[40] The London MOHs took up their posts in April 1856, to be immediately confronted by the tail-end of a typhus epidemic. There is no particular consciousness of this expressed in their reports, but they certainly started on their sanitary labours immediately, and there can be little doubt that the fever-nests and similar poor-class property were quick to receive attention under the Nuisances Removal Act. It is tempting to speculate that this attention was effective: from 1858 to December 1861 typhus admissions to the LFH fell to their lowest-ever levels since records of the disease began (Fig. 7.1), at a time when the national economy, and probably the local, had not yet recovered from the effects of the Crimean War. The continued absence of typhus in these years is the more remarkable because the working-class economy of London was seriously disrupted from July 1859 to March 1860 by the first of the bitter building-trades strikes which accompanied the early trades-union movement in the city.[41]

The three-year period of typhus quiescence was succeeded by nearly a decade of extraordinary typhus activity. Once again social and economic conditions in the city determined the timing and duration of the epidemic. A second building-trades strike in the spring of 1861 further weakened the working-class economy; more critically, three new railway projects were begun in the central and eastern districts of the city. Two were already in progress south of the river, and another was to be begun in the following year, 1862, when the Agar Town slum in St Pancras was razed to make way for St Pancras Station.[42] Some 7,000 persons were affected by the operations north of the river, and a further twelve railway projects, involving more than 18,000 people, were initiated in these central areas in the years between 1862 and 1867.[43] Following the last of these projects, the widening of the North London Railway's City Branch line between Shoreditch and Islington, completed in 1869, no further new works were initiated until 1872, and the pace of railway projects slackened considerably in the 1870s.[44] The dislocation generated by demolition of housing for these railway projects was considerable. Slum-clearances and street-building operations by the Metropolitan Board of Works further aggravated the situation. Overcrowding levels in the central districts soared, and so did rents; the medical officer for Bethnal Green estimated in 1867 that in some cases the latter had risen by as much as 50 per cent.[45]

The social dislocation brought about by the central London railway projects

[40] Murchison, *Continued Fevers*, 52.

[41] For the background to these strikes, see Richard Price, *Masters, Unions and Men: Work Control in Building and the Rise of Labour 1830–1914* (1980), 15–54.

[42] The details of these developments are given in Hardy, 'Urban famine', 404.

[43] H. J. Dyos, 'Some social costs of railway building in London', *Journal of Transport History*, 3 (1957), 21; see also id., 'Railways and housing in Victorian London', *Journal of Transport History*, 2 (1955), 11–21.

[44] Ibid.

[45] *MOAR* St Giles (1863), 16; *MOAR* Shoreditch (1863), 11; *MOAR* Bethnal Green (1867), 4.

provided an exemplary breeding-ground for epidemic typhus. Typhus admissions to the LFH had increased considerably in the spring of 1861, for the winter of 1860–1 had been severe, but it was not until mid-December that the disease became epidemic. Almost all the first cases admitted to the LFH were unemployed men who had come to London in search of work, and many of them had been only a few weeks in the city. Unprotected by immunity acquired in childhood, and unusually exposed to the disease by reason of the exceptional pressure on common lodging-house accommodation occasioned by the railway works, they quickly picked up the infection. Once the disease had established itself among this mobile population it spread rapidly: in January 1862 the number of LFH admissions for typhus was 140, among the highest monthly totals in the hospital's history.[46] From 1862 until 1870 the number of typhus admissions to the LFH, and the number of 'fever' deaths registered in London, remained at epidemic level (Table 7.1).

From the spring of 1862 to November 1863 the typhus epidemic was confined to the poorest and most densely populated parts of the city.[47] In 1862, 53 per cent of the cases admitted to the LFH came from eight districts, with St George-in-the-East contributing 179 cases; St Pancras (where the entire Agar Town slum had just been razed) 162; and the City 157.[48] In 1863 nearly all the cases so far received into the LFH were said to come from the most crowded parishes, from Bermondsey, Lambeth, St George-in-the-East, Rotherhithe, and the City.[49] At the end of October 1863 it was observed that several parishes had experienced marked fluctuations in the incidence of the disease, but St George-in-the-East and St Pancras furnished the 'most constant and equable supply' of patients. Towards the end of November 1863, while patients were still being received mainly from the south and east (from Rotherhithe, Bermondsey, Lambeth, St Saviour, and St George-in-the-East), there were indications that the disease was spreading. A larger number of cases were arriving from Shoreditch and the City, while cases were also being brought in from Hackney and Kensington, which had not furnished cases for months before.[50] By 1864 the epidemic was becoming more generally diffused through the city, although its principal focus remained the poorest areas.[51] In 1865 it was chiefly prevalent in the southern and central districts, and the LFH received an unusual number of patients from the well-to-do districts. The medical officer noted particularly the 'singular way' in which the disease had wandered beyond its 'customary limits', and appeared in districts where there were few of the destitute and filthy class.[52] In 1866, however, the focus of the epidemic shifted back to the eastern districts and remained there until it began to wane. By 1868 typhus cases were coming to the LFH principally from Stepney, Whitechapel, Shoreditch, and other East End districts.[53]

[46] *Lancet* (1862), i. 207–8. [47] *Lancet* (1863), ii. 422. [48] *LFHAR* (1862), 6.
[49] *LFHAR* (1863), 7. [50] *Lancet* (1863), ii. 603. [51] *LFHAR* (1864), 6–7.
[52] *LFHAR* (1865), 14. [53] *LFHAR* (1868), 19.

The LFH's records do not provide a straightforward picture of the distribution of the epidemic. Not only were milder cases generally treated at home, but, although the LFH was the only metropolitan institution for typhus victims before October 1871, cases were not automatically sent to the hospital from all districts in the metropolis. Certain parishes preferred to save the expense of treatment and deal with cases in their own workhouse infirmaries. Significantly, Whitechapel and St Giles were both in this class.[54] Whitechapel provided perhaps the most notorious example of the practice. It was a district inhabited principally by the poorer classes—probably, its MOH observed in 1868, to a greater extent than any other in London—and it was said to be the centre of the metropolitan fever field.[55] In the decade 1851–60 Whitechapel contributed the largest number of metropolitan fever deaths, and the *Lancet* suspected it of playing a 'too prominent' part in fostering the great 1861–70 epidemic.[56]

In 1865 it was estimated that Whitechapel contained 9,000 houses, 5,000 of which were let out as separate lodgings, each house containing on average three families. The total population in 1861 was 79,000; density in the parish was 195 persons per acre. In the Poor Law year (Lady Day to Lady Day) 1864–5, some 37 per cent of this population received indoor or outdoor relief.[57] Until 1866 the Whitechapel authorities made no use of the LFH, and typhus victims were treated either in the workhouse or at home.[58] In either case the practice only contributed to the further spread of infection. The *Lancet*'s own investigations had clearly shown that the treatment of typhus victims in workhouse infirmaries resulted only too frequently in extensive 'in-house' epidemics;[59] home treatment was equally recognized as only multiplying the foci of infection. Vestry policy on the treatment of typhus cases was but one element in the epidemic spread of the disease, and clearly was not the most important.[60] Nevertheless, in the context of the social dislocation occurring among London's working class during the 1860s, the failure of vestries to ensure what was, in effect, the isolation of cases through treatment at the LFH contributed to the continuing epidemic impetus.[61]

[54] *LFHAR* (1866), 13. Three other districts also avoided the LFH charges: Mile End, Lewisham and Poplar. St Giles began sending cases to the LFH on 1 April 1865; Whitechapel on 1 December 1865. Poor-law cases were charged by the LFH at the rate of 1 shilling a day until 1868. Thus the cost to e.g. St George-in-the-East and St Pancras of typhus cases in 1862 came to approximately £161 and £145. 8*s*. respectively.

[55] *MOQR* Whitechapel (2, 1868), 12; *Lancet* (1865), ii. 656.

[56] *Lancet* (1865), ii. 656.

[57] Ibid.

[58] *MOAR*, Whitechapel (1865), 5.

[59] *Lancet* (1865), ii. 656.

[60] Nevertheless, vestry policy was probably important in sustaining the endemic level of the disease. The LFH's early experience of the impossibility of eliminating typhus from certain courts may have been due to repeated importation from uncontrolled areas of the city, or to inefficiencies of disinfection. See Bynum, 'Hospitals', 106.

[61] This element should not be exaggerated. Many typhus cases undoubtedly remained unknown to the authorities. In 1869, the first year for which such a calculation is possible, admissions to the LFH constituted 17% of estimated London cases; in 1870, 13%. This calculation is based on the

The waning of the epidemic in the later 1860s was not due to any change in the virulence of the disease. In a recent essay analysing the decline of typhus, Bill Luckin examined and convincingly dismissed the possibility of autonomous change in the nature of the disease, and suggested that the behaviour of typhus might be linked to waves of Irish immigration.[62] Irish colonies certainly provided a habitat for typhus in nineteenth-century cities, including London, but although contemporaries often blamed Irish immigrants for bringing epidemic typhus with them, and typhus remained a significant problem in Ireland itself for most of the period, most major typhus epidemics could not be traced back to Ireland. Neither in 1856 nor in 1861 is there reason to suppose that Irish immigration, rather than changing conditions in the city, provoked the epidemic, and while proportionately the numbers of Irish-born were falling in London in the latter decades of the century, the numbers arriving continued to increase.[63]

The ending of the London typhus epidemic in 1870–1 was sudden, but no more so than in 1848 or in 1857. In both the latter years the disappearance of the epidemic was attributed by contemporary observers to the restoration of normal market conditions.[64] In 1870–1 the situation was not so simple: Murchison, for example, had no retrospective explanation to offer.[65] If bread prices stabilized in the early 1870s, they did not fall dramatically.[66] It is possible that, having affected some 190,000 persons in the inner city in the years 1862–9, typhus had effectually diminished the pool of accessible, non-immune potential victims;[67] but the ending of major railway works was probably critical. While general levels of overcrowding did not diminish in the city, London experienced a period of comparative quiet prosperity during the 1870s[68] which probably resulted in less short-term-expediency overcrowding and reduced the likelihood of epidemic typhus. Endemic typhus, meanwhile, remained active in the poorer quarters of the city. There were several local outbreaks in the early 1870s: in Whitechapel in 1873, in Bloomsbury and St Olave in 1873–4, and in Greenwich in 1874; but none of these was on any significant scale.[69]

contemporary assumption of a case-fatality rate of 1 in 10. The form of the disease in London was less virulent than that present in Lancashire, where mortality was *c*.23%: *MOAR* LGB, PP 1863, xxv, app. 2, pp. 229, 304.

[62] Luckin, 'Typhus and Typhoid', 113–14.

[63] Hardy, 'Urban famine', 414.

[64] Murchison, *Continued Fevers*, 51–3; Creighton, *Epidemics*, ii. 205.

[65] Murchison, *Continued Fevers*, 54.

[66] B. R. Mitchell and P. Deane, *Abstract of British Historical Statistics* (Cambridge, 1971), 498.

[67] The figure of 190,000 has been arrived at by taking the total typhus admissions to the LFH in 1862–9 and assuming, on the basis of note 61 above, that these represented 15% of total cases. The importance of provincial immigration in refreshing the non-immune pool was perhaps limited: such immigrants tended to settle in the outer suburbs of the city: Jones, *Outcast London*, 130. In 1870 Murchison observed that the marked decline in typhus was 'to some extent' due to the elimination of susceptibles: *LFHAR* (1870), 8; but he did not offer any retrospective confirmation of this observation.

[68] Jones, *Outcast London*, 276–7.

[69] *MABMP*, vii (1873–4), 97, 181, 214, 373, 401.

THE DISAPPEARANCE OF TYPHUS AFTER 1871

The local outbreaks of the early 1870s suggest once again the effectiveness of local preventive action against typhus when conditions in the city were normal. During these years the transfer of responsibility for pauper typhus cases from the LFH to the Metropolitan Asylums Board hospitals at Homerton (opened October 1871) and Stockwell gave an added impetus to local medical officers tackling typhus, for the MAB's medical officers were well aware of their preventive functions and duties. They were active in informing medical officers of health of raised typhus admissions from their districts and, if cases continued to appear, would remind local Poor Law authorities as well as the sanitary departments of the need for action. This happened in 1873–4, for example, when the parishes of Bloomsbury and the Strand continued, over the months from August 1873 to January 1874, to send a steady trickle of cases to the Stockwell hospital.[70] Although it often took time to eliminate such manifestations of endemic typhus, it is plain that medical officers acted directly in response both to the manifestation itself, and to prompting from the MAB. In August 1873 John Liddle of Whitechapel wrote in response to a letter from the MAB that typhus had been prevalent in the Royal Mint Street district for the past five months, and that ever since its first appearance his attention had been directed to that locality because of it: 'Works of improvement have been carried out there, which will, I believe, have the effect of preventing the spread of the disease. At all events, all that can be effected by me to that end shall be done.'[71]

There was nothing temporary about the preventive objectives of the MAB medical officers. They clearly saw themselves as forming an integral part of a London preventive system; and their vigilance was undoubtedly useful in detecting local problems before the effective introduction of notification: in Camberwell in the later 1880s MAB medical officers were instrumental in stimulating local sanitary activity to bring a series of typhus cases to an end.[72] Although the MAB came under the aegis of the Poor Law Board in these years, and this was in some ways to its disadvantage, there were some preventive compensations. With typhus cases, for example, it very frequently happened that whole families were sent to the hospital even though only one or two members had the disease,[73] and in this way the spread of the disease between individuals could be limited, while the cleansing and disinfecting by the local authority of infected housing was facilitated.

While the experience of the 1860s, demonstrates that the local sanitary organization had no effective means of controlling epidemic typhus when social conditions favoured a major escalation, the gradual disappearance of the dis-

[70] *MABMP*, vii (1873–4), 153, 214, 373.
[71] Ibid. 181.
[72] *MOAR* Camberwell (1886–7), 92–4.
[73] *MABMP*, v (1871–2), 409.

ease after 1870 bears witness by contrast to improving social conditions and the long-term significance of sanitary improvement, and suggests the importance of the major structural upheaval of the 1860s railway-building projects in creating the epidemic ecology. For urban crises did not disappear after 1870. Cyclical depression, unemployment, and distress returned in 1878–9, aggravated by the exceptionally severe winter.[74] During the 1880s London experienced a particularly prolonged period of social crisis, at its worst in the years 1884–7.[75] Throughout this period, overcrowding in the working-class areas of the city improved little. Average real wages, however, began to rise steadily,[76] and the post-1870 London crises differed from those of the pre-1870 period: there were no bread riots or semi-violent distress, and there were no typhus epidemics: the disease continued its steady decline. Yet typhus had declined substantially before. In the years 1803–15 it was very markedly absent in England as a whole,[77] just as it was very rare in London between 1858 and 1860. The decline of typhus in the 1870s was not so sudden or dramatic that it was regarded by contemporaries as anything more than a temporary respite. In 1875, for example, the MOH of the Stockwell hospital, noting that there had been less typhus in London in that year than in any of the preceding fifteen years, warned: 'It is, however, improbable that this comparative immunity will continue for any lengthened period, the number of typhus cases in a community being liable to rapid and extensive fluctuations.'[78] Although the death-rates indicated a declining incidence, the preventive authorities were well aware that the disease still maintained a vital presence in the city in the 1870s: even the seventy-odd deaths registered in London in 1879 and 1880 represented in terms of contemporary calculation some 700 cases.[79] It was fully recognized that a deterioration in social conditions might yet provoke a major resurgence of the disease: indeed, the distress in London in these years caused the *Lancet* to warn particularly against the outbreak of epidemics.[80]

The final decline of typhus in London dates not from the early 1870s, but from the late 1870s and early 1880s, when the disease failed to escalate in step with the return of more unsettled social and economic conditions in the city. The 1870s was a crucial decade, in which the established ecology of typhus in London was finally destroyed. The destruction was not accomplished by any single factor or development, but through a variety of sanitary improvements, including improvements and structural change in the city's housing and water

[74] Jones, *Outcast London*, 46, 277.
[75] Ibid. 281–2.
[76] Mitchell and Deane, *British Historical Statistics*, 345–6. See Michael S. Teitelbaum, *The British Fertility Decline* (Princeton, NJ, 1984), 37–44.
[77] Creighton, *Epidemics*, ii. 162–7.
[78] *MABMP*, ix (1875–6), p. 571.
[79] In 1878 the *Lancet* calculated on the basis of 25% mortality among 179 completed cases at the Metropolitan Asylums Board hospitals that there were 636 cases of typhus in London in 1877: *Lancet* (1878), i. 324. There were 151 registered typhus deaths in London in 1877, giving, on this basis, 604 cases.
[80] *Lancet* (1879), i. 63, 385–6.

TABLE 7.1. *Typhus admissions to MAB hospitals, 1871–1900*

Year	Typhus admissions	% total	Year	Typhus admissions	% total
15 months to 31. 12. 72	134	15.4	1886	10	0.50
1873	401	35.0	1887	35	0.50
1874	536	25.1	1888	1	0.02
1875	65	3.6	1889	23	0.40
1876	139	10.0	1890	16	0.20
1877	170	14.1	1891	18	0.20
1878	168	10.7	1892	19	1.10
1879	48	2.3	1893	2	0.01
1880	28	1.1	1894	6	0.04
1881	219	9.4	1895	3	0.02
1882	148	5.2	1896	9	0.04
1883	45	1.7	1897	2	0.01
1884	29	1.1	1898	9	0.04
1885	53	2.9	1899	11	0.04
			1900	13	0.05

Source: MAB Statistical Committee annual reports.

supplies, and the extension of hospital facilities, as well as changes in the nature of social dislocation within the city. In all these areas important developments during the 1870s undermined the epidemic potential of the disease.

Although very little improvement occurred in housing conditions for the poorest of the London working classes in the later nineteenth century, developments in the late 1860s and 1870 were significant for the typhus habitat. In the first place, there were the demolitions for railways and street improvement, and these were supplemented, after the passing of the Artisans Dwellings Act 1875, by vestry- or MOH-sponsored clearance schemes aimed specifically at fever-nests. In St Giles, for instance, the old fever-dens of Great Wild Street and Little Coram Street had been swept away by 1883, and the clearance of two more (Shelton Street, Drury Lane, and the Colonnade), was contemplated.[81] In 1881 Samuel Lovett, MOH since 1875, remarked that all the typhus outbreaks with which he had had to deal had occurred in condemned areas, but that as soon as the sick were removed to hospital and the houses closed by magistrate's order the spread of the disease was checked.[82] In 1887 the *Lancet* went so far as to remark that the St Giles clearances had cleared typhus out of London.[83]

[81] *MOAR* St Giles (1883), 73. Shelton Street went in 1889: ibid. (1889), 21.
[82] *Lancet* (1881), ii. 1,047. [83] *Lancet* (1887), i. 632.

Meanwhile, although the provisions for the regulation of houses in multiple occupation under the Sanitary Act 1866 had proved almost unworkable,[84] steps were being taken by sanitary departments within the context of existing legislation to remedy the worst superficial conditions as far as possible. This was done by the improvement of specific sanitary defects under the Nuisance Removal Acts, and more generally by getting houses cleaned and lime-washed. In St Martin-in-the-Fields, Dr Beale during the later 1860s 'nearly succeeded' in having every tenement house cleansed and whitewashed at least once a year. Conditions in some courts, he admitted, continued to be 'disgraceful', but he stated that from year to year he found the cleansing and repairing of tenement houses less difficult. In 1867 notices to cleanse had been attended to with 'tolerable exactness', and in no instance had it been necessary to call on the magistrates for aid.[85] In St Giles in 1875–83, 12,573 improvement orders were issued, and 7,770 houses cleansed—some 971 per annum.[86] St Giles had only 3,968 inhabited houses in 1881: apparently some 24.5 per cent of its housing stock was cleansed yearly.

The combination of fever-nest demolition and regular cleansing went some way to removing the old typhus habitat. If low-level non-epidemic typhus was sustained between epidemics by the survival of *Rickettsia prowazeki* in dried louse faeces, and by the continuous flow of newcomers into (and out of) poor-class lodgings, demolitions and the regular cleansing of this type of housing would have its effect in breaking the cycle of transmission. In Liverpool, for example, it was said that regular cleansing and supervision had eliminated typhus from the city's common lodging houses between 1848 and 1863.[87] It may also be relevant that in the years 1868–79 the London MOHs had to contend with three successive major outbreaks of recognized infectious epidemic disease: scarlet fever in 1868–70, and smallpox in 1870–3 and 1876–8. A direct result of these epidemics was widespread house-to-house visitation in search of contacts and unvaccinated children; and equally widespread disinfection of the houses, bedding, and clothing of victims throughout London, on a scale never experienced before. The implementing of these preventive policies was undoubtedly particularly thorough in the poorest areas, which were the most vulnerable to sanitary supervision.

The 1870s also saw the first extension of constant piped-water supplies into the poorest areas of London, enabling the poor the better to cleanse their bodies, clothes, and homes themselves. By 1880 company-supplied constant service was widely provided in the eastern, though less so in the northern, districts.[88] The pioneering work of the East London Water Company in this

[84] See below Chap. 8, 'Tuberculosis'.

[85] *MOAR* St Martin (1867), 19. Beale found that these houses rapidly became dirty again: ibid (1868), 18.

[86] *MOAR* St Giles (1883), 73.

[87] *MOAR* LGB, PP 1865 (*c*.3484), xxvi, appendix 8, p. 478.

[88] Hardy, 'London's water supply in the nineteenth century', in W. F. Bynum and R. S. Porter (eds.), *Living and Dying in London*, *Medical History*, supplement no. 11 (1992).

regard was already making an impact by the end of the 1860s. In 1868, for instance, John Liddle recorded that the poorer parts of Whitechapel were now probably better provided with water than 'any other district in London'.[89] Beginning in 1869, the East London Company's policy of extending constant service throughout its district meant that by 1883 all houses supplied within its metropolitan district had access to a constant supply. Although in the poorest courts it was often the case that water was supplied by stand-pipe rather than being laid on to houses, the convenience of a constant supply, with the alteration in patterns of water-usage which this entailed, became widely available throughout East London in the 1870s. It is difficult to assess how far the provision of constant supply changed habits of personal cleanliness for the better, for in working-class homes one bath and one clothes-wash a week remained the custom well into the twentieth century.[90] While it is clear from evidence before, for example, the 1884 Royal Commission on Housing[91] that water supply continued to be a difficulty in some of the poorer districts of the city, where stand-pipe facilities or one water-source per house rather than per household meant that domestic water supplies still had to be laboriously carried upstairs to individual units, the provision of constant water supplies, together with the growing cult of cleanliness among the respectable working class, may have been important in the matter of household cleanliness, a contributary factor to the typhus ecology.

Hospital provision was the third area in which developments significant in the typhus context occurred. The work of the MAB hospitals from the 1870s added, as we have seen, a further dimension to the preventive information network, but already in the 1860s changes were made in hospital use which may have contributed to the ending of the typhus epidemic in that decade. At the beginning of this period most London vestries relied on their own workhouse infirmaries to treat cases of fever occurring among the poor. The pressure which the 1860s epidemic brought to bear on workhouse services in its early years caused many districts to resort to LFH treatment for their typhus cases, but it was an expensive proceeding for economy-minded guardians to sanction. The situation altered with the passing of the Metropolitan Poor Act of 1867, which introduced rate-equalization as a means of spreading the financial burden of London's poor more evenly. Money spent on the hospitalization of infectious-disease victims could now be reclaimed from the Metropolitan Common Poor Fund; and so inhibitions about excess spending were removed.[92] The number of admissions to the LFH certainly rose sharply in 1868 over 1867 (typhus admissions increased to 449 from 254 in the three months

[89] *Lancet* (1868), i. 273.

[90] Martin Daunton, *House and Home* (1983), 42.

[91] *RCHWC*, PP 1884–5 xxx, *Report*, p. 13. It should be noted that local authorities had no power to compel the supply of water for domestic purposes, only for sanitation. Domestic water provision thus remained a frequent difficulty in small houses whose owners were reluctant to pay 3*d* a week for it: ibid., q. 9632; in any case the supply was generally of cold water only.

[92] Metropolitan Poor Act 1867, 30 & 31 Vict. c.60, ss. 61–9.

June–August), but as the numbers of typhoid admissions and of registered fever deaths also rose, the impact of the new legislation in this area cannot be quantitatively assessed. In terms of the etiology of the disease, however, increased hospitalization seems likely to have been a more effective preventive measure for typhus than for the genuinely infectious diseases such as scarlet fever and smallpox; and the extension of hospital provision for fever patients with the opening of the MAB hospitals may have contributed significantly to reducing the incidence of the disease.[93]

Finally, during the 1870s the pressure of railway demolitions eased. Although quite large railway displacements continued to be made in the 1870s, these were not on the same scale, or as concentrated in time, as those which took place in the central and eastern districts in the early to mid-1860s. Between 1867 and 1885 some 19,000 persons were displaced by railway schemes, compared with 37,000 between 1859 and 1867.[94] Pressure on housing in the centre did not ease, because railways, street improvements, slum-demolition, and warehouse construction continued relentlessly,[95] but the impact of these operations was more diffused and the degree of social dislocation less acute in the years after 1870 than at almost any time in the previous decade. In this sense, and with the temporary return to balance of the metropolitan working-class economy, the crisis of the 1860s passed in London in the 1870s, and with it the essential conditions for the continuance of epidemic typhus. Rising real wages meanwhile took the edge off urban distress in the later years of the century, and prevented large-scale 'stress' overcrowding. Poverty and misery did not disappear in London, but bread riots, semi-violent distress, and epidemic typhus did.[96]

Yet if crucial environmental and preventive improvements undermined the epidemic capacity of typhus during the 1870s, the disease was not finally dislodged from its seats of residual survival before the twentieth century. Isolated outbreaks continued to occur in London and other cities in the 1880s and 1890s. There were outbreaks in St Giles and St Saviour in 1879 which demonstrated respectively the effectiveness of house-closure and of thorough disinfection. In St Saviour, the victims, a family who lived in one of the most crowded courts, were all removed to hospital; all their furniture was burnt, the paper torn from the walls, and the room fumigated. The whole episode was, wrote Robert Bianchi, a lesson on the need for caution in washing infected linen: the first victim, the mother of the family, had in another part of London washed the linen of a child just removed to hospital with typhus.[97] There was a prolonged outbreak in Lisson Grove, Marylebone, in the autumn of 1881,

[93] G. M. Ayers, *England's First State Hospitals* (1969), part 1.

[94] Dyos, 'Railways and housing', 14.

[95] Jones, *Outcast London*, chap. 8; A. S. Wohl, *Endangered Lives: Public Health in Victorian Britain* (1983), chap. 2.

[96] Jones, *Outcast London*, 45, 54.

[97] *Lancet* (1879), i. 69.

which the *Lancet* described as being 'eminently discreditable' to the local sanitary administration; and indeed Wynter Blyth, MOH since 1879, although he subsequently had a distinguished career, seems to have been eminently pig-headed in his insistence that the lack of powers to deal with 'the single suit of rags' was the cause of his failure to end the series of cases.[98] There were also episodes in Camberwell in 1885–6, in St Olave in 1890, in Kensington in 1898, and in St George's, Southwark in 1899. In none of these instances was there any significant extension of the disease; and the Kensington outbreak is instructive. Here typhus had been present in Western Buildings, Ladbroke Grove, Notting Hill since Christmas 1897, but it was not until a young medical man attending some of the cases and an undertaker arrived as patients at the Western Hospital in mid-March that the presence of the disease was recognized. Until then it had been thought to be influenza. Despite this three-month period of grace, however, there was no wider extension of the disease 'beyond those most directly exposed to the contagion': Reginald Dudfield attributed this limited spread to the general improvement of conditions of life among the people.[99]

Typhus was the only one of the communicable diseases in the nineteenth-century preventive canon which had ceased to be a significant cause of concern by the end of the period. Its virtual disappearance represents one of the most significant social gains made by English urban populations during these years. Not only were the working classes relieved of a periodic scourge, but those members of the middle class who came into regular contact with the poor ran a greatly reduced risk of succumbing to the disease after the mid-1880s. While it would evidently be extreme to argue that the burgeoning of middle-class interest in the problems of the working classes and the poor at this time took place because the fear of typhus had receded, it is not out of place to remark that the mass of philanthropic and social work undertaken by the better-off, and especially by their women, would have been considerably more hazardous had typhus had continued to prevail as it had done before 1870. If the survival of endemic and epidemic urban typhus in the first six decades of the nineteenth century reflected the extent to which economic instability and social dislocation were still a part of English industrial society, its disappearance indicated the arrival of more settled conditions as well as improving sanitation, and permitted the development of a far wider degree of middle-class interventionist social effort than had been possible or acceptable when the disease formed an active component of urban poverty. In this final disappearance of epidemic typhus, London's preventive organization played a crucial part, for it was through its efforts in cleansing and whitewashing, improving, or demolishing poor-class property in the city that the disease was gradually dislodged from the habitats which permitted its endemic survival.

[98] *Lancet* (1881), ii. 806, 1,018. [99] *Lancet* (1898), i. 1,016.

8
Tuberculosis

Pure Air, and plenty of it, is the grand prophylactic of this destructive disease. Without it, like the monkeys, of old in the unventilated rooms, of the Zoological Gardens, we 'rot and rot, and drop and drop'.

(Samuel Pearce, 1862)

The Strand and St Giles triple the [death] rate for Lewisham and Hampstead. London stands almost alone in its tremendous contrasts.

(Sir Hugh Beevor, 1899)

INTRODUCTION: THE HISTORICAL AND ETIOLOGICAL DEBATE

During the entire nineteenth century, the scourge of tuberculosis was widely felt and widely feared through all levels of society. Tuberculosis has an ancient history, and in its dominant respiratory form, which primarily affects those in the prime of life, has had an incalculable effect on human societies and individual destinies. It is an infectious disease, although this was not accepted in England until the end of the nineteenth century. Like typhus, its incidence is closely related to environment and domestic habit; like typhus, it too declined during this century, but this decline was far less dramatic, and in all its forms tuberculosis was still the leading killer, after heart disease, in 1900.

In the decline of tuberculosis, however, may lie the clue to the nineteenth-century mortality decline, and the heart of a puzzle which has fascinated many historians. It was identified by Thomas McKeown as the central feature of the mortality decline and, because McKeown considered the decline of tuberculosis to have begun before the effect of the nineteenth-century sanitary reform movement began to be felt, as a prime indicator that the general mortality decline was initiated by rising standards of living.[1] While scholars have subsequently deliberated on the respective influences of housing and nutrition in tuberculosis mortality,[2] McKeown's interpretation has recently been challenged by several scholars, notably by Simon Szreter, Neil McFarlane, and Allan Mitchell.[3] Szreter and McFarlane argue that direct social intervention was as

[1] Thomas McKeown, *The Modern Rise of Population* (1976), 68.

[2] Gillian Cronje, 'Tuberculosis and mortality decline in England and Wales, 1851–1900', in R. I. Woods and J. Woodward (eds.), *Urban Disease and Mortality* (1984); id., 'Captain of the Men of Death: pulmonary tuberculosis in the economy of England and Wales, 1851–1910', unpublished Ph.D thesis, University of London (1990); J. M. Winter, *The Great War and the British People* (1986); Linda Bryder, *Beneath the Magic Mountain: A Social History of Tuberculosis in the Twentieth Century* (Oxford, 1988); F. B. Smith, *The Retreat of Tuberculosis 1850–1950* (1988).

[3] Simon Szreter, 'The importance of social intervention in Britain's mortality decline

important as the indirect benefits of rising living standards in bringing about the reduction in tuberculosis deaths, while Mitchell has pointed to the example of France, which was much less successful than either Britain or Germany in combating the disease at this period. In Mitchell's view it is unlikely that the English and the Germans were significantly better nourished than the French, and he suggests that the key to improvement lay in local sanitary measures and national health reforms, in both of which France lagged behind England and Germany. Against this background, a closer examination of tuberculosis mortality in London is topical, for the local circumstances of English tuberculosis mortality have yet to be investigated in any detail.[4]

Tuberculosis is a chronic infectious disease which may manifest itself in different forms: as respiratory (pulmonary) tuberculosis (also known as phthisis, or consumption), scrofula, lupus, tuberculosis of the bones and joints, or tubercular meningitis. In addition to being chronic (the period from the active manifestation of the disease to its termination in death lasts for years rather than weeks or months), it is a cruelly debilitating disease with a most complex etiology.[5] It is caused by the bacillus *Mycobacterium tuberculosis*, discovered by Robert Koch in 1882, but there are five types of tuberculosis affecting different animal types, of which only two, the human and bovine, cause disease in man. The human type was by far the most common source of disease in this period, although contemporaries believed until 1901 that tuberculosis of bovine origin was more common, and that the disease was increasing rapidly among the bovine population.[6] In fact human tuberculosis was responsible for around 98 per cent of all cases of pulmonary tuberculosis, and for some 70 per cent of non-pulmonary cases; bovine tuberculosis, which is transmitted primarily in infected milk and is associated more particularly with the disease in infants and children, was responsible for the rest.[7]

c.1850–1914: a reinterpretation of the role of public health', *Social History of Medicine*, I (1988), 1–39; Neil McFarlane, 'Hospitals, housing and tuberculosis in Glasgow', *Soc. Hist. Med.*, 2 (1989), 59–85; Allan Mitchell, 'An inexact science: the statistics of tuberculosis in late nineteenth-century France', *Soc. Hist. Med.*, 3 (1990), 387–403.

[4] An honourable exception to this generalization may be found in Linda Bryder, 'Silicosis, tuberculosis, and the slate industry in North Wales 1927–1939', in P. Weindling (ed.), *The Social History of Occupational Health* (1985), 108–26; see also Cronje, 'Captain of the Men of Death'.

[5] The most impressive description of what it was like to be a tuberculosis victim is to be found in Pierre Guillaume, *Du Désespoir au salut: les tuberculeux aux XIX et XX siècles* (Paris, 1986), 14–21. The myth of the disease as a gentle killer has a long history: e.g. in 1882 the *Lancet* cited a passage from the letters of Edgar Allan Poe in which the poet wrote of the death of a consumptive friend: 'It is a path I have prayed to follow. I would wish all I love to perish of that gentle disease. How Glorious!' The journal declared its object in quotation was 'not to criticise this romantic view of phthisis, but to record it': *Lancet* (1882), i. 555. A more realistic assessment was presented by Sir William Broadbent, who described phthisis as a tedious and trying way of leaving the world, often so painful and distressing, and most expensive: *Lancet* (1898), ii. 1,101.

[6] Arthur Newsholme, *Fifty Years in Public Health* (1935), 239; *Lancet* (1880), i. 923.

[7] Ministry of Health, *A Memorandum on Bovine Tuberculosis in Man with Special Reference to Infection by Milk*, Reports on Public Health and Medical Subjects, 63 (1931), 23 (cited in Bryder, *Mountain*, 3).

Human tuberculosis is spread by droplet infection, in the fine saliva spray expelled when speaking, coughing, or sneezing. Three routes of transmission for the bacillus have been described: dried, as dust particles; in moist droplets; or as droplet nuclei, formed when the liquid content of small droplets has evaporated quickly, leaving dried 'droplet nuclei' so small that they remain suspended in the air for a considerable time. The relative importance of these three routes is uncertain,[8] although most authorities agree that infection is generally airborne.[9] The risk of infection is clearly related to the duration and intensity of the individual exposure to the bacillus. Although a small percentage of cases are particularly infectious, tuberculosis is not in general a highly infectious disease; it is principally where people are crowded together in poorly ventilated conditions that the risk of infection from active cases is great.

Infection with tuberculosis is not, however, synomyous with the development of active disease. Most infected individuals successfully overcome infection, and remain unaware of their encounter with *Mycobacterium tuberculosis*, although healed lesions in the lungs bear witness to the encounter. In the early twentieth century some 90 per cent of Britain's population was estimated to have been infected with tuberculosis at some time, although only 1 per cent of these developed active disease.[10] The factors which lead to disease, whether by activation of existing infection or by re-infection, are known to include personal and domestic hygiene, diet, overcrowding, occupational exposure to infection, environmental exposure to agents liable to cause lung damage, and the effects of previous infectious-disease episodes. In seeking to explain the decline of tuberculosis, structural factors such as fertility and migration may be added to these social determinants of mortality.[11] The balance of these factors in determining the overall pattern of, and regional variations in, tuberculosis mortality is unclear. Economic conditions, as much as social, plainly play a crucial part in the equation,[12] but within this generalization the respective roles of housing and diet remain debateable. In general terms, the reasons for the decline of tuberculosis have been well defined by F. B. Smith: 'Better nutrition, housing, nurture, lessening of fatigue, smaller family size, acting synergistically in varying permutations through time and place hold the answer.'[13] Yet such a general answer remains unsatisfactory. The continuing challenge of historical tuberculosis research is to achieve a finer evaluation of the balance of factors driving the decline of the disease.

[8] W. W. C. Topley and G. S. Wilson (eds.), *Principles of Bacteriology, Virology and Immunity*, seventh edn. (1984), iii. 38.

[9] Matthew O. Lock, 'Tuberculosis', in F. H. Top and P. H. Wehrle (eds,) *Communicable and Infectious Diseases*, ninth edn. (St Louis, Miss., 1981), 675–6; G. P. Youmans, *Tuberculosis* (1979), 357.

[10] Sheridan Delepine, *Astor Committee Final Report*, 2 (1913), 27 (cited in Bryder, *Mountain*, 4).

[11] Topley and Wilson, *Principles*, iii. 38; Cronje, 'Tuberculosis', 97.

[12] M. Greenwood, *Epidemics and Crowd Diseases* (1935), 358; Bryder, *Mountain*, 129.

[13] Smith, *Retreat*, 244.

The problem of respiratory tuberculosis dominated the nineteenth-century preventive approach to the disease, and is that which will principally concern us here. In seeking to understand the decline of the disease, however, an issue of outstanding importance is the reliability of recorded mortality figures. McKeown and his colleagues accepted the registrar-general's data without question. Indeed, McKeown claimed that deaths from respiratory tuberculosis were declining even before registration began, although the evidence for this is slender, and shaky in the extreme.[14] McKeown also adduced a continuous decline in respiratory tuberculosis from the beginning of registration in 1838. It is this assertion which has been challenged by Simon Szreter, who pointed out that McKeown's own figures indicate that registered phthisis mortality did not begin a sustained fall until after 1866–7.[15] This is consistent with the pattern of the disease in London, and in the city's individual registration districts (Figs. 8.1, 8.2*a–c*). Szreter has argued that the fall in mortality discerned by McKeown for the years 1847–50 was a short-term fluctuation in the overall mortality pattern, and that a strong resurgence of phthisis mortality in 1850–6 and no clear trend decline in the following decade represented a return to the *status quo*. A closer examination of the reliability of the nineteenth-century mortality figures for respiratory diseases suggests not only that Szreter's argument is valid, but that the beginning of the decline in phthisis mortality may be pushed even further forward, towards the 1880s. Although there was dis-

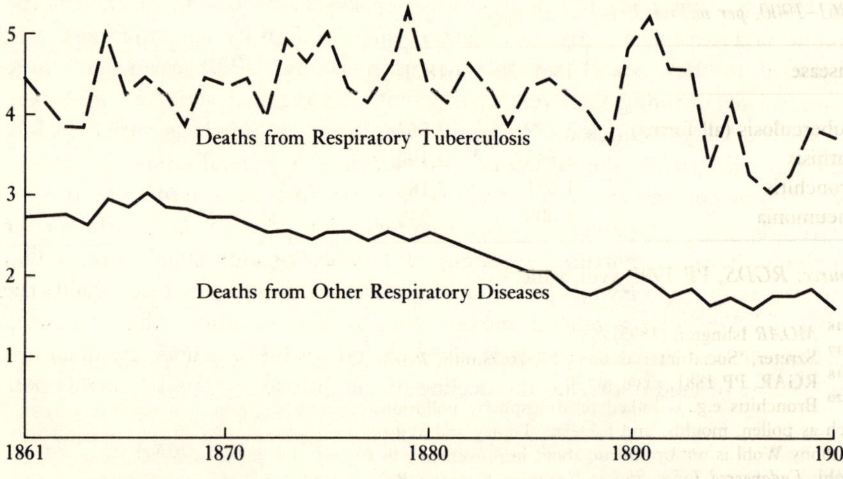

FIG. 8.1. *Deaths from respiratory diseases in London, 1860–1900, per 1,000 population.*

[14] I have elaborated this point in 'Diagnosis, death and diet: the case of London 1750–1914', *Journal of Interdisciplinary History*, 18: 3 (Winter 1988), 387–401.

[15] Szreter, 'Social intervention', 15.

cussion and some disagreement among contemporaries on the reliability of the figures and the nature and dating of the beginnings of decline, at least one observer in the 1890s dated his local decline in phthisis from 1870.[16]

There are, however, other reasons for treating a mortality decline adduced from the registration data with reservations, for there is still the problem of differential contemporary diagnosis between phthisis and bronchitis and other respiratory diseases.[17] Until the 1880s deaths from the latter rose in counterbalance to the decline in respiratory tuberculosis, so that, as the registrar-general remarked in 1881, 'the sum of the two shows no progressive decrease'.[18] (Table 8.1; Fig. 8.1) It was only when the continuing and accelerating decline in phthisis after 1880 was accompanied by a reduction in other respiratory diseases that the *Lancet* thought it worthwhile to call attention to the 'undoubted decline' in mortality from the former.[19] The causes of this reduction in deaths from other respiratory diseases are obscure, and probably as complex as those for phthisis, but may include some diminution in atmospheric pollution, better nurture, and housing conditions improved through regular lime-whiting, making houses less hospitable to moulds.[20] Some of these factors may also have influenced tuberculosis mortality; it is notable that it was only in the 1880s that deaths from non-respiratory tuberculosis began to decline.[21]

TABLE 8.1. *Death-rates from tubercular and respiratory disease in England and Wales, 1861–1900, per million living at all ages*

Disease	1861–70	1871–80	1881–90	1891–1900
Tuberculosis (all forms)	3,239	2,862	2,429	2,010
Phthisis	2,545	2,190	1,775	1,391
Bronchitis	1,691	2,186	2,081	1,811
Pneumonia	1,008	948	1,041	1,227

Source: *RGDS*, PP 1905 xviii, table 5.

16 *MOAR* Islington (1895), 55.

17 Szreter, 'Social intervention', 13, 16; Smith, *Retreat*, 21, n. 13, 14; Hardy 'Diagnosis', 392–4.

18 RGAR, PP 1881, xxvii, p. 30.

19 *Lancet* (1889), i. 954.

20 Bronchitis e.g. is linked to atmospheric pollution, cigarette smoking, and sensitizing agents such as pollen, moulds, and bacteria: Topley and Wilson, *Principles*, iii. 399. It may be noted that Anthony Wohl is not optimistic about improvements in atmospheric pollution at this period: A. S. Wohl, *Endangered Lives: Public Health in Victorian Britain*, (1983), 217. Improvements in nurture are less than easy to demonstrate, but see below; in 1874 the MOH for St Giles noted that the mortality from bronchitis and pneumonia among the poor was not surprising—it was not uncommon for them to come home drunk and lie down on the floor or stairs in wet clothes: *MOAR* St Giles (1874), 38.

21 Smith, *Retreat*, table 3, p. 10; the point was emphasized by H. Timbrell Bulstrode, 'Report on sanatoria for consumptives and certain other aspects of the tuberculosis question', *MOAR* LGB, Supplement, PP 1907 xxvii, pp. 33, 34.

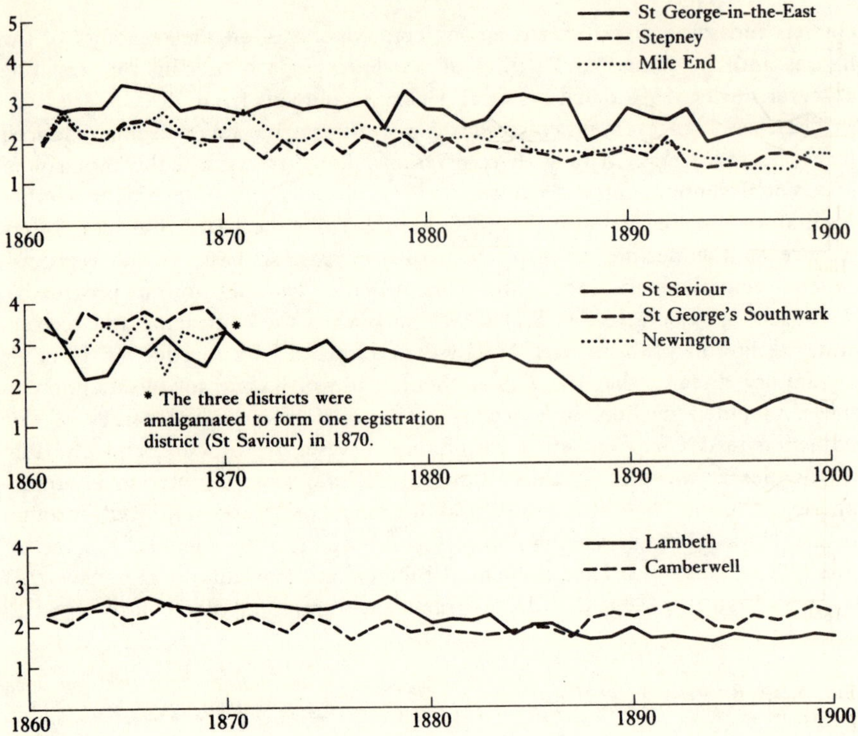
St George-in-the-East
Stepney
Mile End
1860
1870
1880
1890
1900
St Saviour
St George's Southwark
Newington
* The three districts were amalgamated to form one registration district (St Saviour) in 1870.
Lambeth
Camberwell

a

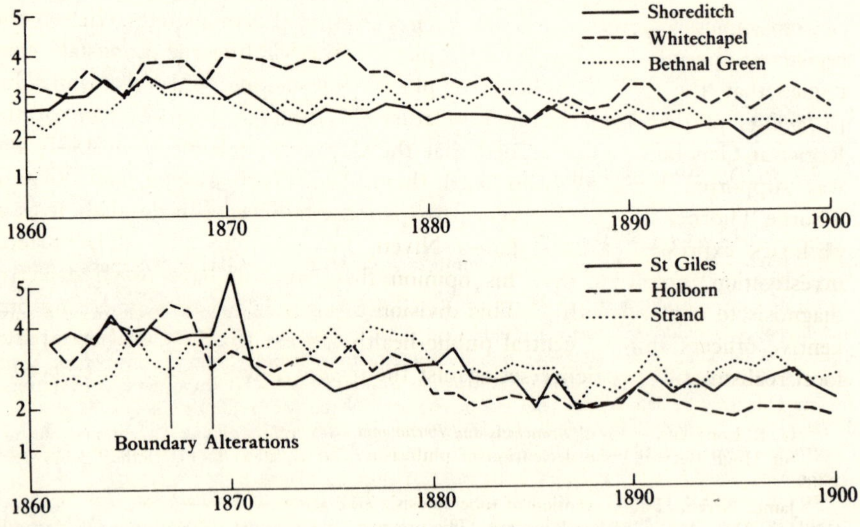
Shoreditch
Whitechapel
Bethnal Green
1860
1870
1880
1890
1900
St Giles
Holborn
Strand
Boundary Alterations

b

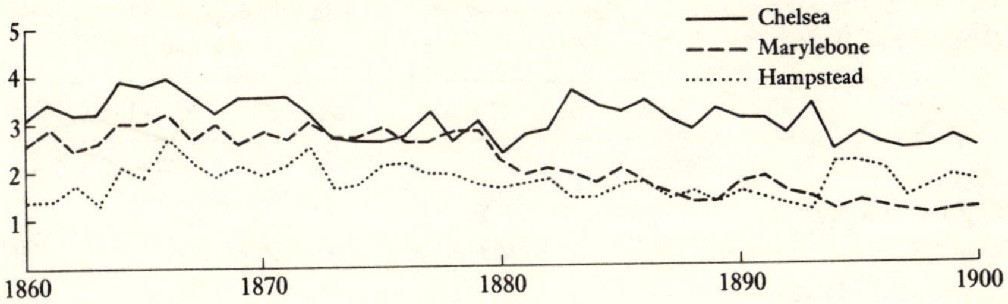

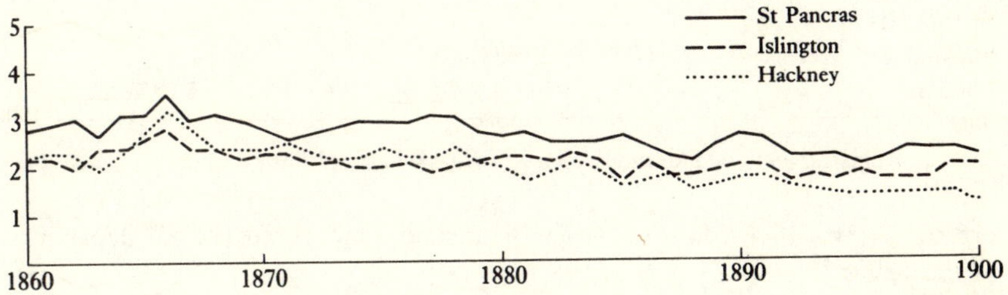

FIG. 8.2a–c *Respiratory-tuberculosis deaths in London registration districts, 1860–1900, per 1,000 population.*

Contemporary observers, as the *Lancet*'s attitude demonstrates, viewed the registered mortality figures with suspicion. In 1883 George Longstaff concluded that 'the apparent decline' in phthisis rates since 1851 was mainly due to 'points of diagnosis and nomenclature'.[22] Although John Tatham of the Registrar-General's Office argued that the data were reliable from 1851, and was supported by some who used them, like Hugh Beevor and Richard Thorne Thorne,[23] acute observers perhaps more familiar with the daily lives of phthisics expressed doubts. James Niven, for example, after diligent local investigation, noted in 1897 his opinion that 'we still have much defective diagnosis to contend with'.[24] This division of attitude between practising preventive officers and the central public-health officers suggests, perhaps, partly local realism and experience set against the overall view; it may also reflect the

[22] G. B. Longstaff, *Phthisis, Bronchitis and Pneumonia* (1884), 6.

[23] Sir Hugh Beevor, 'The declension of phthisis', *Lancet* (1899), i. 1,005; see also (1898), ii. 1,489.

[24] James Niven, 'The prevention of tuberculosis', *Transactions of the Epidemiological Society*, 16 (1896–7), 214; see also Arthur Ransome, 'The prospect of abolishing tuberculosis', *Public Health*, 2, (1892–3), 293–4.

TABLE 8.2. *Phthisis and respiratory disease death-rates per 1,000 living for London and England and Wales, 1861–1900*

	1861–70	1871–80	1881–90	1891–1900
Phthisis				
England and Wales	2.5	2.2	1.8	1.4
London	2.8	2.4	2.1	1.8
Respiratory Disease excluding phthisis				
England and Wales				
London	4.3	4.6	4.3	4.0
Bronchitis				
England and Wales	1.7	2.2	2.1	1.8
London	2.4	2.9	2.6	2.1

Sources: Registrar-general's annual reports; *MOAR* LCC (1900), 42.

pressures for self-justification of the financially beleagured central departments in the 1890s.[25]

A phthisis mortality decline dating from at least 1851 must, in view of the evidence, be viewed with suspicion. There were, of course, local variations, but if the date for the beginning of the national decline is moved back to the later 1860s, or even to 1880, then McKeown's argument for the primacy of the disease in the British mortality decline falls flat, and the case for causative factors other than improved diet is reopened.[26] Szreter has suggested that sanitary reform was indeed significant in reducing tuberculosis levels, notably in terms of reducing the impact of infectious diseases predisposing the development of active tuberculosis.[27] In particular, he argues that the reduction in the 'filth diseases'—typhoid and typhus—and the disappearance of cholera from the later 1860s was critically important, resulting in fewer post-primary tuberculosis breakdowns. In Szreter's view it is likely that tuberculosis was only a subsidiary element in a vicious cycle of sanitation-related diseases, which was broken in 1867–8 as a result of the labours of the sanitary reform movement.[28]

Szreter's thesis has the devastating charm of simplicity, and makes an important contribution to our understanding of nineteenth-century tuberculosis. None the less, it probably accounts for only part of the truth. Although there are close similarities between the pattern of tuberculosis's national decline and that of some other infections—in timing, for example, with typhoid, typhus, scarlet fever, and whooping cough; and in sex-incidence with

[25] For the difficulties experienced by Thorne Thorne as medical officer to the Local Government Board, see R. M. MacLeod, 'The frustration of state medicine 1880–1899', *Medical History*, 11 (1967), 15–40.

[26] Szreter, 'Social intervention', 16–17. [27] Ibid. 17. [28] Ibid.

typhoid, as mortality fell faster among women, closer examination of local patterns of tuberculosis, typhus, typhoid, and cholera mortality reveal that the links between them are far from clear-cut—as might be expected from a disease with as complex an etiology as tuberculosis. Indeed, the history of registered tuberculosis mortality in mid-nineteenth-century London demonstrates the justice of Gillian Cronje's warning that the causes of local tuberculosis mortality must have been very various.[29]

LOCAL VARIATIONS

London was throughout the century one of the principal centres of pulmonary-tuberculosis mortality, with average annual death-rates in excess of those for England and Wales. Relatively high tuberculosis mortality was a characteristic which the city shared with the four other major areas of economic growth: the northern textile counties, the north-east coalfield, Birmingham and the Black Country, and Glamorgan and the South Wales coalfield.[30] In common with the national trend, London's mortality fell, from an average of 2.9 per 1,000 living in the decade 1851–60 to 1.8 in 1891–1900.[31] Within the city, however, mortality was unevenly distributed, lower in the peripheral districts, higher in the centre; lower in the well-to-do west, higher in the East End; and while the long-term trend of the city's mortality decline followed that of the rest of the country, within the different parishes mortality peaks and lows by no means followed a common pattern (Figs 8.2*a–c*).

Detailed examination of the various mortality patterns of different diseases demonstrates the difficulties of such local analyses, and can result in spectacular confusion. Even setting aside the complications of other respiratory diseases, and the fact that the available figures are uncorrected for deaths in institutions until the 1890s, the registered phthisis death-rates show considerable local individuality. The pattern of the 1860s is especially interesting, because it was in these years that London experienced its last major urban crisis on the pre-industrial model, accompanied by a major typhus epidemic and interrupted by an outbreak of cholera.[32] In decennial terms there was little to choose between 1851–60 and 1861–70: Shirley Murphy calculated a phthisis mortality of 2.86 per 1,000 for the former, of 2.84 for the latter.[33] Annual mortality figures are not consistently available before the later 1850s, but it seems that phthisis mortality did swing up, from a fairly stable level in the later 1850s, to peaks in 1864 and 1866, before falling to its former level by 1870, and declining quite steadily thereafter until the 1890s. (One may note

[29] Cronje, 'Tuberculosis', 94. [30] Ibid. 97. [31] *MOAR* LCC (1900), 42.

[32] Anne Hardy, 'Urban famine or urban crisis? Typhus in the Victorian city', *Medical History*, 32 (1988), 401–25.

[33] *MOAR* LCC (1900), 42.

with interest that the death-rates for other respiratory diseases follow the curve of phthisis quite closely in the 1860s (Fig. 8.1), before registration practices were further tightened in 1874.) The typhus epidemic of the 1860s, which began in 1862, peaked in 1864 and 1867, and ended in 1868, may have been at least as important as cholera in determining the phthisis pattern of the decade, according to the Szreter argument.

The experience of the local registration districts suggests some link between typhus and tuberculosis, but correlations cannot be made specific because of the absence of typhus-mortality figures in these years. A link between cholera and tuberculosis may in some cases be suggested more clearly, except for the problem of *duration*: post-primary tuberculosis breakdown, precipitated by a cholera (or typhus) incident, would take between two and perhaps four years to reach termination. However, let us look at the data for the typhus epidemic, which began in the East End of London in the spring of 1862. In that year registered 'typhus' deaths in the central and eastern districts uniformly soared (Fig. 7.1). Phthisis deaths peaked in Shoreditch, Stepney, and Mile End in 1862; in Whitechapel in 1863; in Bethnal Green in 1864; and in St George-in-the-East not until 1865. St Giles and the Strand, also fever-ridden and, like Whitechapel, full of common lodging houses sheltering the poorest of the poor, also registered phthisis peaks in 1862. That of the Strand, however, was only a hiccup compared with the maximum registered in 1865. Holborn and St Giles achieved substantial phthisis peaks in 1864. The link between mortality peaks for typhus and for phthisis is not obviously demonstrated by local experience: it seems clear that other factors must have been at least as important as the former in determining the latter; and typhoid and cholera peaks are no more easily correlated with phthisis in any specific fashion. Typhoid was epidemic in both England and London between 1865 and 1868;[34] among the East End districts most seriously affected by cholera in 1866, phthisis peaks were recorded in Shoreditch, Bethnal Green, and Whitechapel in 1866, but not in St George, Stepney, and Mile End; in the two former the peak had begun in the previous year. Several northern districts beyond any but incidental effects of the cholera epidemic also registered phthisis peaks in 1865–6 (Fig. 8.2*c*).

While further detailed investigation of the circumstances of local tuberculosis mortality in the metropolis is evidently required, and the interaction of different disease organisms in human bodies remains unclear, an overview of the case of London in the 1860s suggests some connection between the social and economic circumstances of the city and phthisis mortality, as well as the more general observation that the city was unusually riddled by epidemic disease during that decade. To make a more specific connection between diet and the disease is less easy. Nutritional levels in working-class London certainly fell

[34] *LFHAR* (1868), 9.

during the building-trades strikes of 1859–61,[35] and might be thought to have borne some responsibility for the phthisis peaks of the early 1860s, except that the building trades were no more strongly represented in the districts experiencing phthisis peaks in 1862 than in districts where phthisis peaked later.[36] Although prices were very high in 1865, placing meat almost beyond the reach of the poor, employment was reported to be good.[37] In 1866 work was slack in the East End; in 1868 and 1869, also, trade was bad and employment wanting.[38] In parallel, Gillian Cronje's observations on tuberculosis and the condition of Lancashire during the 1860s are of considerable interest.

By contrast with London, conditions in Lancashire were far more clear-cut. The cotton famine began in 1861, but incipient typhus epidemics in the cotton towns in 1862–3 were apparently quelled by the generous relief which poured into the area from a sympathetic public, and which prevented serious social dislocation.[39] The famine ended in 1864, but many cotton operatives had meanwhile suffered serious nutritional deprivation,[40] and phthisis mortality in the urban districts of Lancashire rose sharply in the years 1864–7. Significantly, the rural district of Garstang experienced a continuous decline in tuberculosis mortality during the 1860s.[41] Cronje suggests that the case of Lancashire demonstrates the influence of nutrition; yet other factors, such as the stress of unemployment and altered patterns of social behaviour, may have been at least as important in determining this mortality, and remain to be evaluated.[42] Whatever the precise social balances influencing the raised tuberculosis mortality of these years in London and urban Lancashire, the experience of these two substantial districts in the 1860s, when increased phthisis mortality was associated with economic and social distress, suggests that a closer examination of registered, and qualified, tuberculosis mortality in the context of social and economic conditions may indicate this mortality perhaps represents a return to *status quo* rather than the interruption of a recently established pattern of decline.

The delicacy of such intricate analyses of local phthisis mortality as I have attempted above is enhanced by the more esoteric features of tuberculosis etiology, as well as by specific local social and economic factors which may have

[35] Hardy, 'Urban famine', 404.

[36] According to the 1861 census, the percentage of men over 20 employed in building-related trades was approximately as follows: Shoreditch, 30%; Bethnal Green, 22%; Stepney 21%; Mile End 14.5%; and the others of lesser significance.

[37] *MOAR* St Saviour (1865), 7; *MOAR* St George-in-the-East (1865), 22.

[38] *MOAR* St George-in-the-East (1866), 19; ibid. (1868), 22; *MOAR* St Saviour (1869), 11.

[39] Hardy, 'Urban famine', 421.

[40] Derek Oddy, 'Urban famine in nineteenth-century Britain: the effect of the Lancashire cotton famine on working-class diet and health', *Economic History Review*, second ser. 37 (1983), 68–86.

[41] Cronje, 'Tuberculosis', 172.

[42] Oddy's analysis of the effects of the cotton famine on diet and health does not, in my view, make a convincing case for the raised incidence of infectious disease at this time being related to diet as opposed to behavioural factors.

had a bearing on the timing and extent of local phthisis mortality. In Bethnal Green, for example, the presence of the City of London Hospital for Diseases of the Chest (founded in 1848—later the Victoria Park Hospital), affected registered mortality not only through deaths in the hospital, but through the large number of out-patients who came to reside locally while receiving treatment.[43] In districts containing, or close to, phthisis hospitals, hospital deaths may have been of small account compared to the presence of numerous out-patients: by the later 1860s, for example, the Brompton Hospital was said to be attracting over 10,000 new cases a year, and the City Hospital some 14,000; in the later 1880s, similarly, the North London drew nearly 3,000 for treatment annually at its out-patient premises in Tottenham Court Road.[44] If anything, the distorting effect of this mortality grew as time went on: in 1858 the Brompton registered 1,038 new out-patients; by 1889 the figure was 13,377;[45] at the North London, weekly out-patient attendance was 700 in 1871, 'and rapidly increasing'.[46] Such cases, while probably attracted from the nearest localities, may have come from all over London and further afield, their infection and eventual death reflecting less on the London district where the death was registered than on the local conditions and stresses in their district of origin.[47]

Problems caused by the variability and etiology of tuberculosis are less easy to demonstrate in a specific local context, yet may have serious implications of the local 'tuberculosis ecology'. Rates of survival for open phthisis cases are, for example, a considerable complicating factor. Chronic cases survived much longer than galloping cases—between fifteen and thirty years after developing; experienced physicians were agreed that galloping cases, those terminated by death in a year or less from diagnosis, were relatively rare.[48] French authorities like Laennec (1781–1826), Andral (1797–1876), and Louis and Bayle (1774–1816), estimated the duration of life after the onset of active phthisis as on average twenty-three to twenty-four months. English research modified these estimates, however, producing some interesting differentials of expectancy by social class. James Pollock of the Brompton Hospital, whose out-patient clinics embraced patients of all social classes below the wealthy, gave the average duration of 129 cases ending in death as from two years nine months to three years; these cases (7 per cent) were among 3,566 patients, the remainder of whom were still living at the end of two-and-a-half years.[49] Charles Theodore Williams, himself attached to the Brompton, and son of the phthisis specialist Charles J. B. Williams, noted significantly that in terms of

43 *MOAR* Bethnal Green (1878), 25.

44 *Lancet* (1868), i. 455; (1874), i. 821; (1887), i. 1,258.

45 *Lancet* (1858), i. 254; (1889), i. 1,218.

46 *Lancet* (1871), i. 870.

47 In 1863 the Brompton was said to be attracting patients from all parts of London and many distant places in the country: M. Davidson and F. G. Rouvray, *The Brompton Hospital* (1954), 66.

48 C. T. Williams, 'The duration of phthisis pulmonalis', *Medico-Chirurgical Transactions*, 54 (1871), 97.

49 Ibid. 116–17.

the few deaths and duration of life for the survivors, Pollock's findings were 'the most favourable results for the lower classes ever published'.[50]

Among C. T. Williams's own patients, 'mostly of the upper and middle class', the duration of life was apparently greater, although the terms of his and Pollock's projects are not strictly comparable. Among the thousand individuals covered by Williams, 198 died (20 per cent), after an average survival of eight years, while the 102 who remained as his patients had on average lived eight years and two months since first consulting him.[51] It is possible that, had Pollock extended the terms of his study, he might have found a mortality of 20 per cent over eight years, and a survival rate of 80 per cent, but this seems improbable in view of the findings of Dr Fuller of St George's Hospital, which appropriately balance the two extremes. Fuller found that the greater number of his 118 hospital patients died between three and eighteen months after the onset of the disease; in his private practice, however, forty-six cases survived variously between one and seven-and-a-half years. The discrepancy between the two groups of cases was clear, but was not, according to Fuller, wholly due to social position (by which he presumably meant nutritional and occupational status), but rather to the greater care with which the upper and more educated classes were wont to watch their health and note the earliest inroads of disease.[52]

While class differentials in the survival of phthisis victims may complicate the assessment of factors determining local death-rates, the conclusions of these English doctors on survival-rates during the 1850s and 1860s have wider implications.[53] Indeed, with the rise of the middle classes in this period, with the extension of suburbia, and the spread of ideals of 'respectability' and 'privacy', it may be suggested that mortality-rates from tuberculosis in the later decades of the century were increasingly affected by rising living standards less directly through improved diet, than through the changing standards of domestic behaviour which accompanied this social development. 'Respectability' was no less a god to the working classes than to the lower middle class by the end of the century.[54] The significance of these intangible factors to the history of phthisis cannot be proven, only suggested; and the evidence may also be used in support of the role of improved nutrition.[55] It appears, however, that phthisis mortality-rates were slower to fall among the well-to-do than among the general population. The four septennial reports of the Scottish Widows Fund showed the same percentage of deaths on lives at risk between 1860 and 1888; only in the final report of the century, that for 1889–95, was an improvement discernible. Among the legal and medical professions,

[50] Ibid. 118. [51] Ibid. 113. [52] Ibid. 116.

[53] C. T. Williams's study was published in 1871 (see n. 48 above); Pollock's work probably dates from the early 1860s. His book *The Elements of Prognosis in Consumption*, from which Williams drew his information, was published in 1865 and favourably reviewed by the *Lancet* on 9 December of that year (*Lancet* (1865), ii. 649–70). I have been unable to trace a copy.

[54] Wohl, *Endangered Lives*, 65. [55] Beevor, 'Declension', 1,008.

meanwhile, there was little reduction in the phthisis death-rate in the age-group 25 to 45 between 1871 and the mid-1890s; and in the medical profession itself, deaths from phthisis were in the same proportion to deaths from all causes at each age in 1890–2 as they had been in 1873–82.[56] For what they are worth, the (uncorrected) registered death-rates from phthisis in the well-to-do western districts appear to have been slower to fall (Table 8.3), but although the poorer classes in these areas may have departed to their own homes when

TABLE 8.3. *Phthisis mortality per 1,000 living in London registration districts, 1861–1900 (uncorrected figures)*

District	1861–70	1871–80	1881–90	1891–1900
Kensington*	2.8	2.1	1.9	1.7
Chelsea	3.5	2.8	3.2	2.6
St George's, Hanover Square	2.6	2.6	2.4	2.0
Westminster*	3.3	2.8	2.0	1.2
Marylebone	2.9	2.4	1.7	1.3
Hampstead	1.9	1.9	1.5	1.7
St Pancras	3.0	2.8	2.4	2.2
Islington	2.4	2.1	2.0	1.8
Hackney	2.5	2.2	1.8	1.5
St Giles	4.0	2.7	2.4	2.5
Strand	3.2	3.6	2.7	2.8
Holborn*	3.8	3.0	2.1	1.9
City*	3.7	3.0	2.7	2.1
Shoreditch	3.1	2.6	2.3	2.0
Bethnal Green	2.8	2.7	2.7	2.3
Whitechapel	3.5	3.6	2.8	2.8
St George-in-the-East	3.0	2.8	2.7	2.3
Stepney	2.3	1.9	1.7	1.5
Mile End	2.4	2.4	1.9	1.5
Poplar	2.9	3.0	2.5	2.1
St Saviour*	4.1	2.8	2.2	1.5
St Olave*	4.2	3.0	2.3	2.2
Lambeth	2.5	2.7	2.0	1.6
Wandsworth	2.1	1.9	1.5	1.2
Camberwell	2.3	2.0	1.9	2.2
LONDON	2.9	2.6	2.1	1.8

Note: *Collective district or district with boundary changes.
Source: Registrar-general's annual reports.

[56] Beevor, 'Declension', 1,008.

TABLE 8.4. *Deaths from other respiratory diseases per 1,000 living in London registration districts, 1861–1900 (uncorrected figures)*

District	1861–70	1871–80	1881–90	1891–1900
Kensington*	3.6	4.1	3.7	3.6
Chelsea	4.5	5.1	4.4	4.6
St George's, Hanover Square	3.7	4.7	4.3	4.0
Westminster*	4.2	4.6	4.2	3.2
Marylebone	4.8	5.1	4.1	3.6
Hampstead	2.1	2.7	2.1	1.7
St Pancras	4.4	4.7	4.2	4.1
Islington	3.9	4.1	3.8	3.7
Hackney	3.4	3.7	3.3	3.1
St Giles	6.4	6.5	5.4	4.1
Strand	5.5	5.9	5.7	5.4
Holborn*	5.7	5.2	4.7	4.3
City*	5.3	5.0	5.0	5.1
Shoreditch	4.8	5.4	5.5	5.4
Bethnal Green	4.5	5.0	5.5	5.1
Whitechapel	5.7	6.4	6.8	6.3
St George-in-the-East	5.0	6.1	7.0	5.8
Stepney	4.4	5.2	5.6	4.8
Mile End	4.6	4.9	4.8	4.0
Poplar	4.3	5.0	4.5	4.8
St Saviour*	4.7	5.7	5.4	4.7
St Olave*	5.1	5.5	5.5	5.3
Lambeth	4.4	4.7	4.2	4.0
Wandsworth	3.0	3.6	3.3	2.9
Camberwell	3.4	3.8	4.0	3.9
Greenwich	4.0	4.3	4.0	3.4
LONDON	4.3	4.6	4.3	4.0

Note: *Collective district or district with boundary changes.
Source: Registrar-general's annual reports.

they fell ill, the changing social composition of many of these districts included a growing proportion of lower-middle and working class which may help to distort the mortality statistics.

CONTEMPORARY MEDICAL OPINION

The slower decline in phthisis among the well-to-do may be what should be expected if nutritional improvement were responsible for the reduction in deaths from the disease. If so, it also demonstrates the limitations of better nutrition; yet it seems likely too that improvements in *nurture*, in personal care, were less marked among this class than among their social inferiors in this period, and were equally likely to be greater among the under-25 age-group where reduced phthisis death-rates were most marked, since this age-group was less likely—and increasingly, with the falling birth-rates, less likely—to be subjected to the stress of enforced employment to support wives or families. Fuller's observation on the importance of the management of the course of the disease in prolonging life can be echoed from other sources, despite the gloomy assessment of recent historians on the likely effect of medical treatment in this period.[57] Thus in 1875, Ballard of Islington—no mean student of epidemiology—suggested that a small improvement in registered phthisis mortality might be 'in the main due' to the increased facility of diagnosing the disease at earlier stages, to more perfect knowledge of the pathology of tubercule, and to the fact that patients and their friends were 'more alive now than formerly' to the need for early treatment and constant watchfulness and attention.[58] Twenty years later his successor noted the steady decline in the disease since 1870 as 'most satisfactory . . . the modern hygienic treatment of the disease has had good effect'.[59] In 1893 George Nicholas recorded that 'precautions of some kind' were now frequently taken by the friends of phthisics to prevent the spread of the disease.[60] There is evidence to suggest that doctors were indeed giving advice on measures of personal and community hygiene to persons at risk from phthisis by the 1870s,[61] but such specific advice was also increasingly given in a context of greater consciousness of hygiene. The importance of this general development was underscored by J. Edward Squire, physician to the North London Consumption Hospital, in 1889, when he observed that more careful attention to the sanitary and hygienic conditions of life had already had an appreciable effect in reducing the mortality from phthisis. As a rider, however, he added that this improvement had essentially resulted from measures directed in a great part against other diseases, especially the common infectious diseases, or from 'sanitary

[57] Smith, *Retreat*, chaps. 1, 2, et seq.
[58] *MOAR* Islington (1875), 8.
[59] Ibid. (1895), 55.
[60] *MOAR* Wandsworth (1893), 200.
[61] See below, n. 126.

regulations adopted on general principles'.[62] Between the two—measures taken against other diseases and hygienic practices directed against phthisis—medicine may have made more of a contribution to the decline of the disease than has generally been allowed.

The role of 'care' in the survival of the tuberculous individual is emphasized by another factor in the etiology of the disease which puzzled contemporaries. Unlike the associated respiratory conditions of bronchitis and pneumonia, phthisis mortality followed no seasonal pattern, nor was its annual mortality influenced by climactic factors.[63] Phthisis was, in fact, a disease which was responsive to the internal economy of the individual, as it were, and was unaffected by external conditions. The observation was more scientifically formulated by Buchanan and Mitchell in 1880, who discovered on investigation that the range of variation in weekly phthisis deaths during a year was only 25 per cent—smaller than for any conditions other than cancer and premature birth.[64] It was as if, Longstaff commented, 'the inexorable diseases, phthisis and cancer, keep their victims alive . . . until they have finished with them, jealously resenting any interference'.[65] The regularity of the weekly curve suggests indeed that once tuberculosis had been activated in an individual its course, although it might be prolonged by care, inherited resistance, or by the nutritional status of the individual, or hastened by continued work or habitual undernutrition, was unlikely to be immediately concluded by any short-term crises of stress or deprivation; these in themselves could activate the disease, but would not determine its conclusion.

The possible influence of the elements of 'care' and the spread of a greater consciousness of cleanliness and hygienic practices in reducing tuberculosis return us to the links between that disease and typhus: there may be more of a connection between the declining mortalities of these two diseases than can be demonstrated by statistical correlations, or by postulating interactions between them. Tuberculosis and typhus are both causally linked with housing conditions, with poverty and overcrowding. Epidemic typhus is closely associated with stress overcrowding and changes in social behaviour; tuberculosis is more generally associated with overcrowding and poor hygiene. Like typhus, phthisis may be transmitted by infected dust, but even more effectively by close contact with active cases where domestic overcrowding is accompanied by poor ventilation. Stress overcrowding, such as that which generated typhus epidemics in the years before 1870, might also be expected eventually to lead to heightened tuberculosis mortality, perhaps through psychological stress, but also by subjecting individuals to massive doses of tuberculosis bacilli in their

[62] J. E. Squire, 'The prevention of phthisis', *Transactions of the Epidemiological Society*, 8 (1888–9), 48.

[63] Longstaff, *Phthisis, Bronchitis and Pneumonia*, 6. On this basis, which is supported by the evidence of other observers, it seems clear that the pattern of registered phthisis mortality in the 1860s (Fig. 8.1) cannot be disassociated from that of the other respiratory diseases.

[64] Ibid. 8–9. [65] Ibid.

home environments. Social and economic conditions in London in the 1860s provided an ideal ground for raised tuberculosis mortality.

By contrast with the situation in the 1860s, the accelerating—or confirmed—decline in tuberculosis death-rates from 1880 is parallelled by the virtual disappearance of endemic typhus. The behaviour of typhoid in London in these years was meanwhile much more erratic. The similarity of pattern between phthisis and typhus is interesting, notably because their means of transmission were of the same type, by dried droplet nuclei or dried louse faeces, in the atmosphere or in dust. The factors which contributed to the disappearance of epidemic urban typhus may equally have contributed to the simultaneous decline in tuberculosis mortality. Tuberculosis did not disappear, because it was more extensively distributed through British society than typhus had ever been or, with its less flexible etiology, had ever been capable of becoming. None the less, the demolition of the old slum areas in the 1860s and 1870s to make way for railways and new housing, the wider availability of constant water supplies in working-class areas from the 1870s, and the activities of medical officers of health, not only against overcrowding but towards the cleaning, maintenance, and ventilation of dwelling-houses, may have been significant in terms of tuberculosis mortality.

It is even possible that some of these preventive activities, taken in response to typhus, smallpox, scarlet fever, and other infectious diseases, were in part covertly directed at tuberculosis. The emphasis placed by MOHs on ventilation, although partly directed against typhoid on the basis of the sewer-gas theory, and against other diseases on grounds that overcrowding helped both to spread them and intensify their effects, may also have been motivated by the desire to do something towards diminishing the more serious mortality of tuberculosis, an affliction which many, already by the 1860s, considered rightfully to belong among the preventible diseases. It is often assumed that MOHs and general practitioners paid little attention to tuberculosis, viewing it as 'a commonplace, intractable' problem.[66] There may be truth in this, for many individuals in many areas; certainly the disease does not feature prominently among the *recorded* concerns of preventive officers. On the other hand, there is evidence to suggest that the concern of these members of the profession was veiled because of—as it was frequently obstructed by—the prevailing social conventions and mythology of tuberculosis.

It is well known that the belief that tuberculosis was hereditary dominated nineteenth-century English attitudes to the disease, with terrible results.[67] The significant qualification, that the hereditary factor was thought to be the *susceptibility* to the disease, rather than the disease itself, is often overlooked. Yet this distinction is important, for it shaped both preventive and individual

[66] The phrase is F. B. Smith's: *Retreat*, 244.

[67] R. and J. Dubos, *The White Plague: Tuberculosis, man, and society* (1953), 6; Smith, *Retreat*, 36–40.

responses to phthisis, and permitted activity against the disease, rather than sanctioning apathy towards it. In 1858, in a passage frequently quoted into the age of bacteriology, Sir John Simon called for the mortality from phthisis to be jealously criticized, for, 'the tendency to tubercular disease is one which transmits itself from parent to child; and thus, if in any one generation the disease be artificially engendered or increased, that misfortune does not confine itself to the generation which first suffers them'.[68] Thirty years later Henry Welch, MOH for Blackpool, declared the most generally accepted doctrine on the etiology of phthisis—that supported, he claimed, by Virchow, Koch, Orth, Woodhead, and others—to be that, '*it is the vulnerability of tissue that is inherited, and not the actual disease*'.[69] The belief in hereditary susceptibility was less severe than that of direct heredity: it allowed for preventive action to be taken, by affected individuals and their families in the first instance,[70] and more broadly by official preventive work aimed at ameliorating those conditions known to enhance the likelihood of development of the disease.

The belief in hereditary transmission nevertheless effectively spiked any direct preventive action. Families would give false addresses or move house to avoid medical inquiries.[71] Of the patients who consulted Charles Theodore Williams for the first time in 1863, some 57 per cent made only one consultation, presumably to have the diagnosis confirmed, and thereafter disappeared.[72] Phthisis deaths were, as we have seen, often registered as from a different cause. James Niven, observing that they were not infrequently registered as bronchitis or pneumonia, almost exonerated the general practitioner: 'It is very natural to wish to protect people from the dread which attends the knowledge that consumption is "in the family".'[73] Niven himself was often told by people that they had had no tuberculosis death in the family, but that their relations had been supposed to have died from consumption: he felt justified in concluding that the practice of concealing the occurrence of tuberculosis from families was as real as it was reasonable to anticipate that it should be: it obviously happened all the time.[74] Nor were other respiratory diseases the only possibility of alternative diagnosis. Temperature and diarrhoea, common symptoms of advanced phthisis, often permitted the diagnosis of typhoid; and pressure from concerned relatives and family was not infrequently a factor in such apparently erroneous decisions: 'In many cases the wild terror of the

[68] General Board of Health, *Papers Relating to the Sanitary State of the People of England*, PP 1857–8 xxiii, p. xxii.

[69] Henry Welch, 'Modern views on the etiology of phthisis', *Practitioner*, 64 (1890), 229.

[70] See Smith, *Retreat*, 37–8; *MOAR* Camberwell (1857–8), 29.

[71] J. Niven, 'The aetiology of consumption', *Practitioner*, 68 (1891), 62.

[72] Williams, 'The duration of phthisis', 98.

[73] Niven, 'Inquiry into the conditions under which the infection of consumption is operative', *Public Health*, 3 (1890–1), 463.

[74] Ibid.

householder, especially in the case of servants prevents sufficient delay to occur to properly establish the diagnosis'.[75]

The complex web of concealment and collusion practised by phthisical families and their medical attendants, and, no doubt, their own respect for these formulae, led preventive officers to adopt an unspoken (or at least unrecorded) non-interventionist policy towards tuberculosis until the later 1880s, and in most cases until the mid- to late 1890s. This is not to say that medical officers were unaware of the problem of phthisis, or that they did not attempt, within the limitations of their powers, to ameliorate the conditions which they felt encouraged the development of the disease. The appointment of the first London MOHs came at a time when the environmental causes of tuberculosis were evoking much interest. Improper diet and impure air had long been considered the two most important stimulants of the disease,[76] and from the beginning of sanitary interest in it links had been made between the incidence of phthisis and urban conditions. In his second report, the registrar-general drew attention to the connection between population density and high mortalities from phthisis and other respiratory diseases; in his third, he noted that the excess of deaths from consumption caused by 'the insalubrity of towns', was greatly in excess of deaths from the other major urban killer, typhus.[77] In the late 1850s and early 1860s a series of epidemiological investigations re-emphasized the importance of impure air, otherwise often known as 'rebreathed air'. The idea had first been popularized in the context of the sanitary movement by Florence Nightingale,[78] and, in its variations, was to prove durable and popular with the preventive establishment.[79] The investigations of Headlam Greenhow, published in 1857 and 1860–1 under the aegis of the General Board of Health and the Privy Council, were the first—and for long isolated—studies of the local and occupational incidence of tuberculosis.[80] It was, however, the outcome of the Army Sanitary Commission of 1858 that made the most decided impact on the way in which phthisis was viewed by the preventive establishment.

The findings of the Army Commission were, indeed, startling (Table 8.5), indicating in the clearest terms that the risks of death from respiratory disease were far higher in the ranks than among the ordinary civilian population.[81] The impact of this revelation was the greater because the army represented

[75] Edmund Gwynn, 'Diagnosis in relation to the notification of infectious diseases', *Public Health*, 10 (1897–8), 143.

[76] Sir James Clark, *A Treatise on Pulmonary Consumption* (1835), 229.

[77] *RGAR*, PP 1840 xvii, p. 84; PP 1841 sess. 2, vi., pp. 99–100.

[78] Smith, *Retreat*, 31; Florence Nightingale, *Notes on Matters Affecting the Health of the British Army* (1858), 501.

[79] It was also immensely influential in France: Guillaume, *Désespoir*, 157.

[80] E. Headlam Greenhow, 'The different prevalence of certain diseases in different districts in England and Wales', part A, in General Board of Health, *Papers Relating*, 315 ff.

[81] *Report of the Commissioners into the Regulations affecting the Sanitary Condition of the Army etc.*, PP 1857–58 xviii, p. xv. See also *MOQR* St George's, Southwark (1, 1858), 2.

TABLE 8.5. *Respiratory disease in the British Army, 1853 (death-rates per 1,000, mean strength)*

Cause	Household cavalry	Dragoons	Foot guards	Infantry	Civilians*
Inflammation of lungs, pleurisy and acute catarrh	0.2	0.7	1.3	1.3	0.5
Spitting of blood, consumption, chronic catarrh, asthma	6.4	6.6	12.5	8.9	5.8
All causes:	11.1	13.6	20.4	17.9	11.9

Note: *In twenty-four large towns.
Source: *Report of Royal Commission on the Regulations Affecting the Sanitary Condition of the Army* (1857–8), xviii, p. xv.

picked lives: not only were they men in the prime of life, but they had been especially selected for their fitness and physique. Further, the available figures were favourable, since they did not include men invalided out on similar grounds, who then died outside the service. The conclusion that close and confined barrack accommodation was responsible seemed inescapable.[82] Improvements in accommodation rapidly followed. Twenty-five years later Edmund Parkes, a scrupulous observer, recorded a 67 per cent decline in mortality from pulmonary disease among British troops, from 7.86 per 1,000 in the seventeen years to 1846, to 2.2 per 1,000 in the twenty-two years to 1880. The only condition capable of explaining this change was, Parkes noted, the level of overcrowding in barracks: 'It is the only condition which has undergone a decided change both at home and abroad.'[83]

It is evident from contemporary medical literature that the findings of the Army Commission made a considerable impact on those interested in preventive medicine,[84] including the London MOHs. Thus Edwin Lankester (St James's, Westminster) was able to write in 1858 that 'all medical writers are agreed that impure air, from want of ventilation, is the most potent of all causes of consumption.[85] Samuel Pearce (Bethnal Green), who by 1862 was

[82] John Hogg, *Observations on the Prevalence of Consumption* (1860), 88. In fact, the Commission's conclusion was rather more broadly miasmatist: 'that the ravages committed in the ranks of the army, by pulmonary disease, are to be traced in a great degree to the vitiated atmosphere generated by overcrowding and deficient ventilation, and the absence of proper sewerage in barracks' (*Army Sanitary Commission*, p. xvi). In respect of ventilation, the findings of an investigation by P. Juillerat for Paris in 1906 are interesting: the correlation between the number of doors and windows per inhabitant in the various districts of the city and the number of deaths from tuberculosis was remarkably close (Guillaume, *Désespoir*, 150). For a deservedly brief discussion of the Victorian correlation of deficient sewerage and tuberculosis mortality, see Smith, *Retreat*, 32–3.

[83] Edmund Parkes, *Hygiene*, sixth edn. (1883), 607.

[84] See e.g. J. T. Hammack, 'The relation between density of population and mortality from consumption', *Transactions of the National Association for the Promotion of Social Science* (1859), 563–9.

[85] *MOAR* St James's, Westminster (1858), 16.

placing even more emphasis on pure air, considered that: 'Where not derived hereditarily—in-door occupations, close heated rooms and deprivation of pure air are the most potent causes of "this mammoth disease".'[86] In the 1870s William Hardwicke (Paddington) considered poor ventilation among the prime causes of consumption: many cases came to his notice that could not be traced to any hereditary tendency, 'but were distinctly brought on by the continued breathing of foul atmosphere'.[87] Most interestingly, he noted that, 'where more than one consumptive case has occurred in the same household, it has appeared to the ordinary observers to have been caught from the sick person'. This observation suggests that the belief in heredity was not entirely solid, and permits the speculation that hygienic advice (for example, on improving ventilation) might indeed find favourable ground. Hardwicke's own opinion was firm, though likely to lead to hygienic advice: the true cause of the disease was 'an endemic one arising from the ill-ventilation and re-breathing of bad air in bed-rooms, shops and factories'.[88] Orme Dudfield, his colleague in Kensington, was more inclined to favour heredity, but was not unaware of environmental problems and social distinctions: among the lower classes, he considered, tubercular disease occurred because of hygienic conditions as well as heredity; among the upper classes, cases were 'usually' traceable to heredity.[89]

Many medical officers voiced their concern with phthisis in these years,[90] and it is probable that they, among others, took the view that tuberculosis was a preventible disease. William Rendle of St George's, Southwark, for example, taking his lesson explicitly from the Army Commission, observed in 1858 that 'it has recently become prominent how very preventable a disease this is'.[91] For Rendle, the origins of tuberculosis were 'no doubt' inherited, but he stressed that the disease must 'be produced before it can be bequeathed': its principal causes were obvious: sleeping in ill-ventilated rooms, overcrowding, and bad ventilation in general. He pointed out that houses were commonly tightly shuttered all night (to conserve heat and exclude dangerous draughts), and were sickeningly offensive to enter in the mornings. His own experience in visiting the poor and the sick (he had previously been a Poor Law medical officer), as well as the numerous complaints he had received as MOH, proved to him that this condition was commonplace.[92] St George's was one of the poorest districts in London, and one of the least amenable to sanitary education: nearly twenty years later Rendle's successor, Henry Bateson, was still inveighing against draught-excluding practices, and the 'stale, stinking air which stunts the intellect and deteriorates the body'.[93]

86 *MOAR* Bethnal Green (1858), 8; ibid. (1862), 8.
87 *MOAR* Paddington (1870–1), 8.
88 Ibid.
89 *MOAR* Kensington (1879), 52.
90 See *MOAR* Camberwell (1857–8), 29; *MOAR* Shoreditch (1862), 12; *MOAR* Holborn (1865), 41; *MOAR* Marylebone (1868), 9.
91 *MOQR* St George's, Southwark (1, 1858), 2.
92 Ibid.
93 *MOAR* (1874–5), 19–20. See also *MOAR* Camberwell (1883–4), 167–8.

PREVENTIVE HEALTH AND EDUCATION MEASURES

Although no specific preventive policies were developed against tuberculosis before the later 1880s, when Niven at Oldham and Ransome at Manchester initiated pioneering anti-tuberculosis schemes, it is clear that medical officers, philanthropists, and interested sanitarians were promoting measures designed to reduce tuberculosis mortality from the 1860s onwards. The phthisis motive was necessarily covert, but was present none the less. The package of relevant measures was outlined by James Hammack as early as 1859: the erection of model dwellings, the improvement of work-rooms and their proper construction to ensure ample cubic space, provision of parks and playgrounds, and the encouragement of outdoor exercise.[94] In all these areas steps began to be taken from the 1860s which, while far from solving the problem or achieving major improvements, at least initiated a process of reform. The philanthropic promotion of open spaces in urban areas, of parks and playing-fields, and the growth of the gospel of physical education, initially to the greater benefit of the better classes, were a part of this process, as were the model-dwellings movement and developments in the history of housing. More specifically, the Workshops Regulation Act of 1867 and the Regulations for Houses Let in Lodgings may have had a more direct effect on the ecology of tuberculosis, although neither has yet received the investigation it deserves.

The Workshops Regulation Act was administered by the metropolitan local authorities for nearly three years (1868–71) before being re-allocated to the city's sub-inspectors of factories.[95] Taken together with the provisions of the 1866 Sanitary Act,[96] these regulations governing working conditions in manufacturing businesses employing fifty or fewer persons gave the sanitary authorities ample opportunity for surveillance of industrial working conditions in London. Overstretched as most sanitary departments were, it is unlikely that the local authorities made energetic attempts to enforce these regulations, yet the medical officers' reports bear witness that workshop inspections were made, and that handbills describing the chief points in respect of which the masters of workshops had been made liable were circulated.[97] Nor did the medical officers' work in this area cease after 1871, for the provisions under the Sanitary Act remained, and they continued to deal with complaints about overcrowding and sanitary defects in work-rooms made by medical men in attendance on sick working people.[98] Conditions in workshops continued to be a sanitary problem throughout the rest of the century, but a degree of supervision, and the publicizing of sanitary standards for work-rooms, may have resulted in some local improvement. Much, however, still depended on the

94 Hammack, 'Consumption', 368.

95 Workshops Regulation Act 1867, 30 & 31 Vict., c. 146, s. 9.

96 Ibid., and Sanitary Act 1866, 29 & 30 Vict., c. 90, s. 19 (ii).

97 See e.g. *MOAR* Camberwell (1868–9), 36–7.

98 *MOAR* Paddington (1872–3), 16.

success and standing of individual employers: Beatrice Webb's inquiry into conditions in the East End tailoring trade in 1888 'brought one fact into strong relief': that the sanitary condition and general comfort of the workshop depended more on the importance and wealth of the contractor than on the quality of the work he turned out.[99]

The effectiveness of the Lodging Houses Regulations was equally in some measure dependent on landlords, but the responsibility of enforcing them remained with the local authorities in this period. These 'Lodging House Clauses' as they were known, established under Section 35 of the Sanitary Act 1866 and Section 47 of the Sanitary Law Amendment Act 1874, were possibly of greater sanitary significance than the Workshops Regulations, and were certainly more problematic for the preventive authorities. Houses let in lodgings were an integral part of London's housing market in the nineteenth century, as they still are today. A wide range of house-types were included in the category, from the tenements of the poorest poor, let by the room on a weekly rental, to the homes of the respectable indigent middle class, including tradesmen, doctors, and clergy. At the lower end of the scale houses let in lodgings represented a considerable sanitary problem, different from that of the common lodging houses (a bed in a dormitory in return for a nightly fee), but not unrelated to it.[100] It was in this type of accommodation that the infectious diseases of adults flourished, and it was in the poorest type of houses let in lodgings that stress overcrowding commonly occurred, with two or three families sharing a room normally occupied by one, when under- or unemployment, high prices, or housing shortages made themselves felt.

Under the Nuisances Removal Act 1855, London's local authorities had been empowered to abate overcrowding in houses let in lodgings or occupied by more than one family, but the subsequent legislation enabled them to place such houses on a register, to make by-laws to regulate their management and conditions in them, and to subject them to inspection.[101] In the early years of the scheme only two authorities, Hackney and Chelsea, made any effective attempt to enforce these provisions.[102] Both were moderately well-to-do districts with, as yet, limited amounts of really poor-class housing. The lack of enthusiasm of other authorities is not surprising. In the first place, the process of registration was exceedingly expensive and laborious. The secretary of state refused to sanction proposed vestry regulations unless they fixed a minimum

[99] Beatrice Potter, 'The tailoring trade', in Charles Booth (ed). *Life and Labour of the Poor in London* (1893), iv. 48.

[100] The common lodging houses were under the supervision of the Metropolitan Police: Common Lodging Houses Act 1851, 14 & 15 Vict. c. 28, s. 3.

[101] Nuisances Removal Act 1855, 18 & 19 Vict., c. 121, s. xxix; Sanitary Act 1866, 29 & 30 Vict., c. 90, s. 35; Public Health Act 1875, 38 & 39 Vict., c. 55, ss. 76–90.

[102] RCHWC, PP 1884–85 xxx, Report, p. 26; Francis Sheppard, *London 1808–1870: The Infernal Wen* (1971), 290.

of 300 cubic feet of space for each adult,[103] and registration thus entailed entering and measuring every room in every house to be placed on the register. Andrew Whyte Barclay, the conscientious MOH for Chelsea, found it impossible to make a selection of suitable houses for registration under the Act, and was obliged to register whole streets as well as courts and alleys; he vouchsafed that the process of registration involved very considerable labour.[104]

Yet if the actual process of registration was laborious, the decisions it entailed and the continuing administration of the regulations were fraught with practical and social problems. Although several vestries intended to implement the Lodging House Clauses, and wrestled fruitlessly with these complications, enforcement of the regulations was limited.[105] The situation was not improved when, in 1883, the Local Government Board issued revised guide-lines and declared the provisions of the 1866 and 1874 Acts in force in those parishes and districts of the city which were not already operating them.[106] There was much consternation, and a good deal of indignation, among medical officers at the new recommendations, and many protestations that they were unworkable.[107] It is possible to sympathize with the medical officers, but the LGB's 1883 proposals do illustrate the standards which were beginning to be considered a desirable minimum: 400 cubic feet of space per person; windows in each sleeping room to be kept fully open for at least two hours every day; the floor of every sleeping room to be thoroughly swept at least once a day and thoroughly washed at least once a week.[108]

The proper administration of the Lodging House Regulations required a devotion of inspector-power which most London vestries were neither willing, nor perhaps able, to provide.[109] Although sanitary departments were enforcing improvements in ventilation as a regular part of their programme of inspection, cleansing, and maintenance of poorer-class property,[110] the impact of these measures on tuberculosis is hard to assess. On the one hand the

[103] Standards for overcrowding were first set in 1866, when the Strand District obtained a magistrate's ruling that overcrowding should be deemed to exist in a legal sense whenever the air-space available to a family should be less than 400 cubic feet per member in a single room: *MOAR* Strand (1866), 6. See also Enid Gauldie, *Cruel Habitations* (1974), 92.

[104] *MOAR* Chelsea (1867–8), 181; see also *MOAR* Hackney (1868), 4.

[105] A. Wilkinson, 'The beginnings of disease control in London: the work of the medical officers of health in three parishes, 1856–1900', unpublished D.Phil. thesis, University of Oxford (1981), 51–8.

[106] *MOAR* Camberwell (1883–4), 'Report to the Sewers and Sanitary Committee on houses let in lodgings', 105–6.

[107] See e.g. ibid. 107–14; *MOAR* Holborn (1884–5), 34–7.

[108] *MOAR* Camberwell (1883–4), 'Report . . . on houses let in lodgings', 109.

[109] *MOAR* Hammersmith (1886), 150.

[110] *MOAR* Holborn (1884–5), 35; John Tripe, 'The sanitary condition and laws of medieval and modern London', *Transactions of the Society of Medical Officers of Health* (1881–2), 21. Since 1855, Tripe reported, 'additional means of ventilation' had been supplied to 2,939 houses in his own district of Hackney. For these additional means of ventilation, see A. W. Blyth, *A Manual of Public Health* (1890), 73–8.

measures were not confined to multiple-occupancy houses or houses on the register; on the other, the numbers of houses registered for supervision were relatively few before 1883, and in the years thereafter tended to fluctuate.[111] Even in the 1890s a quarter of London districts still avoided implementing them (Table 8.6). Meanwhile, the educational efforts of sanitary inspectors, philanthropists, and others working among the poor may also have reaped some dividend: Hugh Beevor, for example, declared that there had been an improvement in habits of ventilation among the poorer people, although it was by no means general, 'and on all sides one hears how deep the public ignorance is or their negligence in this respect'.[112]

Indeed, the issue of fresh air was a continuing concern to the medical officers. At the mid-century, fresh air in the home was by no means a priority for English households. 'The fear of a draught is alike the bane of rich and poor', wrote Edwin Lankester in 1858.[113] All social classes were prejudiced against fresh air, and their prejudices were not without foundation. First, on quasi-medical grounds that are still with us, there was the fear of draughts: the draughts which produce the great British chill, an affliction unknown to the rest of the civilized world. More practically, the introduction of fresh air into the home also unavoidably resulted in the introduction of the 'blacks' which floated so plentifully in Britain's polluted skies and which smeared and fouled the surfaces they touched; and of the dust which lay so plentifully in the streets and which filtered through every open crevice. Finally there was the belief that the air which entered was saturated with the gases given off from open ditches (sewers), filthy streets, graveyards, and cesspools. Summing up these factors before his employers, Henry Bateson, medical officer for St George's, Southwark, noted that as he was speaking the windows of the Vestry hall were tightly closed.[114] In the homes of the poor the maintenance and preservation of warmth was an added consideration, which led to the stopping-up of chimneys with sacks, the sealing of windows with list, the fixing of upper sashes, and other devices. 'Who may count', demanded Bateson rhetorically on another occasion, 'the thousands of deaths brought about by closed doors, closed windows, fire board, list and sandbags?'[115] Lack of fresh air particularly affected women and children, most of whose lives were spent indoors. 'Indoor life is the great calamity of our wives, sisters, and children, in all grades of society', wrote Charles Lord of Hampstead in 1867.[116] Physically, he

[111] See e.g. *MOAR* St George's, Hanover Square (1887–99). The number of houses registered changed yearly in this district. It was a wealthy area and the numbers on the register averaged only around 75.

[112] Beevor, 'Declension', 1,010.

[113] *MOAR* St James's Westminster (1858), 22.

[114] St George's, Southwark *VM*, 23 June 1856; see also Wohl, *Endangered Lives*, pp. 208, 404 (note 2).

[115] *MOAR* St George's, Southwark (1873–4), 18. List was a wooden or woollen fabric border or edging fixed to exclude draughts around the edges of doors and windows (*OED*). See also *MOAR* Fulham (1864), 11; *MOAR* Limehouse (1863), 13.

[116] *MOAR* Hampstead (1867), 64.

Table 8.6. *Houses registered as let in lodgings in London sanitary districts, 1897*

District	Number of houses on the register
Kensington	1,500
Hammersmith	201
Fulham	24
St George's, Hanover Square	95
Westminster	1,190
St James's	18
Marylebone	931
Hampstead	840
St Pancras	166
Islington	400
Hackney	48
St Giles	610
St Martin	168
Strand	75
Holborn	35
St Luke	16
Shoreditch	96
Whitechapel	64
St George-in-the-East	17
Limehouse	69
Mile End	180
St Olave	11
St George's, Southwark	336
Bermondsey	307
Rotherhithe	18
Wandsworth	36
Camberwell	154
Greenwich	9
Lewisham	27
Woolwich	91
Plumstead	6

Note: Districts where lodging houses were not registered: Bethnal Green, Lambeth, Lee, Newington, Paddington, Poplar, St Saviour, Stoke Newington, Battersea, and Chelsea.

Source: *MOAR* LCC (1897), app. 2, p. 1.

was almost certainly right. The children, deprived of what sunlight filtered through the city's polluted skies, developed rickets, were early infected by tuberculosis, and were weakened in their resistance to concentrated doses of the common infectious diseases; while the women, mewed up in their airless parlours and kitchens, were only too likely to succumb to heavy doses of tuberculosis. Despite much sanitary concern, the prejudice lingered until at least the early years of the twentieth century: don't leave your windows open at night, the young Molly Hughes was warned; it's enough to give you the cholera.[117]

The evidence suggests that quite strenuous efforts were being made to enlighten public ignorance on the importance of ventilation in the last three decades of the century. From the 1870s members of the Sanitary Institute were seeking to drive home the dangers of poor ventilation to their audiences. In 1879, for example, H. J. Strong, after discussing the dangers of high concentrations of carbon dioxide in the atmosphere, exclaimed: 'What more fruitful source of consumption is there than sleeping in a small ill-ventilated and perhaps crowded sleeping-room? Our barracks and men-of-war have demonstrated this.'[118] Bedroom doors, Strong revealed, were more frequently left open than windows as a source of ventilation.[119] A few years later Countess de Viesca was urging her listeners to try to sleep with their window open—'a couple of inches at the top is enough'—and recommending that windows should be opened as soon as the room was vacated in the mornings.[120] The significance of these reminders may have been especially great for the class at which they were principally aimed: the respectable wage-earning class. In 1868 James Whitmore noted the health and robustness of the children of the destitute classes who spent the entire day in the open air from their earliest infancy, compared to the debility of the children of the respectable poor, who were kept indoors in confined and ill-ventilated rooms, that they might 'avoid the contamination of the little Street Arabs'. These children showed all the signs of bodily weakness and the development of tubercular disease.[121] It was part of the educational effort of the sanitary movement to spread the gospel of fresh air, and although the evidence suggests that progress in this area was slow, and was probably largely confined to the classes most receptive to sanitary instruction, a greater consciousness of the contribution of adequate ventilation to the maintenance of good health may have resulted.[122]

[117] Molly Hughes, *A London Child of the 1870s* (Oxford, 1977), 97.

[118] H. J. Strong, 'The importance of thorough ventilation in dwellings', *Transactions of the Sanitary Institute*, 1 (1879), 83.

[119] Ibid.

[120] Countess Dolores de Viesca, 'Sanitary House Management', *Trans. San. Inst.*, 7 (1885–6), 131–2.

[121] *MOAR* Marylebone (1868), 9. Similarly, J. J. Rygate observed that the front doors of the very poor were usually open, while those of the respectable poor were kept closed, and for this reason the former did not suffer as severely or as generally from scarlet fever as the latter: *MOAR* St George-in-the-East (1869), 6.

[122] Beevor, 'Declension', 1,010.

Efforts to improve domestic hygiene in respect of ventilation were paralleled by attempts to reform domestic nursing practices. Nursing was an area almost certainly encompassed in the 'modern hygienic treatment' of tuberculosis, and practices do seem to have been changing under pressure from sanitarians in these years. The dangers of close attendance upon the consumptive sick had long been known—the case of John Keats is classic. In 1860 John Hogg noted specifically of the consumptive context that, 'the atmosphere of a sick-room is always unhealthy; and the strongest and most robust persons soon suffer while in close attendance on invalids . . .'[123] The traditional nursing method for respiratory tuberculosis may be described as 'close' nursing, and was applied not only to those in whom the disease was active, but to those who were regarded as incipient consumptives. Persons who were suspected of carrying the hereditary taint of phthisis were habitually protected, kept in close, stuffy rooms, and shielded from fresh air. Once the disease developed, sick-rooms were kept curtained, light and air rigorously excluded. It was common for one member of the family to assume the duty of nurse and companion to the invalid; such companions were not only expected to pass their days in the sick-room, but frequently their nights as well. By the early twentieth century, however, observers were speaking of such practices as the ignorance of the past.[124]

The preventive community may well have been instrumental in accomplishing this change. Close nursing, while ideal for communicating phthisis, also evidently helped to spread other infectious diseases, and could be actively discouraged. The fear of phthisis, as Strong's remarks on ventilation illustrate, could be used to press home a general sanitary point without offending the social taboo, but tact often dictated that the subject be avoided before the public. Benjamin Ward Richardson, for example, made no specific reference to the disease when he addressed a gathering of wage-earners at the Sanitary Institute in 1879, and insisted that, 'to make the sick room a dark cell in which all kinds of impurities may be concealed day after day, is an offence to nature which she ever rebukes in the strongest manner'.[125] Belief in the evil of rebreathed air naturally suggested caution in restricting the ventilation of sick-rooms or in associating too closely with consumptive patients. There is evidence to suggest that the practice of sleeping with sick relatives was being actively discouraged by medical practitioners: in 1872, for example, Francis Kilvert was told by 'pretty Mrs Prosser' that she had been warned by her medical attendant not to sleep with her sister, who was dying of consumption; she had disregarded his warning, and was now in the same case herself.[126]

[123] Hogg, *Observations*, 68.

[124] W. H. Symons, 'Local statistics', *Public Health*, 12 (1899–1900), 343; John Vinrace, *The War Against Consumption* (1901), 21.

[125] B. W. Richardson, 'Health at home', *Trans. San. Inst.* 1 (1879), 284–5.

[126] Francis Kilvert, *Diary*, ed. W. Plomer, 3 vols. (1939), ii. 207 (9 June 1872). See also Smith, *Retreat*, 37, 47.

Although shared bedrooms continued to be the norm in working-class housing into the twentieth century, shared sleeping accommodation in itself did not invariably result in the transmission of active tuberculosis. Other habits of household practice were evidently important, for the Williamses noted that there was little evidence of transmission between husbands and wives.[127]

The significance of changing nursing practices may be greater than that of general domestic ventilation habits for the history of tuberculosis. The ideals of the infant sanatorium movement, which began in Germany around 1860, stimulated new directions in the treatment of consumptives,[128] and probably assisted in the development of the more wholesome approach to the care and management of invalids.[129] The new popular preventive approach initiated by the Sanitary Institute in the late 1870s was actively focused on improving working-class habits in this area; and with the proliferation of voluntary sanitary and philanthropic workers in the years after 1880, the dissemination of improved hygienic practices probably quickened.[130]

THE OVERCROWDING, HOUSING, AND POVERTY NEXUS

While the effects of the spread of hygienic nursing and reformed attitudes towards ventilation must be largely speculative, and the problems of domestic cleanliness and fresh air which underlay them were not class-specific, they were none the less closely associated with a major preventive, essentially class-specific, problem: overcrowding. In terms of tuberculosis etiology, both domestic overcrowding and housing density are significant.[131] In neither respect did conditions in central London improve significantly during this period, and the fall in tuberculosis mortality occurred notwithstanding. None the less, the effects of overcrowding on the distribution of the disease within the city were marked. Allowing for the hospital factor, the distribution of heaviest tuberculosis mortality changed little in London from the 1860s to the 1890s. The worst affected districts, in the decade 1861–70, were still, though in different degrees, the worst affected in the later 1890s (Table 8.3). Sir Hugh Beevor's calculations, based on figures provided by Shirley Murphy, reveal the close link between overcrowding as defined in the 1891 census, and phthisis mortality. Beevor's figures were corrected for hospital mortality, but even so his data, based on sanitary district returns, obscure the precision of the link, for within the individual districts there were striking variations in housing conditions and the corresponding phthisis mortality.

127 C. J. B. and C. T. Williams, *Pulmonary Consumption*, second edn. (1887), 87; Smith *Retreat*, 37.

128 Smith, *Retreat*, 97–8.

129 C. T. Williams and P. Horton-Smith, *The Climates and Baths of Great Britain* (1902), ii. 72.

130 See above, Chap. 1, 'Whooping Cough'.

131 For the effects of housing density, see Smith, *Retreat*, 170.

Medical officers of health naturally knew of the link between social conditions and disease: it was easily demonstrated in their own districts. In St James's, Westminster, for example, a district uncomplicated by hospital or common-lodging-house factors, and with a high tuberculosis mortality, the differences stand out clearly. The district was composed of three divisions: St James's Square, with an average of 1.5 families per house, and a density of 134 per acre in 1861; Golden Square, with 5 families per house and 262 to the acre; and Berwick Street, with 3 families per house and 432 per acre.[132] The population of the latter divisions was almost entirely skilled artisan, earning high wages. Their social security was reflected in their immunity from typhus, but they were terribly ravaged by tuberculosis.[133] The average tuberculosis mortality for the three districts was respectively 18, 28, and 29 per 100 deaths; in the decade 1861–70 the total annual tuberculosis mortality for St James's district stood at 3.25 per 1,000 living, against 2.85 in Marylebone and 2.29 in Limehouse, both parishes with much higher typhus rates.[134] Significantly, deaths from bronchitis and pneumonia in St James's followed the same pattern of distribution as tuberculosis.[135] In St Giles, similarly, the contrasts were shocking. Starkly formulated by George Ross, the phthisis death-rate of the parish ranged from 1 death per 1.08 houses per annum in Queen Street, to 1 per 41 houses in Woburn Square.[136] Until the mid-1870s or so the poor districts of St Giles were, however, also a nest of typhus infection, and the poverty and insecurity which this implies, together with its constantly shifting population, obscure the connection so evident in St James's between domestic overcrowding without poverty, and high tuberculosis mortality.

Levels of domestic overcrowding, the presence of hospitals treating phthisics, and also the occupations of the residential population all affected tuberculosis mortality-rates in different parishes, quite apart from the socio-economic status of their inhabitants. In addition, the Strand, Westminster (St Margaret and St John), St Giles, and Whitechapel all had their mortality swollen by the presence of numerous common lodging houses within their boundaries. These were frequented by the poorest of the poor, the tramps and the homeless, and were recognized as the last alternative to the workhouse for those with incurable maladies; consumption always prevailed 'to an extreme extent' in districts where such houses were common.[137] In 1899 the occupants of these lodging houses were said to die of phthisis twice as frequently as the occupied males of London.[138] In Westminster one-seventh of all phthisis deaths registered in 1898 occurred in the common lodging houses, which were situated chiefly in the St John's sub-district.[139] In the Strand, ten of the eleven common lodging houses in the district were situated in the Strand

132 *MOAR* St James's, Westminster (1858), 15.
133 Ibid. (1863), 45.
134 Ibid.
135 Ibid. (1858), 19.
136 *MOAR* St Giles (1870), 11.
137 Ibid. (1863), 11.
138 Beevor, 'Declension', 1,010.
139 *MOAR* Westminster (1898), 47.

sub-district in 1897. The tuberculosis death-rate in that sub-district was 4.78 per 1,000 in 1897, as against 2.55 in St Anne's Soho, where the remaining such establishment stood.[140] In St Giles, again with three sub-districts, tuberculosis deaths in Bloomsbury were a third of those in South St Giles, just as in general mortality the former ranked with the healthiest districts in London, the latter with the least healthy.[141] The southern part of the district, at least until the clearances of the 1870s, was inhabited by the humblest class of labourers, and was among the oldest, most densely populated, and most deteriorated parts of the city. In North Drury Lane, Short's Gardens, and Church Lane common lodging houses ensured repeated high phthisis mortality.[142]

It was not until the last decade of the century, with the arrival of the MOH of the London County Council as a co-ordinating force for London prevention, that the correlations between overcrowding and phthisis mortality in the city as a whole were given any systematic attention. From 1894, when the registrar-general began to issue corrected mortality figures, with deaths in institutions distributed to the districts where they belonged, Shirley Murphy paid increasingly close attention to phthisis. Already in that year Murphy drew up correlations between overcrowding levels and phthisis mortality in the London sanitary districts,[143] and by 1896 he was able to record that death-rates from the disease were 'remarkably consistent' year by year in overcrowded dwellings.[144] This clearly pointed to the operation of some constant cause or causes, but he found it impossible to say whether this was overcrowding itself, or the other adverse social conditions with which it was usually associated. It might be, for example, that the disease, by adding to family expenditure or by diminishing wage-earning capacity, left less money available for rent and thus brought about overcrowding.[145] Two years later he had reached the conclusion that, however much other reasons might contribute to phthisis: 'There is ample reason for thinking that the dwelling itself and the manner in which it is occupied are important factors in determining the prevalence of the disease.'[146] The correlations between overcrowding and phthisis mortality in the London districts were certainly striking (Fig. 8.3). Hugh Beevor drew the conclusion that 'in the face of overcrowding the declension of phthisis cannot proceed', and argued that this was probably why London had not improved as much as the country as a whole.[147] For Beevor overcrowding meant deficient ventilation, yet he admitted that it was also associated with poverty, and that

[140] *MOAR* Strand (1897), 130.

[141] *MOAR* St Giles (1877), 37; (1867), 7.

[142] Ibid. (1863), 11. Detailed information on the geography and population of the common lodging houses over time is lacking, but there were said to be about one thousand, accommodating 31,651 persons in 1891. At this time the MOH for Whitechapel estimated that 10% of his district's population was housed in common lodging houses, i.e. some 7,700 individuals. Like the Salvation Army Shelters, the common lodging houses frequently served as feeders to the union infirmary and workhouses: *Public Health* (1891), Supplement to the Seventh International Congress on Hygiene and Demography, 3, 25.

[143] *MOAR* LCC (1894), 43.

[144] Ibid. (1896), 49.

[145] Ibid.

[146] Ibid. (1898), 48.

[147] Beevor, 'Declension', 1,010.

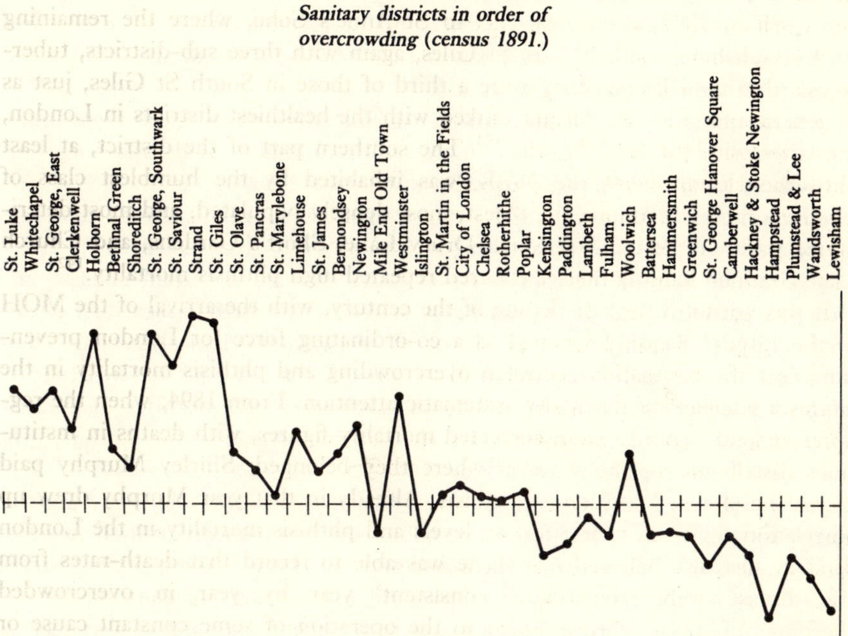

FIG. 8.3. *Mortality from respiratory tuberculosis in relation to overcrowding in London districts, 1898. Source: MOAR* LCC 1898, diagram 20.

poverty was a factor where higher mortalities were found than might have been expected from the amount of overcrowding.[148]

The poverty factor affected individual London district death-rates quite specifically. In the first place, tuberculous families tended to drift downwards in the social scale, into poorer localities, and often eventually into the workhouse.[149] A district like St Saviour, with a 'wonderful array' of charities,[150] would inevitably find itself with an excessive phthisis rate, almost certainly unrelated to sanitary conditions in the district.[151] This drift may also help explain the curious statistics reported from Bethnal Green, where in the 1860s the gentry died at a higher rate from phthisis than did artisans and labourers.[152] Perhaps gentry residence in Bethnal Green was related to established phthisis in the family, the result of poverty or of a desire to escape the stigma

[148] Ibid. 1,010, 1,020.

[149] Niven, 'Inquiry', 464. The point was often used later: Smith, *Retreat*, 169.

[150] *MOAR* St Saviour (1891), 47.

[151] Sanitary conditions in St Saviour were none the less not good, despite the valiant efforts of its understaffed sanitary department: *MOAR* LCC (1893), app. iv, p. 63.

[152] *MOAR* Bethnal Green (1858), 8; (1862), 8.

of decline in their own milieu. The various parishes containing workhouse infirmaries belonging to other districts might also expect an unfairly raised phthisis mortality, although this was not noted by contemporaries, unlike the problem of the common lodging house.[153]

The complex series of factors which determined mortality-levels from phthisis in individual London districts increases the difficulty of determining what the salient factors influencing overall mortality-levels were. In the 1890s preventive officers battling with the same problem were often inclined to return to the theory of the epidemic streets; as Henry Welch declared in 1890: 'Every physician has noticed that phthisis repeatedly appears in certain houses', and that this pattern could often be related to the house itself, rather than to any one family.[154] Frank Payne, president of the Epidemiological Society, drew attention to the many researches that showed that: 'a special incidence of phthisis attaches to particular dwellings, so that special localities in a town, special streets, special houses in a street, even rooms in a house, appear as the nurseries of tubercular disease.'[155]

Just as Shirley Murphy came to stress the importance of the house and the way it was used, so Arthur Ransome, one of the two pioneers of local tuberculosis studies, also believed that the house and the rooms where people gathered together were 'the most important medium for propagating consumption'.[156] The predominance of rural phthisis among the female population was seen as further evidence for the influence of house-infection.[157] Although some modern authorities argue against this means of transmission,[158] the phenomenon probably existed, but may not have been widespread. The house that was in itself tuberculous may have accounted for a relatively small proportion of cases: Niven's researches suggested that infection did not linger sufficiently long in most instances to produce fatal consequences in new tenants, although in highly infectious cases (an unknown percentage of victims) this may have been less true.[159]

Evidence for house-infection was produced by a number of authorities at this period, including the influential American tuberculosis expert Lawrence

[153] It was strongly suggested by Arthur Newsholme that the Poor Law infirmaries bore a special responsibility for reducing tuberculosis mortality: A. Newsholme, 'An inquiry into the principal causes of the reduction in the death-rate from phthisis', *Journal of Hygiene*, 5 (1906), 304–84. F. B. Smith finds Newsholme's thesis attractive (*Retreat*, 239). However, since these institutions bore the considerable stigma of the Poor Law—the more so, because they made a pauper funeral inevitable—they only received those whose all other means of support had failed. In this respect they seem unlikely to have much reduced the damage done by active cases, or to have had much success in prolonging life by means of care. Gillian Cronje has recently argued that the administration of the Poor Law in fact helped to maintain tuberculosis death rates in this period: Cronje, 'Captain of the Men of Death', chap. 7.

[154] Welch, 'Modern views', 230–2. See also *MOAR* Strand (1893), 135.

[155] J. F. Payne, 'Tuberculosis as an endemic disease', *Trans. Epid. Soc.*, 12 (1892–3), 9–10.

[156] *Lancet* (1890), i. 688; (1898), i. 14–17.

[157] Payne, 'Tuberculosis', 18.

[158] Youmans, *Tuberculosis*, 357.

[159] Niven, 'Inquiry', 464.

TABLE 8.7. *Houses and deaths from tubercular diseases in Bath, 1866–1898*

	Number of houses	Deaths per house
	1	8
	7	6
	12	5
	47	4
	112	3
	473	2
	1,813	1 = 51.4%
TOTAL	3,529	2,576

Source: W. H. Symons, 'Local Statistics', *Public Health*, 12 (1899–1900), 343.

Flick.[160] In London this type of transmission might explain the experience of Plumstead, where the medical officer noted that consistently higher phthisis death-rates in the western district could only be accounted for by the supposition that old houses, which composed the housing stock there, were less healthy than new ones, which were general in the eastern district.[161] The high phthisis rates of England's cathedral cities,[162] with their ancient housing stock, might find a similar explanation. However, an investigation of phthisis cases in Bath over a period of twenty-two years produced no confirmatory evidence of this phenomenon, although it failed to distinguish between cases where the possibility of direct personal infection existed (Table 8.7). Nevertheless, this study showed that multiple phthisis deaths occurred in over 49 per cent of houses where phthisis deaths occurred at all, and the investigator, W. H. Symons, found that while some streets had no deaths from any form of tuberculosis over a thirty-year period, in others they were numerous. In one particular street, furthermore, improvements made to the housing stock had significantly accelerated the decline in tuberculosis mortality.[163]

TUBERCULOUS GROUPS IN THE POPULATION

The culpability of particular houses infected by intense doses of virulent tubercule bacilli in spreading and maintaining tuberculosis is attractive, especially because typhus was similarly sustained, and because the thesis seems to

[160] *Lancet* (1922), ii. 302; see also B. A. Whitelegge and G. Newman, *Hygiene and Public Health*, rev. edn. (1905), 409–10.

[161] *MOAR* Plumstead (1893), 101.

[162] Beevor, 'Declension', 1,013.

[163] Symons, 'Local statistics', 343, 360–1.

be borne out by reduced mortalities following on house demolitions or improvement in specific areas. Yet similar arguments were never extended to working premises, even though the general significance of overcrowding and ventilation was accepted as being reinforced by the evidence of occupational mortality. In London itself the occupations followed by a significant proportion of the working class probably contributed to the city's phthisis mortality. The early investigations of Headlam Greenhow for the General Board of Health had revealed high phthisis mortalities among those working in dusty or gritty occupations;[164] this finding is perhaps reflected in the concern of London MOHs where fur-pulling was a local industry.[165] More specifically, studies in the early 1860s by William Ord and Edward Smith on the sanitary circumstances prevailing in the London tailoring and printing trades confirmed that close crowding in work-rooms and the exclusion of fresh air operated powerfully in inducing high phthisis mortalities.[166] Among the printers the effect of poor working conditions was particularly prominent: they received high wages and had a low general mortality (a sign of their general good health), yet were subject, in the 1860s, to a phthisis mortality nearly double that of the ordinary London community.[167] In 1860 and 1861 phthisis accounted for 47 per cent of the deaths recorded by the printers' sick societies, and lung diseases in general for 70 per cent.[168] Like the skilled artisans of St James's, their highly paid status and satisfactory nutritional intake did not prevent them being ravaged by tuberculosis. Among the needle trades, the vitiated atmosphere of the work-rooms, condemned by James Hammack in 1858 as 'one of the worst forms of overcrowding', wrought dreadful havoc: according to William Rendle, phthisis was rife among tailors and milliners 'solely from the unhealthy state of their workrooms'.[169] Charles Williams similarly found that of 3,214 males who became inmates of the Brompton Hospital in a single decade, 56 per cent had been in indoor employments. Among his outpatients, the numbers of male clerks, compositors, tailors, and shoemakers and female milliners and dressmakers were 'very great'.[170]

The geographical distribution of the trades traditionally associated with phthisis within the city reinforced the evil cycle of domestic overcrowding, poverty, and insanitary practices; it was very similar to those of both over-

164 Greenhow, 'The different prevalence of certain diseases', part A.
165 St George's, Southwark *VM*, 31 Jan. 1859.
166 *MOAR* LGB, PP 1864 xxviii, app. 10: William Ord, 'The sanitary circumstances of dressmakers and needlewomen in London', 371–2, 374; app. 11: Edward Smith, 'The sanitary circumstances of London printers', 407, 414; app. 12, Edward Smith, 'The sanitary circumstances of London tailors', 427.
167 Smith, 'Printers', 407. See also M. Cairns and A. Stewart, 'Pulmonary tuberculosis in the printing and shoemaking trades. Historical Survey 1881–1931', *British Journal of Social Medicine*, 5 (1951).
168 Ibid., 406.
169 Hammack, 'Consumption', 368; *MOAR* St George's, Southwark (1859–60), 13.
170 Williams and Williams, *Pulmonary Consumption*, 77.

crowding and high phthisis mortality. In the years between 1861 and 1901, however, the proportionate share of the traditional 'overcrowded' trades in the total employment of London declined. In 1861 female needleworkers, of whom there were about 98,000 in the capital,[171] were concentrated in the West End and west central districts, and in the East End. In the former, including Marylebone, St Pancras, St James's, Westminster, Strand, St Giles, and St Luke, they represented some 10 per cent of the female population aged over 20; in the East End, excluding Poplar, over 16 per cent. South of the river, 10 per cent of the adult female population of both St George's, Southwark and Newington were also employed in these trades. By 1901, although total numbers had increased to some 116,000, the proportionate share of the needleworking trades in female employment had declined, to an average of just under 7 per cent in the west and central districts, to nearly 9 per cent in the East End,[172] and to 6 per cent in Southwark. In Marylebone alone the figure remained almost constant, at just over 10 per cent. In the Metropolitan Borough of Stepney, which was roughly comparable to the group composed of the districts of Whitechapel, Stepney, Mile End Old Town, and St George-in-the-East, the proportion of needleworkers to total female working population declined from 16.1 per cent in 1861 to 12.3 per cent in 1901, although actual numbers rose from just under 12,000 to 13,597. Although the two censuses are not strictly comparable, because 1901 referred to the female population over 10 years old, the inclusion of the 10–19 year-old group cannot mask the declining relative share of needleworking in London's employment market.

Among males a similar decline occurred in the proportionate share of tailoring to total employment. In 1861 some 22,000 males were employed in tailoring, on average 3.2 per cent of occupied males. By 1901 the employed numbered some 31,000, but their proportionate share of the job market had fallen to 1.6 per cent. In the borough of Stepney alone were there any significant increases: here the numbers engaged in tailoring rose from just over 2,000, representing 2.8 per cent of the employed, to over 12,000, representing 10.6 per cent employed in 1901. This concentration was mainly in Whitechapel, following the expansion of the retail ready-made industry.[173] In the West End and central districts the proportion of males employed in tailoring declined sharply in 1861–1901. In the borough of Westminster it declined from 7.2 per cent in 1861 to 3.5 per cent in 1901; in Finsbury and Holborn, from an average of 4.7 per cent to 1.4 per cent. The residential focus of the tailoring trade shifted slightly in these years, from Holborn and Finsbury, where actual numbers declined, into the north-eastern districts, where in St Pancras, Islington, Hackney, and Hampstead numbers noticeably increased.

[171] P. G. Hall, *The Industries of London since 1861* (1962), 60.

[172] The boroughs of Shoreditch, Bethnal Green, and Poplar averaged just over 8%; the total was increased by Stepney with 12.3%.

[173] Hall, *Industries*, 57.

The needle trades were not alone in experiencing a relegation within the hierarchy of London employment. Changing occupational patterns affected other London occupations carrying a high tuberculosis risk in this period. The numbers of male printers swelled from some 9,000 in 1861 to about 39,000 in 1901; but their proportionate share of employment fell from 3.4 per cent to 2.2 per cent. Print-workers became more widely distributed through London, although the main concentrations remained largely the same: Holborn and Finsbury (3.4 per cent, 1861; 4.8 per cent, 1901); Shoreditch, spreading into Bethnal Green by 1901; Islington and St Pancras, with new focuses in Hackney and Stoke Newington by 1901; and an expanding sector south of the river, Southwark alone increasing from some 2.75 per cent in 1861 to 5.8 per cent in 1901. The City and Westminster, which housed notable concentrations in 1861 (in West London, 9 per cent of males over 20 were printers), on the other hand declined to no more than average proportions of 1.5 and 1.2 per cent respectively. By contrast, the numbers of shoemakers declined somewhat, from about 29,000 in 1861 to 23,000 in 1901. In 1861 the industry had already been concentrated in the East End, but was also more widely spread throughout the city; by 1901, with the disappearance of the old bespoke trade from the West End and the replacement of primary leather manufacture by sweated wholesale assembly work,[174] it had retreated largely to the East End and Hackney, with more-minor concentrations south of the river and in Holborn and Finsbury.

The declining employment share of the London industries traditionally associated with high phthisis mortality, combined with their greater geographical concentration, carried implications for the distribution of tuberculosis mortality in the city. On the one hand, relatively fewer people in each registration district were employed in these trades, and relatively fewer were therefore exposed to working conditions conducive to the spread of tuberculosis; on the other, this occupationally associated mortality was intensified in particular areas: notably in those which had the highest percentage of domestic overcrowding. The developing pattern of industry and employment could thus be critically linked with the pattern of phthisis: declining overall mortality related to a declining employment-share of high-risk occupations, with continuing high local mortality associated with the survival, and local concentration, of such employment. In a situation such as that found in later nineteenth-century London, where domestic overcrowding in the poorest areas is not thought to have improved at all in the latter part of the century (and in some grew worse),[175] and where shared bedrooms were still the norm in working-class

[174] See P. G. Hall, 'The East London footwear industry: an industrial quarter in decline', *East London Papers*, 5 (1962), 3–21.

[175] Jones, *Outcast London*, 174–8; Wohl, 'Working class housing', 24–5.

accommodation, occupation was perhaps as important as housing in maintaining raised tuberculosis mortalities.[176]

While the residential pattern of the needle trades, printing, and shoemaking remained broadly stable between 1861 and 1901, and their proportionate share of employment declined, the numbers of both males and females occupied as clerks soared. Office-work was the great creation of Victorian business and philanthropic interests. In 1861 some 16,000 males were employed as clerks in the metropolis; by 1901, their numbers had risen to over 82,000, and they had been joined by more than 18,000 women. The residential distribution of these workers contrasted with that of the manual trades: in 1861 the highest concentrations of clerks were to be found in Chelsea, Islington, Hackney, the City, and Camberwell; by 1901 they lived in significant numbers in all areas of the capital. Socially, it may be assumed that most clerks were above the poorest class—they were among those who benefited from the growth of suburbia, with its greater share of fresher air and new houses, and the development of suburban railway networks—but their conditions of work increased their risk of tuberculosis, and may have helped to raise or maintain phthisis mortality in their districts of residence. The rising numbers of clerks may, for example, help to explain the rise in registered (uncorrected) tuberculosis mortality in Camberwell from around 1887 (Fig. 8.2b): in 1861 the district contained 858 male clerks, representing 5.2 per cent of its male population over 20; by 1901 it contained 7,238 male (7.7 per cent) and 1,354 female (1.3 per cent) clerks.

The prevalence of types of employment giving a heightened phthisis risk among the working and lower middle class should not distract from the less easily charted, but none the less present, mortality among the upper classes. Although it is in certain respects true to say, as is often said, that the disease affected 'rich and poor alike',[177] by the 1930s, and almost certainly for centuries before, phthisis had affected the poorer classes proportionately more severely than the rich. The causes of this class-differential mortality are impossible to gauge precisely because of the complex etiology of the disease. As Charles Theodore Williams observed of the sample of 1,000 upper- and middle-class cases drawn from his private practice, although their social status exempted them from 'absolute want', it by no means released them from other injurious influences. Among his cases were men of every profession: members of parliament, lawyers, doctors, army and navy officers, businessmen, and clergy.[178] Better nutrition does not protect against infection by, or the development of, tuberculosis, but it probably increases resistance. It is, however, extremely difficult to disentangle the significance of nutritional status from

[176] Cronje, 'Tuberculosis', 98–9, argues that diet and occupation were probably more important in influencing decline, while housing, less open than occupation to regulation and less responsive than diet to increased prosperity, probably helped to maintain the death rates.

[177] T. D. Brock, *Robert Koch: A Life in Medicine and Bacteriology* (1988), 117.

[178] Williams, 'Duration', 115–16.

other, especially related social, factors which can contribute to the disease. In the words of F. B. Smith, where the relationship between poor diet and the development of infection are concerned, 'beyond broad correlations the mechanisms are little understood'.[179] Any explanations of the behaviour of phthisis which hinge on nutritional status should be treated with caution.[180] As far as the role of improving dietary standards in the nineteenth century is concerned, the doubtful validity of the decline in phthisis much before 1870 or even 1880 adds force to the warning issued by Bill Luckin in respect of typhus: that it is unwise to seek even tentative links between bread prices and the incidence of disease.[181]

Housing and occupation, and more problematically diet, are all social factors which played a conspicuous part in London's nineteenth-century tuberculosis mortality. Less conspicuously, structural factors of fertility and migration may also be significant.[182] While London's birth-rate, like that of the country as a whole, declined from around 1870, work on family size and birth-rates in the city at district level remains to be done; emigration, though more tangible, is also an under-explored subject. Gillian Cronje has discussed the possible effects of internal migration in general terms, and F. B. Smith that of emigration abroad.[183] However, London's population history includes substantial immigration from abroad, a factor which has been associated with increased mortalities in American cities.[184] The effects of emigration abroad are impossible to assess at district level, or to disentangle from migration within the city, but rural immigration may have affected the age-distribution of phthisis mortality: James Hammack, for example, explained the city's unusually low phthisis death-rates at ages 15–35 as due to less than half that population being 'native' and immigrants being rarely sickly.[185] Good health was essential to

[179] Smith, *Retreat*, 171.

[180] It seems to me, for example, that the question of why the disease behaved differently during the two World Wars of the 20th cent. needs further critical examination; e.g. Linda Bryder's view that 'the major difference between the two wars . . . was clearly related to nutritional levels' (*Mountain*, 112), does not take account of substantial changes in domestic behaviour and hygienic standards between 1914–18 and 1939–45.

[181] Luckin, 'Typhus and Typhoid', 113. Correlations between falling wheat prices and declining phthisis were made by Arthur Newsholme in 1906, and between the declining phthisis and rising standards of living by Hugh Beevor and R. J. Ewart: Newsholme, *Journal of Hygeine*, (1903), 451; Beevor, 'Declension', 1,008; Ewart, *Proceedings of the Royal Society of Medicine*, 16 (1922–3), parts 1–2, section for Epidemiology and State Medicine, 13–16. Although the correlations by Newsholme and Ewart have been stressed by Smith (*Retreat*, 171, 243), it is notable that Newsholme later dismissed improved nutrition as a factor ('An Inquiry', 374), while Ewart's argument was severely criticized by the distinguished epidemiologist Major Greenwood: *British Medical Journal*, 1 (1922), 868; *Proc. Roy. Soc. Med.*, 16 (1922–3), parts 1–2, Section for Epidemiology and State Medicine, 16–17.

[182] Cronje, 'Tuberculosis', 99–100; Smith, *Retreat*, 241, 244.

[183] Cronje, 'Tuberculosis', 100; Smith, *Retreat*, 241.

[184] Richard A. Meckel, 'Immigration, mortality and population growth in Boston, 1840–1880', *Journal of Interdisciplinary History*, 15: 3 (Winter 1985), 393–417.

[185] Hammack, 'Consumption', 367.

servants, for example, and in 1861 there were 220,000 servants in London; further, such young and unmarried persons, when they became afflicted with tuberculosis, returned to their homes in the country to die.[186] The latter was a common observation,[187] and in London was also extended to the army of assistants in the warehouses and retail shops of the city.[188] But although this pattern of behaviour can be substantiated with smallpox cases, specific examples are almost unknown for tuberculosis.[189] Among the nineteenth-century investigators, Hugh Beevor found that migration of this type had no effect on county rates,[190] while Symons was unable to explain the different mortality-rates experienced by young men and young women in Bath on the basis of this type of illness-induced re-migration.[191] The peculiar age-distribution of phthisis in London was considered by Beevor rather to demonstrate that 'overcrowding produces its effects only in a small degree on growing lungs'.[192] It may be that improving nutrition enabled the young to resist the assault of adverse environmental influences, only to succumb under the greater pressures of the middle years of life.

The evidence does not suggest that rural immigrants succumbed to phthisis at a greater rate than native-born Londoners; although rates in districts with high concentrations of native Londoners cannot usefully be set against those with low, since various social factors invalidate the comparison. Nor can the distribution of foreign immigrants confirm any closer association between the fact of immigration and susceptibility to tuberculosis.[193] London's Irish population was reported to have a higher general mortality than the English,[194] but this is likely to be linked to Irish life-styles (or possibly inherited racial resistances), since a high proportion of the city's Irish were in fact English-born. The Irish had an infamous reputation for typhus, but there is no suggestion that the London Irish were particularly vulnerable to phthisis, even though the disease remained a formidable problem in Ireland itself.[195] London's considerable German population came in for no special medical notice,[196] while the

[186] Ibid. [187] Cronje, 'Tuberculosis', 95. [188] *MOAR* St Giles (1873), 29.

[189] An extremely—perhaps invalidly—local example may be found in Kilvert's *Diary* for May Eve, 1876 (iii. 279): 'At Whitty's Mill I found dear Hannah Price dying. Dying of Consumption in the same chair in the same corner where her dear sweet sisters Margaret and May had sat waiting so long and patiently for death.' While there was probably a Price family history of tuberculosis, Hannah had been a servant at the Swan Inn, Clyro, and her mistress there, Mrs Prosser, had previously died of the disease.

[190] Beevor, 'Declension', 1,013–14. [191] Symons, 'Local statistics', 364.

[192] Beevor, 'Declension', 1,010.

[193] For an overview of the effects of migration movements in London, see Richard Lawson, 'Urbanisation and change in nineteenth-century England', in J. Patten (ed.), *The Expanding City* (1983).

[194] *MOAR* Marylebone (1885), 14.

[195] Henry Whitaker, 'The excessive mortality from phthisis in Ireland', *Public Health*, 8 (1895–6), 10. Timbrell Bulstrode also noted that there were 'certain data which point in the . . . direction as regards the proneness of the Irish to tuberculosis' ('Report', 6).

[196] There was no German quarter in London which would have facilitated such an investigation. The German-born colony was widely distributed throughout the city, although there were

Lancet's special investigation into the compact and self-sufficient Italian community of Primrose Hill revealed no unusual susceptibility to disease.[197] Towards the end of the century it was thought that tuberculosis was increasing among the Jews of East London, but on closer investigation the increase was apparently in chest diseases generally among the poorer Jewish workers. The trades showing this increase were reported, significantly, to be tailoring, boot-making, and fur-dressing; the victims were mostly Russians and Poles, and there was the usual account of poor conditions in work-rooms—unventilated, overcrowded, and overheated, together with the fear of draughts so common among working people. The Committee of the Jewish Board of Guardians nevertheless issued recommendations for limiting the spread of tuberculosis.[198]

The increasing concentration of Jewish immigrants in East London in the 1890s, as well as contemporary evidence, suggests that they participated in the high tuberculosis mortality of those districts, although whether in any exceptional degree is impossible to assess. Whitechapel had always had high death-rates from phthisis and other respiratory diseases, and the mass immigration of Jews from Eastern Europe in the years after 1880 appears to have had little influence on registered phthisis mortality. Major peaks in Jewish immigration in 1881–2, 1891–2, and 1896[199] are not reflected in the phthisis data; indeed, death-rates began to fall in Whitechapel in 1883, and although they peaked again in the early 1890s, the rise preceded the major immigration movement (Fig. 2b). By the 1890s Whitechapel was, according to its MOH, entirely changed in character by the Russian and Polish immigrants[200], and MOHs in other East End districts were beginning to detect the same pattern: the West Ward of Mile End Old Town had become a Jewish quarter,[201] and both Bethnal Green and St George-in-the-East experienced major influxes of Jewish immigrants.[202] In some of these districts at least, the arrival of the immigrants was associated by MOHs with further structural change in the parish: houses formerly occupied by one family deteriorated into lodgings.[203] The newly arrived immigrants were generally agreed to have dirty and unhygienic habits, but it was also apparent that the Jewish Board of Guardians was making valiant and, in some degree, successful efforts to educate them in sanitary mat-

more in some districts (e.g. St Pancras, Islington, Whitechapel, St George-in-the-East, Hackney) than in others: Arthur Shadwell, 'The German Colony in London', *National Review*, 26 (1896), 809.

197 *Lancet* (1879), ii. 590.

198 *Public Health*, 11 (1898–9), 213. The committee's recommendations were based on Dr J. A. Russell's *Hints about the Prevention of Consumption* (Glasgow, 1896).

199 V. D. Lipman, *A Social History of the Jews in England* (1954), 85–6.

200 *MOAR* Whitechapel (1894), 3.

201 *MOAR* Mile End (1888–9), 69; (1891), 11.

202 *MOAR* Bethnal Green (1893), 6; (1898), 6; *MOAR* St George-in-the-East (1896), 30; (1899), 34.

203 *MOAR* St George-in-the-East (1894), 71; *MOAR* Mile End (1888–9), 61.

ters.[204] Despite the changing nature of their local populations, tuberculosis mortality in the East End parishes sustained its declining curve, suggesting that the immigrant populations had little substantial effect in increasing mortality. Whatever immunities or susceptibilities the Jewish immigrants brought with them, there is no discernible difference in their collective reaction to the high-risk occupational and housing conditions of the East End.[205]

The living and working conditions of immigrant Jewish workers in the East End brings us full circle, to overcrowding, poor ventilation, and insanitary practices, and to the combination of factors involving these which weighted the distribution of tuberculosis mortality in London. The complex circumstances of tuberculosis causation and incidence in this period must be gleaned from a limited literature, yet it is clear from the available sources that the disease was considered preventible and was a focus of active, though necessarily covert, preventive interest from the later 1850s at least. When Sir James Simpson declared in 1867 that phthisis was a disease for prevention not cure, more fitted for sanitary than medical treatment, he meant it in a very limited sense: the hereditary disposition to the disease could be negated by the judicious selection of occupation or trade, residence, and the conduct of life.[206] For most of the period, and for most people, tuberculosis was seen as an individual concern, to be prevented and treated by the individual and his family, rather than as a social problem to be tackled by the state on behalf of society. The emergence of the new bacteriology in the 1880s permitted the eventual erosion of the old taboos against tuberculosis, together with widening acceptance among the medical profession of the social preventability of the disease.[207] For the preventive sector, where the latter had long been recognized, the revelation of a specific origin for phthisis resulted in a reassessment of existing concepts of the way in which the disease behaved, and created new possibilities of preventive action.

[204] *MOAR* Mile End (1891), 11. See also Lipman, *Social History*, 105; Jerry White, *Rothschild Buildings: Life in an East End Tenement Block 1887–1920* (1980), 16–17.

[205] According to several authorities, phthisis appeared to be rare among Jews: Whitelegge and Newman, *Hygiene and Public Health*, 407.

[206] Sir James Young Simpson, 'Public Health', *Transactions of the National Association for the Promotion of Social Science* (1867), 117.

[207] F. B. Smith notes that British delegates to the International Congress on Tuberculosis in Berlin in 1899 declared the one clear fact about phthisis to be that it was 'not "catching" in the popular sense of the word'. According to Smith, the turn of opinion on the spread of the disease did not come until about 1905. It is my feeling that he is being severe on the 1899 delegates to Berlin: tuberculosis is *not* 'catching' in the popular sense, i.e. with the immediacy and directness that smallpox, measles, and whooping cough are. This point was expressed more clearly by Hugh Beevor in 1903, when he observed that 'the term infectious is too loose a term to apply to both measles and tuberculosis', and suggested that 'sub-infectious' was the most appropriate term for the latter (*Lancet* (1903), i. 85). Arthur Whitelegge and George Newman, two distinguished health officers, similarly described phthisis as 'a true infective disease but a sub-infectious one': *Hygiene and Public Health*, 411.

THE PUBLIC-HEALTH MOVEMENT AND TUBERCULOSIS BACTERIOLOGY, 1880–1900

The first excitement over the possibilities of the new bacteriology pre-dated Koch's epoch-making discoveries of the bacilli of anthrax (1876) and tuberculosis (1882). Although British medical and popular opinion subscribed to the hereditary theory of tuberculosis, this had never been accepted in southern Europe, where belief in the infectiousness of the disease prevailed. Elsewhere in Europe and America opinion was more divided.[208] The idea of tuberculosis as a communicable disease was thus continually present, if in opposition to general British beliefs. By the late 1870s, however, the idea was beginning to be taken more seriously in England, since both experiments on the infectivity of tuberculosis on the continent and the observation of respected English authorities suggested that the disease might be transmitted through the inhalation of fine particles of tuberculous sputa, 'atomised in the air by the patient's cough'.[209] The publication, in April 1880, of Julius Connheim's pamphlet *Tuberculosis as an Infectious Disease*, quickened attention. In the words of James Russell, Connheim was the first to popularize the idea of infection with regard to tuberculosis: he argued the case for infection with the greatest clarity possible before the discovery of the bacillus.[210] The summer of 1880 witnessed a spate of comment and investigation in the English medical press.[211]

In spite of the excitement over Connheim's publication, and perhaps because of the twin dominance of re-breathed air and heredity, Koch's discovery of the tubercule bacillus two years later made little immediate impact in England. Although it was admitted that the discovery of the bacillus placed tuberculosis on the 'lengthening list of bacterial diseases',[212] it was several years before this revelation resulted in any developments in public-health policy, although a few local preventive officers may have acted earlier.[213] The *Lancet* leader celebrating the publication of Koch's work marks little movement from the pre-bacillus view: 'There are undoubtedly dispositions to phthisis and inherited tendencies, but these do not disprove the fact that the real *disease* can only be acquired.' Disinfection, the journal continued, was the only means of coping with the 'virus' outside the body, and suitable precautions should be taken when dealing with the sick. Prevention was an easier course than the 'impossible feat of slaying this microscopic parasite'.[214] The implications of the knowledge that tuberculosis could only be acquired were, however, far-reaching, and needed some digesting by the medical establishment. The statistically minded George Longstaff noted that Koch's discovery had 'set all

[208] Bulstrode, 'Report', part 1; Guillaume, *Désespoir*, 34–42, 120; Smith, *Retreat*, 33.
[209] *Lancet* (1878), i. 844; ii. 741. See also Smith, *Retreat*, 36.
[210] J. A. Russell, *On the Prevention of Tuberculosis* (Glasgow, 1896), 6.
[211] *Lancet* (1880), ii. 726, 793, 870; (1881), i. 825, 1,108.
[212] *Lancet* (1884), i, 481.
[213] Ibid. 480.
[214] Ibid.

men a-thinking', before concluding, in April 1884, that the evidence of English and Welsh mortality statistics on the communicability of phthisis was, so far as it went, negative.[215] By 1888, however, some consensus had been reached. In that year the new journal of the Society of Medical Officers of Health announced that, whatever differences existed on the detail of etiology and pathology, the leaders of preventive medicine were agreed that tubercule was the local expression of a parasite, that the parasite was a bacillus of a distinctive kind, and that it gained entry to the body by being inhaled, or taken in food, or occasionally by accidental cutaneous inoculation with tuberculous matter: 'The doctrine of the contagion of phthisis and tubercule generally must be preached from the house-tops until the knowledge . . . has filtered down to the people.'[216]

If the doctrine of the communicability of tuberculosis received official preventive sanction only in 1888, two MOHs had already begun to take radical action on the basis of Koch's discovery. At Manchester, Arthur Ransome (1834–1922), who had long been interested in tuberculosis, had been stimulated to undertake the local studies of tubercular infective areas which were his major contribution to tuberculosis studies.[217] Meanwhile in Oldham, James Niven (1851–1925) became the first officer to take specific preventive action against the disease. Niven, who came to public health from private practice in a southern suburb of Manchester, and was appointed MOH for Oldham in 1886, took immediate practical action on his appointment.[218] He was already 'fully imbued with the more advanced doctrines as to the nature of tuberculosis', and was probably the first MOH prepared to enforce simple preventive measures against the disease. His first annual report for Oldham (1886) made ten practical recommendations for preventing the spread of tuberculosis: that consumptive patients should as far as possible be isolated like fever patients; that kissing and other intimate contact with them should be forbidden; that the rooms inhabited by patients should be well aired, and expectoration

[215] Longstaff, ***Phthisis, Bronchitis and Pneumonia***, 3, 10.

[216] *Public Health*, 1 (1888), 144, 145.

[217] e.g. Arthur Ransome, 'Some evidence respecting tubercular infective areas', *Trans. Epid. Soc.*, ns 5 (1886–7), 124–36; id., *Where Consumption is Bred in Manchester and Salford* (1888); Ransome came of a line of distinguished surgeons, and although on qualifying practised as a physician at Manchester, was from the first interested in preventive medicine. He was associated with Owens College, first as lecturer in hygiene then as Professor of Public Health, 1874–95; during this period he was made an FRS for his invention of the stethometer. He was among the honorary staff of the Manchester Hospital for Consumption, and in this capacity saw daily large numbers of cases of lung disease, including tuberculosis.

[218] Of a remarkable family, whose four sons all became Cambridge Wranglers, Niven had been eighth Wrangler in 1874, and a Fellow of Queens' College, Cambridge. He had originally intended to study engineering, but entered St Thomas's Hospital after Cambridge, gaining his MB in 1880. From 1880 to 1884 he served under the Metropolitan Asylums Board, and in 1894 succeeded John Tatham as medical officer of health for Manchester, when the former acceded to the General Register Office. His obituary named him one of the greatest of medical officers of health, and one of the most useful public servants that Manchester ever had. *Lancet* (1925), ii. 783.

destroyed by fire; that non-consumptives should not sleep with consumptives; that when a medical man had diagnosed consumption, the fact should at once be made known to relatives; and that all workers in rooms filled with irritating dust or fibres should wear respirators, and carry a stock of them so as to be able to change when the respirator they were wearing became clogged. Beyond these personal hygienic measures, Niven recommended that the 'utmost attention' should be paid to draining of subsoil and to the separation of houses from damp; that rooms should be ventilated without draught, and should not be overcrowded; and that every measure should be taken to improve house sanitation. The freer admission of light, the draining and paving of yards, and all such ordinary sanitary measures were, he declared, all directed against consumption. Finally, because there was reason to believe that the disease could be contracted through eating the flesh of diseased animals, a heavy penalty should be inflicted where such flesh was sold for food.[219] In his 1887 report Niven continued to publicize the infectiousness of tuberculosis, and in mid-1888 he and Ransome independently issued sets of rules for the prevention of phthisis, which in Oldham were distributed as handbills to householders.[220]

Just as these small beginnings of preventive action against tuberculosis were burgeoning in Oldham and Manchester, the publication of two papers by George Cornet, one of Koch's co-workers, in November 1888 and February 1889, placed the whole issue of tuberculosis squarely before the preventive medical world, in such a fashion that it could no longer be ignored.[221] Cornet's papers, on the distribution of tubercule bacilli outside the body and the causes of tuberculosis mortality among nurses, were recognized as the most important work on tuberculosis since Koch's discovery of the bacillus seven years earlier.[222] The first paper concluded, after experimental inquiry, that under certain conditions, where matter spat up by consumptives was not destroyed, infective material remained on the walls of rooms in sufficient quantities to convey the disease to guinea-pigs when inserted in very small amounts. In the second paper, Cornet followed up the conclusions of the first by discussing the high death-rates from phthisis among the nursing sisters of the convent hospitals of Berlin; most tellingly, the worst sufferers were the novices, whose duty it was to sweep up dried expectoration from the floors of consumptive wards.[223] Not only was the danger from the inhalation of dried

219 *Public Health*, 1 (1888), 212.

220 *Public Health*, 8 (1895–6), 231–2.

221 George Cornet, 'On the distribution of tubercule bacilli outside the body', and 'On the mortality among nurses and its causes', *Zeitschrift für Hygiene* (Nov. 1888; Feb. 1889).

222 J. Niven, 'On the prevention of phthisis', *Public Health*, 5 (1892–3), 197.

223 The relative immunity from the disease of staff at British consumption hospitals such as the Brompton had long been argued as evidence against the communicability of phthisis; see e.g. Richard Payne Cotton's attack on William Budd, *Lancet* (1867), ii. 550–1; also (1883), i. 323. According to Niven, standards of hygiene at the Brompton were much higher than those of the Catholic hospitals: the wards at Brompton were well lighted, well ventilated, and clean. See Niven, 'Prevention', 208.

sputa seen to be great, but the implication that the disease could be spread by infected household dust was revolutionary.[224]

The immediate result of Cornet's publications was a rash of articles on the prevention of phthisis by a small group of preventive officers who had taken the lesson of its infectiousness to heart, including Niven and Ransome, Henry Welch, MOH for Blackpool, and J. Edward Squire of the North London Consumption Hospital. These papers were intended not, as yet, to educate the public on the infectiousness of phthisis (this was done, if at all, by handbill), but to convert their colleagues to the necessity of taking action against the disease. The reports of the London medical officers suggest, however, that it was not until the late 1890s that the generality of these colleagues began to take active measures, although there is some evidence indicating that measures begun in the earlier 1890s went unreported until years later.[225] In 1893 Shirley Murphy remarked, in discussion at the Society of Medical Officers of Health, that Niven's work 'brought the Society face to face with a large question that in some way or another phthisis ought to be of more immediate concern to the M.O.H. than it was'.[226] For most medical officers, however, the established social and medical defences for coping with tuberculosis remained a fundamental obstacle to action. The outraged cry of the practitioner William Dale of Lynn, following the report of Connheim's work in 1880, illustrates the degree of resistance to the idea, as well as some popular misconceptions:

> I cannot imagine a more lamentable thing than that the public at large should get the idea that phthisis is contagious . . . for seeing the disease is so widespread, and seizes young, delicate and helpless girls and women chiefly . . . [it is] a barbarous and unwarrantable thing to raise the question in the public mind in connexion with it, and on evidence which I believe to be utterly worthless.[227]

Although the British were to prove less resistant on this point than the French,[228] there was, throughout Europe, a strong element of caution in the attitude of the bulk of the medical profession towards the practical implications of the new discoveries. In their anxiety to achieve the application of desired hygienic reforms, the supporters of Koch and Cornet were inclined, as

[224] F. B. Smith draws attention (*Retreat*, 48) to the observations made by William Thomson of Melbourne, who detected the personal infectiousness of phthisis and its ability to spread through infected dust, and whose work was published in 1882. The virtual failure to notice Thomson's work in Europe, regretted by Smith, is a reflection of Thomson's unknown standing there, and of the vastness of the generally worthless literature published throughout this period purporting to have discovered cures for, or means of preventing, tuberculosis. Cornet's researches were made under the aegis of the most highly respected bacteriological laboratories in Europe, and were published in Koch's own journal. This background gave his work a substance and authority which ensured that it would be taken seriously, where Thomson's failed to attract attention.

[225] *MOAR* LCC (1898), 47.

[226] *Public Health*, 5 (1892–3), 201.

[227] *Lancet* (1881), ii. 1,108.

[228] Guillaume, *Désespoir*, 204–5: the French ethical dilemma on the infectivity of tuberculosis effectively paralysed prevention action until the 1960s.

James Russell, MOH for Glasgow, observed, to 'out-Herod Herod',[229] and such rigorous insistence on the preventive forms dictated by the new bacteriology cannot have endeared their methods to doctors beset by ethical anxieties and wrestling with the traditional beliefs of their communities.

The very nature of the revolutionary advances being made by the new bacteriology, in addition, caused those not immediately enthused by its ideas to view its progress with detachment. As Russell observed (and there were evidently many who agreed with him), there was 'always an element of danger' in the enthusiasm generated by a new discovery. Their caution is in the circumstances comprehensible, for the implications of the latest research were far-reaching. As Russell observed: 'When the issues concern interference with human conduct, and involve the personal liberty of a considerable section of the community, even on the plea of the safety of the remainder, we are bound to ask if the game is worth a candle.'[230] In view of the very great sensitivity of the British middle and upper classes to the possibilities of any kind of infection, many MOHs were concerned not to generate a tuberculosis scare.[231] Indeed, Arthur Ransome, who produced a leaflet on *The Prevention of Consumption* for the Manchester and Salford Sanitary Association in 1894,[232] felt it necessary to produce another the following year, on *The Consumption Scare*. In this he argued that infectivity had lately gained too much prominence, and stressed the virtues of pure air and light, especially sunshine, as 'nature's preventive'.[233] The balance between raising public alertness and generating public alarm was a fine one; it preoccupied preventive officers and delayed the application of the new preventive techniques to tuberculosis throughout the 1890s and into the first decade of the twentieth century.

The evidence suggests that there *was*, in fact, a tuberculosis scare in the mid-1890s, at least among the educated classes. Ransome admitted, in January 1895, that public agitation on the infectivity of phthisis might then 'justly be designated as a "scare"'.[234] Persons with almost any chest disease had difficulty in obtaining places as servants; the difficulty in finding sites for consumption hospitals was becoming almost as great as for fever hospitals.[235] According to James Russell, the fear of infection was widespread in the West End of London.[236]

However, if Cornet's researches had opened the door to the fear of tuberculosis infection, they also offered a way out. By implicating the *dried* sputa of the consumptive as the medium of transmission, Cornet in fact resolved the

[229] Russell, *The Prevention of Tuberculosis*, 6. [230] Ibid. 34.

[231] *Public Health*, 5 (1892–3), 307–9 shows Charles Paget (Salford) and Louis Parkes (Chelsea) in debate with Niven and Ransome on alarmism and phthisis as well as on the exact method of communication of the disease and the measures to be taken against it.

[232] *Public Health*, 7 (1894–5), 132. I have not been able to trace a copy of this pamphlet. According to the journal, it contained the necessary information, but was 'not alarmist'.

[233] *Lancet* (1895), i. 298. [234] *Public Health*, 7 (1894–5), 128.

[235] Ibid. [236] Russell, *On the Prevention of Tuberculosis* (Glasgow, 1896), 25.

problem: he himself stressed that the consumptive individual was harmless, and only harmful through bad habits.[237] By the mid-1890s Ransome and Russell were emphasizing the central importance of the dried sputa, and the role of natural disinfectants such as light and fresh air: the disease was said not to be directly infectious.[238] Sir William Broadbent, speaking at Huddersfield Technical College, stated explicitly that the disease was not communicated directly from person to person by breathing the same air or sleeping in the same room. There was no need, he said, to aggravate the sufferings of the phthisical patient by treating him as a public danger. It was dust that was the danger, and in spite of the bacillus's inability to resist heat, light, and fresh air, it could survive indefinitely in dust: 'We do not realise how ubiquitous dust is . . . In every breath we take we inhale an incalculable number of motes . . .'[239] By thus emphasizing the role of dust, the British preventive organization sought to minimize the social damage occasioned by the discovery that tuberculosis was an infectious disease. The concept of infection through dust could be directly related to existing sanitarian teachings on the importance of cleanliness, and permitted the application of preventive measures workable at the personal level.[240]

The deflection of attention from the idea of the infectious tubercular individual was the more important because at this stage any active measures against the disease had to be initiated and developed by local medical officers relying on existing information networks and on the educational power of personal relations, just as had been the case for the other infectious diseases before the enactment of the Infectious Diseases Notification Act. It is possible that some progressive medical officers had been practising such measures for years already, but that these had been of a covert nature: Shirley Murphy reported that there had been increasing attention to measures for the prevention of tuberculosis since 1882.[241] It is likely that the publicity generated by the new bacteriological research, with the wide press coverage which it received, gradually eroded the taboos which had limited public discussion of any means of preventing the disease. This new situation only began to emerge during the 1890s. A few medical officers began to discuss the disease and its prevention more fully in their reports in the early years of that decade, and from 1896 the MOH for Newington began to attach spot maps of local phthisis deaths to his annual reports.[242]

237 Ibid. 39–40.

238 Ibid. 31; Ransome, *Lancet* (1895), i. 298; (1898), i. 14–17.

239 *Lancet* (1898), ii. 1,101.

240 Bryder, for example, notes the contemporary preventive view that 'nothing was to interfere with the drive to reform the habits of the poor' (*Mountain*, 21).

241 *MOAR* LCC (1898), 47.

242 See e.g. *MOAR* St Giles (1894), 98; *MOAR* Paddington (1895), 242–51.

TUBERCULOSIS BECOMES 'RESPECTABLE': THE BATTLE FOR NOTIFICATION

A turning-point for local tuberculosis prevention was reached in 1898, with the foundation of the National Association for the Prevention of Tuberculosis. Although this event must be seen in the wider context of concern for the physical condition of the people as affecting national efficiency, which stimulated the wider health movement of the early years of the twentieth century,[243] the ground for this very specific and much-publicized philanthropic association had been prepared by the bacteriological revolution. It was not so much the acceptance of germ theory which was the important element here, as the way in which private reservations about a socially sensitive disease had crumbled under public discussion of the issues of the new bacteriology. The formation of the association, but even more its patronage by the Prince of Wales, signalled the emergence of tuberculosis as an open subject for action and discussion; it is a phenomenon familiar today, when English royalty still undertakes to dispel taboos surrounding diseases like AIDs and leprosy, which carry a status similar to that of tuberculosis in nineteenth-century society.

The impact of the foundation of the National Association for the Prevention of Tuberculosis is clearly reflected in the reports of local MOHs. The first substantial mentions of tuberculosis prevention occur in 1898 in, for example, the reports of the medical officers for the Strand, Mile End Old Town, and Fulham, and in 1899 in those of Hackney, Kensington, and St Luke.[244] In these years too, the first traces of direct action in London appear. In 1898 the disinfection of premises and linen after a phthisis death was offered by the sanitary departments of Kensington, Marylebone, Stoke Newington, St Luke, Shoreditch, Mile End, St George's, Southwark, Newington, Lambeth, Battersea, Camberwell, and Plumstead.[245] In Plumstead disinfection had been made available for phthisis deaths in 1894;[246] in St Luke specific measures were instituted in the early months of 1898; one may speculate that the inauguration of the NAPT on 20 December gave George Yarrow the impetus to describe them in his report. None the less, from early 1898 enquiries were made in St Luke into the occupation, habits, and environment of every death certified as from phthisis. The co-operation of local medical men was solicited, and in the event of such a death the offer was made (as it was in every other case of known infectious disease) to disinfect rooms, bedding, and clothing. In only five instances among the 144 phthisis deaths registered was the offer accepted.[247] However, the department persevered, issuing circulars on disinfec-

[243] Bryder, *Mountain*, 21–2. For the formation and work of the NAPT, see ibid. 15–22 ff.

[244] *MOAR* Strand (1898), 212–15; *MOAR* Mile End (1898), 35–7; *MOAR* Fulham (1898), 22–4; *MOAR* Hackney (1899), 4–52; *MOAR* Kensington (1899), 113–30; *MOAR* St Luke (1899), 234.

[245] *MOAR* LCC (1898), 47.

[246] *MOAR* Plumstead (1896), 116.

[247] *MOAR* St Luke (1899), 234.

tion and prevention to both medical men and the general public.[248] In Plumstead, take-up rates of disinfection were similarly poor, and the medical officer also resorted to handbills and pamphlets in an attempt to educate his constituency.[249]

The unenthusiastic public response to preventive measures against phthisis in Plumstead and St Luke illustrates the continuing deep social prejudice against the disease, and suggests that disinfection procedures were not generally accepted when offered in these years. Such specific preventive measures as were offered against tuberculosis in the closing years of the nineteenth century can have contributed little to furthering the decline, and few medical officers were as resolute in their educational attempts as James Niven, whose handbills were boldly headed 'Consumption is an Infectious Disease'.[250] None the less, public education was seen as of crucial importance in the campaign against tuberculosis. An editorial in an early issue of the medical officers' journal *Public Health*, declared in 1888 that: 'It must become a matter of common knowledge that not alone tuberculous meat and milk are dangerous, but also the close intercourse of the healthy with the diseased.'[251] As we have seen, however, the constraints of popular attitudes towards tuberculosis limited this ambitious programme; indeed, medical officers themselves needed educating. James Niven was active in demonstrating to his colleagues and urging upon them the need for more concerted preventive action, but it seems plain that many were reluctant to follow his example. The recognition before 1898 that the findings of the new bacteriology required action from the preventive sector of the medical profession was due to the efforts of a small group of able and energetic preventive officers, most of them young, who were afterwards among the most distinguished public servants of their profession.

In fact, during these years there were moves afoot to make tuberculosis an officially recognized part of the preventive officers' duties by bringing it into line with current policy on the other infectious diseases. The general recognition of tuberculosis as a preventable infectious disease raised the question of its suitability to be brought within the scope of the Infectious Diseases Notification Act soon after the enactment had been made in 1889. In 1890 Robert Philip, the Scottish pioneer of tuberculosis dispensaries, urged the adoption of the compulsory notification of tuberculosis in Edinburgh; and in 1891 John Burdon Sanderson argued for its inclusion in the IDNA on the grounds that information on the actual prevalence of the disease was still wanting.[252] Compulsory notification, however, implied that isolation should be enforced as a logical corollary, according to the canons of current preventive

[248] Ibid. [249] *MOAR* Plumstead (1896), 116; (1897), 109; (1898), 107; (1899), 23.
[250] *Public Health*, 5 (1892–3), 170. [251] *Public Health*, 1 (1888), 145.
[252] British Medical Journal, 1 (1934), 1,106; J. Burdon Sanderson, *Public Health* (1891), Supplement on the Proceedings of the Seventh International Congress on Hygiene and Demography, part 2, p. 135.

thinking, and there were many who balked at both the social and practical consequences of such a move. It is indicative of the sense and sensitivity of the progressive officers that both Ransome and Niven were in favour of some form of notification for phthisis cases, without being convinced that it was necessary to go all the way to compulsion.[253]

The ethics of notification for a disease as socially sensitive as tuberculosis were extraordinarily delicate, and constituted a formidable barrier to its introduction. When Niven tried to introduce voluntary notification in Oldham in 1893 with the full co-operation of the local medical men, the scheme was rejected by the town council.[254] Fears that notification would reinforce the idea of the direct contagiousness of the disease, and result in patients being regarded as lepers, their 'social and industrial freedom . . . seriously shackled', produced widespread doubt about the wisdom of notification among the profession,[255] and restrained the enthusiasm of MOHs, who were not prepared to sanction the terrible individual tragedies which they foresaw would inevitably result from the measure.[256]

At the turn of the century most of the profession was still opposed to notification for phthisis,[257] and the Local Government Board was actively obstructing progressive local authorities who wished to introduce compulsory notification for the disease.[258] In his Harben Lectures for 1898, Richard Thorne Thorne, then LGB medical officer, made a forceful statement of the arguments against notification.[259] None the less, the LGB found itself forced to sanction the voluntary notification of phthisis cases in February 1900.[260] Reinforcing the point, *Public Health* drew attention to the old preventive mechanism whereby Poor Law medical officers informed MOHs of cases of sickness occurring among pauper patients. In respect of phthisis, the journal observed (and in doing so made its contribution to a modern myth), this tool was especially valuable, 'as it is among the poorer classes that the disease chiefly prevails'.[261]

Public Health's virtual definition of phthisis as a disease of poverty in 1900 may be seen as an early manifestation of what later became a more public campaign to strengthen the preventive case by associating the disease primarily with poverty.[262] It has recently been suggested that the declining death-rates from tuberculosis in the later nineteenth-century threw into relief the association of the disease with poverty—with overcrowding and poor diet—that led in

[253] *Public Health*, 4 (1891–2), 322.

[254] Newsholme, *Fifty Years*, 252.

[255] Ibid. 246.

[256] *Public Health*, 11 (1898–9), 205, 324.

[257] See the responses to Arthur Newsholme's paper, 'Notification of consumption, its pros and cons', *Jnl. San. Inst.* 21 (1900), 56–61.

[258] R. Thorne Thorne, *The Administrative Control of Tuberculosis* (1899), 54–72.

[259] Ibid. 204–5; Newsholme, *Fifty Years*, 250.

[260] *Public Health*, 12 (1899–1900), 305.

[261] Ibid.

[262] Timbrell Bulstrode, writing around 1904, clearly sought to diminish the role of phthisis among the better classes, while stressing the connection of the disease with poverty: Bulstrode, 'Report', 82–6. For NAPT propaganda on these lines, see Bryder, *Mountain*, 20.

the twentieth century to its being defined as a disease of poverty.[263] The achievement of that definition was more deliberate, and more politically motivated, than is generally apparent, although it sprang from a recognition of the realities of the social distribution of the disease. If preventive programmes for phthisis were to have a chance of success without disrupting the fabric of society, then the well-to-do classes' frantic fear of infection—'indiscriminating, even to absurdity'—must be diffused, and the stigma of infection relieved. The preventive authorities sought to achieve this by emphasis on transmission through dust, but also by stressing the connection of the disease with poor hygiene and poverty. Notification, sputum tests, disinfection, and associated preventive paraphernalia could be disassociated from the better classes by judicious propaganda. The health of the more prosperous section of the community, wrote Niven, was due not just to their better sanitary circumstances but largely to the 'quality which makes for prosperity, namely, a faculty of attention to many details' to which, he suggested, 'the harder worked section of the community have neither the ability nor the energy to bestow'.[264] In Niven's view (and he was almost undoubtedly right), the extent to which the well-to-do suffered from phthisis was small compared with the great bulk of the community. Thus, on grounds of their relative immunity, and of their greater personal care and hygiene, he was content that the 'terrors of the West End may be safely left to the assuaging care of the skilful physician to whom it will conduct its victims'.[265] Thus the doctrine of the epidemic streets, of the fever-nest, was brought skilfully into play, to exonerate the better classes from the burdens of prevention. It was a far cry from the old preventive idea that the wealthy were as careless of infection as the poor, from the *Lancet*'s dispassionate observation of 1859 that, if gin, close rooms, and overcrowding existed among the poor, then overheated ballrooms and claret cup were too prevalent amongst the rich.[266] By 1900 the *Public Health* editorial was declaiming: 'By the destruction of "rookeries" in great cities and by the erection of sanitary dwellings in the poverty-stricken districts of large towns is the campaign against tuberculosis satisfactorily to be waged . . . sanitary precautions are of the highest importance in stamping out tuberculosis . . .'[267] From being a socially indiscriminate disease transmitted by hereditary tendency and/or adverse environmental circumstance, tuberculosis was well on the way to becoming a social disease, determined by poverty and all the unfortunate hygienic habits which poverty induced.

Against this background of the subtle restructuring of the public perception of phthisis, pressure from progressive medical officers gradually succeeded in

[263] See the discussion in N. J. Tomes, 'The white plague revisited: essay review', *Bull. Hist. Med.*, 63 (1989), 471–2.

[264] Niven, 'Prevention', 233.

[265] Ibid.

[266] *Lancet* (1859), i. 270.

[267] *Public Health*, 13 (1900–1), 713.

undermining opposition to notification. Brighton was the first town officially to introduce the voluntary notification of phthisis, in 1899. In his memoirs Arthur Newsholme gave an illuminating account of the process by which he softened up his constituency in the years between 1893 and its final acceptance of the measure in 1899.[268] Between 1899 and 1903 Sheffield, Manchester, and Liverpool followed Brighton's example, and in 1903 Sheffield secured a local act of parliament to make notification compulsory.[269] By the time of his retirement in 1908, William Power, Thorne's successor at the LGB, was coming to recognize the value of these local experiments,[270] but it was with the appointment of Arthur Newsholme as his successor, taking office in January of that year, that the implementation of progressive methods with respect to tuberculosis on a national basis became reality. Newsholme immediately embarked on the policy of gradually initiating compulsory notification which he had found so successful in Brighton. In 1908 the LGB, adopting the suggestion made by *Public Health* in 1900, required Poor Law medical officers to report their phthisis cases to the local MOH.[271] Eventually, following the recommendations of the Royal Commission on Tuberculosis, the disease was made compulsorily notifiable in 1913.[272]

CONCLUSIONS

The achievement of compulsory notification in 1913 marks the culmination and conclusion of nineteenth-century preventive action against tuberculosis. The campaign against the disease was carried on in the twentieth century by diverse means, not least following the NAPT's precept that the force of law should not be used to carry out preventive objects in connection with tuberculosis.[273] Active preventive concern with phthisis on any scale dates only from the 1890s, and it is clear that specific preventive measures against the disease had little influence on its declining mortality in this period. None the less, there was considerable covert concern among the preventive community over tuberculosis from the time of the establishment of the London preventive service, and many of the preventive activities which sanitary departments undertook throughout this period—improving domestic ventilation, supervising house construction, cleansing, disinfecting, and instructing the public in healthier ways of living—encompassed tuberculosis in their preventive intention.

In the event, the tuberculosis experience of a city as complex and diverse as

[268] Newsholme, *Fifty Years*, 252–4.
[269] Bryder, *Mountain*, 42; Smith, *Retreat*, 68.
[270] Newsholme, *Fifty Years*, 250.
[271] Ibid.; Bryder, *Mountain*, 42.
[272] Bryder, *Mountain*, 42–3. The results of the measure were none the less far from satisfactory: Smith, *Retreat*, 69–70.
[273] Newsholme, *Fifty Years*, 248. This characteristically British attitude still undermines preventive campaigns against infectious diseases today.

London assists little in the historian's preoccupation to determine the respective roles of housing, nutrition, and other factors influencing the decline in mortality. Overwhelmingly, the Victorians themselves associated the disease with housing—not simply with conditions of squalor and overcrowding, but with the way in which houses were built and occupied over and above any association with poverty. In part this may have been a reflection of the possibilities of preventive action; housing improvements fell within the perceived scope of Victorian public-health reform, whereas the diet and social condition of the people were beyond state control. It was also the result of observation, of the continuing concern with specific diseases and their physical environment which had helped to generate the public-health movement, and which persisted in the policies of prevention during the rest of the century. Foreign observers, too, singled out housing as a central issue in tuberculosis mortality, and singled out English efforts in this area for special praise. Pierre Brouardel, dean of the Faculty of Medicine in Paris, spoke of the English effort in laudatory terms in 1901, pushing the frontiers of specific preventive effort further back than I have dared to do, or than was perhaps justified in terms of the effectiveness of legislation:

> Before the scientists . . . had actually made known their discoveries, you English people had already begun the struggle. Convinced by observation that tuberculosis throve in dark and damp dwellings, in 1836 . . . you passed a law providing for the construction of healthy homes. [Since then more than ten Acts of Parliament] have rendered salubrious the dwellings of the poor, the workshop, the town . . . You have diminished mortality in England from tuberculosis by 40 per cent.[274]

If the nineteenth-century perspective exaggerates the role of housing in tuberculosis mortality, standards of housing and the ways in which houses were used were important elements in that mortality. In whatever respects the resistance of the individual to the development of active tuberculosis was increased by improving diet or diminishing fertility, the fact remains that tuberculosis is an infectious disease and that the intensity and duration of exposure are critical determinants in overcoming individual resistance.[275]

As with typhus, whose etiology appears in many ways to have been similar to that of tuberculosis, the efforts of London's MOHs, in terms of demolishing old housing stock, cleaning houses, improving domestic ventilation, and educating the public, seem to have played a critical role in reducing the impact of the disease. Similarly, the improving standards of personal and domestic

[274] *Public Health*, 13 (1900–1), 797–8. The warning issued by John Burnett, that it would be unwise to attempt to assign a quantifiable 'weight' to the specific influence of the house on health, is apposite here: John Burnett, 'Housing and the decline in mortality', in R. S. Schofield *et al.* (eds.), *The Decline of Mortality in Europe* (Oxford, 1991), 176.

[275] The effects of relative exposure to other infectious diseases, although an important issue, cannot be explored here for reasons of space. Its probable significance has further been emphasized by Szreter: see Simon Szreter, 'Healthy government? Britain, *c*.1850–1950', *Historical Journal*, 34 (1991), 502.

hygiene which undoubtedly contributed to the relatively faster reduction among women of deaths from typhoid, seem likely also to have contributed to the same pattern of sex-related decline in tuberculosis. Varying patterns of decline across the country may owe much, not only to differing local educational processes, but also to differing traditions and patterns of coping with the disease itself. Unlike typhoid, where the rate of mortality decline was very similar in both rural and urban districts, rural districts were in general slower to improve their tuberculosis mortality than urban areas. As the registrar-general remarked of this trend,

> The country is in fact more primitive and 'old fashioned' than the towns in regard to phthisis mortality as well as in other matters. It is tempting to speculate whether such differences may be in any degree due to the prevalence in the rural districts of more old fashioned views regarding the disease, but any such assumption would probably be unsafe.[276]

Despite the registrar-general's disclaimer, it seems likely that some such effect was indeed at work. Local social and economic circumstances ensured that improvements in mortality-rates varied in timing and extent district by district, but it is clear that London's medical officers were involved in a discreet campaign against tuberculosis from the later 1850s. Even though the direct effects of that campaign cannot be quantifiably assessed, it remains possible that the improving rates of phthisis deaths among women from the 1860s reflect in some degree the success of the wider preventive campaign for sanitary education. Beyond this the evidence of the sanitary literature, and the pattern of the decline of the disease in the city, suggest that local sanitary measures, within the framework of national legislation, were crucial factors in instigating the decline of tuberculosis mortality in nineteenth-century Britain.

[276] *RGDS* (1919), part III, p. lxxiv. It is notable that the GRO regarded the registration of phthisis deaths in London to be more reliable than elsewhere in the country, reflecting the higher levels of medical expertise in the city.

9
The Impact of Local Preventive Medicine

> The great object of sanitary administration should be to educate and lead the people to a knowledge of the value of Sanitation . . . one good lesson [is] capable of producing much better results than many harsh and coercive proceedings.
>
> (The philosophy of H. G. Sutton, MOH, Shoreditch, 1866–91, in Shoreditch *VAR*, 1890–1.)

The essential function of the Victorian preventive authorities was to attempt to control the infectious diseases through surveillance, sanitary reform, and stamping out. Alongside these epidemiological measures, however, lay an awareness of two broad social questions which at once extended the scope of preventive work and complicated its pursuit: the need for popular education, and the problem of poverty. The recognition of these two factors consolidated the preventive package, and contributed fundamentally to the wider success of the preventive campaign.

POPULAR IDEAS ON ILLNESS, DISEASE, AND DEATH

The work of the local sanitary departments in implementing both nuisance reform and more especially any version of the stamping-out policy, could only take place with the broad co-operation of the people, the general public, for whose ultimate benefit the system was designed. The gradual transition from the popular concepts, or lack of them, of hygiene and disease of the earlier Victorians to those entertained today, in a society which may be fairly said, in terms at least of domestic and personal hygiene, to be house-trained, has been a neglected study.[1] For the large part of London's population, it is probable that the transition from one state to the other was accomplished during the Victorian period. In 1898 the MOH for the City contrasted the current positive response to public-health measures with the days when the endeavours of his predecessor, Henry Letheby, were held up to obloquy as 'mischievous sentimentalism, fettered by the fantastic rules of a visionary system of hygiene'.[2]

The history of ideas of disease causation, as entertained by educated medical

[1] For this process in late 19th cent. America, see N. J. Tomes, 'The private side of public health: sanitary science, domestic hygiene, and the germ theory, 1870–1900', *Bulletin of the History of Medicine*, 64 (1990), 499–539.

[2] *MOAR* City (1857–8), 16; (1898), 79.

persons, is only one aspect of society's beliefs about disease. For the history of disease prevention, popular ideas about disease, and popular concepts of personal and domestic hygiene and of the nature of the home, are of great importance. Evidence for these intimate personal beliefs is scarce and care must be taken in its evaluation, for different beliefs and practices existed within and between the different sections of society.

It is clear, however, that one concept of great significance dominated the domestic perceptions of all classes, that of the Englishman's home as his castle, a phrase which encapsulated for many a widespread, ill-defined, and popular belief in the liberty of the subject. The origins of this notion date at least from the sixteenth century, when the great jurist Sir Edward Coke (1552–1634) twice made use of it, and it is probably much older.[3] The idea of the Englishman's liberties—his freedom from 'slavery'—certainly developed and spread, if in a rather ill-defined way, during the seventeenth and eighteenth centuries.[4] With the coming of the Industrial Revolution, urban expansion, and the growth of middle-class culture in the later eighteenth and early nineteenth centuries, the notions of liberty became involved with refinement of social distinctions and the search for privacy.[5] By the mid-nineteenth-century the idea of domestic privacy had become widespread through all classes, even if, among the lowest social groups, it might be more manifest as a dislike of outside intervention.

Resolution of the antagonism between this sense of privacy, allied with antisocial habits of cleanliness and concepts of disease, and the ideals of public-health reform and preventive medicine which informed the work of the sanitary departments was essential if the transition from an insecure, low-expectancy, high-mortality urban society to a stable, high-expectancy, low-mortality one was to be successfully accomplished. Simon Szreter has speculated that there was, in this respect, 'some kind of sea-change' in the relevant aspects of class relations following 'the turbulent 1880s';[6] examination of the preventive literature, one of the few accessible (if external) sources for this sea-change, suggests that the process was more diffused than Szreter visualized, beginning before the 1880s in some social groups, but reaching some kind of climacteric during that decade, after which the positive acceptance of preventive methods became more rapid, and more socially pervasive, during the 1890s and beyond.

It is evident from the writings of the preventive officers that domestic pri-

[3] The *OED*'s earliest citation is 1567 (s.v. 'castle', 3(e)).

[4] George Rudé, 'The London "mob" of the eighteenth century', *Historical Journal*, 2 (1959), 13–14, 17; E. P. Thompson, *The Making of the English Working Class* (Harmondsworth, 1968).

[5] On the importance of privacy, see L. Davidoff and C. Hall, *Family Fortunes; Men and Women of the English Middle-Class, 1750–1850* (1987), chap. 8.

[6] Simon Szreter, 'The importance of social intervention in Britain's mortality decline *c*.1850–1914: a reinterpretation of the role of public health', *Social History of Medicine*, 1 (1988), 32–33.

TABLE 9.1. *Death-rates for England and Wales in decennia, 1841–1910*

Decade	Crude death-rate per 1,000 living	Standardized death-rate per 1,000 living
1841–50	22.4	21.6
1851–60	22.2	21.2
1861–70	22.5	21.3
1871–80	21.4	20.3
1881–90	19.1	18.6
1891–1900	18.2	18.1
1901–10	15.4	15.2
1911–20	14.0	13.5

Source: *RGDS*, 1921, part 3, p. xliii, table XXII.

vacy was extensively valued, and the intrusions of the preventive administration widely resented or resisted through all levels of society. While, on the one hand, medical officers found it very difficult to ascertain the incidence of infectious diseases, especially dangerous, antisocial ones like smallpox and typhoid, among the well-to-do, they met with more express resistance among lower social classes.[7] Thus, incidents of concealed cases of infectious disease may be found in local records throughout the period. By the 1890s, when the evidence suggests that many of the barriers to preventive intervention were at last crumbling, there were still limits to what was acceptable, as angry reactions to the Infectious Diseases Notification Act showed.[8] Social reticence about the presence and nature of illness within the family is well documented for respiratory tuberculosis, but also existed for other infectious diseases, like scarlet fever and chickenpox. This consciousness perhaps varied between different social groups; but for the rising lower middle class at least, infectious disease was still an event to be kept as closely as possible within the family, or at least the familiar locality, at the beginning of the 1890s.[9] Such attitudes do not appear to have seriously interfered with the work of the Metropolitan Asylums Board in this decade, but their survival demonstrates that acceptance of the new procedures of prevention was as yet incomplete.

The insistence on domestic privacy was, however, generally accompanied by a disregard for all but the most serious and incapacitating degrees of illness itself; an attitude inevitable, perhaps, in a society accustomed to varying degrees of ill health. Minor and chronic illnesses were widespread in the population, and helped to mask the early stages of more serious infectious disease.

[7] *Lancet* (1871), i. 284; *MOQR* Whitechapel (1, 1878), 13; *MOAR* St George-in-the-East (1872), 37.

[8] Newington *VAR* (1891–2), 79.

[9] Ibid.

Insanitary conditions, noted John Bristowe, 'produce in many persons states of ill-health which make life irksome, but which do not necessarily end in death'.[10] For Charles Meymot Tidy, crude death-rates were an unsatisfactory indication of the degree of deterioration suffered by a population: 'men may rot without dying'.[11] Such illnesses were not simply the result of sanitary circumstances: a wide range of medical conditions, easily alleviated today, were a continuing part of daily life in the days before antibiotics, minor surgery, and scientific medical practice.[12] The existence of these conditions, and people's long familiarity with them, inevitably constituted a formidable obstacle to preventive success. These were, no doubt, among the factors behind the apathy which William Rendle observed in the middle years of the century: 'There is a great deal of carelessness touching human life, and a great want of common sense or serious thought in the preserving of it: much is left to chance: there is a fatalism or stolid indifference upon the matter, pervading English society.'[13] It was an indifference born partly of stoicism, but it was bolstered by the financial pressures and economic conditions prevailing in a society where social security was largely a matter of individual providence and good fortune, and such safety-nets as were available were widely unpopular.

For sheer familiarity with ill health was one part of the 'indifference' equation, but specific disincentives to the admission of genuine ill health existed among the various different social classes. Medical officers frequently reported the small attention paid to illness of all kinds among the various social classes; and where attention was paid, it was often in the form of concealing cases of infectious disease from co-residents, friends, and authorities, because of the dread of loss of income if business or occupation were interrupted.[14] Even middle-class families were not exempt from these pressures, for a sizeable number of them were relatively poor, but with social standards to maintain.[15] Among the well-to-do, also, social life and religious observances were carried on normally, despite the presence of infectious disease in households, and children continued to be sent to school when siblings were ill, or as soon as the worst symptoms were over.[16] As the *Lancet* remarked, the wealthy were often remarkably careless and selfish in this respect.[17]

Among the working classes and the poor the incentives to ignore disease were far stronger. In 1886 Francis Egan reported that the dread among the poor of being deprived of work through infectious disease remained 'an insuperable barrier' to limiting its spread.[18] Financial pressures fuelled the stoic

[10] *MOAR* Camberwell (1860–1), 14.

[11] *MOAR* Islington (1875), 8 ff.

[12] See Hilary Marland, *Medicine and Society in Wakefield and Huddersfield, 1780–1870* (Cambridge, 1987), 196–7; F. B. Smith, *The People's Health* (1979).

[13] *MOAR* St George's, Southwark (1857), Supplement, 2–3.

[14] *MOAR* St James's, Westminster (1871), 45; *MOAR* Lambeth (1877–8), 20; *MOAR* Fulham (1886), 142.

[15] See *Lancet* (1879), i. 784.

[16] *MOAR* St James's, Westminster (1858), 10; (1868), 41.

[17] *Lancet* (1875), ii. 141.

[18] *MOAR* Fulham (1886), 144; see also *Lancet* (1897), ii. 881.

tendency. As William Iliff observed in dismay: 'Washing, mangling and needlework go on as usual in many an infected home, children, aye adults also, the sick and the sound, mix indiscriminately.'[19] These practices, which were common among working people, were replicated in slightly different forms among other social classes.[20]

The whole tenor of life among all social classes was to ignore infectious disease: to admit its presence was to disrupt social life and business; to interrupt children's schooling; to suffer inconvenience, boredom, or loss of essential income. At the same time this 'indifference' helped to maintain infectious disease in families, and so spread infection broadcast around them, through such media as laundries, cabs, clothing, food and drink, and personal contacts. Extreme examples are not difficult to find,[21] and there is ample evidence that such practices were common up to the end of century. In Islington in 1894, A. E. Harris discovered a total of 995 cases of infectious disease in houses where a trade was simultaneously being carried on, ranging from an artificial florist's to a veterinary surgeon's and a wine broker's;[22] and in 1896, 1,252 children were found to be attending school while suffering from infectious disease.[23]

The disruption of customary practices in the case of illness and death was a further cause for concealment. Visiting and gossip were an integral part of the experience of illness among the working classes and the poor,[24] and this custom was intensified where local communities were close-knit, as in culs-de-sac or the small crowded courts of the poorest districts.[25] As late as 1896 Frederick Waldo found social customs implicated in the maintenance of a diphtheria outbreak in Cornbury Street, Southwark, where patients were freely visited by neighbours, including children, and funerals became the subject of special gatherings in the houses of mourners.[26]

Customary behaviour towards illness was reinforced on two levels, partly by popular beliefs concerning infectious diseases themselves (for example, that a saucer of Condy's Fluid beneath the bed removed all danger),[27] but perhaps more importantly by the possibility of death. The rituals surrounding death, whether simply of proper mourning and burial, or of the extended celebratory wakes enjoyed by the Irish community, were critical in determining responses to preventive involvement. The celebration of death remained an integral part

[19] *MOAR* Newington (1871–2), 112; see also *MOAR* Clerkenwell (1862), 15.

[20] *SCALDI*, PP 1881 vii, q. 630.

[21] See A. Wilkinson, 'The beginnings of disease control, in London: the work of the medical officers of health in three parishes, 1856–1900', 22; *Lancet* (1872), ii. 173.

[22] *MOAR* Islington (1894), table 37, pp. 33–6.

[23] Ibid. (1896), table 87, p. 141.

[24] *MOAR* St George-in-the-East (1875), 44; *MOAR* St Giles (1886), 70; *RCHWC*, q. 2,150.

[25] Henry Mayhew, *London Labour and the London Poor* (reissue, New York, 1968), i, pp. 15, 58.

[26] *MOAR* St George's, Southwark (1896), 34.

[27] W. L. Hunter, 'Slipshod sanitation', *Public Health*, 6 (1893–4), 361.

of English social custom throughout the nineteenth century,[28] but for the preventive authorities, anxious to implement the stamping-out policy, deaths from infectious disease were deaths fraught with danger. They considered smallpox corpses to be infectious, and for caution's sake assumed the same of other bodies dead from infectious disease.[29] Certainly, where infection remained among the family of the deceased, it was frequently passed on to friends during pre-burial gatherings.[30]

It was the fear of infectious corpses, as well as a more general concern for decency in crowded working-class accommodation, where the corpse would share a room with the surviving family before burial, that lay behind the Victorian provision of municipal mortuaries. The local authorities were first empowered to provide mortuaries under the Sanitary Act 1866,[31] and in the years following London's medical officers are to be found repeatedly urging the building of mortuaries, which their vestries were generally reluctant to provide. By 1893 eighteen districts were equipped with mortuary accommodation deemed satisfactory by the LCC; a further eight had mortuaries which did not include a separate chamber for infectious-disease corpses; three were improving their facilities, and others providing them.[32] Mortuaries were apparently an effective preventive weapon. The wakes with which the Irish traditionally celebrated the departure of the dead were a recognized hazard in spreading infectious diseases,[33] but mortuary provision seems to have succeeded in breaking this traditional form of mourning: John Rygate, for example, was relieved to discover that the trouble his officers took in removing bodies to the parish mortuary had the effect of diminishing these celebrations.[34]

Festivities apart, there were often sentimental or financial inducements for delaying burial. There was a general reluctance to part with the dead,[35] and among the poor it was common practice to delay burial for a week or more.[36] The practice arose partly 'from the strange pleasure of the excitement of having the dead in the house and of anticipating a funeral', and partly from the need to raise the money for burial.[37] The rooted objection to pauper burials meant that bodies could be kept in the house unburied for up to a fortnight at a time, and all the while (frequently for most of the night) large numbers of

[28] J. S. Curl, *The Victorian Celebration of Death* (1976); for the rituals of death and burial, see Ruth Richardson, *Death, Dissection and the Destitute* (1988), chap. 1.

[29] See e.g. E. Slade-King, 'Notes on the spread of diphtheria', *Transactions of the Sanitary Institute*, 2 (1880–1), 61.

[30] *MOAR* St George's, Southwark (1896), 34.

[31] Sanitary Act 1866, 29 & 30 Vict., c. 90, s. 27.

[32] *MOAR* LCC (1893), 59.

[33] *MOAR* St George-in-the-East (1878), 43; *Lancet* (1877), ii. 741; (1878), ii. 896; (1886), i. 186.

[34] *MOAR* St George-in-the-East (1878), 43.

[35] *MOAR* St Martin-in-the-Fields (1867), 20.

[36] *Lancet* (1866), ii. 45.

[37] Ibid.

friends and relatives thronged the room where the corpse lay.[38] Such practices often resulted in unhygienic and even dangerous situations.[39] Thus, Henry Bateson discovered the coffin of a child dead of smallpox, with its lid partly pushed aside, being used as a work-table by a family of four living in one room.[40] It might be argued that such cases were relatively rare, because rarely reported; it is likely, however, from the MOHs' concern for mortuaries, that they were rather common, and often escaped official notice.

The importance of burial rituals, and indeed of the whole social process of illness and dying, created formidable obstacles to the prosecution of any stamping-out policy in regard to the infectious diseases. In the years following the legislation of the later 1860s several refinements were introduced to preventive practice which were apparently designed to discourage popular traditional practices where infectious diseases were involved. Most of these refinements occurred in the area of hospital practice. Whereas, for example, voluntary institutions like the London Fever Hospital were powerless to detain patients who wished to leave, the Metropolitan Asylums Board hospitals had full powers to prevent their departure unless ordered by one of the hospital's medical officers.[41] Initially, bodies were returned from the board's hospitals to their vestry mortuaries for burial, but by the early 1880s most of those who died in the MAB hospitals were being buried from the hospital.[42] Such practices, together with the pauperization policy of 1871–86, helped to generate resistance to hospital care. It was partly, as Dr Rygate observed, that the poor did not see why they should be removed, when others stayed ill at home.[43] The disruption of community customs was perhaps more serious. Thus, the death of a friend away from home had 'the most deterrent effect' on local applications for medical assistance, especially from the Poor Law medical officers, who alone had the power of removal. Many cases went untreated, or only by 'a little medicine procured from a chemist', lest the presence of infectious diseases should become known in any way.[44] If a death occurred at, say, Homerton Hospital, 'an unpleasant feeling' long persisted in the neighbourhood, and set up a great reluctance in parting with those subsequently ill.[45]

Resistance to removal was strengthened by the same popular beliefs that permitted the social customs of sick-visiting to continue for infectious disease. It was widely believed among the poorer classes that if any particular contagion was not feared, it could not be caught; also, that there was little or no danger of disease being communicated by mild cases.[46] Thus, mothers would deliberately expose their children to apparently 'mild' cases of infectious

[38] *RCHWC*, qq. 5,388, 5,289, 5,390; James Amos, *Nine Years in Kent Street* (1870), 19–20. For the reasons behind the objections to pauper burial, see Richardson, *Death*, chap. 1.

[39] *MOAR* Newington (1872–3), 118; *MOAR* Bethnal Green (1880), 15.

[40] *Lancet* (1869), ii. 164.

[41] *MOAR* St Giles (1876), 47.

[42] *MOAR* Hackney (1883), 83.

[43] *MOAR* St George-in-the-East (1875), 44.

[44] Ibid. 45.

[45] Ibid (1879), 40; see also *MOAR* Mile End Old Town (1882–3), 5.

[46] *MOAR* Lambeth (1877–8), 19.

disease. The public, wrote Arthur Downes, 'speak broadly of a good or bad "sort" of measles and the like, and frequently prove the sincerity of their belief by exposing their children to what they deem a favourable infection'.[47] Such beliefs positively encouraged sick-visiting and other habits which medical officers were anxious to discourage. George Bate (Bethnal Green) described how even a hospital removal itself was open to objection, because as soon as an ambulance drove up to a house for this purpose 'a mob of idle persons speedily collects, and the patient is frequently carried across the pavement between a double row of spectators'. In Lisbon Street, Bethnal Green, an outbreak of sixteen cases of smallpox was clearly traceable to this cause.[48]

Although infectious disease was commonly treated with much indifference, this could be disrupted by the appearance of severe forms of almost any infection, especially smallpox. A panic reaction to 'zymotic' disease was well recognized by contemporaries; it was seen at its most extensive during cholera outbreaks, but also occurred more locally. As *The Times* observed of the London smallpox outbreak of 1863: 'Let the public be alarmed by all means; but let them be alarmed into action, not into panic.'[49] Panic involved extreme preventive measures, including flight from the affected locality, and often a greater co-operation with the preventive authorities. In 1854, for example, black flags were hung from the windows of houses in Clerkenwell affected with cholera.[50] With the endemic diseases, such panics seem to have developed only where a more virulent disease-strain manifested itself, or in neighbourhoods unaffected for some time; smallpox, being particularly hideous and virulent, was also more likely to provoke panic reactions among local populations. The disinclination for hospital removal was much less, indeed it was rarely opposed, when the case was one of smallpox.[51]

The intricate web of custom and popular belief surrounding infectious illness and death was one of the principal problems confronting the medical officers at mid-century. It was difficult to impose a stamping-out policy upon a public imbued with customary responses and insufficiently impressed with the value of the necessary sanitary measures.[52] In 1879 David Davies, the very able medical officer for Bristol, noted forcefully that the management of infectious disease was

> comparatively easy among educated people who are prepared to carry out the preventive measures recommended by the Public Authorities or their private Medical Advisers, but when they [infectious diseases] appear in force among the undisciplined classes

[47] Arthur Downes, 'Notes on diphtheria', *Transactions of the Epidemiological Society*, ns 7 (1887–8), 205.

[48] *MOAR* Bethnal Green (1884), 8–9; *MOAR* Newington (1884–5), 126.

[49] Cited in *Lancet* (1863), ii. 499.

[50] *MOAR* Clerkenwell (1869), 15.

[51] *MOAR* St-George-in-the-East (1875), 44; T. O. Dudfield, *Two Sanitary Addresses* (1889), 31.

[52] *MOAR* Mile End Old Town (1868–9), 8.

the Sanitarian finds his endeavours thwarted on every hand by gross carelessness or blind fatalism.[53]

The transmission of sanitary knowledge was a problem. There were hopes of the new public elementary schools, established under the 1871 Education Act,[54] but pessimistic views on the speed with which ingrained ignorance could be undermined: in 1872 the *Lancet* reported gloomily that, 'on a sanguine view', it would take ten to twenty years of School Board work 'before the mass of people are intelligent enough to take the trouble to use vaccination' as extensively as was necessary to prevent major epidemics.[55] Indeed, the difficulties of successfully imparting this kind of information is reflected in numerous MOH reports.[56] Yet by the early 1880s John Bristowe had observed improvement in attitudes and domestic habits among the better-off and middle classes, the small tradespeople, clerks, and artisans;[57] and by the end of the decade this new awareness of the benefits of sanitation and prevention was extending further down the social scale.

The wider recognition of the importance of prevention and satisfactory domestic sanitation was at least in part the result of concerted attempts at public education by the medical officers and other interested government agencies. Education was seen as a crucial part of the preventive scheme, and the availability of information as central to the success of both educational effort and the preventive process. The publication of the weekly tables of mortality for London was, for example, one device by which the General Register Office sought to abort 'explosions of terror in times of epidemic'. The value of the practice was proved, it was felt, by comparison with the Continental determination to conceal such factual information: there was no panic in London over cholera in 1854 or 1866 to compare with those which occurred in Paris, Marseilles, and Naples in 1866.[58] Education was important, for, as Edward Ballard noted, no vigilance of the sanitary authority could entirely prevent the outbreak of epidemics or modify the ill effect of extremes of temperature on old and young: 'To provide a remedy against these influences is the province of *private* hygiene, assisted where useful by public liberality.'[59] It was in this precise area, in encouraging private hygiene by the discreet exercise of public liberality, that the sanitary departments made their most lasting contribution to public health.

It is clear that medical officers by and large contributed significant inputs of

[53] David Davies, *Typhoid Fever in Bristol* (Bristol, 1879), 19.

[54] e.g. in Westminster, Barnard Holt urged those members of his vestry who would join local school boards to demand that 'before every other secular subject' pupils be taught the structure and functions of the human body: *MOAR* Westminster (1869), 56.

[55] *Lancet* (1872), ii. 158.

[56] e.g. *MOAR* St George's, Southwark (1879–80), 35; *MOAR* Islington (1863), 4; *MOAR* Islington (1868), 7.

[57] *MOAR* Camberwell (1883–4), 159.

[58] *RGAR*, PP 1867 xvii, p. 61.

[59] *MOAR* Islington (1863), 4.

time and energy to the broader education of their constituencies. It was a long-term, often discouraging, task. Andrew Whyte Barclay put his faith in 'the power of patience and perseverance', and consoled himself with the thought that the children who grew up under the influence of periodical visitations and cleanings would, when adult, take a greater interest in and care about sanitary matters than their parents, 'who were educated in a state of things so utterly different'.[60] William Iliff, meanwhile, found that 'a little pains in explaining the true state of things, will cause prejudice and opposition to give way'.[61] Apart from the personal efforts of the MOH, the educative value of the sanitary inspections should not be forgotten,[62] nor the labours of the MOH in getting these accepted. Here, techniques varied. In Putney, R. H. Whiteman's 'best efforts' were focused from the beginning of his tenure on 'teaching the indigent how to use and not abuse' the advantages of sanitary supervision.[63] By contrast, David Davies kept himself out of sight as much as possible, 'because familiarity breeds contempt'; he preferred that his sanitary inspectors should be able to use his name as a weapon to get things done.[64]

The personal efforts of the sanitary staff were commonly reinforced by the distribution of handbills, tracts, and leaflets. Every sanitary authority distributed instructions on the prevention of infectious disease in their thousands with the arrival of any serious epidemic outbreak, but more general literature on hygiene and prevention was almost certainly also widely distributed. In the Strand, for example, a paper describing simple precautions against infectious disease was distributed to every house in the district where such a case was known.[65] In Hampstead, Charles Lord, a very moral man (one of the few MOHs to be very obviously so), was giving out tracts with titles such as *How do People Hasten Death*, and *The Black-hole in our own Bedrooms*.[66] The very existence of such pamphlets argues an active interest in the education of the masses on these subjects. Lord issued them, and organized public lectures on similar themes, with the specific purpose of 'training the public mind'.[67] Other medical officers also organized lectures,[68] as did the Sanitary Institute, which also held ladies' meetings and open sessions for the working classes.[69] And there was a wide range of charitable bodies working towards the same objects: the Ladies Sanitary Association, founded in 1857, is perhaps the best known.[70] The numerous, active branches of this organization visited the homes of the poor with pails of whitewash and scrubbing brushes, and distributed 'intelligible tracts' on the laws of health to 'the stolid and ignorant': in 1864 alone the

[60] *MOAR* Chelsea (1869–70), 148; *MOAR* Islington (1863), 6.

[61] *MOAR* Newington (1860–1), 21; see also *MOQR* Whitechapel (1, 1881), 11.

[62] *MOAR* Clapham (1886), 56.

[63] *MOAR* Putney (1858), 20.

[64] *RCHWC*, q. 6,913.

[65] *MOAR* Strand (1869–70), 10.

[66] *MOAR* Hampstead (1878) 49.

[67] Ibid.

[68] e.g. Camberwell *VM* (23 Mar. 1881); (22 June 1881); (14 Dec. 1898).

[69] See *Transactions of the Sanitary Institute*, 1879–93.

[70] A. S. Wohl, *Endangered Lives: Public Health in Victorian Britain* (1983), 36–7, 67–9.

association distributed 100,000 such tracts.[71] In addition to the efforts of the sanitary departments and voluntary associations, some vestries took an active part in public health education.[72]

Although the way was hard and long, and a great deal of ignorance and resistance survived,[73] evidence of public improvement surfaces occasionally in the preventive literature. The *Lancet* observed in 1878 that: 'Sanitary knowledge is extending rapidly among the people',[74] and the occasional references from medical officers confirm that this was probably the case. In 1886 the medical officer for Clapham felt there to be 'abundant evidence' that the public was beginning to view sanitary inspections 'not as an inquisition into their private affairs, but as a safeguard to health'.[75] By the 1890s A. E. Harris of Islington had become aware of new middle-class standards: 'They will not tolerate the sanitation of a few years ago; indeed they expect that the houses they live in will be at least rendered safe against the entrance of sewer gas, and themselves safeguarded against infectious disease.'[76] Indeed, Harris was astonished by the keen interest the middle classes took in the condition of their homes, and by

> the knowledge they exhibit of drains, soil pipes, ventilation and like matters. They are thoroughly up to date in their information, and they understand, as a rule, how much the Public Health Authority can do for them, and indeed, they do not hesitate, often in trivial matters, to invoke its assistance.[77]

These people, Harris added, counted the cost of bringing up children, and did not bring into the world children for whom they could not provide. Middle-class Islington in the 1890s already exhibited many of the traits accepted as distinguishing the middle classes in the 1980s and 1990s.

Improvements were also observed in practices relating to the control of infectious diseases. In Kensington, Orme Dudfield observed his people going to hospital 'reluctantly, for the benefit of the community' in the mid-1880s, as well as 'the happiest results' following the de-pauperization of MAB hospital relief by the 1883 Disease Prevention (Metropolis) Act.[78] In 1880 the bulk of the sick had been kept at home: eight years later the pattern had been reversed throughout London.[79] The hospitals too noticed the difference: in 1890 the increased public demand for accommodation led the London Fever Hospital to restrict its intake to patients from the MAB area: it had become 'manifestly impossible' for the Fever Hospital to provide for an indefinite area outside

[71] *Lancet* (1863), i. 559; (1865), i. 79.

[72] See e.g. St James's, Westminster *VAR* (1884–5), 156; (1885–6), 52–3.

[73] e.g. Wohl gives a most gloomy impression: *Endangered Lives*, chaps. 2 and 3; see also above, Chap. 1, 'Whooping Cough', and Chap. 2, 'Measles'.

[74] *Lancet* (1878), ii. 814.

[75] *MOAR* Clapham (1886), 56; *MOAR* Newington (1881–2), 181.

[76] *MOAR* Islington (1895), 15.

[77] Ibid.

[78] *MOAR* Kensington (1885), 45.

[79] Ibid. (1888), 23.

metropolitan London.[80] Increased public awareness of the benefits of hospital treatment seems also to have been matched by higher standards at home: in 1885 George Bate observed a greater nursing intelligence bestowed on patients and a greater hygienic care on homes, 'which counts for so much in the successful treatment and eradication of infectious diseases'.[81]

While all these efforts were going on, and some improvements being recorded, there remained room for a more broadly based educational attack, such as developed from the later 1880s. The emergence of this educational movement, aimed very much at women, and more specifically at working and poor-class women, can clearly be traced in the sanitary literature of the period. The *Transactions* of the Sanitary Institute began to carry, mainly in abstract form, numerous communications from women on the subject of improving the domestic environment, sanitary and cooking practices, and the education of children. Women had been neglected by the early sanitary movement, with its emphasis on the externals of improvement. Educated women were frequently as ignorant as the uneducated.[82] From the 1880s, however, with increasing attention to domestic conditions, the education and training of women in domestic hygiene and preventive practices came to be seen as the means of educating yet more women by their training and example. By the early 1890s women were making a considerable contribution to the proceedings of the Sanitary Institute. Indeed, their endeavours go far to confirm the words of the lady mayoress of Liverpool, Mrs W. B. Bowring, who remarked in her opening address to the Ladies Conference on Domestic Hygiene of 1894 that there had never been a time when sanitation, or health in the house, had been as much talked of: 'One might almost say it has become a fashionable craze.'[83]

It was a craze which Mrs Bowring endorsed: although she had no wish 'to trench upon the province of men', she advocated that every girl should have a thorough training in domestic economy, and that the subject should include domestic drainage, ventilation, and lighting; the purity of water, milk, and meat; the proper preparation and cooking of food; cleanliness of house and person; the care of children, nursing of the sick, and management of infectious diseases.[84] The London Board schools had already inaugurated a scheme of training in such rudiments of sanitation at this date, and it was her wish that similar schemes should be adopted in the provinces, just as the employment of lady 'health lecturers' and health missionaries already had been in some areas.[85] The call by *The Times* a few years earlier, for sanitary reformers now

[80] *LFHAR* (1890), 11; see also *MABAR* (1889), 26.

[81] *MOAR* Bethnal Green (1884–5), 4.

[82] Frances Johnstone, *The Prevention of the Spread of Fevers* (1883), 1.

[83] Mrs W. B. Bowring, 'Address', *Journal of the Sanitary Institute*, 15 (1894), 414.

[84] Ibid.

[85] Ibid. 414–16. I should be noted that the LSB's initiative in hygiene education (perhaps distinct from the 'domestic science' Mrs Bowring spoke of) was not a success: see Kaye, 'Hygiene', n. 86 below, 486.

to educate rather than legislate, 'to make the mass of the people in some degree at least participate in the knowledge of the causes of preventable disease and death',[86] was beginning to be met.

The effectiveness of all this health propaganda is very difficult to assess. Parliamentary investigations and other sources give ample indication that there was still a long way to go in training urban man by the 1890s; in 1910 Alice Ravenshill and Margaret Schiff, representing the new socially conscious, reforming woman, could still draw attention to a 'dense mass of ignorance and apathy' and urge the need for public education in hygiene and sanitary science, for the awakening of the individual sanitary conscience 'at an age when habits and ideals are still unformed'.[87] The rise of the middle-class reformer, of social investigation, and enhanced legislative concern, partly reflect the success of training in the better classes of society, but suggest that this perhaps widened the gulf between comprehension and ignorance. As an anonymous correspondent of *The Times* noted irritably of the London Poor in 1883: 'Professional philanthropists often fall into grievous error from failing to understand the depth and width of the gulf which separates such people from the members of a middle class family, or even from the family of a decent working man.'[88] As general standards of hygiene rose, the public perception of the as-yet sanitarily unconverted altered.

Yet the success of 'training' at all levels was at least in part a question of opportunity. An instructive illustration comes from Marylebone, suggesting the extent to which hygiene propaganda had penetrated Victorian society, even if occasionally economic incentives—Ballard's 'public liberality'—were needed to prove the effectiveness of sanitary education. Following the Cleansing of Persons Act 1897, which permitted local authorities to expend any reasonable sum on buildings, appliances, and attendants requisite for the cleansing of persons infested with vermin, Marylebone Vestry decided, as an experiment, to establish such a facility. A single bath was installed, because, it was assumed, it would rarely be used. Soap and warm water were provided, and arrangements were made for the bather's clothes to be disinfected by steam while he was bathing. Rather to the vestry's surprise, the bath proved most popular among the 'denizens of lodging houses, Salvation shelters and those who on warm nights sleep in the Parks, open spaces and doorways', a fair percentage of whom were subsequently able to obtain work on the Central Railway, having previously been refused because of their dirty condition; the disinfection of clothes, perhaps for this reason, was apparently a major attraction of the establishment. Startled but not dismayed by the success of their scheme,

[86] *The Times*, 11 Aug. 1891: see also J. R. Kaye, 'Hygiene in elementary education', *Jnl. San. Inst.*, 18 (1897), 482–5; Tom Blundell, 'The sanitary inspector as a teacher of sanitation', *Jnl. San. Inst.*, 20 (1899), 79–80.

[87] A. Ravenshill and M. Schiff, *Household Administration* (1910), 225–7.

[88] *The Times*, 30 Nov. (1883).

Marylebone made plans to increase the number of baths, and to extend the facilities to women.[89]

The success of Marylebone's bathing-and-disinfection establishment among the class commonly regarded as the city's lowliest denizens is suggestive of the extent to which the concept of personal hygiene had percolated through Victorian society. No longer was hygiene the message of eccentric visionaries; it had become an accepted standard, not always obtainable, among ordinary people. The emergence of local-authority services directed more towards social than environmental problems, of preventive policies which extended beyond the stamping-out principle to encompass health and welfare on a more generalized basis than infectious disease alone, was made possible by the success of earlier sanitary policies. In the balance of probabilities, the evidence for continuing poverty and ignorance, dirt, and disease remains substantial if often impressionistic; it may be too easy to exaggerate them at the expense of the positive evidence for changing perceptions of the nature of the care that might be bestowed upon the infectious sick and dead, of evidence for a greater awareness of the dangers of disease, of the processes which produced it, and of the possible means of limiting its effects.

POVERTY AND SOCIAL BEHAVIOUR

If educational standards are one significant determinant of popular habits, economic factors are certainly another; and poverty, exploitation and underemployment, insanitary housing, and chronic under-nutrition represent a familiar package to students of Victorian urban life. Poverty was a problem which the preventive organization could not tackle, but which it had to understand, and work with, in its effort to control disease. And in the observation of many preventive officers, it was not poverty itself but the way in which the life of poverty was lived that was salient to disease and premature death. The relationship between poverty and infectious disease in Victorian cities was a complex one, more complex than the common assumption among modern observers and historians that poverty leads to malnutrition, which in turn lowers resistance to infection and disease.[90]

Modern studies of disease behaviour in developing countries have led to a general belief that malnutrition aggravates the severity of infection; there are indications, however, that for this relationship to operate, malnutrition must be

[89] A. Wynter Blyth, 'The Cleansing of Persons Act, 1897, 60 & 61 Vict., Ch. 31', *Jnl. San. Inst.*, 20 (1899), 31–3; see also Wohl, *Endangered Lives*, 70–1.

[90] See e.g. Wohl, *Endangered Lives*, 56, and the WHO literature which he cites; D. J. Oddy, 'Urban famine in nineteenth-century Britain: the effect of the Lancashire cotton famine on working class diet and health', *Economic History Review*, second ser. 37 (1983), 68–86.

severe.[91] For historians interested in the demographic transition, in answering the question why death-rates began to decline in the nineteenth century, McKeown's master statement, *The Modern Rise of Population*, established nutrition as of crucial importance. A few years before McKeown's book was published, however, Andrew Appleby's interest in the relationship between dearth and disease opened a new field of inquiry to early-modern economic and demographic historians. The fruits of research in this area are now leading to the revision of historical perceptions of the relationship between famine and disease, and to a new emphasis on the importance of social behaviour rather than nutritional status as the determinant of disease patterns. The work of John Post on the eighteenth-century subsistence crises, and more especially John Landers's recent studies of London, have contributed significantly to establishing this new approach.[92] Modern medical studies, meanwhile, have also begun to show a greater awareness of the importance of social factors as opposed to nutritional status in determining levels of infection and disease-outcome.[93] Examining the recent evidence for links between malnutrition and epidemic infectious disease, John Post concluded that they are 'neither conclusive nor unambiguous'.[94] In particular, Post was impressed by the evidence of John and Anne Murray, which throws doubts on the assumption that malnutrition inevitably aggravates infection.[95] Many assumptions about the relationship between disease and malnutrition in the past have been based on medical research done in the developing countries of the modern world; and as Post observes, there may be a methodological problem in carrying findings made in contemporary developing countries into the European past: 'significant environmental, behavioural, and cultural differences' exist between the two types of society, 'which may affect any interpretation of the relationship between famine and disease'.[96] Post's scepticism is shared by Walter and Schofield, whose assessment of recent work in this area provides a definitive summary of the current historical position.[97]

[91] For the nutrition/disease assumption, see e.g. David C. Morley, 'Nutrition and Infectious Disease', in E. J. Clegg and J. P. Garlick (eds.), *Disease and Urbanisation* (1980), 38.

[92] John D. Post, *Food Shortage, Climatic Variability, and Epidemic Disease in Preindustrial Europe*, (Ithaca, NY, 1985); John Landers, 'Mortality, weather and prices in London 1675–1825: a study of short-term fluctuations', *Journal of Historical Geography*, 12 (1986), 347–64; id., 'Mortality and metropolis: the case of London, 1625–1825', *Population Studies*, 41 (1987), 59–76; Landers and A. Mouzas, 'Burial seasonality and cause of death in London 1670–1819', *Pop. Stud.*, 42 (1988), 59–83.

[93] See e.g. Peter Aaby *et al.*, 'Overcrowding and intensive exposure as determinants of measles mortality', *American Journal of Epidemiology*, 120 (1984), 49–63.

[94] Post, *Food Shortage*, 271.

[95] Ibid.; John Murray and Anne Murray, 'Suppression of infection by famine and its activation by refeeding—a paradox?', *Perspectives in Biology and Medicine*, 20 (1977), 475–8.

[96] Post, *Food Shortage*, 272.

[97] John Walter and Roger Schofield, 'Famine, disease and crisis mortality in early modern society', in Walter and Schofield (eds.), *Famine, Disease and the Social Order in Early Modern Society* (Cambridge, 1989), 17–21.

The growing doubts among early-modern historians of the validity of assuming a direct link between famine, disease, and death, have recently received notable reinforcement from Alexander de Waal's revolutionary study of the famine in Darfur, Sudan, in 1984–5.[98] After reassessing the British interpretation of the word 'famine', de Waal argues that the deaths which occurred during the Sudanese famine were not due to starvation, but were caused by outbreaks of disease brought about by the social dislocation which followed the famine: death occurred *in parallel* to destitution, not because of it. He concludes that the priority for people in the famine-stricken rural areas was not to save every possible life, but to preserve their way of life for the future.[99] While John Post's methodological warning should be remembered, de Waal's observations have striking affinities with the conclusions which Post and Landers have reached on eighteenth-century disease behaviour, and with those which my own work on the nineteenth-century epidemic diseases has suggested; social dislocation and social behaviour are important in determining the patterns of both epidemic and endemic disease. In the case of nearly all the infectious diseases, social behaviour is more important to infection and outcome than nutritional status.

The implications of these recent findings by medical and development observers and early modern historians have not yet been explored by nineteenth-century historians, whose demographic and medical interests and techniques generally diverge from those of the earlier period. The assessment of the relevance of nutritional status to the performance of specific communicable diseases may none the less throw light on McKeown's claims for the role of dietary improvement in the nineteenth-century mortality decline. Thus Simon Szreter has convincingly argued, by reassessing the chronology of mortality decline from tuberculosis, that McKeown wrongly emphasized the centrality of respiratory tuberculosis against that of mortality caused by poor sanitation and hygiene, and so distorted the balance of causality towards nutrition rather than social intervention as an explanation of mortality decline.[100] Tuberculosis is one of the few communicable diseases whose association with nutrition continues to be considered positive, if obscure. By contrast, the diseases caused by poor sanitation and hygiene are independent in their epidemiology and mortality determinants of nutritional factors. In neither typhoid, an endemic disease, nor cholera, an imported epidemic, is the issue of death or recovery influenced by nutritional status. In typhus, a disease both endemic and notably epidemic, long associated with famine and deprivation, incidence is determined by the social consequences of famine and deprivation rather than by famine and deprivation themselves. The nutritional status of the individual

[98] Alexander de Waal, *Famine that Kills: Darfur, Sudan, 1984–1985*, (Oxford, 1989).
[99] Ibid. 187–94.
[100] Szreter, 'Social intervention', 1–37.

is irrelevant to individual resistance and outcome; social behaviour is the factor which determines the epidemic escalation of residual endemic typhus.[101]

If we look more closely at one of the few recognized English 'famines' of the nineteenth-century, the Lancashire cotton famine, it is apparent that it provides no convincing proof that hunger, rather than altered social behaviour through greater domestic crowding, or the coincidence of a severe winter in 1862–3, was responsible for an increase in the incidence and mortality of epidemic diseases.[102] True, the central medical department's inspector, George Buchanan, listed bad diet among the causes of this prevalence, but only as part of a recognized package of contributory factors, among which 'bad air, and want of cleanliness' were probably of greater significance to the epidemic-disease ecology.[103] Examination of the mortality determinants of the other important communicable diseases further reduces the significance of nutritional status. In smallpox, scarlet fever, and diphtheria, it is the intrinsic virulence of the infecting strain of the disease which determines issue. There remain measles and whooping cough. Modern experience in developing countries had generally been thought to confirm that death from measles was associated with nutritional deprivation, until the work of Aaby and his colleagues redirected attention to the malign influence of overcrowding and intensive exposure.[104] Nineteenth-century observers were more inclined to blame measles mortality on inadequate nursing, which resulted in fatal secondary infections; McKeown himself admitted that mortality in measles is largely due to invasion by secondary organisms.[105] Fatalities in whooping cough are not generally thought to be linked to nutritional status, but this disease, like measles and diarrhoea, actually *reduces* nutritional status, and as a result of this and a similar age-incidence on very young children, has a curious relationship with both measles and nutrition.[106] The historical evidence suggests that rickets was an important factor in nineteenth-century whooping-cough mortality, so that nutrition cannot be entirely dismissed from the consideration of the causes of whooping-cough mortality. None the less, the balance of evidence on whooping cough suggests that in this disease too, social conditions which resulted in non-immune children receiving high doses of the infectious agent were also an important factor.

[101] Anne Hardy, 'Urban famine or urban crisis? Typhus in the Victorian city', *Medical History*, 32 (1988), 412–13.

[102] Oddy, 'Urban famine', 83–4; Hardy, 'Urban famine or urban crisis'.

[103] *MOAR* PC, PP 1863 xxv, app. V.i: George Buchanan, 'The Cotton Famine', 303.

[104] Aaby *et al.*, 'Overcrowding', 49. See also the work of David Morley, for example, D. Morley, M. Woodland, and W. J. Martin, 'Measles in Nigerian children', *Journal of Hygiene, Cambridge* 61 (1963), 115–31, and above, Chap. 2, 'Measles'.

[105] Thomas McKeown, *The Modern Rise of Population* (1976), 97.

[106] D. Morley and M. Woodland, *See How They Grow: Monitoring Child Growth for Appropriate Health Care in Developing Countries* (1979), 92–3; E. Smith, 'Whooping Cough', in T. C. Allbutt (ed.), *A System of Medicine* (1897), ii. 239.

For the communicable diseases as a group, therefore, with the possible exceptions of tuberculosis and the measles/whooping-cough axis, levels of nutrition had a minimal effect in determining the outcome of disease episodes. Reservations about the historical relationship between 'starvation' and infectious disease apply equally to that between chronic under-nutrition and infectious disease. In one respect only, with regard to the specific deficiency-disease rickets, may this opinion be modified. Contemporary medical observers were decidedly of the view that rickets was a contributory factor in whooping-cough mortality; according to Arthur Newsholme in 1913, rickets was very commonly the factor determining a fatal result when children were attacked by infections.[107] As we have seen, rickets was endemic in Victorian urban areas, and although not specific to the working classes, was responsible for the poor physique of so many of these classes into the twentieth century.[108] A dietary deficiency of vitamin D was one factor in its epidemiology, but sunlight deprivation was perhaps more critical in determining the distribution of rickets in these years.[109]

The differential social impact of rickets was, however, brought about by differences in diet and behaviour between the classes. For many working families, the dairy products which constitute an alternative source of vitamin D were too expensive to be purchased regularly, and the persistence of pigeon chests, contracted pelvises, knock knees, and bow legs into adulthood suggests the presence of severe deprivation: in milder cases the bony deformities usually correct themselves as growth proceeds.[110] Rickets was frequently found among the well-to-do,[111] although its effects were generally not apparent by adulthood: dietary vitamin D, residence in less-smoky areas, and holidays by the sea or in the countryside helped to compensate for deprivation suffered in infancy. Hospital out-patient figures, reflecting the poorer city people, suggested a rickets-rate of between 30 and 50 per cent.[112] Family behaviour could, however, tip the balance independently of general nutritional standing. In a survey in 1917, Margaret Ferguson found 27 per cent of rachitic families 'markedly neglected', compared with 44 per cent who were apparently well cared-for: maternal anxiety, however, had often resulted in a child being confined indoors for a protracted period.[113] The implications of this general prevalence of rickets for the resistance of small children to childhood infections and other dis-

[107] *MOAR* LGB, PP 1914–15, xxv, p. 19; and see above, Chap. 1, 'Whooping Cough'.

[108] Wohl, *Endangered Lives*, 56–7.

[109] W. F. Loomis, 'Rickets', *Scientific American* 6 (1970), 77–91; Dame Harriette Chick, 'The discovery of vitamins', *Progress in Food and Nutrition Science*, 1 (1975), 10–13; H. Jolly and M. Levene, *Diseases of Children* (1985), 505; R. Summitt, *Comprehensive Pediatrics* (St Louis, Miss., 1990), 160–1. I have discussed the question of rickets further in 'Rickets and the rest: Child-care, diet and the infectious children's diseases', *Social History of Medicine* 5 (1992), 389–412.

[110] Davidson, *Human Nutrition*, 279–80.

[111] *Lancet* (1880), ii. 814.

[112] G. F. Still, *Common Disorders and Diseases of Childhood* (1909), 82.

[113] Margaret Ferguson, 'A study of the social and economic factors in the causation of rickets', *Medical Research Committee Report*, no. 20 (1917–18), 52.

eases may be serious: the untreated rachitic child is a weakling, with an increased risk of infections, especially broncho-pneumonia.[114]

The relationship between rickets-prevalence and the mortality patterns of the infectious diseases of childhood is far from straightforward, for rickets was not the only factor affecting outcome in these diseases.[115] The balance of these various factors in influencing mortality from the various children's diseases in the past is almost impossible to assess. Our knowledge of the general nutritional status of England's population in the second half of the nineteenth century is fragile, and likely to remain so. There is a consensus that rising real incomes, free trade, and advances in food technology led to improved nutritional status for a significant proportion of the population in the years after 1870. Yet, although the period was one of remarkable growth in average standards of living,[116] not all classes benefited equally. In London, where the problems of casual labour and low-productivity domestic industry remained unresolved,[117] relatively high rates of under- and unemployment held back living standards for a notable proportion of the working classes. Exactly what proportion of the working classes lived in chronic poverty and were inadequately fed is open to debate, but it seems likely that the very poor constituted less than 10 per cent of the city's population by the 1880s.[118] The problem is further compounded by the uneven distribution of food within families: wives and children were commonly less well fed than the bread-winner, upon whose strength the entire family depended. In the opinion of one recent historian, the conclusion is 'inescapable' that women and children were undernourished in families whose income amounted to thirty shillings a week or less. In what degree they were undernourished is less certain.[119]

The imperceptible decline in the combined fatalities of measles and whooping cough, both diseases which, through the presence of rickets at least, were amenable to some nutritional influence, confirms the suggestion of other contemporary evidence that there was perhaps little amelioration in the nutritional

[114] Davidson, *Human Nutrition*, 279–80; see also Florence J. Greenwood, 'The mortality of infants and children under five years', *Jnl. San. Inst.*, 23 (1902), 634.

[115] See above, Chaps. 1, 'Whooping Cough'; 2, 'Measles'. See also Hardy, 'Rickets and the rest'.

[116] Charles Feinstein, 'What really happened to real wages?: trends in wages, prices and productivity in the United Kingdom, 1880–1913', *Ec. Hist. Rev.*, second ser. 63: 3 (1990), 329–55; id., 'New estimates of average earnings in the United Kingdom, 1880–1913', *Ec. Hist. Rev.*, second ser. 63: 4 (1990), 595–643.

[117] G. S. Jones, *Outcast London* (1972), chap. 4.

[118] Estimates of poverty in London at this period are drawn from Charles Booth's great study *Life and Labour of the People* (1891).

[119] D. J. Oddy, 'A nutritional analysis of historical evidence: the working class diet, 1880–1914', in D. J. Oddy and D. S. Miller (eds.), *The Making of the Modern British Diet* (1976), 219–25. Recent research indicates that birth cohorts in the period *c.*1820 to 1870 were of shorter stature than those born at the end of the 18th cent., but that mean heights recovered in the latter years of the 19th cent. Assessing the balance between diet and other factors influencing such a pattern is difficult, however: R. Floud, K. W. Wachter, and A. Gregory, *Height, Health and History: Nutritional Status in the United Kingdom, 1780–1980* (Cambridge, 1990), 182–95, 304–9.

and physical condition of London's poorer children in the second half of the nineteenth century.[120] Yet the experience of some of the city's immigrant communities, by contrast, confirms the importance of social behaviour in influencing mortality from these diseases. Both the Jews and the Irish, for example, laid great stress on the care of young children, and their offspring 'usually stand apart in poorer neighbourhoods from the usual degeneracy'.[121] Rickets was rare among the Jews; they were cleaner, and 'their round and ruddy faces' presented a strong contrast to the pale, scrofulous countenances of the English children who lived in the same crowded courts.[122] In 1884 the Revd R. C. Billing, rector of Christ Church, Spitalfields, described how the 10,000 foreign Jews in his parish mostly lived in a state of great degradation and dirt, but were often not as poor as the English poor, and 'anything like contagious disease is not known among them, and that has been a great puzzle to the medical officers'.[123] Different social beliefs, differing domestic traditions and practices, probably lay behind the perceived low childhood mortalities of the Irish and Jewish communities. All Jews, but especially the poorest, it was said, dreaded a death because it was associated with ritual privation and absolute cessation from work for several days.[124] These factors were an evident incentive to special nursing care for the sick, in contrast to the customs of continuing normal life despite illness and bereavement, and the celebration of the latter, which were so widely practised among London's Gentiles.

Although they often remarked on social behaviour, London's medical officers made little comment on the dietary habits of their people, on their nutritional condition or its relation to infectious disease. The pioneering studies of Edward Smith show that the nineteenth-century health reformers were not unaware of the public-health problem of malnutrition,[125] but there was no widespread preventive action taken to remedy or alleviate it through education or political activity. Most often, the attitude adopted by medical observers was that made infamous in the 1930s: that working-class ineptitude at cooking and general domestic management lay at the root of the evil.[126] Ineptitude was not the whole story, however; nor was poverty. English dietary habits and prejudices were seen as bearing some measure of responsibility for working-class undernourishment. Reviewing the habits of London's Italian colony in 1880, a *Lancet* observer noted: 'The English poor live irregularly and starve themselves half the week because they cannot afford a joint or steak every day.'[127] The Englishman's beef, that symbol of his status and relative wealth, made its own contribution to his nutritional disadvantage.

[120] See e.g. the evidence before the *ICPD*, 1904.

[121] *ICPD*, q. 475.

[122] *ICPD*, q. 517; J. H. Stallard, *London Pauperism Amongst Jews and Christians* (1864), 11.

[123] *RCHWC*, q. 4,995.

[124] Stallard, *Jews and Christians*, 13.

[125] Edward Smith, 'The nourishment of distressed operatives', in *MOAR* PC, PP 1863 xxv, app. V.3, pp. 320–456; Buchanan, 'Cotton Famine', 303.

[126] *Lancet* (1859), i. 86; (1873), ii. 163.

[127] *Lancet* (1880), i. 260.

The difficulty of disentangling nutritional influences on mortality from others confounded Victorian observers as it has done historians. Studies of immigrant groups with relatively low mortalities, for example, revealed a variety of differing social and dietary practices, but no single, definable crucial variable. London's Italian community was poor, but despite filth, overcrowding, and bad drains, its death-rate was not high. This, it was observed, was partly because they had regular and plentiful meals, and they were not proud about joints and steak.[128] But other critical factors could have been Italian prudence and personal habits: they were mostly single men, who dressed well, and who 'do not encumber themselves with wives and children whom they are unable to support'.[129] Marriage patterns, indeed, were obviously a critical determinant in sustaining levels of poverty or affluence within and between different social groups and classes. John Tripe, for example, noted that very few clerks earning as little as thirty shillings a week would marry, nor did they have large families, in contrast to mechanics, who did both: the clerks knew that it would 'pull them down more than anything else to have large families to support'.[130]

The social behaviour of the Jews was almost certainly a contributory factory to that low mortality, even among new immigrants, which so puzzled observers in the last two decades of the century. The Jewish immigrants lived in poverty, they were overcrowded, their tenements were dirty, and they had 'bad habits generally', yet, the *Lancet* noted: 'The Jews in London die slowly. It is a considerable trouble to our Medical Officer of Health . . . Mr Shirley Murphy cannot make out why in Whitechapel they die no faster than in other parts of London.'[131] Despite the outward trappings of squalid urban poverty, the Jewish immigrants had inestimable advantages in a religious tradition in which cleanliness was most important. There were the regulations surrounding the raising, slaughter, and distribution of meat; the ritual ablutions and changes of clothing; the Sabbath feast and the passover house-cleansing: all of which contributed to greater personal and domestic hygiene than was to be found among other urban immigrants, notably the Irish. The Mosaic Code even provided for the isolation of infectious-disease cases, and for disinfection, though how far these precautions were practised in everyday life may be debatable.[132] According to Ernest Hart, the Jews were noted for a 'remarkable immunity from intermittent fevers', from cholera and other filth diseases; from convulsions and tabes mesenterica in children; and from phlegmasia (inflammation accompanied by fever) of the respiratory organs.[133] Sir James Crichton-Browne

[128] *Lancet* (1880), i. 260; for the life of London's Italian colony, and the public-health problems it posed, see Lucio Sponza, *Italian Immigrants in Nineteenth Century Britain: Realities and Images* (Leicester, 1988), esp. chap. 7.

[129] *Lancet* (1880), i. 260. [130] *RCHWC*, q. 9,012. [131] *Lancet* (1890), i. 260.

[132] Ernest Hart, 'The Mosaic code of sanitation', *Sanitary Record*, 1 (1877), 183.

[133] Ibid. 198.

confirmed the Jews' comparative freedom from all forms of tuberculosis;[134] and many observed their remarkable immunity to cholera.[135] Hygienic practices and higher levels of family care were certainly a factor in this apparently greater resistance to communicable diseases, but poor Jews, and especially the Russian and East European immigrants, did not share the British preoccupation with meat; they made use of a wide range of cereals, pulses, and vegetables, as well as of fish, eggs, and milk;[136] and this freedom from the dominance of meat may, it seems, have been an important factor among their poor in achieving a nutritionally satisfactory diet. It is, however, impossible to disentangle the relative significance of dietary and hygienic practices. If the Jews had a greater freedom from respiratory tuberculosis, which might be taken to be significant of better diets, their freedom from cholera and fevers undoubtedly signified superior domestic and personal hygiene, and domestic hygiene is also important in the etiology of tuberculosis.

The disease and mortality experience of London's immigrant groups, like so much of the city's nineteenth-century mortality history, merits further detailed investigation. The nutrition and social practices of individuals, for example, are only one contributory factor to the city's overall disease experience. No city exists in isolation, and the external context of its life, the pressures of wider population movements, of economic change, and technological development, may affect its disease experience over time. Yet the steady decline in London's crude death-rate from the later 1860s, and the peaks of mortality occurring between 1870 and 1900, bear little obvious relation to such external influences, and are generally determined by an escalation in deaths from one or another (sometimes several) of the communicable diseases (Fig. 9.1). The trade depressions of 1866–7, 1879, and 1884–7 appear to have had an impact on cycles of mortality; but the epidemic peak of 1866 was caused by cholera, whose import was independent of economic movements. The effects of the depressed years of the 1890s on morbidity and mortality perhaps deserve closer scrutiny than can be given them here: compared with the smooth downwards mortality curve of the 1880s, the 1890s were evidently years of greater mortal instability.[137]

None the less, the experience of the 1890s demonstrates the effectiveness of the Victorian preventive system. The massive Jewish immigration into London in the last decades of the nineteenth century, especially during the 1890s when

[134] Sir James Crichton-Browne, 'The prevention of tubercular disease', *Jnl. San. Inst.*, 15 (1894), 455. This is not to claim that the Jews were immune from tuberculosis. In the closing decades of the century immigrant Jews were proving susceptible to infection in the terrible conditions of the sweat-shops where they worked: see above Chap. 8, 'Tuberculosis'; Jerry White, *Rothschild Buildings: Life in an East End Tenement Block 1887–1920*, (1980), 152–3.

[135] *Lancet* (1855), i. 50; *South London Press*, 18 Aug. 1866.

[136] White, *Rothschild Buildings*, 153–4; E. Mellanby, 'Accessory food factors (vitamines) in the feeding of infants', *Lancet* (1920), i. 861.

[137] The details of London's trade cycle have been drawn from Jones, *Outcast London*, 278, 281–2, 347–8.

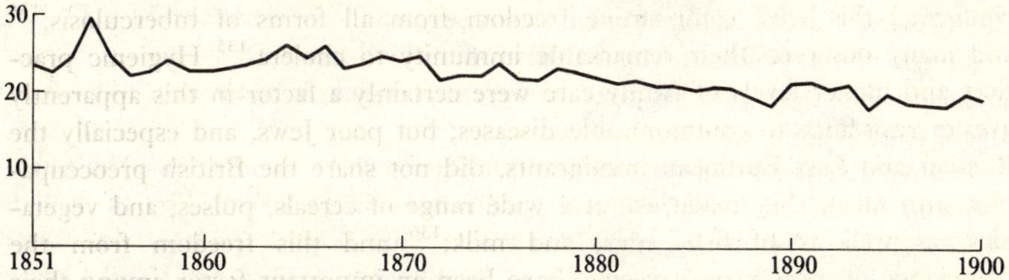

FIG. 9.1. *Crude death-rate in London, 1851–1900, per 1,000 population.*

economic depression also threatened the city's mortal stability, had a minimal demographic and epidemiological impact. The epidemic peaks of 1890s London cannot be matched to the waves of Jewish immigrants,[138] a fact which suggests the extent to which the public-health administration now regulated the flow of forces that determined the city's infectious-disease profile. In the years before 1870, and for centuries before that, unusual migration and immigration had been critical elements in disrupting the social economy and disease ecology of both town and countryside. Such population movements caused social dislocation and brought about outbreaks of epidemic disease. In the 1860s economic depression and unusual rural immigration had been instrumental in creating an epidemic climax in London.[139] The city's preventive organization, barely four years old in 1860s, had neither achieved sufficient sanitary improvement, nor acquired sufficient epidemic experience, to influence the course of events or to modify the impact of disease. By the 1890s it was a different story; by then, the sanitary organization had gained effective control of the city.

CONCLUSION: INFECTIOUS DISEASE AND THE MODERN RISE OF POPULATION

The importance of social intervention in changing the pattern of disease-incidence and mortality in nineteenth-century England is only now becoming recognized by historians. Simon Szreter's thesis has provoked other historians to consider wider sources for the history of mortality, and to set McKeown's arguments in a fresh perspective. Allan Mitchell, notably, has drawn attention to the anomalous experience of nineteenth-century France, where tuberculosis death-rates failed to fall down to 1914. A comparison of the different patterns

[138] In America, Irish and European immigrants had an impact on epidemic patterns: see R. A. Meckel, 'Immigration, mortality and population growth in Boston, 1840–1880', *Journal of Interdisciplinary History*, 15 (1985), 393–417.
[139] Hardy, 'Urban famine', 403–5.

of tuberculosis deaths in France, Germany, and England leads, Mitchell argues, to the opposite of McKeown's conclusion: that local sanitary measures and national health reforms were of key importance in reducing deaths from this disease.[140]

In England, the down-turn in national death-rates coincided with the establishment of the national preventive organization in the 1870s. This in itself is not conclusive: the history of the major infectious diseases shows no one factor to have been of overriding importance in reducing death-rates. If we look at the eight major diseases and their behaviour in the years 1850 to 1900, two sets of distinctions can be made. One is between the diseases which principally affected adults and the infectious diseases of childhood. The former were affected by preventive intervention, the latter were not. Within the childhood group, moreover, there is a division between scarlet fever and diphtheria, in which the virulence of the infective organism determined the pattern of incidence and mortality, and measles and whooping cough, in which social factors determined fatality.

All four children's infections depend for their transmission on close personal contact, and are either infectious before symptoms make the nature of the disease clear, or are transmitted by asymptomatic carriers. In the absence of immunization therapy, they pose an insoluble preventive problem. By contrast the 'adult' group of infections are clearly amenable to specific measures of prevention, whether through improved personal and domestic hygiene, better water supplies, or, in the case of smallpox, vaccination. It was in this group that the potential for effective preventive action lay.

The impact of Victorian attempts to intervene in the natural course of the principal infectious diseases was, therefore, rather various. With regard to the children's diseases, the only certainty is that direct preventive intervention was of little significance in changing their pattern of behaviour. Taken as a package, the story of measles and whooping cough suggests little in the way of improved living standards among children of the poorest classes before 1914, while that of scarlet fever and diphtheria reflects the shifting potency of disease strains and changing patterns of dominance between them. The established interpretation, which sees the advent of antitoxin as initiating the reduction in diphtheria deaths, has little foundation in fact. Milder strains of the disease were already displacing the virulent in the early 1890s, before antitoxin became widely available or was effectively used. A coincidence of timing permitted the 'triumph of antitoxin' to become established as a successful medical myth.

The limitations which epidemiological reality imposed on preventive attempts to control the childhood infections contrasts with preventive effectiveness against the other major infections. The impact of smallpox, typhoid, and typhus, and (more arguably) of tuberculosis, was significantly reduced

[140] Allan Mitchell, 'An inexact science: the statistics of tuberculosis in late nineteenth-century France', *Social History of Medicine*, 3 (1990), 403.

through the activities of the preventive administration. This is perhaps most clearly seen with smallpox. The combination of vaccination and the stamping-out policy, together with local and international surveillance, brought the disease under control in the 1880s. The task of the preventive authorities was undoubtedly made easier because victims were not infectious during the incubation period, and were most so at the height of their fever. None the less, the later nineteenth-century reduction in smallpox incidence was a considerable triumph for the preventive authorities. Infant vaccination alone, as practised in Britain without any provision for systematic re-vaccination, could never have been as effective as the stamping-out policy proved to be after 1870. The great epidemic of 1870–1 was itself proof of the fundamental inadequacy of vaccination policy as a preventive measure, in a society where the liberty of the individual, and more especially of the consenting adult individual, remained a potent political philosophy.

The preventive contribution to the reduction in deaths from typhoid, typhus, and tuberculosis was equally substantial, if less clear-cut. The variety of factors involved in maintaining endemic typhoid in nineteenth-century communities was great, and it is hardly surprising that their discovery and elimination was a gradual process, piecemeal over fifty years and more. The virtual elimination of typhus was assisted by its limited local survival in non-epidemic years, which facilitated the detection and control of outbreaks. This enabled the preventive authorities, through continued vigilance and the application of stamping-out measures, to ensure that there was no further epidemic escalation of the disease. The reduction in deaths from both typhoid and typhus through diligent local activity and public-health education was a major achievement of the Victorian preventive administration. And for tuberculosis, similarly, general sanitary improvements, in the sense of slum-clearances, new housing, constant water supplies, and the growing emphasis on domestic cleanliness, were probably important. Environmental and occupational factors were clearly of considerable significance in determining its incidence and fatality, and the Victorian evidence suggests that these were more potent in influencing the behaviour of the disease than improved resistance resulting from a nutritionally satisfactory diet.

Although the story of tuberculosis is fraught with unquantifiable variables, it clearly belongs with that of the other major infectious diseases, and is part of the story of preventive medicine. Nor was the effectiveness of the preventive organization limited to the diseases discussed in this book: England's freedom from cholera epidemics after 1870 was due to the efforts of the medical officers, and it may be, too, that they assisted in the eventual down-turn in deaths from infant diarrhoea.[141] All the activities which the Victorian preventive authorities undertook in the name of sanitary improvement and disease

[141] For cholera, see Hardy, 'Cholera, quarantine and the English preventive system, 1850–1895', *Medical History*, 37 (July 1993); the full story of infant diarrhoea remains to be explored.

prevention were of fundamental importance in breaking up established disease habitats and routes of transmission, and in opening up private homes and private lives to a consciousness of health and cleanliness. The force of nineteenth-century preventive medicine lay, not in national policies enunciated by a central administration, but in the persevering implementation of local measures based on local observation by a body of professional men whose sole responsibility was to their local community.

Examination of the local epidemiological factors determining patterns of infectious disease in England reinforces the significance of preventive measures and of the natural behaviour of infections. Rather than confirming the influence of improved nutrition, this study suggests that England's population was essentially above the critical threshold of under-nutrition below which resistance to infection is affected. The local history of the major infectious diseases does not support McKeown's thesis, as summarized by Mitchell, of 'a steady amelioration by natural causes, especially by better nutrition'. Indeed, it may be suggested that the possibility of amelioration by natural causes was a chimera. Whatever the natural patterns of infectious disease before the nineteenth century, the phenomenon of massive, unregulated urban growth and expanding national and international transport systems in that century destroyed the pre-industrial world and most of the natural systems of checks and balances for the infectious diseases as a group.

Above all, detailed examination of the nineteenth-century sources for historical epidemiology demonstrates the importance of establishing proper criteria for their use. McKeown's failure fully to evaluate the reliability of the registrar-general's statistical series seriously flawed his argument as regards the nineteenth century. Even supposing that tuberculosis deaths did decline under the influence of improved nutrition after 1840, the compensating ground-swell of deaths from bronchitis indicates that chronic, long-term disease did not diminish as a factor complicating resistance to other infectious diseases before the 1880s at least. The influence of chronic disease on mortality patterns, and the impact of infections upon each other are thorny historical problems, and cannot be discussed here. The epidemiological record clearly suggests, however, that it was not better nutrition that broke the spiral of deaths from infectious disease after 1870, but intervention by the preventive authorities, together with natural modifications in disease virulence, which reduced exposure to several of the most deadly infections. The opposition of vested interests to sanitary reform, which has been demonstrated by several historians,[142] was successful in temporarily delaying local measures of improvement but did not significantly compromise the overall impact of preventive medicine.

McKeown's work was in many respects polemical: he himself wrote of the

[142] Wohl, *Endangered Lives*; W. Luckin, *Pollution and Control: A Social History of the Thames* (Bristol, 1986); David Owen, *The Government of Victorian London, 1885–1889: The Metropolitan Board of Works, the Vestries and the City Corporation*, ed. R. M. MacLeod (1982).

problem of modern population history, that it should be regarded as a canvas 'on which a comprehensive interpretation is sketched, at an early stage', and that detailed work could subsequently be used to fill in the outline where necessary.[143] Many facets of nineteenth-century mortality patterns remain to be explored, and the time has perhaps not come for a comprehensive revision of McKeown's comprehensive interpretation. Clearly, however, some such re-evaluation will be necessary, as scholarly activity continues to modify various aspects of McKeown's argument. Wrigley and Schofield's monumental work on English population history has already rendered obsolete his dismissal of fertility as the instigator of population growth in the eighteenth century. Where McKeown argued that increasing food supplies led to a reduction in infectious-disease deaths, and hence to a rising population in that century, Wrigley and Schofield found rather that increased nuptiality, and hence higher fertility, in an increasingly politically and economically stable society, was the primary source of rising rates of population growth, supported and sustained by increasing food supplies.[144] These findings were the result of meticulous historical investigation, and displace McKeown's essentially unhistorical assessment of the role of fertility in eighteenth-century population growth. McKeown was a scientist speculating on historical phenomena, and his unfamiliarity with historical realities cannot but raise wide questions about the validity of his arguments. The central players in the drama of modern population growth—fertility, mortality, and infectious disease—must be thoroughly examined and set in their historical context before their respective contributions can be properly assessed.

The history of the infectious diseases in modern times remains inextricably intertwined with the history of the cities that spawned them. There are indications that improvements in urban environments in the eighteenth century led to stabilizing disease-rates, even while medical men were becoming increasingly aware of the problems of disease among the poor.[145] In the early nineteenth century, increased exposure to infection and to environmental factors which further enhanced the fatality of many infections drove an increase in infectious mortality. In the struggle to overcome endemic infections which got under way after 1840, mastery over urban environments and understanding of the processes of disease were crucial to success. The problems of nineteenth-century cities called for a systematic and professional administrative response,

[143] McKeown, *Modern Rise*, 11. For a recent assessment of his position on medical intervention and the historical debate, see S. J. Kunitz, 'The personal physician and mortality decline', in R. S. Schofield, D. Reher, and A. Bideau (eds.), *The Decline of Mortality in Europe*, (Oxford, 1991), 248–62. See also Robert Woods, 'Public health and public hygiene', in ibid. 244–6.

[144] E. A. Wrigley and R. S. Schofield, *The Population History of England 1541–1871* (Cambridge, 1981).

[145] Penelope Corfield, *The Impact of English Towns 1700–1800* (Oxford, 1982), chap. 10; William McNeill, *Plagues and Peoples* (1976), chap. 6; J. C. Riley, *The Eighteenth-Century Campaign to Avoid Disease* (1987); Roy Porter, 'Cleaning up the Great Wen', in W. F. Bynum and R. S. Porter (eds.), *Living and Dying in London, Medical History*, supplement no. 11 (1991).

which was provided with the establishment of sanitary authorities and, more especially, of medical officers of health in London in 1855 and elsewhere in 1872. The medical officers of health played a central part in the transformation of England's disease experience during the last decades of the nineteenth century. It was they who spearheaded the Victorian struggle against infectious disease, and it was their initiative and their labours which led to the eventual eradication of the epidemic streets.

Appendix: Statistical Note

A note of caution must be sounded about nineteenth-century mortality statistics. The subject has already been treated in a pioneering article by Bill Luckin,[1] but needs further exploration in the local context. The basis of all mortality calculations for this period are the annual and decennial reports of the registrar-general, supplemented by census material. There are no reliable figures for disease incidence before the provisions of the 1889 Notification Act were tightened up in 1892; until this date the records of the London Fever Hospital and, from 1871, the Metropolitan Asylums Board must be used to supplement the registration data. None of these sources is completely trustworthy. The registrar-general's reports, as Luckin warns, must be treated 'with a high degree of caution and scepticism'. Luckin draws attention to three particular difficulties with the registration material: the categorization of disease; failure to allocate deaths to district of residence rather than to the district in which death occurred; and failure to indicate the incidence of non-fatal illness.[2] With the census material, on which calculations of mortality-rates proportionate to population are based, there is a related problem: depending on the season at which the census was taken, population figures for the individual districts (notably those with a well-to-do population) may be too low. Finally, with regard to disease incidence, the available material for the pre-1892 period is extremely difficult to use at district level, and is better seen in aggregate relation to the general city experience: there was no systematic district admissions policy to either the London Fever Hospital or the MAB hospitals, and the number and nature of cases arriving from the different unions differed widely.

Problems with the categorization of disease are a well-recognized feature of historical mortality studies. In the registration period (post-1837) these are less acute than for earlier centuries for which the Bills of Mortality are the only reference, but some caution should none the less be exercised in the use of registration categories. For the communicable diseases as a group, the registration data categories may, on the whole, be taken as fairly reliable. There are, of course, exceptions, notably in the registration of deaths from respiratory tuberculosis (phthisis); typhoid and typhus; and diphtheria. For the sake of brevity and clarity, specific problems with the various diseases will be discussed under individual headings below.

Whooping Cough

The mortality figures for whooping cough may be considered essentially reliable. The disease is distinctive in its symptoms, and it was a widespread, very familiar disease of childhood.

[1] W. Luckin, 'Death and survival in the city', *Urban History Yearbook* (1980), 53–62.
[2] Ibid. 55.

Measles

Figures for measles may be accepted as a generally reliable indicator of the epidemic prevalence and fatality levels of the disease. Again, it was a familiar childhood disease with a distinctive rash, which might be distinguished from other infection-induced rashes without too much difficulty. However, measles fatalities were often due to subsequent respiratory complications in this period, and registered measles deaths may underestimate mortality levels by a factor of deaths attributed to respiratory disease.

Scarlet Fever

Diagnoses are likely to have been reliable, despite the variability of the disease; some deaths may have been allocated to complications such as nephritis, but since these generally occurred within the recognized period of the disease (as indicated by the desquamation of the convalescent case), they are likely to be insignificant statistically. It should be remembered, however, that scarlet fever and diphtheria were not separated in the registration tables until 1859, so that figures for the years 1856–8, after the reappearance of diphtheria in England, are for both diseases.

Diphtheria

Registration data for diphtheria is less reliable than for the other three children's diseases, and its mortality levels should be viewed in conjunction with those for croup and quinsy. It was a 'new' disease when it appeared in 1856, and its reliability in registration consequently suffered, gaining in stability perhaps only in the 1880s.

Smallpox

Registration of smallpox was essentially reliable; it was a well-known and generally distinctive disease. Some under-registration is indicated by deaths ascribed to chickenpox, which is hardly ever fatal. The curve of chickenpox deaths moves with that of smallpox; the actual figures are statistically insignificant. Smallpox attributions become less reliable in the 1890s, by which time the disease was relatively rare, and outside the experience of many young practitioners.

Cholera

Being an imported disease of distinct and limited epidemics, and with sensational symptoms, cholera attributions are essentially reliable in the known epidemic years. Some diarrhoea mortality may be associated with cholera in these years. The epidemics were of what was known to contemporaries as 'Asiatic cholera'; this is a different disease from that known as 'English cholera', a variant of diarrhoea, and attributions to 'cholera' in non-epidemic years should be ascribed to the latter.

Typhoid and Typhus

Typhoid and typhus are very similar in symptom, and were generally confused until distinguished by Sir William Jenner in 1846. It was, however, not until after Wunderlich's temperature studies had facilitated differential diagnosis that the two diseases were distinguished in the registrar-general's reports after 1869. Attributions of typhus, at least, should still be treated with some caution in the registration data after this date, while typhoid was sometimes used as a disguise for tuberculosis. The records of the London Fever Hospital distinguished typhus from typhoid after 1847, permitting assessment of the relative epidemic prevalence of the two diseases in London in the years 1847–70.

Tuberculosis

Registration data for respiratory tuberculosis should be treated with great caution, and preferably in conjunction with that for other respiratory diseases. Although diagnosis became more precise during the course of the century, with the advent of auscillation and the stethoscope, the social taboos surrounding the disease led to many deaths being registered as bronchitis, pneumonia, or even typhoid, depending on the symptoms present in the final stages.

Following on from questions of categorization, the second problem with the registrar-general's figures for individual registration districts is, as Luckin points out, that deaths were allocated to the district in which they occurred, rather to that in which the person concerned had lived (and acquired his disease). A number of complicating factors are thereby introduced into the mortality picture, and the crude mortality-rates cannot be accepted unannotated as a real reflection of the sanitary condition and health status of the local population. In the first place, there were deaths occurring in hospitals. Districts in which major, or specialist, hospitals were situated registered disproportionate numbers of certain deaths. Thus Islington, in the years before 1870, appears to have a much higher than average fever and smallpox mortality because of the presence of the London Fever Hospital and the Smallpox Hospital. With the opening of the Metropolitan Asylums Board hospitals from 1870, this factor comes to affect other districts; by the end of the century there were infectious-disease hospitals in Fulham, Hampstead, Hackney, Lambeth, and Greenwich. The Evelina Hospital, in St George's, Southwark, also took infectious cases, as did the general hospitals, though only in small numbers, mainly typhoid, and then largely before 1870. Quite a number of districts came to possess consumption hospitals although only the Brompton (Kensington, Chelsea) and perhaps the North London (Hampstead) were large enough to make a significant impact on local mortality figures.[3] During the later decades of the century London became a centre for small specialist hospitals, and some districts, notably Marylebone, eventually had quite a few of these. Other districts also felt the effects of this development. In St James's, Westminster, for example, there were large numbers of hotels and superior lodging houses in the fashionable quarters near the great clubs of St James's and Pall

[3] Besides their inmates, they attracted a large number of out-patients, who often came to reside close to the hospital. See above, Chap. 8, 'Tuberculosis'.

Mall. Invalids from all over the country came here in attendance on eminent London physicians and surgeons; and James Edmunds, the MOH, complained that it was often difficult to draw the line between residents and non-residents, in order to achieve a correct picture of the district's mortality.[4] It would, however, be a mistake to assume that these 'foreign' deaths always operated to a district's disadvantage; there was also the deceptively beneficial factor of local deaths occurring outside the district. Thus, Mile End Old Town discovered in the mid-1880s that its death-rates were far less favourable than they appeared to be, because of the number of parish deaths which took place in institutions beyond its own boundaries.[5]

TABLE App. 1. *MAB* hospitals, 1871–1900

Hospital	District	Opening date
North-Western	Hampstead	1870
South-Western	Stockwell	1871
Eastern	Homerton	1871
Western	Fulham	1877
South-Eastern	Deptford	1877
Northern	Winchmore Hill	1882
Hospital Ships		1883
Fountain	Tooting	1893
Brook	Woolwich	1896
Park	Lewisham	1897
Grove	Lower Tooting	1899

Source: MABAR.

Apart from the hospitals with a direct association with infectious-disease deaths, large institutions such as prisons and barracks could influence the general mortality of a district in various ways. Barracks, for example, contained a population of 'picked lives'—young, healthy males, and might be expected to exercise a beneficial influence on local death-rates, but before the Army Sanitary Commission Inquiry of 1858, men in barracks were peculiarly prone to die from respiratory tuberculosis. After the reforms introduced subsequent to the inquiry, their tuberculosis mortality was less than average.[6] The Woolwich Barracks, however, where there were also military families on site, proved to be a continuous source of infectious disease and sanitary anxiety.[7] Workhouses also, especially workhouse infirmaries, may have influenced mortality levels, and where districts housed the workhouse population of others (Islington, for example, contained the Holborn Union Infirmary), they may have distorted local mortality figures.[8] There were also non-institutional factors in operation. A district with many poor lodging houses, like Westminster or Strand, attracted a low population that may have suf-

[4] *MOAR* St James's, Westminster (1895), 154.

[5] *MOAR* Chelsea (1885), 136.

[6] See above, Chap. 8, 'Tuberculosis'.

[7] For problems at the Woolwich Barracks, see *Lancet* (1874), ii. 813, 850, 880; (1875), i. 351; *Daily News*, 12 Dec. 1874.

[8] See above, Chap. 8, 'Tuberculosis'.

fered disproportionately from tuberculosis. Camberwell was on the tramp routes from Surrey and Kent, and its workhouse was known for its liberality: John Bristowe clearly felt that it attracted an unfair number of persons suffering from typhus and other infectious diseases, especially during the hop-picking season.[9] Similarly, St Saviour's, Southwark found its 'wonderful array' of charities a mixed blessing. A 'very short residence' was required to apply for these, with the result, as James Herron saw it, that 'large numbers of people whose health has broken down' through age or deprivation crowded into the poorer and cheaper tenements to become eligible for the charities. They were people who could not withstand the strain of any serious illness, and their presence drove up the district's mortality-rate beyond its true level.[10] Herron's sense of injustice (at a time when aggregate mortality figures were still regarded as the index of a district's health and sanitary achievement) was aggravated by the consequences of the opening of a new infirmary at Champion Hill: the magnificent hospital, with its extensive range of accommodation and treatment, attracted a 'steady and increasing flow' of social outcasts into the district.[11] Even districts without ancient charities had problems with undesirable immigrants: Putney, for example, had a reputation for 'pure suburban atmosphere' which attracted tuberculosis victims.[12]

The attraction of residents undesirable because of their low health status was likely to result in unfavourable mortality statistics, but may at least represent a fairly continuous influence on mortality in affected districts. This factor should, however, be borne in mind when assessing the relative healthiness of any district, and its achievements in areas such as housing or disease control, where death-rates from specific diseases might be taken as an indicator of success. More difficult to pin down is the influence of seasonal mobility on annual death-rates; this behaviour pattern affects the reliability of census material as well. In certain districts, notably in the West End during the summer months, and the East End during the fruit- and hop-picking seasons, a considerable section of the community removed itself for months or weeks at a time. The 1861 census was taken during the hop-picking, and Henry Letheby complained that this resulted in a serious underestimate of the City population.[13] Similarly, in 1891 Orme Dudfield refused to accept the official figures, which showed a decrease in the sub-district of St John's, Paddington, because a large number of families had been 'out of Town'.[14] Ten years earlier the decrease in St John's had been attributed, not to the incursion of railways or the opening up of new roads, but to the wealthy displacing the 'more numerous' poor.[15] The influx of East European refugees into the East End lent a particular doubtfulness to the 1891 figures: the difficulty which the Whitechapel's sanitary inspectors encountered in obtaining correct particulars, even by carefully visiting each tenement, led the MOH to doubt the accuracy of the census returns.[16] It may be that deaths occurring away from home during the hop-picking were more than compensated for by deaths occurring subsequently from diseases acquired in Kent, but these non-institutional deaths, especially in the well-to-do districts, evidently exercised an artificially healthy influence on registered mortality.

The social composition of a district also qualifies the significance of its registered

[9] *MOAR* Camberwell (1869–70), 50.
[10] *MOAR* St Saviour (1891), 48.
[11] Ibid. 47. This was probably the Dulwich Hospital (1887).
[12] *MOAR* Wandsworth (1865), 46.
[13] *MOAR* City (1860–1), 8.
[14] *MOAR* Paddington (1890), 177.
[15] Ibid. (1880), 26.
[16] *MOAR* Whitechapel (1894), 3.

mortality figures. As John Bristowe put it, 'by a kind of process of natural selection, the young and able-bodied tend to accumulate in certain localities, while the infants and the aged, and it may be the sickly, remain in undue proportion in other localities'.[17] It may be that this effect was more marked at sub-district than at registration-district level; further work on the population composition of London's registration districts is evidently required. Bristowe took the examples of Dulwich and Peckham within his own district to illustrate the point. Dulwich had a remarkably low death-rate, Peckham a relatively high one, but 'I do not for one moment believe that the difference in their death-rates indicates a corresponding difference in their healthiness'. Differences in structure between the two populations affected the significance of registered mortality. While the population of Dulwich was swollen by numerous servants in the prime of life, its mortality did not include that of the servants, but only of the resident families. The servants died in hospital, or in their own homes. In the poor households of Peckham, where there were no domestic servants, older and adult children generally quitted home, often to become servants elsewhere, and the vitality of the family was, in a statistical sense, diminished, by their efflux. Peckham households consisted disproportionately of the very young, the old, and the sick, because the young adults returned home when they fell ill.[18] Further, the poorer classes married earlier and had more children. As children up to 4 or 5 'even under the most favourable circumstances', suffered a higher mortality than any other age-group, their presence also raised the general death-rate.[19] Indeed, as Bristowe warned at the conclusion of this exercise: 'The fact is that the sanitary condition of a locality is more truly measured by the comparative prevalence in it of certain forms of disease than by mere variations of death-rate.'[20]

These 'mere variations in death-rate' are, however, in most cases the only indications of the respective prevalence of different diseases. Unfortunately, the hospital factor means that district-level mortality figures become increasingly distorted for the infectious diseases in the years after 1870. Before 1870 deaths from smallpox occurring at Highgate, and from typhus, typhoid, and scarlet fever at the London Fever Hospital were probably relatively low enough, at district level, not to contribute any substantial distortion to the district figures. With the arrival of the MAB hospitals from the 1870s, and especially with the dramatic rise in hospitalization of cases of scarlet fever, diphtheria, and typhoid after 1891, district mortality figures for these diseases become increasingly doubtful; by the 1890s they are often meaningless. The clearest example of this fallacy in the registration data comes with smallpox. Following preventive anxiety about the role of the MAB smallpox hospitals in spreading the disease in the localities in which they were situated, the managers established hospital ships, moored at Long Reach on the Thames, to which all smallpox cases were transferred in the years after 1884. Thereafter, the number of smallpox deaths registered in London dropped to virtually none. By contrast, the number registered in the Kentish district of Dartford rose sharply, and thereafter was frequently noticeably higher than in the surrounding countryside.

Correcting the district mortality rates to allow for the accelerating rate of hospital transfers for infectious cases is a task of great complexity. Until the Infectious Diseases Notification Act 1889 was implemented, there are no records of disease incidence as

[17] *MOAR* Camberwell (1863–4), 29. [18] Ibid. 29–31. [19] Ibid. 31.
[20] Ibid. 31–42.

opposed to mortality, and hospital mortality rates are a notoriously unreliable indicator. The admissions records of the London Fever Hospital furnish the historian with a reasonable indication of the relative prevalence of typhoid and typhus in the city as a whole for the years 1859–79, and those of the MAB hospitals give insight into scarlet fever, smallpox, and eventually diphtheria, for the period after 1870. Nevertheless, the MAB, while it published the number of cases entering its hospitals, and the mortality rates experienced for each disease, did not publish deaths differentiated by disease according to the local authority district to which they belonged. In 1888 the MAB's Statistical Committee warned against taking the crude admissions figures from the various districts too seriously:[21]

> It must be remembered that the number of cases being sent by the various Parishes and Unions should not be regarded as absolute standards of the relative presence of disease in them, owing, among other reasons, to the great difference in the number of population, also to the different practices adopted with regard to the proportion of patients making use of the Managers' Hospitals or being treated elsewhere.

Although the managers collated the total death-rates from all diseases for individual districts, these are not much help in determining the relative fatality of specific diseases locally; indeed, as the Statistical Committee further warned, the condition of patients with regard to their general health, and the stage of the disease reached before their transfer to hospital varied 'sensibly' in different districts.[22] The very list of districts contributing the highest and the lowest numbers of cases to the hospitals in proportion to population in that year serves as a warning. The highest contributors were Fulham, Westminster, St Pancras, Holborn, Whitechapel, Lambeth, and Wandsworth; the lowest Hampstead, Islington (where the London Fever Hospital was situated), and Stepney.[23]

The MAB data are thus of rather limited use in any attempt to correct registration data or to supplement the picture it provides of disease incidence in any particular locality. Disease-specific hospital death-rates among the Whitechapel poor, for example, cannot be compared with those of the Marylebone poor, although the death-rates for the various diseases of different hospitals (which had geographical catchment areas) did vary. The most that can be done is to apply the death-rate of the relevant hospital to the annual case totals of individual districts. This formula has been used by Bill Luckin to evaluate the relative incidence of typhoid and typhus for the city's districts from the 1870s.[24] None the less, it is a technique which, besides being immensely laborious, seems to contain serious flaws, as indicated by the Statistical Committee's ruminations cited above. Statistical series acquired by this method should be treated with caution. I have shamelessly, and perhaps incautiously, made use of Bill Luckin's calculations for typhoid in the relevant chapter.[25] I have not had the energy or the confidence to attempt to replicate his work for scarlet fever and diphtheria, preferring to gain an impression of the general prevalence and seriousness of these diseases in different districts from consideration of the combination of registered death-rates, hospital admissions, and the notification figures when they become available. The historical study of infectious diseases cannot be fully undertaken without a statistical component; it is unfortunate that this is one of the least-satisfactory forms of evidence regarding them.

[21] *MABAR* (1888), 13. [22] Ibid. 14. [23] Ibid.
[24] Luckin, 'Typhus and typhoid', in R. I. Woods and J. Woodward (eds.), *Urban Disease and Mortality* (1986), 118–19. [25] See above, Chap. 6, 'Typhoid'.

Bibliography

Place of publication London, unless otherwise shown.

PRINTED PRIMARY SOURCES

Reports of the London Medical Officers of Health, 1856–1900.

Annual Reports of the Medical Officer for London, 1890–1900.

Annual Reports of the Statistical Committee of the Metropolitan Asylums Board, 1887–1910.

Minutes of Proceedings of the Metropolitan Asylums Board.

Annual Reports of the London Fever Hospital.

Parliamentary Papers

Registrar-General's Annual Reports, 1855–1900 (and decennial supplements, 1861–1920).

John Simon, *Papers Relating to the History and Practice of Vaccination* (1857).

General Board of Health, *Papers Relating to the Sanitary State of the People of England* (1857–8).

Reports of the Medical Officer of Health to the Privy Council 1859–1870.

William Pole, *Report . . . to the Board of Trade and to the Home Office on the Constant Service System of Water Supply* (1872).

Reports of the Medical Officer of Health to the Local Government Board, 1872–1902, 1917–18.

Annual Reports of the Water Examiner to the Board of Trade.

Commission on the Influence of Smallpox and Fever Hospitals, 1882.

Royal Commission on the Housing of the Working Classes, 1885.

Royal Commission on Vaccination, Report, 1896.

Interdisciplinary Committee on Physical Deterioration, 1904.

Journals and Newspapers

British Medical Journal.

Glasgow Medical Journal.

Journal of the Royal Statistical Society.

Journal of the Sanitary Institute.

Journal of the Royal Sanitary Institute.

Journal of State Medicine.

Lancet.

London Statistics.

Medical Research Committee Special Report Series.

Medical Times and Gazette.

Medico-Chirurgical Transactions.

Nineteenth Century.

Practitioner.
Public Health.
South London Press.
The Times.
Transactions of the Epidemiological Society.
Transactions of the National Association for the Promotion of Social Science.
Transactions of the Pathological Society.
Transactions of the Sanitary Institute.
Transactions of the Society of Medical Officers of Health.
West London Medical Journal.

CONTEMPORARY ARTICLES AND MONOGRAPHS

Journal articles of special importance only have been included as separate items in the bibliography.

AMOS, JAMES, *Nine Years in Kent Street* (1870).

ARMSTRONG, H. E., *Port Sanitary Administration on the Tyne* (1888).

ASHBY, H., and WRIGHT, G. A., *The Diseases of Children*, fifth edn. (1905).

—— 'The prevention of smallpox in the metropolis', *Journal of the Sanitary Institute*, 23 (1902).

BALME, HAROLD, 'The signs and symptoms of measles in relation to diagnosis and prognosis', *Practitioner*, 73: 2 (1904).

BEETON, ISABELLA, *The Management of Children in Sickness and in Health* (1873).

BEEVOR, Sir H., 'The declension of phthisis', *Lancet* (1899), i.

BLYTH, A. W., *A Manual of Public Health* (1890).

BOOTH, CHARLES, (ed.), *Life and Labour of the People* (1892).

BOOTH, W., *In Darkest England* (1890).

BRETONNEAU, P., *Des Inflammations spéciales du tissu muqueux, et en particulier de la dipthérite* (Paris, 1826).

BUCHAN, A., and MITCHELL, A., 'The influence of weather on mortality from different diseases at different ages', *Journal of the Scottish Meteorological Society*, 4 (1875).

BUDD, W., *Typhoid Fever* (1861).

CARPENTER, ALFRED, *Hints On House Drainage*, third edn. (1866).

CHEADLE, W. B., *The Artificial Feeding of Infants* (1889).

CLARK, Sir JAMES, *A Treatise on Pulmonary Consumption* (1835).

COLLIE, ALEX, *On Fevers* (1887).

CORFIELD, W. H., *The Etiology of Typhoid Fever and its Prevention* (1902).

CORNET, G., 'On the distribution of tubercule bacilli outside the body', *Zeitscrift für Hygiene* (Nov. 1888).

—— 'On the mortality among nurses and its causes', *Zeitscrift für Hygiene* (Feb. 1889).

CREIGHTON, CHARLES, *A History of Epidemics in Britain*, 2 vols. (Cambridge, 1894).

CROOKSHANK, EDGAR M., *The Prevention of Smallpox, with Special Reference to the Origin and Development of the Stamping-Out System* (1894).

DAVIES, DAVID, *Typhoid Fever in Bristol* (Bristol, 1879).

DIBDIN, W. J., *The Purification of Sewage and Water* (1897).

DOWNES, ARTHUR, 'Notes on diphtheria', *Transactions of the Epidemiological Society*, ns 7 (1887–8).

DRINKWATER, HARRY, *The Epidemic of Measles Prevalent in Sunderland* (Edinburgh, 1885).

DUDFIELD, T. O., 'Metropolitan sanitary administration', *Transactions of the Society of Medical Officers of Health* (1884–5).

—— *Two Sanitary Addresses* (1889).

—— 'History of the Society of Medical Officers of Health', *Public Health*, Jubilee Issue (1906).

FERGUSON, M., 'A study of the social and economic factors in the causation of rickets', *Medical Research Committee Special Report*, 20 (1917–18).

GAMGEE, J., *The Cattle Plague* (1866).

GLADSTONE, CATHERINE, *Healthy Nurseries and Bedrooms* (1884).

GOODALL, E. W., and Washbourn, J. W., *A Manual of Infectious Diseases* (1908).

GREENHOW, E. H., *Diphtheria* (1860).

GRESSWELL, D. A., *The Natural History of Scarlet Fever* (Oxford, 1890).

GWYNN, E., 'Diagnosis in relation to the notification of infectious diseases', *Public Health*, 10 (1897–8).

HAMMACK, J. T., 'The relation between density of population and mortality from consumption', *Transactions of the National Association for the Promotion of Social Science* (1859).

HART, ERNEST, 'The Mosaic code of sanitation', *Sanitary Record*, 1 (1877).

—— *Report on the Influence of Milk in Spreading Zymotic Disease* (1897).

—— *Waterborne Typhoid* (1897).

HELLYER, S. S., *The Plumber and Sanitary Houses*, fourth edn. (1884).

HEWITT, G., *The Pathology of Hooping Cough* (1855).

HIRSCH, A., *Handbook of Geographical and Historical Pathology* (1886).

HOGG, JOHN, *Observations on Consumption* (1860).

HOUSTON, A. C., *Studies in Water Supply* (1913).

JENNER, Sir W., *Lectures and Essays on Fever and Diphtheria* (1893).

JOHNSTONE, FRANCES, *The Prevention of the Spread of Fevers* (1883).

KENWOOD, HARRY, 'The notification of measles', *Journal of the Sanitary Institute*, 18 (1897).

KILVERT, FRANCIS, *Diary*, ed. W. Plomer (1939).

LAING, JAMES S. 'Whooping cough: its prevalence and mortality in Aberdeen', *Public Health*, 13 (1901–2).

LATHAM, B., *Sanitary Engineering* (1873).

LONGSTAFF, G. B., *Phthisis, Bronchitis and Pneumonia* (1884).

MCVAIL, J. C., *Half a Century of Smallpox and Vaccination* (Edinburgh, 1919).

MUNRO, A. C., 'Measles: an epidemiological study', *Transactions of the Epidemiological Society*, 10 (1890).

—— 'The notification of measles', *Public Health*, 4 (1891–2).

MURCHISON, C. 'The etiology, pathology, and treatment of scarlet fever, *Lancet* (1864), i.

—— *Continued Fevers of Great Britain*, fourth edn. (1884).

MURPHY, S. F. (ed.), *Our Homes and How to Make Them Healthy* (1882).

NEWSHOLME, ARTHUR, *Epidemic Diphtheria* (1898).

—— 'An inquiry into the principal causes of the reduction in the death-rate from phthisis', *Journal of Hygiene*, 5 (1906).

NIGHTINGALE, FLORENCE, *Notes on Matters Affecting the Health of the British Army* (1858).

NIVEN, J., 'Inquiry into the conditions under which the infection of consumption is operative', *Public Health*, 3 (1890–1).

—— 'On the prevention of phthisis', *Public Health*, 5 (1892–3).

—— 'The prevention of tuberculosis', *Transactions of the Epidemiological Society*, 16 (1896–7).

PALMBERG, A., *A Treatise on Public Health and its Applications in Different European Countries* (1893).

PARKES, EDMUND, *Hygiene*, sixth edn. (1883).

PARKES, L. C., 'The common house fly (*Musca Domestica*)', *Journal of the Royal Sanitary Institute*, 32 (1911).

PAYNE, J. F., 'Tuberculosis as an endemic disease', *Transactions of the Epidemiological Society*, 12 (1892–3).

POWER, W. H., 'Thoughts on the nature of certain observed relations between diphtheria and milk', *Transactions of the Pathological Society*, 30 (1879).

RADCLIFFE, J. N., 'The prevalence, distribution and limitation of scarlet fever in England', *Transactions of the Epidemiological Society*, 2 (1864).

RANSOME, ARTHUR, 'The prospect of abolishing tuberculosis', *Public Health*, 2 (1892–3).

—— *Where Consumption is Bred in Manchester and Salford* (1888).

RAVENSHILL, A., and SCHIFF, M., *Household Administration* (1910).

REECE, R. J., 'Scarlet fever', *West London Medical Journal*, 9, (1904).

REEVES, M. P., *Round About a Pound a Week* (repr. 1979).

RENDLE, W., *London Vestries and their Sanitary Work* (1865).

REYNOLDS, Sir J. R. (ed.), *A System of Medicine*, second edn. (1870).

RICHARDSON, B. W., 'Health at home', *Transactions of the Sanitary Institute*, 1 (1879).

—— *The Field of Disease* (1883).

RUSSELL, J. A., *Hints about the Prevention of Consumption* (Glasgow, 1896).

—— *On the Prevention of Tuberculosis* (Glasgow, 1896).

SCOVELL, C. A., 'The isolation of infectious diseases in the metropolis', *Journal of the Sanitary Institute*, 17 (1896).

SHADWELL, ARTHUR, 'The German colony in London', *National Review*, 26 (1896).

SIMON, J., *English Sanitary Institutions* (1889).

SIMPSON, Sir J. Y., *A Proposal to Stamp Out Smallpox* (Edinburgh, 1868).

SLADE-KING, E., 'Notes on the spread of diphtheria', *Transactions of the Sanitary Institute*, 2 (1800–1).

SMITH, EDWARD, 'English statistics of hooping-cough', *Medico-Chirurgical Transactions*, ns 37 (1854).

—— *Handbook for Inspectors of Nuisances* (1873).

SNOW, J., *On the Mode of The Communication of Cholera* (1855).

SQUIRE, WILLIAM, 'Measles' and 'Whooping Cough', in Richard Quain (ed.), *A Dictionary of Medicine* (1882).

STALLARD, J. H., *London Pauperism among Jews and Christians* (1864).

STILL, G. F., *Common Disorders and Diseases of Childhood* (1909).

SWITHINBANK, H., and NEWMAN, G., *The Bacteriology of Milk* (1903).

SYKES, J. F. J., 'The control of infectious diseases', *Transactions of the Sanitary Institute*, 7 (1886–7).

—— 'The causes of the increase of diphtheria mortality in London', *Public Health*, 6 (1893–4).

—— *Public Health and Housing* (1901).

—— *Smallpox in London in 1901* (1901).

SYMONS, W. H., 'Local statistics', *Public Health*, 12 (1899–1900).

THOMPSON, T. S. L., 'The collection and disposal of house and trade refuse', *Journal of the Royal Sanitary Institute*, 32 (1911).

THORNE, R. THORNE, *Diphtheria: Its Natural History and Prevention* (1891).

—— *The Administrative Control of Tuberculosis* (1899).

VACHER, FRANCIS, *A Healthy Home* (1894).

VALLIN, E., 'L'Hygiène de Londres', *Revue d'hygiène*, 5 (1883).

VIESCA, Countess DOLORES DE, 'Sanitary house management', *Transactions of the Sanitary Institute*, 7 (1885–6).

VINRACE, JOHN, *The War Against Consumption* (1901).

WALDO, F. J., and WALSH, D., 'Murder by measles', *Nineteenth Century*, 39 (1896).

WARREN, ELIZA, *How I Managed my Children from Infancy to Marriage* (1865).

WELCH, HENRY, 'Modern views on the etiology of phthisis', *Practitioner*, 64 (1890).

WEST, CHARLES, *Lectures on the Diseases of Infancy and Childhood*, seventh edn. (1884).

—— *The Mother's Manual of Children's Diseases* (1885).

—— *How to Nurse Sick Children*, new edn. (1908).

WHITELEGGE, B. A., 'Measles epidemics, major and minor', *Transactions of the Epidemiological Society*, 12 (1892–3).

—— and NEWMAN, G., *Hygiene and Public Health*, rev. edn. (1905).

WILLIAMS, C. J. B., and WILLIAMS, C. T., *Pulmonary Consumption*, second edn. (1887).

WILLIAMS, C. T., 'The duration of phthisis pulmonalis', *Medico-Chirurgical Transactions*, 54 (1871).

—— and HORTON-SMITH, P., *The Climates and Baths of Great Britain* (1902).

SECONDARY PRINTED BOOKS AND ARTICLES

AABY, PETER, *et al.*, 'Overcrowding and intensive exposure as determinants of measles mortality', *American Journal of Epidemiology*, 120 (1984).

—— 'Severe measles: a reappraisal of the role of nutrition, overcrowding, and virus dose', *Medical Hypotheses*, 18 (1985).

—— 'Severe measles in Sunderland, 1885: a European–African comparison of causes of severe infection', *International Journal of Epidemiology*, 15 (1986).

ACKERKNECHT, E. H., 'Anti-contagionism between 1821 and 1867', *Bulletin of the History of Medicine*, 22 (1948).

AYERS, G. M., *England's First State Hospitals* (1969).

BEHAR, M., 'A deadly combination', *World Health* (Feb.–Mar. 1974).

BETT, W. R. (ed.), *The History and Conquest of Common Diseases* (Norman, Okla., 1954).

BLOOMFIELD, A. L., *A Bibliography of Internal Medicine: Communicable Diseases* (Chicago, 1958).

BOOTH, D., 'Mortality differentials within large American cities in 1890', *Human Ecology*, 7 (1979).

BREESE, B. B., and BREESE HALL, C., *Beta Haemolytic Streptococcal Diseases* (Boston, 1978).

BRIGGS, A., 'Cholera and society in the nineteenth century', *Past and Present*, 19 (1961).
BRIMBLECOMBE, PETER, *The Big Smoke* (1987).
BROCK, T. D., *Robert Koch: A Life in Medicine and Bacteriology* (1988).
BROOKS, G. F., and BUCHANAN, T. M., 'Pertussis in the United States', *Journal of Infectious Diseases*, 122 (1970).
BRUNDAGE, A., *England's Prussian Minister: Edwin Chadwick and the Politics of Government Growth, 1832–1854* (University Park, Pa., and London, 1988).
BRYDER, LINDA, 'Silicosis, tuberculosis, and the slate industry in North Wales 1927–1939', in P. Weindling (ed.), *The Social History of Occupational Health* (1985).
—— *Beneath the Magic Mountain: A Social History of Tuberculosis in the Twentieth Century* (Oxford, 1988).
BUCHANAN, I. H., 'Infant mortality in British coal mining communities, 1880–1911', unpublished Ph.D thesis, University of London (1983).
—— 'Infant feeding, sanitation, and diarrhoea in colliery communities, 1880–1911', in D. J. Oddy and D. S. Miller (eds.), *Diet and Health in Modern Britain* (1985).
BURKITT, D., and TROWELL, H. C. (eds.), *Refined Carbohydrate Foods and Disease* (1975).
BURNETT, JOHN, *A Social History of Housing 1815–1985*, second edn. (1986).
—— *Plenty and Want: A Social History of Food in England from 1815 to the Present Day*, third edn. (1989).
—— 'Housing and the decline in mortality', in R. S. Schofield *et al.* (eds.), *The Decline of Mortality in Europe* (Oxford, 1991).
BURNETT, Sir MACFARLANE, and WHITE, DAVID O., *The Natural History of Infectious Disease*, fourth edn. (Cambridge, 1972).
BUSVINE, JAMES, *Insects, Hygiene and History* (1976).
BYNUM, W. F., 'Hospital, disease and community: the London Fever Hospital 1801–1850', in Charles Rosenberg (ed.), *Healing and History* (1979).
CAIRNS, M., and STEWART, A., 'Pulmonary tuberculosis in the printing and shoemaking trades. Historical Survey 1881–1931', *British Journal of Social Medicine*, 5 (1951).
CHALMERS, A. K., *The Health of Glasgow, 1818–1925* (Glasgow, 1930).
CHAPMAN, C. B., 'The year of the Great Stink', *Pharos* (July 1972).
CHAVE, SIDNEY, *Recalling the Medical Officer of Health* (1987).
CHICK, Dame HARRIETTE 'The discovery of vitamins', *Progress in Food and Nutrition Science*, 1 (1975).
—— HUME, M., and MACFARLANE, M., *War on Disease: A History of the Lister Institute* (1971).
CLEGG, E. J., and GARLICK, J. P. (eds.), *Disease and Urbanisation* (1980).
CLIFF, A., and HAGGETT, P., 'Island epidemics', *Scientific American*, 250 (May 1984).
CORFIELD, PENELOPE, *The Impact of English Towns 1700–1800* (Oxford, 1982).
CRONJE, GILLIAN, 'Tuberculosis and mortality decline in England and Wales, 1851–1900', in R. I. Woods and J. Woodward (eds.), *Urban Disease and Mortality* (1984).
—— 'Captain of the Men of Death: pulmonary tuberculosis in the economy of England and Wales, 1851–1910', unpublished Ph.D thesis, University of London (1990).
CURL, J. S., *The Victorian Celebration of Death* (1976).
DAUNTON, MARTIN, *House and Home* (1983).
DAVIDOFF, L., and HALL, C., *Family Fortunes: Men and Women of the English Middle-Class, 1750–1850* (1987).

DAVIDSON, M., and ROUVRAY, F. G., *The Brompton Hospital* (1954).

DAVIS, J., *Reforming London: The London Government Problem 1855–1900* (Oxford, 1988).

DEARDEN, C., HARMAN, P., and MORLEY, D., 'Eating more fats and oils as a step towards overcoming malnutrition', *Tropical Doctor*, 10 (1980).

DICKINSON, H. W., *A History of Water Supply* (1954).

DIXON, CYRIL, *Smallpox* (1962).

DWORK, DEBORAH, *War is Good for Babies and Other Young Children* (1987).

DYOS, H. J., 'Railways and housing in Victorian London', *Journal of Transport History*, 2 (1955).

—— 'Some social costs of railway building in London', *Journal of Transport History*, 3 (1957).

—— 'The slums of Victorian London', *Victorian Studies*, 11 (1967).

EYLER, J. M., *Victorian Social Medicine: The Ideas and Methods of William Farr* (1979).

—— 'Scarlet fever and confinement: the Edwardian debate over isolation hospitals', *Bulletin of the History of Medicine*, 61 (1987).

FEE, E., and ACHESON, R. (eds.), *A History of Education in Public Health* (Oxford, 1991).

FEIGIN, R. D., and CHERRY, J. D., *Textbook of Infectious Diseases*, second edn. (Philadelphia, Pa., 1987).

FEINSTEIN, C., 'What really happened to real wages?: trends in wages, prices and productivity in the United Kingdom, 1880–1913', *Economic History Review*, second ser. 63: 3 (1990).

—— 'New estimates of average earnings in the United Kingdom, 1880–1913', *Economic History Review*, second ser. 63: 4 (1990).

FINER, S. E., *The Life and Times of Sir Edwin Chadwick* (1952).

FISHMAN, W. J., *East End 1888* (1988).

FLOUD, R., WACHTER, K. W., and GREGORY, A., *Height, Health and History: Nutritional Status in the United Kingdom 1780–1980* (Cambridge, 1990).

FORFAR, J. O., and ARNEIL, G. C. (eds.), *A Textbook of Paediatric Medicine* third edn. (Edinburgh 1984).

FRASER, STUART, 'Leicester and the smallpox', *Medical History*, 24 (1980).

GASTELL, BARBARA, 'Measles: a potentially finite history', *Journal of the History of Medicine*, 28 (1973).

GAULDIE, ENID, *Cruel Habitations* (1974).

GOODALL, E. W., GREENWOOD, M., and RUSSELL, W. T., *Scarlet Fever, Diphtheria and Enteric Fever, 1895–1914*, Medical Research Council Special Report, no. 137 (1929).

GREAVES, J. P., and HOLLINGSWORTH, D. F., 'Trends in food consumption in the United Kingdom', *World Review of Nutrition and Dietetics*, 6 (1964).

GREEN, A. F., 'The problem of London's drainage', *Geography*, 41 (1956).

GREENWOOD, M., *Epidemics and Crowd Diseases* (1935).

GUILLAUME, PIERRE, *Du Désespoir au salut: les tuberculeux aux XIX et XX siècles* (Paris, 1986).

HALL, P. G., *The Industries of London since 1861* (1962).

—— 'The East London footwear industry: an industrial quarter in decline', *East London Papers*, 5 (1962).

HALL, S. A., 'The cattle plague of 1865', *Medical History*, 6 (1962).

HAMLIN, C., *What Becomes of Pollution? Adversary Science and the Controversy on the Self-Pollution of Rivers in Britain, 1850–1900* (New York, 1987).

—— *A Science of Impurity: Water Analysis in Nineteenth-century England* (Bristol, 1990).

HARDY, ANNE, 'Smallpox in London: factors in the decline of the disease in the nineteenth century', *Medical History*, 27 (1983).

—— 'Water and the search for public health in London in the xvii and xix centuries', *Medical History*, 27 (1984).

—— 'Urban famine or urban crisis? Typhus in the Victorian city', *Medical History*, 32 (1988).

—— 'Public health and the expert: the London Medical Officers of Health, 1856–1900', in R. M. MacLeod (ed.), *Government and Expertise: Specialists, Administrators, and Professionals, 1860–1919* (Cambridge, 1988).

—— 'Diagnosis, death and diet: the case of London, 1750–1914', *Journal of Interdisciplinary History*, 18 (1988).

—— 'Parish pump to private pipes: London's water supply in the nineteenth century', *Medical History*, Supplement no. 11 (1992).

—— 'Rickets and the rest: childcare, diet, and the infectious children's diseases, *Social History of Medicine*, 5 (1992).

—— 'Tracheotomy versus intubation: surgical intervention in diphtheria in Europe and the United States, 1830–1930', *Bulletin of the History of Medicine*, 66 (1992).

HENNOCK, E. P., 'Poverty and social theory in England: the experience of the eighteen-eighties', *Social History*, 1 (1976).

HIGGINS, T. T., *Great Ormond Street* (1952).

HOEPRICH, P. D. (ed.), *Infectious diseases*, (Haverstown, Md., 1977).

HORSFALL, F. L., and TAMM, I., *Viral and Rickettsial Infections of Man* (1965).

HOWE, G. M., *Man, Environment and Disease in Britain* (Harmondsworth 1976).

HUGHES, MOLLY, *A London Child of the 1870s* (Oxford, 1977).

JOLLY, H., and LEVENE, M., *Diseases of Children* (1985).

JONES, G. S., *Outcast London* (1971).

LAMBERT, R. S., 'A Victorian national health service: state vaccination, 1855–71', *Historical Journal*, 5 (1962).

—— *Sir John Simon, 1816–1904, and English Social Administration* (Bristol, 1965).

LANDERS, JOHN, 'Mortality, weather and prices in London 1675–1825: a study of short-term fluctuations', *Journal of Historical Geography*, 12 (1986).

—— and MOUZAS, A., 'Burial seasonality and cause of death in London 1670–1819', *Population Studies*, 42 (1984).

LAWSON, RICHARD, 'Urbanisation and change in nineteenth-century England', in J. Pattern (ed.), *The Expanding City* (1983).

LEES, L. H., *Exiles of Erin* (Manchester, 1979).

LEWES, F., 'The G.R.O. and the provinces in the nineteenth century', *Social History of Medicine*, special issue (Dec. 1991).

LEWIS, R. A., *Edwin Chadwick and the Public Health Movement* (1952).

LILIENFELD, A. M., 'The French influence on the development of epidemiology', *Bulletin of the History of Medicine*, ns 4, supplement (1980).

LILIENFELD, D. E., '"The Greening of Epidemiology": sanitary physicians and the London Epidemiological Society (1830–1870)', *Bulletin of the History of Medicine*, 52 (1978).

LIPMAN, V. D., *A Social History of the Jews in England* (1954).

—— *A Century of Social Service 1859–1959: The Jewish Board of Guardians* (1959).

LOMAX, ELIZABETH R., 'Advances in pediatrics and in infant care in nineteenth-century England', unpublished Ph.D thesis, University of California, Los Angeles (1972).

LOOMIS, W. P. 'Rickets', *Scientific American*, 6 (1970).

LUCKIN, W., 'Death and survival in the city', *Urban History Yearbook* (1980).

—— 'Typhus and Typhoid in London', in R. I. Woods and J. Woodward (eds.), *Urban Disease and Mortality* (1984).

—— *Pollution and Control: A Social History of the Thames* (Bristol, 1986).

MACARTHUR, W. P., 'The medical history of the famine', in R. D. Edwards and T. D. Williams (eds.), *The Great Famine* (Dublin, 1956).

MACDONALD, J. C., 'The history of quarantine in Britain during the nineteenth century', *Bulletin of the History of Medicine*, 25 (1951).

MCFARLANE, Neil, 'Hospitals, housing and tuberculosis in Glasgow', *Social History of Medicine*, 2 (1989).

MCKEOWN, THOMAS, *The Modern Rise of Population* (1976).

MACLEOD, R. M., 'Law, medicine and public opinion: the resistance to compulsory health legislation, 1870–1907', *Public Law* (Summer 1967).

—— 'The frustration of state medicine 1880–1899', *Medical History*, 11 (1967).

—— (ed.), *Government and Expertise: Specialists, Administrators and Professionals, 1860–1919* (Cambridge, 1989).

MCNEILL, WILLIAM, *Plagues and Peoples* (1976).

MADSEN, T., and MADSEN, S., 'Diphtheria in Denmark', *Danish Medical Bulletin*, 3 (1956).

MARLAND, HILARY, *Medicine and Society in Wakefield and Huddersfield, 1780–1870* (Cambridge, 1987).

MECKEL, R. A., 'Immigration, mortality and population growth in Boston, 1840–1880', *Journal of Interdisciplinary History*, 15 (1985).

MELLANBY, E., 'Accessory food factors (vitamines) in the feeding of infants', *Lancet* (1920), i.

MERCER, A. J., 'Smallpox and epidemiological-demographic change in Europe: the role of vaccination', *Population Studies*, 39 (1985).

—— *Disease, Mortality and Population in Transition*, (Leicester, 1990).

MILL, ALAN, 'Flush it or fester', *New Scientist* (3 Jan. 1985).

MITCHELL, ALLAN, 'An inexact science: the statistics of tuberculosis in late nineteenth-century France', *Social History of Medicine*, 3 (1990).

MORLEY, DAVID, *Paediatric Priorities in the Developing World* (1973).

—— 'Nutrition and infectious diseases', in E. J. Clegg and J. P. Garlick (eds.), *Disease and Urbanisation* (1980).

—— 'Severe measles', in N. F. Stanley and R. A. Joske (eds.), *Changing Disease Patterns and Human Behaviour* (1980).

—— and WOODLAND, MARGARET, *See How They Grow: Monitoring Child Growth for Appropriate Health Care in Developing Countries* (1986).

—— and MARTIN, W. J., 'Measles in Nigerian children', *Journal of Hygiene, Cambridge*, 61 (1963).

MULLETT, C. F., 'A century of English quarantine, 1709–1825', *Bulletin of the History of Medicine*, 23 (1949).

Murray, J. and Murray, A., 'Suppression of infection by famine and its activation by refeeding—a paradox?', *Perspectives in Biology and Medicine*, 20 (1977).

Newby, M., *Sick Children's Hospital Nursing in Nineteenth Century Britain*, Occasional Papers in Nursing and Caring, 1 (1987).

Newsholme, Arthur, *Fifty Years in Public Health* (1935).

Oddy, D. J., 'A nutritional analysis of historical evidence: the working class diet 1880–1914', in D. J. Oddy and D. S. Miller, *The Making of the Modern British Diet* (1976).

—— 'Urban famine in nineteenth-century Britain: the effect of the Lancashire cotton famine on working-class diet and health, *Economic History Review*, second ser. 37 (1983).

—— and Miller, D. S. (eds.), *Diet and Health in Modern Britain* (1985).

Owen, David, *The Government of Victorian London, 1855–1889: The Metropolitan Board of Works, the Vestries and the City Corporation*, ed. R. M. MacLeod (1982).

Palmer, Roy, *The Water Closet* (1973).

Panum, P. L., *Observations Made during the Epidemic of Measles on the Faroe Islands in the Year 1846* (New York, 1940).

Parish, H. J., *A History of Immunization* (Edinburgh, 1965).

—— *Victory with Vaccines* (Edinburgh, 1968).

Pelling, Margaret, *Cholera, Fever and English Medicine 1825–1865* (Oxford, 1978).

Porter, Dorothy, 'Stratification and its discontents: professionalisation and conflict in the British public health service, 1848–1914', in E. Fee and R. M. Acheson (eds.), *A History of Education in Public Health* (Oxford, 1991).

—— and Porter, R. S., 'The politics of prevention: anti-vaccinationism and public health in nineteenth-century England', *Medical History*, 32 (1988).

Porter, R. S., 'Cleaning up the Great Wen', in W. F. Bynum and R. S. Porter (eds.), *Living and Dying in London*, *Medical History*, supplement no. 11 (1993).

Post, J. D., *Food Shortage, Climatic Variability, and Epidemic Disease in Preindustrial Europe* (Ithaca, NY, 1985).

Price, Richard, *Masters, Unions and Men: Work Control in Building and the Rise of Labour 1830–1914* (1980).

Prochaska, F. K., 'Body and Soul: Bible nurses and the poor in Victorian London', *Historical Research*, 60 (Oct. 1987).

Richardson, Ruth, *Death, Dissection and the Destitute* (1988).

Riley, J. C., *The Eighteenth-Century Campaign to Avoid Disease* (1987).

—— 'Disease without death: new sources for a history of sickness', *Journal of Interdisciplinary History*, 18 (1987).

—— *Sickness, Recovery and Death: A History and Forecast of Ill Health* (1989).

Rogers, Naomi, 'Germs with legs: flies, disease and the new public health', *Bulletin of the History of Medicine*, 63 (1989).

Rolleston, J. D., *The History of Acute Exanthema* (1937).

Rosen, George, 'Acute communicable diseases', in W. R. Betts (ed.), *The History and Conquest of Common Diseases* (Norman, Okla., 1954).

Rotberg, R. I., and Rabb, T. K. (eds.), *Hunger and History: The Impact of Changing Food Production and Consumption Patterns on Society* (Cambridge, 1985).

Rubinstein, D., *School Attendance in London 1870–1904: A Social History*, University of Hull Occasional Papers in Social and Economic History, 1 (1969).

RUDÉ, GEORGE, 'The London "mob" of the eighteenth century', *Historical Journal*, 2 (1959).

SCHOFIELD, R. S., REHER, D., and BIDEAU, A. (eds.), *The Decline of Mortality in Europe* (Oxford, 1991).

SHEPPARD, FRANCIS, *London 1808–1870: The Infernal Wen* (1971).

SMITH, F. B., *The People's Health* (1979).

—— *The Retreat of Tuberculosis 1850–1950* (1988).

SPONZA, L., *Italian Immigrants in Nineteenth Century Britain: Realities and Images* (Leicester, 1988).

STANLEY, N. F., and JOSKE, R. A. (eds.), *Changing Disease Patterns and Human Behaviour* (1980).

SUMMITT, R., *Comprehensive Pediatrics* (St Louis, Miss., 1990).

SZRETER, SIMON, 'The importance of social intervention in Britain's mortality decline *c.*1850–1914: a reinterpretation of the role of public health', *Social History of Medicine*, 1 (1988).

—— 'Healthy government? Britain, *c.*1850–1950', *Historical Journal*, 34 (1991).

—— 'The GRO and the public health movement in Britain, 1837–1914', *Social History of Medicine*, special issue, (Dec., 1991).

TANSEY, E. M., 'The Wellcome Physiological Research Laboratories 1894–1904: the Home Office, pharmaceutical firms, and animal experiments', *Medical History*, 33 (1989).

THOMAS, MARK G. 'Epidemiology of Pertussis', *Reviews of Infectious Diseases*, 11 (1989).

THOMPSON, E. P., *The Making of the English Working Class* (Harmondsworth, 1968).

THOMPSON, F. M. L., *Victorian England: The Horsedrawn Society* (1970).

TOMES, N. J. 'The white plague revisited: essay review', *Bulletin of the History of Medicine*, 63 (1989).

—— 'The private side of public health: sanitary science, domestic hygiene, and the germ theory, 1870–1900', *Bulletin of the History of Medicine*, 64 (1990).

TOP, F. H., and WEHRLE, P. H. (eds.), *Communicable and Infectious Diseases*, ninth edn. (St Louis, Miss., 1981).

TOPLEY, W. W. C., and WILSON, G. S. (eds.), *Principles of Bacteriology, Virology and Immunity*, seventh edn. (1984).

WAAL, A. DE, *Famine that Kills: Darfur, Sudan, 1984–1985* (Oxford, 1989).

WALTER, J., and SCHOFIELD, R. S. (eds.), *Famine, Disease and the Social Order in Early Modern Society* (Cambridge, 1989).

WATKINS, DOROTHY, 'The English revolution in social medicine, 1889–1911', unpublished Ph.D thesis, University of London (1984).

WEINRAB, B., and HIBBERT, C. (eds.), *The London Encyclopaedia* (1983).

WHITE, JERRY, *Rothschild Buildings: Life in an East End Tenement Block 1887–1920* (1980).

—— *The Worst Street in North London: Campbell Bunk Islington, between the Wars* (1986).

WILKINSON, A., 'The beginnings of disease control in London: the work of the medical officers of health in three parishes, 1856–1900', unpublished D.Phil. thesis, University of Oxford (1981).

WILLIAMSON, J. G., *Coping with City Growth During the British Industrial Revolution* (Cambridge, 1990).

WILSON, L. G., 'The historical riddle of milk-borne scarlet fever', *Bulletin of the History of Medicine*, 60 (1986).

WINGATE, PETER, *The Penguin Medical Encyclopaedia* (Harmondsworth, 1972).

WINSLOW, C. E. A., *The Conquest of Epidemic Disease* (Princeton, NJ, 1943).

WINTER, J. M., *The Great War and the British People* (1986).

WOHL, A. S., 'The housing of the working classes in London, 1815–1914', in S. D. Chapman (ed.), *The History of Working-Class Housing* (Newton Abbot, 1971).

—— *Endangered Lives: Public Health in Victorian Britain* (1984).

WOOD, LESLIE, *The Restoration of the Tidal Thames* (1981).

WOODS, H. M., 'An epidemiological study of scarlet fever in England and Wales since 1900', *MRC Special Report Series*, no. 180 (1933).

WOODS, R. I., and WOODWARD, J. (eds.), *Urban Disease and Mortality*, (1984).

——, WATTERSON, P. A., and WOODWARD, J. H., 'The causes of rapid infant mortality decline in England and Wales, 1861–1921, Part 1' *Population Studies*, 42 (1988); 'Part 2', 43 (1989).

WRIGLEY, E. A., and SCHOFIELD, R. S., *The Population History of England 1541–1871* (Cambridge, 1981).

YOUMANS, G. P., *Tuberculosis* (1979).

Index